D1432809

Date

LOGISTICS OF DISTRIBUTION SYSTEMS

LOGISTICS OF

DISTRIBUTION SYSTEMS

Frank H. Mossman

MICHIGAN
STATE
UNIVERSITY

Newton Morton

KENT
STATE
UNIVERSITY

ALLYN AND BACON, INC.
BOSTON, 1965

To the patience, inspiration,
and constructive help
of Ruth and Laura

LIBRARY OF CONGRESS CATALOG CARD NUM-
BER: 64-8941

PRINTED IN THE UNITED STATES OF AMERICA

PREFACE

Business administration is ever-changing, as its practitioners constantly try to add to their stock of scientific knowledge and to apply this knowledge to business decisions. Art is used here to indicate the ability to combine the factors of business enterprise so that profits are made through differential gain. Since the available combinations of factors are constantly changing, and the desires of society also change, there is an increasing need for both scientific knowledge and artistry in applying this knowledge to the field of business.

These two goals, increasing scientific knowledge and applying this knowledge, have been the objectives of professional colleges of business administration for many years. The approaches have varied over the years, but the discipline has always demonstrated its flexibility in developing and adapting to improvements in both fields. Early curricula in business administration followed primarily the functional approach, giving a highly descriptive orientation of how each function was performed. Later on, as specialization began to occur within each of the functions, these functional courses tended to splinter off into additional descriptive methods courses.

In an effort to overcome some of the obvious deficiencies of such descriptive courses, some professors have attempted to draw heavily upon the behavioral sciences to infuse new vitality into describing the function; others in more recent years have attempted to rely more upon mathematics and quantitative techniques to lend some analytical precision. These two infusions have made it possible for forward-looking individuals in the discipline to implement the functional approach in two significant ways: first, analysis of the interactions which occur between each of the major functions; second, analysis of the functions as creators of change and as adaptors to change. Such an analysis goes far beyond the original descriptive approach.

Fortunately, students of distribution are in the forefront of those studying business administration through the new functional approach. One perspective of functional interaction is from the standpoint of a society within a given geographic or political unit. Here one may analyze the level of economic development as the triangular interaction of human wants and needs, human knowledge and skills, and utilization of available natural resources. A change in any of these forces will trigger a reaction in the other two corners of the triangle. The distribution system is a human skill which overcomes the spatial separation of markets and raw materials, and thus is a fundamental part of the interaction process.

A second perspective of functional interaction is from the standpoint of the individual firm. The changing nature of the market requires that each firm adjust its whole entrepreneurial effort to create differential advantages for itself. In terms of spatial relationships, these adjustments mean constant surveillance of raw material sources, plant locations, warehouse locations, retail outlets, and other parts of the distribution system.

The principal objective of this book is to present distribution as a creator of change in the other parts of the business system, and to show how distribution adapts itself to changes caused by those other parts. Each of the interaction levels indicated above is analyzed with this objective in mind. Part One is devoted to the logistics of macrodistribution systems, involving a study of the technology and application of capital to distribution systems, location of processing centers as related to spatial extent of the market, and population changes in relation to distribution. Part Two is a consideration of regulations and policy as they promote or restrain the ability of each of the distribution forms to meet changing market and technological conditions.

Part Three of the book is devoted to the logistics of microdistribution systems. Since the objective of logistics at this level is to create differential gain for the firm, the subject matter includes the adjustment of the microdistribution system to change, changes of terminal location in the distribution system, and distribution and revenue analysis. Part Four is an analysis of policy in two important areas of microdistribution, warehousing and inventory levels. The use of simulation techniques is presented as the conclusion of this section.

Five special appendices are given after particular chapters in order to provide greater depth of treatment. Some of these involve mathematics, and others are highly technical. Two appendices of a more general nature are included at the close of the book. Many will find this material of interest, particularly if they are majors in the area of distribution logistics.

Our sincerest thanks are due the graduate and undergraduate students who have used much of this material in mimeographed form in distribution logistics classes. Their comments have been invaluable, and have often been the basis for revisions into the present book. We also owe a considerable debt to the very helpful comments and suggestions of the reviewers of the original manuscript.

There are many persons whom we would like to thank for their individual help at various points in the preparation of the manuscript. Due particular thanks for their help with selected materials are Dr. Donald Bowersox, McDonald Stamp Company; Professor James L. Constantin, University of Oklahoma; Professor Melvin Greenhut, Florida State University; Professor Bernard J. LaLonde, University of Colorado. Of special help in providing information regarding regulatory questions were Dr. T. J. Sinclair, Association of American Railroads; Mr. John R. Meeks, Traffic Consultant, and Mr. James J. Broz, Defense Traffic Management Service. Mr. Phil C. Beverly, Atlantic Coast Line Railroad, was helpful in consultation on matters pertaining to railroad consolidations. As a logician and friendly discussant, our thanks are due to Professor Thomas Farrell, Michigan State University, for his help in sharpening up ideas at several points.

Former and present graduate students not only helped to criticize ideas, but were, on occasion, the originators of useful concepts; these individuals are mentioned at specific points. The following were of special help: Richard Bergson, William Brannen, Fred Elam, George Gecowetz, Stanley Hardy, J. Richard Jones, Chunbong Kimm, Gene Losa, Richard J. Lewis.

The following professional associations were of help in furnishing specific information: Air Transport Association, American Transit Association, American Trucking Associations, Inc., American Waterways Operations Association, Committee for Oil Pipelines, Transportation Association of America. Our thanks are also extended to the following for use of published material: Association of Interstate Commerce Commission Practitioners, *Railway Age,* Railway Progress Institute, *Traffic World, Transportation and Distribution Management.*

Sincere thanks are also due to colleagues Professor John L. Hazard and Professor Edward W. Smykay for their contributions.

We hope that this book will stimulate many individuals, particularly those of honors calibre, into the further study of the discipline of distribution logistics. In a competitive world, one soon learns to accept change as a way of life with changing relationships between the component parts of the economic system. The challenge to the individual is to derive analytical solutions to the problems posed by change. Such solutions will be rewarding, both mentally and monetarily, to those who study in this field.

CONTENTS

PART FOUR. MICRODISTRIBUTION SYSTEM POLICY

xii CONTENTS

TABLES

FIGURES

Logistics of Distribution Systems

PART ONE

LOGISTICS OF

MACRODISTRIBUTION

SYSTEMS

CHAPTER ONE

LOGISTICS OF

DISTRIBUTION SYSTEMS

IN THE ECONOMY

Distribution systems constitute a major functional area of our economic system, and the logistics of such systems play a major part in the development of the country. A *distribution system* may be defined as the operation which creates time, place, and form utility through the movement of goods and persons from one location to another.[1] The system encompasses all movement from the shipment of raw material to the final resting point of the finished product. Thus defined, it includes the physical facilities for intercity movement, the physical arrangements for storage, and the terminal properties necessary to equalize demand and supply with respect to the size of the shipment. Rights of way, movement equipment, storage facilities, retail stores, and other terminal properties are thus all part of the distribution system.

Logistics is interdisciplinary, cutting across many scientific fields of speculation. It is the science concerned with the logical arrangement of the functional areas required to achieve a desired goal. In its best known sense, as a military term, logistics refers to the branch of military science concerned with the mathematics of transportation and supply, and the movement of bodies of troops. The military definition has been broadened for use in the study of distribution systems, but retains its essential meaning, as can be seen by substituting the term "logical arrangements." In fact, let us now say "logical conceptual arrangements" in place of "mathematics."

---

[1] Form utility is included in the definition because a change in the quantity of goods available for purchase constitutes a utility to the user of the systems.

Thus, the logistics of distribution systems is the science concerned with the logical conceptual arrangement of the movement system facilities in such a way that a given desired goal is attained. Distribution systems can be approached as general or particular systems. One then speaks of the logistics of *macrodistribution* and the logistics of *microdistribution*. *Macro* is a prefix meaning "large," and *micro* is a prefix meaning "very small."

Macro- and Microdistribution Systems

In the analytical approach to macrodistribution systems, attention is focused on the distribution system as a whole, rather than on its individual components. For example, social scientists are concerned with the aggregative forces at work in the nation considered as a universe. On the other hand, the analytical approach to microdistribution systems is concerned with the various forces at work in sub-segments of a given universe or macrosystem. For example, social scientists may study particular production and distribution problems of an individual firm.

The study of distribution systems should include investigation of both macro- and microdistribution systems if the various parts of the movement system are to serve economically the requirements of the market place. The selection of either approach depends, to a great extent, upon the problems to be studied and the objectives to be attained. For example, the over-all cost of movement in a given intercity movement agency can be determined from the general approach, but the range of cost within the agency must come through the particular approach.

While it is clear that the general approach is concerned with the over-all aspects of a universe and the particular approach deals with an individual system, the dividing line between the general and particular analytical approaches is difficult to discern. It is usually a comparatively arbitrary division at best. Where a relatively small number of firms are interrelated, the same forces that determine the level of interrelationship might apply to both the general and the particular approaches. As the number of firms and individuals increases, so does the complexity of the interrelationships.

The relationships of the forces at work in the larger universe should be studied so that the individual company (or other segment of the system) can tie in its own efforts with the trends of the larger universe. Although it is often extremely difficult to ascertain trends correctly, managements in charge of planning and control often must at least estimate them in order to make commitments for future actions. Examples of this are commitments made by the federal and state governments for the interstate highway system, the construction of airports to handle projected volumes of traffic, and the development of master plans by urban planners.

TRIUNAL INTERACTION AND THE DISTRIBUTION SYSTEM

As pointed out by Professor Erich W. Zimmermann, the level of economic development in a given competitive society is a result of the triunal interaction of human wants and needs, human knowledge and skills, and the available resources which may be transformed into products to satisfy the wants and the needs of the population.[2] The entire interaction process takes place through human beings; it is human wants and desires, human knowledge and skills, and human utilization of resources that interest us. More particularly, it is in the functional grouping of human knowledge and skills that business administration finds its place among the educational disciplines.

Human knowledge and skills can be divided into three principal areas. First, the demand creation skills, aimed at the analysis and satisfaction of desires; second, the transformative skills by which the resources are changed in their form to meet the desires of the population; third, the distribution skills which are aimed at overcoming the obstacle of space, making possible a wider geographic practice of the principle of comparative or absolute advantage.

Each of these three areas must be handled skillfully if the population is to realize a relatively high standard of living.[3] As each of

[2] This is sometimes referred to as the resources approach to the study of an economic system. The person who has done the most in the United States in the development of this approach is the late Erich W. Zimmermann, Professor of Economics, University of Texas. Professor Zimmermann's work is presented in *World Resources and Industries* (New York: Harper Brothers, 1951). Professor John L. Hazard, Michigan State University, has done an outstanding piece of research in applying this technique to the economic potentials of the Great Lakes Region.

[3] The use of the functional approach to the study of Business Administration requires a definition of *function*. A function may be defined as an activity carried on for the purpose of meeting or attaining particular objectives. As

these functions is conducted, a system evolves with a wide variety of alternatives for the individual or the firm to utilize. The objective of each individual and firm in the system is to create differential gain for himself through performing the particular function or functions better than his competitors.

The desires of individuals, and of society in general, are insatiable for certain temporary periods of fulfillment. For example, an individual may be able to consume only a given amount of food at a given time, but his over-all requirements for a given scale of living may be said to be insatiable and subject to change through time. The resources which man transforms or uses to meet some of his requirements are randomly distributed throughout the earth's surface. This randomness is reflected not only in the topography and location of surface lands, but, more evidently, in the location and formulation of mineral deposits—the raw materials of the society. Since materials seldom exist where they can readily be turned into usable products, they must be moved to the processing point. By employing the technology of movement, man is able to overcome the obstacle of space and obtain the materials to create things to satisfy his physical requirements. Thus, distribution serves to move raw materials and supplies to processing points and to move the finished or semi-finished articles to the market place.

The three forces of physical desires, technical skills, and resources interact in an ever-changing relationship which constitutes the economic system. People produce goods and services for actual use, for accumulation of a reserve, or for exchange for other goods and services. What they produce depends upon the kinds, numbers, and intensities of their wants. What people want depends, to a considerable extent, on the availability of goods. Availability is affected by the distribution system.

It is not the purpose here to analyze the social, political, and institutional structures which influence man's desires. It is sufficient to indicate that his wants are insatiable, and that he will exert his technical skills and utilize resources in an effort to satisfy them. This is what is meant by the "triunal" interaction of man's requirements,

---

stated so excellently by Edmund D. McGarry: "The term function should be so defined as to meet the purpose for which it is used. The function of the heart is not simply to beat, which is its activity, but rather to supply the body with a continuous flow of blood." Edmund D. McGarry, "Some Functions of Marketing Reconsidered," a selected essay reprinted in Reavis Cox and Wroe Alderson, *Theory in Marketing* (Homewood, Ill.: Richard D. Irwin, Inc., 1950), p. 267.

knowledge and skills, and resources. If all three factors remain constant, a static economic system will result. In a highly competitive economic system, however, it would be unusual for all three to remain so.

In a competitive world where change is a normally accepted way of life, man's wants, technical skills, and utilization of resources will change. A change in any one of these forces will start a chain reaction in the other two. The dynamics of change in the distribution system in the United States is the object of study in this text.

DISTRIBUTION AND THE PRINCIPLE
OF COMPARATIVE ADVANTAGE

It seems appropriate, at this point, to relate the field of distribution to the *principle of comparative advantage,* which is the basis of trade. This principle states that each individual, region, or nation will specialize in the production of those commodities or services for which it is best fitted, and will exchange the surpluses with the surpluses of other individuals or regions for which it is best fitted. The principle was stated in early classical economic literature by Ricardo,[4] and was later refined by John Stuart Mill.[5]

Mill, in his presentation, clearly distinguished two separate types of cost differences: conditions of equal cost of production and conditions of comparative differences in production costs. These are illustrated in Table 1-1, using the examples presented by Mill.

Assuming that 50 bushels of corn and 200 yards of cloth were produced in each country, there would be no gain in trade with or without territorial specialization, even though the absolute costs were different. Poland's superiority over England in the production of corn was assumed to be as great as her superiority in the production of cloth. If this assumption was correct, neither country would gain by confining its labor to one of the two products and importing the other, as indicated in Illustration I, Table 1-1.

In Illustration II of Table 1-1, the assumed conditions were changed, and it becomes apparent that both countries gain by spe-

[4] David Ricardo, *The Principles of Political Economy and Taxation* (London: John Murray, 1817), Ch. VII.

[5] John Stuart Mill, *Principles of Political Economy* (New York: Longmans, Green and Company, 1911), Bk. III, Ch. XVII.

TABLE 1-1.   *Mill's Illustration of Comparative Advantage from Specialization in Production**

ILLUSTRATION I—EQUAL DIFFERENCES

Days of Labor Required to Produce Equal Quantities of Cloth and Corn in Poland and England:

COUNTRY	CORN	CLOTH
Poland	100 days	100 days
England	150 days	150 days

Without Territorial Specialization:

	CORN		CLOTH
Poland	100 days labor,	50 bu.	100 days labor, 200 yd.
England	150 days labor,	50 bu.	150 days labor, 200 yd.
		100 bu.	400 yd.

With Territorial Specialization:

	CORN		CLOTH
Poland	200 days labor,	100 bu.	
England			300 days labor, 400 yd.
TOTAL		100 bu.	400 yd.

ILLUSTRATION II—COMPARATIVE DIFFERENCES

Days of Labor Required to Produce Equal Quantities of Corn and Cloth in Poland and England:

Poland	100 days	100 days
England	200 days	150 days

Without Territorial Specialization:

	CORN		CLOTH
Poland	100 days labor,	50 bu.	100 days labor, 200 yd.
England	200 days labor,	50 bu.	150 days labor, 200 yd.
TOTAL		100 bu.	400 yd.

With Territorial Specialization:

	CORN		CLOTH
Poland	200 days labor,	100 bu.	
England			350 days labor, $466\frac{2}{3}$ yd.
TOTAL		100 bu.	$466\frac{2}{3}$ yd.

* John Stuart Mill, *Principles of Political Economy* (New York: Longmans, Green and Company, 1911), Bk. III, Chap. XVII.

cializing in those commodities where they have the greatest comparative advantage. In this illustration, a day's labor produced more corn in Poland than in England. A day's labor also produced more cloth in Poland than in England. But a day's labor produced twice as many bushels of corn in Poland as it produced in England and only 1½ times more cloth. Consequently, more corn and cloth in the aggregate would have been produced in the two countries if Poland specialized in corn production and England in cloth production. The net gain from trade indicated in the illustration was 66⅔ yards of cloth. This principle Mill termed the principle of comparative advantage.

Later economists of both the classical and neoclassical schools refined the principle of comparative advantage and incorporated it into the marginal revenue and cost portions of general equilibrium analysis. The original theory, as developed by Ricardo and Mill, was in terms of labor inputs into production. Later economists converted these into monetary units, and pointed out the importance of proportionality among land, labor, and capital in seeking least cost combinations to maximize profit.

Distribution is one of the basic cost factors, and, as such, will enter into determining the proportionality of the various factors for maximizing net profit. In the final delivered cost of the product to the consumer, if distribution cost is high, such costs will be important in determining the comparative advantage of a firm, region, or nation. If distribution costs are proportionately low, these costs will be less important than the other factors to be considered. However, even in those industries in which the transport cost is a low proportion of the commodity's delivered cost, these costs must still be considered in relation to other competition in the economic area.

Distribution assumes more importance in the principle of comparative advantage when the conditions of processing allow lower unit costs with increased volumes to be obtained by applying capital to the transformation process. This can readily be seen if one considers briefly the historical development of our economic system.

When man was a nomad, he was largely concerned with those wants whose satisfaction was necessary to the maintenance of his own existence. During this stage of economic development, man found it necessary to move to resources in order to satisfy his own wants. However, as he began to utilize the resources of the land for producing goods, he became more stationary. Gradually, individuals accumulated goods beyond their own particular needs and began to look around for ways to exchange surpluses for those of other individuals for mutual advantage. In this stage man first attempted to conquer space, since the extent to which he could trade these surpluses was in large part determined by his ability to overcome spatial obstacles.

Trade at first was on a purely local level. As man used surpluses and applied capital, in the form of tools, to the productive process, hence acquiring a declining unit cost curve, he began to spread out geographically in order to trade his products with others who were likewise beginning to specialize. Attempts were made, as trade spread, to bring raw materials from more distant points to the production site and to deliver the finished products to more distant geographic locations. Not until spatial differences were overcome did regional specialization begin to occur.

If the level of economic development is spatially limited to the village or city, the principle of comparative advantage will be worked out only within that particular location. However, if the problem of spatial relationships is overcome, the principle of comparative advantage can operate over a broader geographic area. Thus, movement is significant in determining the extent to which the principle of comparative advantage can operate in the triunal interaction of human requirements, human skills, and utilization of the natural resources of any population.

DISTRIBUTION DEVELOPMENT, POPULATION MOVEMENTS, AND PHYSIOGRAPHY

The triunal interaction of man's requirements, skills, and resources will take place within the framework of the population under consideration and the physiography of the area. Therefore, it seems appropriate to consider the historical movements of population within the United States, and to relate these to the movement skills of the time as a means of overcoming spatial barriers.

The physiography of the United States consists, basically, of two mountain ranges on the eastern and western extremities, with a broad plains area in between these two ranges. On the Eastern Seaboard, the Allegheny and Appalachian mountain ranges run from Maine into the central part of Alabama, with the rivers east of these mountains draining into the Atlantic Ocean. In the western portion of the United States, beginning at approximately 104 degrees longitude (eastern Montana directly south through eastern New Mexico) and extending to the West Coast, there is a series of mountains of varying heights. In both of these ranges, east-to-west surface movement has been limited principally to the available passes through these mountains.

The Great Plains and lowland areas between the two mountain ranges are drained by a waterway system, of which the Mississippi is the principal river. The Mississippi runs north and south from northern Minnesota to New Orleans, and its principal tributaries on the western portion of its drainage basin are the Missouri River, the Arkansas River, and the Red River. Principal tributaries on the eastern portion are the Ohio River, the Cumberland River, and the Tennessee River. All of these rivers are navigable for considerable lengths (although at varying depths), and were potent in bringing unity to the plains region prior to the advent of the railroad. Of considerable significance to the northern central states is the Great Lakes-St. Lawrence waterway, which consists of the five Great Lakes and the St. Lawrence River. This system today can provide for movement of ocean-going ships to nearly all of the Great Lakes ports. Although the channel was deepened only rather recently, the Great Lakes have been an avenue of commerce for the north central states for many decades.

In the seventeenth and eighteenth centuries, most of the settlers in the American colonies lived on the Atlantic seaboard. The settlers were primarily agrarian, and satisfied most of their wants on their own ground in their own way. Goods which were needed and not available on this continent were brought by ship, primarily from Europe. Most of the settlement during this period was on the coast or along the banks of rivers which emptied into the Atlantic Ocean. Water transportation, both internal and external, was the best manner of goods transport at that time.

Several developments occurred in the latter part of the eighteenth and the early part of the nineteenth century in which transportation played a vital part. First, the law of comparative advantage was developing in the Southern agrarian states and the more industrialized British Isles. Second, as Western Europe became involved in wars, the Northern states, which were beginning to industrialize, took advantage of their position and became competitors with foreign imports. Third, the population, particularly in the Northern states, was beginning to move westward, and the rivers and canals facilitated this emigration.

An important westward population movement was developing very rapidly, over the Appalachian and Allegheny Mountains into such areas as the Ohio Valley, to solve man's wants for new farm land, opportunity, and adventure. Once the basic wants of the population were satisfied, new desires for goods were created. In order to satisfy these desires, the population could, through knowledge and skill, either produce the goods themselves or utilize the available resources to bring these goods to them from the older portions of the country or from foreign countries. For a time, the population produced those goods which it could, but eventually goods and services were exchanged with other areas via the Mississippi River, canals, and other waterways.

The continued westward movement of the population in the first half of the nineteenth century is indicated in Table 1-2. The East North Central states, which in 1800 had only one tenth of one per cent of the total population, had 19 per cent in 1850. The East South Central states, which had six per cent in 1800, had 14 per cent by 1850. The development of the railroad network in the second quarter of the nineteenth century was a tremendous factor in this westward movement. Trade became more intensive between regions, and a relative decline took place in foreign trade.

There was also a rapid increase in the technology of production. For the first time, the abilities and resources of one region could be adequately exchanged for those of another with partial disregard for the proximity of water transportation. The waterways and railroads competed fiercely during the second quarter of the nineteenth century.

In the remainder of that century, the railroad network was extended to the other parts of the country. The westward movement of the population continued rather rapidly, as shown in Table 1-2. Although the Eastern seaboard states continued to grow, the availability of the railroad network for the movement of goods and people, semi-independent of the waterways network, helped bring about the tremendous growth of the area west of the Allegheny and Appalachian Mountains. Thus, by the end of the nineteenth century, the transportation system of the United States had evolved from ocean shipping and foot paths, through river and barge canal (including some wagon roads and turnpikes), to the railroad. The geographic center of the population in the United States had shifted from near Baltimore in 1800 to south central Indiana by 1900 (Figure 1-1).

Prior to the development of the railroad network, industry, in a general sense, had been concentrated in the Middle Atlantic states for a variety of reasons. This area had available technical skills and raw materials, an adequate labor supply, energy resources, close proximity to distribution outlets, and good water transportation. The opening up of the railroad network made these requirements more available to other parts of the country. Resources inherent in a given locality, such as the Great Lakes region, could be combined with other required complementary resources made available by the railroad. As these new regions developed industrially, raw materials could more

TABLE 1-2. *United States Population by Region* for Selected Years, 1800–1960

REGION	1800 I	1800 II	1850 I	1850 II	1900 I	1900 II	1930 I	1930 II	1960 I	1960 II
New England	1,233	23.2	2,728	11.8	5,592	7.4	8,166	6.7	10,546	5.8
Middle Atlantic	1,403	26.4	5,899	25.4	15,455	20.3	26,261	21.4	34,269	18.8
East North Central	51	.1	4,523	19.5	15,986	21.0	25,297	20.6	36,340	19.9
West North Central	—	—	880	3.8	10,347	13.6	13,297	10.8	15,425	8.5
South Atlantic	2,286	43.1	4,679	20.2	10,443	13.7	15,794	12.9	26,066	14.3
East South Central	335	6.3	3,364	14.5	7,548	9.9	9,887	8.1	12,073	6.6
West South Central	—	—	940	4.1	6,532	8.6	12,177	9.9	17,008	9.3
Mountain	—	—	73	.3	1,675	2.2	3,702	3.0	6,897	3.8
Pacific	—	—	106	.5	2,417	3.2	8,194	6.7	20,482	11.2
Other	155	—	N.A.		971		1,971		3,231	1.8
TOTAL CONTINENTAL UNITED STATES	5,308		23,192		75,995		122,775		182,337	

CODE: I—Population
II—Per Cent of Population

* The regions follow the classification of the U.S. Bureau of the Census and are as follows: New England—Maine, New Hampshire, Vermont, Massachusetts, Rhode Island, Connecticut; Middle Atlantic—New York, New Jersey, Pennsylvania; East North Central—Ohio, Indiana, Illinois, Michigan, Wisconsin; West North Central—Minnesota, Iowa, Missouri, North Dakota, South Dakota, Nebraska, Kansas; South Atlantic—Delaware, Maryland, District of Columbia, Virginia, West Virginia, North Carolina, South Carolina, Georgia, Florida; East South Central—Kentucky, Tennessee, Alabama, Mississippi; West South Central—Arkansas, Louisiana, Oklahoma, Texas; Mountain—Montana, Idaho, Wyoming, Colorado, New Mexico, Arizona, Utah, Nevada; Pacific—Washington, Oregon, California; Other—Alaska, Hawaii, Puerto Rico.

Sources: U.S. Bureau of the Census, *Statistical Abstract of the United States:* 1937, 1947, 1957 and 1962 (58th, 68th, 78th and 83rd eds.) Washington, D.C., 1937, 1947, 1957 and 1962.

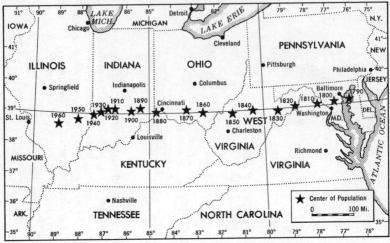

Figure 1-1. *Center of Population for Conterminous United States, 1790 to 1960.* Source: U.S. Bureau of the Census, *Statistical Abstract of the United States* (Washington, D.C.: U.S. Government Printing Office, 1962), p. 7.

easily be transferred from place to place, and finished goods could be distributed on a much more extensive scale.

One can visualize the growth of the transportation industry, the economy, and the nation as a mushroom effect—from embryonic settlements to towns and cities, from small shops to factories, from gardens to large farms, all more or less self-sufficient, to larger and more highly integrated systems which interacted and became more dependent upon each other. Such growth is a striking example of the dependence of the economy upon good distribution system facilities.

Much of this integration was made feasible by the development of an economical, relatively efficient means of solving space problems; namely, the growth of the railroad network in the nineteenth century. It is interesting to conjecture on the possible distribution of our population had the railroads not been developed, and had we been forced to use the existing waterways network for the movement of goods and people. We might have different geographic alignments of the population today.

In the period since 1900, three new forms of transport have been introduced into the movement system: pipelines for liquid and nonliquid products, air transport, and trucking operations over the highways. To characterize the evolution of the transportation system from 1900, one could say that there has been continued interaction, increased integration and complexity, and the possibility of choice among transportation media to serve different needs.

Space problems differ in many factors, including the volume to be moved, unit value of the goods, perishability of the goods, speed required, distance to be moved, and the weight-density of the product. Each medium—whether rail, motor, water, air, or pipe—has its own competitive advantages and disadvantages.[6] Each, however, is suited to performing given tasks in overcoming space problems. As the distribution system performs the job of movement more effectively, it enables individuals and/or regions to produce and market those products and services in which they have their greatest comparative advantage.

Model for the Discussion of the Logistics System

The model for analyzing the logistics of distribution systems will be the consideration of the environment in which the logistics system must operate, the component elements of the system, and environmental conditions. K. H. Schaeffer describes these as the *determiners,* the *components,* and the *integrators.*

The determiners are those elements that affect the system from outside the system proper; they include the inputs that the system must accept, the outputs of the system, and the other constraints external to the system that operate on the system, as for instance the forces of the natural or social environment into which the system is placed. The components are those elements that make up the actual parts of the system. They are the system's subsystems that include the machines, and the humans that function as parts of the system, and the facilities that are internal and integral to the system. The third group of elements comprises those that integrate the system components. These are the various time sequences in which operations or actions occur within the system, the communications within the system, the organization of the system components, and the decision structure within the system. The integrators are thus the principles (or rules) that organize the other system elements to form

[6] See John R. Meyer, "A Comparison of the Advantages and Disadvantages of the Various Modes of Transport," *Technological Change and the Future of the Railways* (Evanston, Ill.: Northwestern University Transportation Center, 1961), pp. 1–14.

them into a whole. The integrators also can be considered to be the grouping principles for the determiners and components.[7]

The determiners, the components, and the integrators are interwoven in the presentation. The determiners may be thought of as wants and needs of the population and the available resources to satisfy these wants and needs. The component elements are the knowledge and skills available to transform and distribute these resources into the satisfaction of the wants and needs. The integrators, or principles of interaction, between the determiners and the components will be considered at appropriate points throughout the book.

Since there are many logical conceptual arrangements of the component parts of the distribution systems under different environments, this book is divided into two parts. The first part deals with the logistics of macrodistribution systems. The second part discusses logistics of microdistribution.

LOGISTICS OF MACRODISTRIBUTION SYSTEMS

The first section of the book is divided into the following sequence: the technology and application of capital to distribution systems, processing centers and spatial extent of the market, and population change as related to distribution systems.

The distribution system is concerned with the concentration and dispersion of products. The requirements for concentration and dispersion are part of the determiners, the wants and needs of society which must be fulfilled by the distribution system. These requirements, and the application of capital to the distribution process, are discussed in Chapter 2.

The location of processing centers, an additional determinant of distribution systems, is analyzed in Chapter 3. The distribution system overcomes space and allows the interaction of human wants, skills, and natural resource utilization. The transformative skills are necessary to change resources into products that can be utilized to satisfy human wants. To a considerable extent, the location of the points at which these transformative skills occur will determine the

[7] K. H. Schaeffer and A. Shapero, "The Structuring and Analysis of Complex System Problems," a paper presented to the Operations Research Society of America, 1961, pp. 6–7.

distance and system required to move each type of traffic. Weight loss or gain in manufacturing and the type of production cost curve of the processing unit are the bases for analyzing processing locations. Emphasis is on the integrators or principles for evaluating changing interrelationships between the determiners of processing center location and the components of the distribution system.

Since interaction occurs through people, the distribution of the population is analyzed in Chapter 4. Sheer population increases often suffice to allow an increase in the total gross product of an economy, both through aggregates and because size permits more specialization. A brief description of the projected population expansion of the United States is given to indicate where transportation markets might develop. The importance of metropolitanization of the population makes it desirable to discuss the structure of metropolitan areas and the effect on transportation requirements. This chapter thus presents population as a determinant of the component structure of the area and the distribution system required to bring these attributes together as a whole.

Following the macroanalysis section, a separate part of the book is devoted to transportation regulation and policy. The intercity transportation agencies are a fundamental part of the distribution structure, and most of the firms operate on a "for-hire" basis to the general public. As such, they come under economic regulation of the various state and federal governments. Economic regulation can promote or restrain the ability of each form of movement to meet changing market and technological conditions. Therefore, it is important to know what state and federal policies are with respect to economic regulation. Also important is the changing use of land for various purposes. Since the distribution system must use land to overcome space, it is important that this determiner be analyzed in the chapter on policy.

Logistics of Microdistribution Systems

Whereas macrodistribution involved the aggregative forces at work as a part of the economic system, microdistribution is concerned with analysis of the systems utilized by the individual firm. The objective in logistics of microdistribution is to arrange the component parts of the system so that differential gain can be created for the company.

To accomplish this objective, the chapter sequence in the second part of the book is as follows: adjustment of the microdistribution system to change, logistics of terminal location in the distribution system, and distribution cost and revenue analysis.

Chapter 8, on the adjustment of the microdistribution system to change, gives primary consideration to the dispersion system of the manufacturer or distributor as the most fruitful area for lowering distribution costs. The chapter starts with an analysis of the changing life styles as they affect the firm's logistics system. Market planning and programming are then related to dispersion, and methods are recommended for selecting suitable dispersion alternatives. A framework for change is presented at the close of the chapter.

Terminals are defined in Chapter 9 as physical locations where the shipment size desires of the distribution system are equalized with the shipment size desires of the customer. Under this definition, retail stores and warehouses are considered to be terminals from a physical point of view, and their locations become important in terms of space preference of the consumers. The objective is to locate at a point where the customer is offered maximum utility with threshold costs of the terminal at a minimum. Beyond this level, the terminal operator will seek to strike a balance between profitable store operation and consumer convenience. Analytical tools are presented for use in seeking such locations.

Since physical movement problems are not distribution's sole concern, consideration is given in Chapter 10 to combining demand creation and the distribution systems in such a way that the objective of differential gain for the individual firm may be more readily realized. Total competitive costs of the firm are obtained on the basis of the factors which cause cost differences in demand creation and distribution. In many instances, these same factors can be used for determination of revenue output with a given amount of cost input.

The ability of the firm to survive rests on its ability to adjust to its environment. Only a few firms are fortunate enough to have the technical knowledge and ability to create and fulfill demand for their products independent of their environment. Most are highly dependent upon their ability to adapt their strategy to a changing environment. Two important areas of adjustment are distribution warehousing and inventory levels. Therefore, policies relevant to these two areas are analyzed in the final part of the book. The use of simulation techniques as an aid to decision making in microdistribution is presented as a conclusion.

Appendix to Chapter One

Some Principles in the Logistics

of Movement

At least ten principles of movement apply to the entire field of distribution and should always be kept in mind in making innovations in the system. These principles will be listed and then discussed individually.

1. A distribution system must operate within the physiographic limitations of its terrain.
2. Continuous rather than intermittent movement is most economical.
3. Wherever feasible, the standardization of methods, types, and sizes of equipment is desirable for distribution efficiency.
4. Movement space is best measured in terms of cubic content if the system involves a single movement unit per power unit; weight, rather than cubic content, is a preferable measurement method if the system involves multiple movement units per power unit.
5. Distribution economies are directly proportional to the size of the load handled per movement.
6. Equipment built for motion should be kept in motion; idle equipment should be as inexpensive as possible.
7. The value of distribution equipment is approximately proportional to its flexibility and adaptability to changing movement requirements of the market.
8. The use of mechanized equipment instead of manpower generally increases efficiency and economy in handling.
9. The ratio of dead weight to payload should be kept to a minimum.
10. Insofar as possible, the equipment should be used for the movement of profitable loads of profitable traffic.

A System Must Operate Within Physiographic Limitations.

The distribution system must operate within the physiographic limitations of its terrain. Until the application of steam to railroad movement, the primary method of movement in the United States was via the rivers and canals of the country. At one time, products of the Ohio Valley had to be shipped downstream on the Ohio and Mississippi Rivers, then via sailing vessels to the East Coast. The construction of canals made it possible, for the first time, to overcome the limitations of the eastern mountain ranges. However, canal building was an expensive procedure that could be accomplished only when there was enough population in the Ohio River Valley to justify the expenditure.[8] The railroad network also had to follow the passes through the mountains, and, in many instances, tunnel construction was delayed until the commercial market justified this expenditure. In modern times, the expense of providing increased power for larger, speedier airplanes has been lessened, at least in part, through the use of military prototypes or subsidization in other ways.[9] Overcoming physiographic or spatial resistance takes place at an increasing cost, although the market may justify such expenditures.

This principle is also true on a smaller scale. The handling system and layout[10] of a terminal or warehouse tend to interact with each other, but physical limitations of the structure often limit both. These limitations include: bearing capacity of the floor, columnar supports, fire lanes, elevators in the case of multi-story operation, and total amount of square and/or cubic footage available for storage.

Continuous Movement Is Most Economical.

Continuous rather than intermittent operation of distribution equipment is most economical whenever this is feasible. The movement of the commodity is most efficiently handled when it approaches a steady flow from production point to consumption point, with a minimum of transfer handling at in between points.

This is illustrated by comparing two airplane flights—one involving ten stops between two points, and another making a non-stop

---

[8] Subsidization did, in some instances, aid in earlier development of facilities. See Chapter 7.

[9] In other instances, such as military necessity, subsidization is desirable to accomplish the national interests of the economy. A good example is the subsidy paid to the U.S. Merchant Marine, which in turn serves for carrying troops in time of war.

[10] Layout relates to such factors as the locations and amount of space devoted to receiving, shipping, selection, storage area, and width of aisles.

flight between those same two points. Considerable cost is involved in bringing the plane down from flying level, landing, taxiing, unloading passengers, and reversing this process, making expenses much higher for the ten-stop flight.

The ideal movement system might be typified by city water systems. As water is released from spigots at consumption points, it is replaced in the supply system by gravity flow from the main reservoir of the city. Unfortunately, the movement system of non-liquid commodities requires some handling on both the concentration and the dispersion sides. This means a higher movement cost.

Standardization of Equipment Is Desirable.

Greater distribution economies are attained when the methods and types and sizes of equipment are standardized. Establishing standard methods for doing given patterns of work permits routine operations to be planned in advance, accomplishing distribution at a much lower cost. The more diverse the types of equipment in use, the greater will be the expense of operation.

This principle can be observed both at the intercity level and in movements within enclosed spaces. When the best way has been determined, standard practice manuals can be prepared for employees, and they can be taught the best way of doing their work. Standardization also allows interchangeability of equipment, simplifies stocking replacement and maintenance and employee training, and may reduce considerably the necessity for transfer of lading. The standard gauge of railroad tracks in the United States shows the desirability of standardization. A railroad car can be operated on the tracks of any Class I railroad in the United States; when a shipment moves between two points, the railroad car may be handled by two or more railroads without a transfer of the goods from the car.

The standardization of equipment should not prevent the possible adoption of new and better equipment and methods. One very real disadvantage of too much standardization and simplification is that it tends to increase resistance to change. Too much resistance makes it less possible to adjust the distribution system to meet the changing requirements of the market place.

Movement Space Should Be Measured in Cubic or Weight Content.

When the operation is a single-movement-unit-per-power-unit type, movement space probably is best measured in terms of cubic content. Movement space requirements are judged on a cubic basis in this type of operation because the available payload space is limited and cannot be expanded for individual movements. Cubic measurement often enters into charges for ocean water transportation in the use of the term "weight or measurement ship's option." The shipping line has the option of using either the weight ton or the measurement ton (40 cubic feet), whichever method will gross for it the largest revenue.

For multiple-movement-units-per-power-unit, some type of weight per square foot measurement probably should be utilized. The concept of weight per square foot can be more readily used for multiple movement units, since the amount of payload space can be expanded within certain physical limits.

Space, with respect to the concentration portions of the distribution operation, is best measured in terms of cubic content. At one time, warehouse operators normally thought of area as the limiting factor in determining storage capacity. The advent of fork-lift trucks, cranes, and other types of overhead handling systems made it possible to store at heights not considered feasible previously.

It is generally less costly to move in only one plane. As applied to warehouse operation, this is evidenced in the desire for single-floor, as opposed to multi-floor, operations. If market requirements permit the operator to do so, it is often desirable to move the warehouse to suburban areas, in order to provide more area on the one-floor level. But if market requirements demand a central location, it may be necessary to maintain the warehouse in a central part of the city and utilize a multi-floor operation.

Distribution Economies Are Proportional to Size of the Load.

Distribution economies generally are proportional to the size of the load. As is readily demonstrable in all systems of distribution, the greater the load per move, the lower the unit cost (within the physical limitations of the system handling the traffic, the legal limitations, and the assumption of excess capacity). We see evidence of this in the lower rates for volume per hundred weight than for less than volume shipments.

Nearly all systems provide some kind of rate incentive to induce volume shipments. The capacity of the system to utilize rate incentives, to some extent, depends upon the amount of payload in relation to the power unit; the possibilities for volume rates are obviously greater as the number of multiple units increases in relationship to a given power unit.

The nodal centers in the transport system, terminal points where assembly and break-bulk operations occur, are probably the costliest single parts of the transportation operation. In these operations, the greater the size of the load, the greater the savings that can be realized. Or, stated a little bit differently, the more pieces carried per handling, the fewer moves required to handle a given volume of merchandise. Many small individual units may be grouped into a single larger unit for more efficient handling; this is generally referred to as the "unitized load" method. The rapid increase in labor costs has added impetus to the development of unitized methods for handling in the concentration and dispersion operations in recent years. In an effort to substitute machinery for labor, both shippers and carriers are developing containers and other forms of unitized loads that can increase the size of the load handled. Advantages of unitized loads include reduced packaging costs, reduced pilferage, fewer stray shipments, reduced loss and damage, and less time involved in taking physical inventory.

There are, of course, physical limitations to the size of the load that can be handled at one time. The load limit of the movement unit must conform to the requirements of the shipper, the terrain over which it operates, and the legal restrictions imposed upon the system. In a warehouse operation, some of the physical limitations would include door widths and heights, column centers, floor load limitations, layout of the warehouse, and requirements of the customer.

Equipment Should Be Utilized as Much as Possible.

One of the prime objectives in selecting distribution equipment is to balance the capital expenditure per unit against the utilization of each unit. An earmark of a successfully operated distribution operation is its ability to relate the capital expenditure for equipment to the use of that equipment. Equipment with wheels is generally more expensive than non-wheeled equipment, and should be kept in motion rather than used for storage. Equipment built for motion should be kept in motion, and idle equipment should be as inexpensive as possible. For example, in the airline industry the movement and power units are combined in one unit which cost several million dollars; the payload per move cannot be expanded, and each piece of equipment must be utilized as much as possible.[11] The construction of a move-

_____

[11] Students often wonder why the helicopter has not been utilized to a greater extent in the short-haul movement of passengers. One of the prime

ment schedule in this kind of operation becomes one of the keys to a successful enterprise.

As another example, motor carriers frequently spot trailers at the shipper's or receiver's dock in order to facilitate loading and/or unloading. If this is done too often, it can become a significant element of cost.

In the assembly and break-bulk processes, a minimum ratio of equipment investment to units of material handled produces the greatest economy. For example, a tractor can handle more units in a given period of time if it is disconnected from a trailer train at the end of each haul, and does not wait for the trailers to be unloaded.

Movement Equipment Should Be Flexible in Use.

One desirable but difficult goal in transportation is to utilize standard equipment and operating methods, but still provide for flexibility to meet changing market conditions. In the principle of standardization, routine procedures are developed to permit movement at a lower per-unit cost. The moment that standardization occurs, however, the danger of inflexibility creeps into the distribution picture. This danger becomes particularly real when a large amount of capital is invested per movement and power unit, and where capital turnover is relatively slow. But the turnover of capital has increased greatly in recent years, in distribution as well as in business generally, and companies have attempted to write off equipment more rapidly than was formerly the case.

Flexibility also applies to materials-handling equipment. Compared to fixed-type handling types of equipment such as conveyors, the fork-lift truck is probably the most flexible piece of equipment in use in a warehouse or terminal. Fork-lift trucks can handle skids and pallets, as well as supporting merchandise both horizontally and vertically. As in intercity transportation, the advantages of standardization must be contrasted with those of flexibility.

Mechanization Is Generally Better Than Manpower.

If mechanized equipment is used instead of manpower, efficiency and economy of handling generally increase throughout the movement

---

reasons for the limited commercial use of helicopters is the fact that the ratio of non-revenue to revenue hours is very high, largely because of maintenance requirements. High cost of equipment is also a factor.

system.[12] This is probably most readily observable in the difference between single and multiple-movement-units-per-power-units. In single units, payload is limited to the capacity of the movement unit, and labor costs can be spread only to the extent of that payload. As more movement units are added per power unit, the cost of labor and power can be spread over additional units of payload.

This same tendency is observable in the terminal and warehouse operations of a carrier. Assembly and break-bulk operations require a good deal of cross movement, and mechanized equipment can quite often be substituted to reduce the unit cost and/or number of such moves.

This principle may conflict with the desired objective of flexibility in the plant. Management must evaluate the importance of each factor in the conflict. However, because of the higher turnover rate of capital, this conflict is not as great in recent years as formerly. Variance in capital turnover among the various distribution systems determines the differing degrees of conflict among these agencies.

Dead Weight Should Be Kept at a Minimum.

The ratio of dead weight to payload in the movement system should be kept as low as possible. In the intercity movement system, this is particularly true when the agency is a single-movement-unit-per-power-unit type of operation. Airlines exemplify the problem in the single-movement-unit type of operation; engine manufacturers have greatly increased the thrust in the power unit, but the ratio of payload to total weight of the planes has been declining. The desired (or required) addition of navigational and other safety aids has increased the amount of non-revenue dead weight and, thus, caused the decline. Motor and water carriers, on the other hand, have progressed considerably by using lighter metals in both the movement unit and the power unit.

The same principle applies to terminal and warehouse operation in that the less the movement equipment weighs, the greater the payload that can be carried. The lower the weights, in the case of fork-lift trucks, trailers, and pallets, the less mechanized power or manpower needed to move them. The use of lighter equipment may also

---

[12] The circumstances under which it is desirable to substitute mechanized equipment for manpower vary greatly. The art of managing a distribution enterprise includes the proper selection of the method that will best perform a given job.

be desirable, but it must be considered against the objective of measuring storage space in terms of cubic content.

*Equipment Should Be Used for Profitable Loads
of Profitable Traffic.*

If a distribution company is to be successful, the loads moved must be profitable to the company. Assurance of profitable traffic will not be a major problem if prices are based on average costs of performing the distribution service. However, if prices are based not on average costs but on value of service, the company will be under constant pressure to juggle the prices on the various segments of business. A distribution company today should constantly be able to determine the traffic on which it is making or losing money. Such information can help distribution managements to reorient company objectives, policies, and operational patterns toward a profitable operation.

CHAPTER TWO

TECHNOLOGY AND

APPLICATION OF CAPITAL

TO DISTRIBUTION SYSTEMS

Man's knowledge and skills constitute the technologies that make available alternative distribution systems to overcome spatial resistances in utilizing natural resources to satisfy human wants and needs. This chapter presents the technologies available for use in the distribution system, and analyzes the development of these systems through the application of capital to the functional distribution processes.

TECHNOLOGICAL CHARACTERISTICS
OF THE DISTRIBUTION SYSTEM

The technological characteristics of the various distribution systems will be discussed in terms of the number of movement units per power unit, the control system, and the use of terminal facilities. While many characteristics help to account for the technological differences between distribution systems, the following are the primary characteristics of each of the major systems. The purpose here is to single out those characteristics which are most important as a basis for cost differences and determine the place a given system occupies in the market allocation of distribution facilities.[1]

[1] The relative importance of each of the intercity distribution systems may be envisioned from the following figures. In 1963, transportation costs were

1. Railroad—multiple-movement-unit-per-power-unit.
2. Motor carrier—single-movement-unit-per-power-unit.
3. Pipelines—the guidance system.
4. Water (inland barge)—multiple-movement-unit-per-power-unit.
5. Water (lake carrier)—single-movement-unit-per-power-unit.
6. Airlines—single-movement-unit-per-power-unit.

Undoubtedly the prime characteristic of the railroad industry is its ability to move a large number of movement units with each power unit. Although the number of cars per unit is variable with the horsepower of the engine and the curvature, grade, and elevation of the track, the entire railroad enterprise is characteristically geared to multiple-movement-unit-per-power-unit operation. Typically, shippers load and receivers unload the cars, so that the railroad is basically involved only with the movement of a carload of merchandise. Switching tracks are maintained from the industrial sidings or public tracks to a classification yard, where the trains are made up into trainload quantity. Power units are then attached and moved as a trainload to various destinations, where the reverse process takes place. The entire operation of the railroad is based on mass movement, including scheduling, methods of control of movement, corporate organization structure, financing, and cooperation with other railroads.

Inland barges are also multiple-movement-unit-per-power-unit operations, but they are not geared quite so closely to automatic operation as are the railroads. The railroads operate on a closed guidance system in which the rails guide the direction of movement. In water transportation, the direction of movement must be maintained by the towboat propelling the various barge units. Another difference between rail and water operation is in the nature of the roadway. The railroads must prepare a rather expensive subgrade and grade, so that the roadway can bear a reasonably heavy load at any point, and yet provide for a maximum of propulsive force in relation to the propulsive resistance. The rail system must also provide for minimization of shock damage, since the movement occurs in a closed guid-

---

8.6 per cent of the gross national product, and were composed of 1461 billion ton-miles of intercity freight and 840 billion passenger miles. The ton-miles of intercity freight was shared as follows: rail, 43.1 per cent; motor carrier, 23.8 per cent; petroleum pipeline, 16.6 per cent; Great Lakes water transportation, 6.6 per cent; inland rivers and canals (including intercoastal and coastwise), 9.8 per cent; and air transportation, .08 per cent. The composition of passenger intercity travel was as follows: automobile, 89.9 per cent; air, 5.0 per cent; bus, 2.6 per cent; rail, 2.3 per cent; and water, .2 per cent. The source of these figures is the Transportation Association of America.

ance system, especially in the terminal operation. The water carriers, on the other hand, do not have to provide for load-bearing characteristics on the roadway, since the water is very buoyant.

The main technological characteristic of motor transport, lake carriers, and air transport is that all are single-movement-units per-power-unit operations. The carrying capacity of a particular unit is limited, and the emphasis must be on obtaining a maximum of propulsive force to overcome propulsive resistance.

The maximum capacity of motor carrier movement units is provided by state statutes which prescribe maximum height, width, length, and axle weights. The additional regulation of a speed limit in effect also prescribes the extent to which they can utilize the propulsive force/resistance as a means of expanding capacity.

Lake carriers have the advantage of a high degree of buoyancy and a low propulsive resistance, but, as in motor transportation, there is a low proportion of cargo weight to dead weight of the vessel or movement unit. This factor, when encountered in ocean transportation, leads to the carrier's exercising "weight or measurement ship's option" for price quotation. Under this option, 40 cubic feet is taken as the standard determining whether charges are assessed on a weight ton of 2240 pounds (as used by many ocean carriers) or on a measurement ton basis of units of 40 cubic feet. If a shipment takes more than 40 feet to stow a weight ton, the ocean carrier will apply the measurement ton basis, as this will provide it with greater revenue. For instance, a weight ton requiring 60 cubic feet for stowage would pay for one and a half measurement tons. Any shipment weighing more than 56 pounds per cubic foot would pay on a weight basis, as that would mean that it would take less than 40 cubic feet to stow a weight ton. This method maximizes the income to the shipping line from a limited amount of shipping space. However, competition in the motor transport field has apparently prevented their adoption of this method of charging. Another probable reason for non-adoption has been that many motor carriers are unfamiliar with the use of the W/M/SO quotation. It must be emphasized that the option rests with the ocean carrier, not with the shipper.

In air transportation there is a low amount of propulsive resistance, but the high propulsive force required to maintain planes in the air (expressed as either high propulsive force per ton or high horsepower per payload) places a severe strain upon the amount of payload space in the plane. In fact, the addition of navigation and other safety devices in recent years to help assure dependability of air operations has reduced the percentage of payload to total load, in spite of the increase in the amount of thrust through the development of jets and other types of air power.

The outstanding characteristic of multiple-movement-unit-per-power-unit operation is that capital can be applied to the movement process in order to obtain lower movement cost per unit. As pointed out, it is possible to attain this on the concentration side, but it becomes increasingly difficult to attain on the distribution side as the goods approach the ultimate consumer. Therefore, the multiple-movement-unit-per-power-unit operations are more suited to the concentration side, and the single-movement-unit-per-power-unit types are utilized more on the dispersion side of the distribution system.[2]

CONTROL SYSTEM AS A FUNCTION OF TECHNOLOGICAL CHARACTERISTICS

The reason for concern with control objectives is that control of movement represents a considerable portion of the expense within the movement system. In general, there are two types of guidance systems—a closed system, in which there is a set course, and an open system, in which there is none. The use of a set course reduces the human element in the guidance system and increases mechanical or automatic controls. The use of a nonset course increases the human element and reduces the opportunities for automatic control.

The four alternative objectives of control are speed, safety, maximum utilization of capacity, and dependability of operation. The following four statements may be taken as basic in the movement system: speed depends on the ratio of propulsive force to propulsive resistance; safety depends on the guidance system; maximum utilization of capacity depends on the number of movement units per power unit; and dependability of service depends on the guidance system selected. Therefore, in view of the primary technical considerations, the primary control objective in each of the movement systems is as follows:

----

[2] The concentration side of the distribution system refers to the concentration of quantities to be assembled into volume quantities for movement, which is typical of the shipment of raw materials. The dispersion side involves numerous small shipments to many points, which is characteristic of the shipment of finished goods.

1. Railroad—maximum utilization of capacity.
2. Motor carrier—speed.
3. Pipeline—dependability of service.
4. Water (inland barge)—maximum utilization of capacity.
5. Water (lake)—speed.[3]
6. Air transport—speed.

Those systems that have multiple movement units per power unit naturally desire to add movement units up to the effective carrying or pulling capacity of the power unit and within the given scale of terminals and roadway. In such systems, the desire for the movement units to be as long as possible affects the kind of control system that will be utilized for movement. Pipelines, railroads, and water carriers operate on a more or less set course. The pipelines have a completely closed guidance system. The railroads have a rail-wheel flange guide which acts as a set course, and barge carriers are forced to follow the channel that is provided on the navigable rivers and lakes. Airlines, and, to a lesser extent, motor carriers, do not operate over set courses. Their problems of guidance are more complex, particularly for the airlines, which operate in three dimensions, rather than two, as is the case for motor transportation.

The control objective for single-movement-units-per-power-unit —motor carriage, lake water carriers, and airlines—is speed, as indicated in the previous section. Speed is basically a function of the ratio of propulsive force to propulsive resistance, and the relative speeds for each system have been listed below. In each instance, the accompanying characteristics will indicate the reasons for comparative cost differences.

1. Air transport—speed is of great importance.
   A. High propulsive force per ton.
   B. High horsepower per pay load.
   C. Low propulsive resistance.
2. Railroad—speed is of medium importance.
   A. Low horsepower per ton.
   B. Low propulsive resistance.
3. Motor transport—speed is of medium importance.
   A. High horsepower per ton.
   B. Low propulsive resistance.
   C. High dead weight to cargo weight.

[3] This objective would be true for a given vessel. However, vessel size might be changed to increase capacity. As size increased, the agency might be increasingly confronted with the problem of maximizing utilization of capacity.

4. Water transport—speed is of lesser importance.
   A. Low horsepower per ton.
   B. Low propulsive resistance.
   C. High cargo weight to dead weight.
5. Pipeline transportation—speed is relatively unimportant.
   A. Low horsepower per ton.
   B. High propulsive resistance.

TERMINALS AS EQUALIZATION POINTS
IN THE DISTRIBUTION SYSTEM

A terminal is a point where movement size requirements are equalized for different parts of the distribution system. Under this definition, four types of services are provided by terminals: *dead storage, assembly, break-bulk,* and *break-bulk and reassembly.*

Dead storage facilities are provided for commodities because of seasonal production, seasonal consumption, or combinations of both. An example of dead storage is the cold storage warehouse, where such items as eggs are stored at the time of production and taken out of storage as needed for consumption.

Assembly terminals are provided for commodities where the shipments do not meet the volume requirements of the carrier; there the commodities are concentrated and handled from there on as volume shipments. An example of an assembly point is the grain elevator in agricultural production centers, where the grain shipments are carried on trucks to elevators and moved as carload quantities from the country elevators to the terminal elevators of milling centers.

Break-bulk terminals are for receiving inbound volume shipments from the distribution system and moving out less than volume shipments into the system again. Beyond the processing point, the requirements of the system are determined by the consumer's purchases of the end product. Since ultimate consumers buy in relatively small quantities and at locations near their own habitats, the distribution system must move successively smaller volumes per shipment from the plant to the wholesaler, wholesaler to retailer, and retailer to consumer. The job, then, from processing point to consumer includes successively breaking down the shipment into smaller quantities. In both the assembly and the break-bulk operations, the institution, by whatever name, is a location that equalizes the movement size requirements for different parts of the distribution system.

The fourth type of terminal facility, *break-bulk and reassembly,* is simply a combination of the second and third types in one physical facility. Break-bulk and reassembly facilities usually occur on the dispersion side of the movement system, in order to serve the many thousands of retailers and/or producers who do a volume of business so small, with consequent small and single shipments, that volume shipments direct from producer to retailer are not economically feasible. Physically, this may serve as an economic justification for the wholesale structure. Shipments of single commodities usually occur in volume to the warehouse or wholesale point. The wholesaler then reassembles these commodities so that there are many commodities in the outbound shipment, and delivery takes place to the retailer.

From the standpoint of movement alone, the presence of a terminal in the movement system is a diseconomy that raises immediate movement costs, but that may be desirable in that over-all total costs are lowered. For example, on the concentration side, a less than volume shipment might be moved direct from the raw material producing point to the processing plant. However, the pooling of these less than volume shipments enables the movement to take place at a lower per unit cost than if each less than volume unit moved as a separate shipment.

The railroads and inland barge carriers are multiple-movement-units-per-power-unit operations. For the most part, on the concentration side the diseconomies of terminals in these operations are offset by the economies from the volume operation. As pointed out earlier, as the movement approaches the end consumer, the average size of the shipment tends to become smaller. In order for the distribution system to serve the customer under these conditions, the movement system must provide adequate terminal and movement facilities.

In more specific terms, this means that as the size of the shipment becomes smaller, there is more need for the single-movement-unit-per-power-unit operation, and for terminals to serve as equalizing points between the requirements of the shippers and the requirements of the movement system. In a sense, the diseconomy of the terminal operation is being compared with the economy of the volume movement operation. If the customer does not buy in large enough quantity to justify direct shipment from the plant he must expect the shipment to travel some distance before he may take possession physically of the goods from the producer or other vendor.[4]

---

[4] As a corollary of this situation, as the size of the shipment becomes smaller, the proportion of variable costs to total costs rises, and the turnover rate on capital also tends to rise.

In the movement system itself, the same four types of terminals are used for the movement equipment. Dead storage facilities must be provided for the movement equipment when it is not in use. Terminal facilities must also be provided for the assembly of movement units at one location, where the power unit is then attached and moved in trainload or other unit quantities. Break-bulk terminal facilities must be provided for breakup of the multiple movement unit or trainload into individual movement unit delivery to the customer at destination. Good examples of these are the classification yards of the railroads, where carloads are assembled from various shippers in a given city and then assembled into trainload quantity, and the reverse process occurs at destination.[5]

Or terminals might be for breaking bulk and reassembling, as in the terminals of many common motor carriers. For example, pickup trucks pick up the shipments from several shippers around a given city and bring them into the motor carrier terminal. At this terminal, these are taken out of the pickup truck and reassembled into line haul units which take the goods to another city, where the reverse process takes place at the destination terminal. Thus, both for the goods themselves and the equipment the terminal is a point at which the shipment size demands of the shippers and the desires of the movement system are equalized.

CONCENTRATION AND DISPERSION SYSTEMS

Fundamentally, two jobs are performed by the commodity movement system: first, the concentration of raw materials into volume quantities for movement to production points; and, second, the dispersion of the finished goods from producer to consumer. In each of these jobs, the size of shipment is an important consideration.

If volume shipments are accumulated as quickly as possible, capital in the form of power, movement units, or rights of way may be applied to the transport of the raw materials and, consequently,

---

[5] Sometimes in the movement system there are assembly, break-bulk, and reassembly operations on either the concentration or the dispersion sides. For example, pool cars of automobile parts from Detroit may be shipped to Kansas City from Detroit, Atlanta, and Cincinnati. There may be widely varying parts in each of the pool cars arriving at Kansas City. The goods would then be broken out of the carloads and reassembled into common destinations for the West Coast.

goods may be moved at a lower cost per unit. Therefore, shipments which do not meet the volume requirements of the carriers (less than volume) are brought into concentration points and handled as volume shipments beyond that point (Figure 2-1). Typical of such shipments

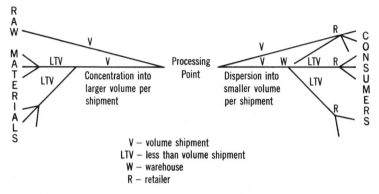

V – volume shipment
LTV – less than volume shipment
W – warehouse
R – retailer

Figure 2-1. *Concentration and Dispersion Systems.*

are grain shipments which, as mentioned earlier, are carried on trucks to elevators and moved as carload quantities from country elevators to the terminal elevators of milling centers. Where the individual shipments are large enough, the concentration process can take place at a single raw material producing point and be moved as a volume shipment to the processing point. For example, in shipping a trainload of coal from a single mine to a utility plant, the coal is concentrated at the mine and moved in trainload quantities, eliminating the necessity for an intermediate point.

As was noted earlier, beyond the processing point the requirements of the movement system are determined by the ultimate consumer. Since the quantities demanded beyond this point are relatively small, the movement system must transport successively smaller volumes per shipment from the plant to the various middlemen. The job, then, from processing point to consumer includes successively breaking down the shipment into smaller quantities.

Since the consumer does not buy in quantities which warrant volume shipments direct from the processing point, the retail structure has come into being as an intermediate point between the two. If the retailer is large enough, he may buy direct from the processor in quantities which will justify volume shipment. However, if the retailer's purchases do not justify the volume shipment, he may buy through a wholesaler or other middleman. Volume shipments can then be made from the processing point to the wholesaler, and less than volume shipments from the wholesaler to the retailer. To summarize, the primary functions of the movement system are: on the concentration side, to concentrate shipments as quickly as possible; on the dispersion side, to break the shipments into successively smaller volumes, in order to serve the consumer.

The extent to which capital may be applied to the movement process in the form of power, movement units, or rights of way differs between the concentration and dispersion operations. The application of capital to movement results in a declining unit cost curve whose shape will depend upon the relationship of fixed and variable costs. The place of fixed and variable costs in movement is considered in the following sections.

FIXED AND VARIABLE COSTS
IN THE DISTRIBUTION SYSTEM

Some authors divide operating cost into the following categories: short-run variable (out-of-pocket) costs, intermediate costs, and long-run variable (fixed) costs. Short-run variable, or out-of-pocket, costs are defined as those traceable to a specific movement of goods. Intermediate costs, then, would concern the replacement of assets which were depreciated over a relatively long period of time. If the period of time is long enough, all costs might be considered variable; therefore, the differences among the three are relative. For our purposes, it is sufficient to make a simple division between variable and fixed, with a full understanding that the time period selected to distinguish between the two is purely arbitrary.

If one assumes the capacity of a given transport medium as fixed for a particular period of time, variable costs will be those which vary with the volume of freight handled by that medium. Such costs, when compared to total costs, are variable in total but remain constant per ton-mile accommodated. Theoretically, these costs may be assigned to a specific volume or movement of freight, i.e., those costs which would not have been incurred if the service had not been rendered. Variable costs are composed of such expenses as fuel, maintenance, and labor.

Fixed costs are those that are fixed in total and, theoretically, are unaffected by increases or decreases in the volume of freight handled. Since these costs are unrelated to volume, they would continue even if all freight movements stopped. Fixed costs might be considered as the capacity cost of a particular distribution system; that is, the cost of providing the physical plant for a given system to handle a given volume of freight within a given geographical area, at a given period of time, and within given time limits. Examples are the capital required for line haul equipment, for terminals, for materials handling equipment, for maintenance shops, and for rights of way.

J. M. Clark illustrates fixed and variable costs in the following analogy:

> The quantity and quality of equipment which it pays to install depends on the amount of use that will be made of it. It may not pay for a settler to lay a water pipe to save carrying three pails of water a day from a spring a few hundred yards from his camp. If the camp grows to a tiny settlement, it may pay to lay some sort of a trough or pipe to save the carrying of one hundred or more pails of water every day, and if the little settlement grows into a town, it will pay to install a reservoir with underground pipes and perhaps a pumping system. A pipe is a fixed expense and the work of carrying pails of water is a variable one, and the fixed expense is for equipment which makes variable expenses unnecessary. This is the type of all labor-saving machinery and all enlargement or development of labor-saving equipment. The saving is measured by the number of pails that have to be carried. If this amount bulks large, it would pay to install a considerable amount of equipment to avoid it, while if it is small, the equipment may be uneconomical.[6]

Summarizing Clark's statement in a different manner, we can say that the average total costs of a process are determined by the relationship of the degree of use of the process with varying proportions of fixed and variable costs. This relationship to the average total cost is illustrated as follows.

Suppose a salesman must rent a car. He has two alternatives. The first rent-a-car service charges ten dollars a day and eight cents per mile. The second charges eight dollars a day and twelve cents per mile. Since both services include gas, insurance, etc., the optimum choice will depend on the expected use of the car. The first service represents higher fixed cost but lower variable cost than the second. The salesman should (on a cost basis) be indifferent between the two

[6] Reprinted from *Studies in the Economics of Overhead Cost* by J. Maurice Clark by permission of University of Chicago Press. Copyright © 1923 by the University of Chicago Press. See also W. Arthur Lewis, *Overhead Costs* (New York: Rinehart and Company, 1949).

services if he plans to drive fifty miles. If he plans to drive more than fifty miles, he should choose the second plan. The two levels of fixed costs (FC_1 and FC_2) are illustrated in Figure 2-2. The corresponding total costs of each plan are represented by TC_1 and TC_2. The areas between the FC and TC lines represent the variable costs which vary directly with the number of miles traveled. These are converted into unit costs, and the effect of the varying proportions of fixed to variable costs and the relationship to the degree of utilization can be seen in Figure 2-2.

The principle illustrated is that when two cost structures are compared to each other, with one having higher fixed costs but lower variable costs, the one with higher fixed costs causes the average total cost curve to decline at a more rapid rate than the lower fixed cost alternative. If enough use (beyond the break-even point) can be made of a process with such a cost structure, the initial higher fixed costs cause lower average total costs. In the salesman's case, the expenditure of ten dollars in fixed costs provides him with lower average total costs for any use beyond fifty miles.

If the producer can realize lower variable costs by increasing the proportion of fixed costs, and enough utilization of the productive factors is possible, he will obtain lower average total costs. Hopefully, lower costs mean a more competitive position. A second result of such a cost structure arises when a producer sets his price on the basis of variable costs. Pricing to cover variable costs allows lower prices to be quoted. Therefore, the relationship of fixed and variable costs with utilization can have a direct relationship to the competitive position of a producer, in terms of the prices he must charge to cover variable or total unit costs.

THE CONCENTRATION MOVEMENT AND FIXED COSTS

In an earlier part of this chapter, it was pointed out that one objective of the distribution system is to concentrate goods into large volumes per shipment as quickly as possible for the purpose of applying capital, in the form of machinery, to the movement process. Four factors which determine the extent of capital application to the movement process include: the total volume of the resource to be moved, the characteristics of the goods, the extent to which the movement operations are repetitive, and speed in transit.

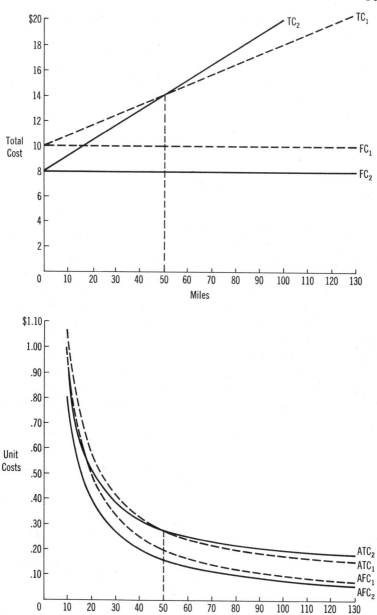

Figure 2-2. *Fixed Costs as a Part of Total Costs.*

Volume is used in two separate ways in the discussion. The first meaning refers to the sheer quantity of the natural resource available for shipment; the second refers to the amount of goods offered for single shipments. The resources referred to in the concentration movement are generally coarse, unrefined, or semi-refined materials such as lumber, coal, iron ore, bauxite, taconite, and other bulk materials. In general, as the volume available for shipment increases, it is possible to apply larger amounts of capital in the form of machinery to the movement process, with a resulting increase in the proportion of fixed costs to total costs. As the volume available decreases, smaller amounts of capital will be applied, usually resulting in a higher proportion of variable costs to total costs.

Characteristics of the goods to be moved refers to those factors that determine the transfer characteristics of the commodity in the movement system. From an engineering point of view, it is generally easier to apply machines to the movement of raw materials than to the movement of finished goods. Raw materials are often homogeneous and uniform commodities, shipped in bulk or unpackaged units, and, as a result, are susceptible to the application of the gravity flow principle. Finished goods tend to move in packaged form as discrete units. In such movement, the transfer into and out of the movement units requires more care to minimize loss and damage, with a resulting increase in the handling costs. For example, it is often possible to apply gravity loading and unloading to rail cars for such materials as coal, wheat, and iron ore, whereas it would be very difficult to apply these to finished packaged commodities.[7]

Repetitive nature of the operations is in a sense a corollary of the characteristics of the goods. Capital is more readily applied in movements which can be routinized so that a given process can be performed repeatedly, without a substantial change in the arrangements for right-of-way, movement equipment, and terminals. Transfer operations are often necessary on both the concentration and dispersion sides of distribution to either assemble or break-bulk the individual shipments. These tasks are more readily accomplished with bulk or unpackaged units (typical of the concentration side) than with the packaged units (typical of the dispersion side). As noted, the repetitive nature of the line-haul operation phase of the movement is a corollary of the volume to be moved. If the volume to be moved is

[7] Other factors which might also be included under characteristics of the goods include: density, possibility of damage to equipment or other commodities in the movement unit, perishability.

small, either as a total amount or as an individual shipment, there is little possibility of a repetitive operation. As the volume per shipment increases, so does the possibility of a repetitive operation and applicability of capital.

Speed must also be considered in applying capital to the movement process. Since it is difficult to vary transportation space or carrying capacity from load to load, an optimum size of power unit, movement unit, and roadway is selected, and one must work within the physical transport limitations of the engineering alternatives. For example, the ratio of space to the rate of movement of that space will vary with the physical means available and is usually designed or constructed to fit the physical limitations. Great quantities of goods can be moved at a slow speed on a Great Lakes ore carrier, or smaller quantities might be moved faster via rail. Another example is a pipeline where the cross sectional circumference of the pipe times the rate of movement of the liquid or gas through that space is the volume. By varying both space size and the movement of the cube at various rates within the economic factors of cost (pipe and pumping), one can arrive at the size of the pipe to be used in the installation. In general, the attainment of speed in movement comes at an increasingly high cost and sometimes requires more than proportionately higher investments of capital.

The element of time, aside from speed in transit, has not been included in the above list because it will be governed by such factors as availability of funds in the capital markets for particular kinds of investments, engineering capabilities of the movement machinery, and applicable tax laws that may determine depreciation rates. Time in this context has two aspects: first, the total period of time over which the machinery will be used; and, second, the rate of use of that machinery within the period of time selected. If the life of the movement machinery is longer, it becomes more feasible to apply large amounts of capital; and if a shorter period of time is selected, a smaller amount of capital may be applied.[8] For example, if the machinery is to be written off over five years, as opposed to ten, then the amount which can be expended will be less for the five year period than for the ten year period.

The utilization of the equipment will also affect the amount of capital applied to movement. If utilization is high, it will tend to en-

---

[8] This refers to the period of time over which the machinery will be depreciated. The depreciation period may be affected by technological obsolesence as well as by the capabilities of the machine.

hance the application of capital to movement, while low utilization tends to restrict its application.

A low unit value of resources makes it more desirable to accumulate such materials into relatively large volumes for single shipments. This allows the carrier to apply power to the movement process. Another contributing factor would be the small number of buyers and sellers of a commodity being shipped. This is clearly the case in the extractive industries such as petroleum, copper, and aluminum where either there is an integration of the mining and production processes into one company or there are few buyers and sellers at the mining and production levels. In the perennial industries, such as lumber, there is less tendency towards oligopoly, and in the agricultural industries there are thousands of producers but a relatively small number of processers. Thus, since the number of buyers and sellers are usually fewer on the concentration than on the dispersion side of distribution, the accumulation of commodities into larger volumes per shipment is more easily performed on the concentration side.

A recent example of applying capital to a concentration movement process is the development of integral trains. The integral train utilizes 100 ton quick unloading hopper cars with a single destination. The application of the integral train idea to the movement of coal is ideally suited for the application of capital.[9] The new 100 ton hopper cars cost $17,500 each ($175 per ton) compared with $11,000 ($157 per ton) for a conventional 70 ton hopper car. The use of additional capital per unit moved in the new hopper cars is justified in several ways.

The volume to be moved, in terms of both the quantity of the resource available and the amount per shipment, is large. The characteristics of coal make bulk handling methods utilizing gravity practical and allow for rapid loading and unloading methods. The rate of use of coal at the plant provides a highly repetitive demand for movement which allows scheduling of trains between the mine and plants to provide for maximum utilization of equipment. Scheduling integral trains between given points for a single commodity reduces switching

[9] The Louisville and Nashville Railroad inaugurated such a service of 50 hopper cars with 100 tons capacity between a coal mine in Paradise, Kentucky and a power plant in Widow's Creek. The unloading and return trip (a 450 mile round trip) requires twenty-four hours. Before beginning this service, the L and N was using two trains of 64 hopper cars with 70 tons capacity. One train of cars was being unloaded at the point of destination while the other was being loaded at the mine.

time, classification time, etc., and results in faster speeds and less time in transit, which also results in greater utilization of equipment.[10] Therefore, all four factors favoring the application of capital are present.

ADAPTABILITY OF AGENCIES POSSESSING HIGH FIXED COSTS

Fixed costs are considered a characteristic of concentration movements, although there are minor qualifications to this statement. High capital investment in rolling stock, right-of-way, and motive power creates a high proportion of fixed costs. This cost is a capital outlay for space, and in concentration movements it is often a very high proportion of the total cost of movement. Thus, for each increment of movement units, the capital cost for equipment to move it will be high. As more movement units are added to a given power unit, the operating cost per unit will become successively lower. Also, because of capital outlay for the movement facilities, a high utilization of the equipment through time must be accomplished before profits can be realized. If one goes to the other extreme and pays very little for the movement facilities, there is generally a high operating cost for each particular movement of space. A low investment in fixed facilities can also come from subsidization, e.g., some airline terminals, or some physical advantage such as support of the movement unit, e.g., support of a barge by the water.

The movement system depends to a large extent upon the economic characteristics of the industries it serves. When major changes occur in the economic complexion of the market, transport systems with a heavy investment in existing facilities may find it difficult to adapt to these changes. A higher ratio of fixed costs to total costs tends to bring with it an economic rigidity which may prevent a reallocation of space and weight movement capabilities, and can result in non-utilization of that space.

Those agencies or carriers possessing lower levels of fixed investment have great flexibility of physical equipment and can adapt more readily to these changes, but only at a higher unit cost for the

---

[10] It has been estimated that the average hopper car in ordinary freight service carries an average of 1200 tons per year, while shuttle service hoppers move 15,300 tons per year and the 100 ton integral train hopper car can carry 25,600 tons per year. See "Integral Trains Herald a Rail Revolution," *Railway Age*, Vol. 154, June 3, 1963, pp. 32–34.

article or commodity moved. Generally, investment in transportation equipment is based upon the expectation of a lower cost for each particular movement. Where this expectation is high, or at least with low risk, a greater outlay is feasible. When the demand for movement is uncertain, less outlay is made in the form of a smaller load capacity. Yet there is an advantage to smaller space facilities, in that small quantities permit greater speed or rate of movement of that space. Definitively, the nature of the investments made in fixed facilities will limit the spectrum of commodities each mode of transportation can carry.

THE DISPERSION MOVEMENT AND FIXED COSTS

The dispersion system, which successively subdivides a shipment into smaller quantities, is largely due to the relatively short distance customers drive in order to purchase commodities, the small average sale per customer at the retail level, and the emphasis on merchandise turnover at this level. The application of capital, in the form of machinery, from processing point to consumer still depends upon the volume to be moved, the characteristics of the commodity to be shipped, the extent of repetitive operations, and speed in transit. In the movement process, however, the application of these factors to the dispersion side differs from application to the concentration side, since practice must be changed to meet the needs of the consumers.

CONSUMER EFFECT ON THE DISPERSION STRUCTURE

Even on the dispersion side, the objective will still be to ship in as large a volume per shipment as possible so that capital can be applied in the form of machinery to the movement process to obtain minimum cost. The extent to which this may be done will be determined by the needs and desires of the consumers of the product. Let us, therefore, consider the distance the customer will travel to make a retail purchase, the average sale per customer at the retail level, and merchandise turnover in the retail store.

Very little definitive work has been done on the distance that a customer will travel to a particular kind of retail store for a particular commodity. This is readily understandable when one considers the tremendous number of variables, including the many hundreds of different types of commodities, the many types and locations of retail outlets, and the many different human reactions to spending time in travel for a particular kind of commodity in a given type of store.

In order to show the relative variation between the time-space factor and the type of commodity, consider the differences among goods of the marketing classification: convenience, shopping, and specialty goods. Convenience goods are items which the customer desires to buy with a minimum of effort at the most accessible location. Shopping goods are items for which he is willing to exert a little extra effort to compare prices, quality, or some other characteristic. Specialty goods are similar to shopping goods, except that price comparison by the consumer is less important. The customer will not travel as far for a convenience item as for either a shopping or a specialty item. In recent years, city retail structures have been forced to relocate nearer to the customers, who have tended to move into suburban areas.[11]

Average sale per customer at the retail level also influences the size of shipment from the producer to the consumer. Generally, the customer buys only a very small amount of goods at any one time. Normally, the customer has enough goods in his own home to meet his needs for current consumption. Of course, the extent of this inventory will vary with the nature of the goods and the income level of the individual concerned. For example, bread may be purchased with relative frequency, but an automobile or a refrigerator may be purchased infrequently. An automobile may be kept on hand for a relatively long time by a low-income family, but be traded in for a new model rather regularly by a high-income family.

Pressure within the retail and wholesale structures to lower operating expenses through increased merchandise turnover also affects the size of shipment. Merchandise turnover is defined as the ratio of sales to the average amount of inventory on hand for any particular period of time. This may be computed in either dollars or physical units. For example, if a retail store had sales of merchandise of $100,000 for a month and an average inventory of $25,000 on

[11] Paul E. Smith surveyed 21 major shopping centers in the United States and found the following: "The median distance for 70 per cent of the customers to the shopping center was 8 miles and the time 20 minutes. More than 50 per cent of the customers lived within an even smaller radius of 5 miles. The median population within an 8 mile radius was 300,000." Paul E. Smith, *Shopping Centers, Planning and Management* (New York: National Retail Dry Goods Association, 1956), p. 48.

hand at all times, the merchandise turnover for that period would be four times ($100,000/$25,000).

The desirability of increasing merchandise turnover may be seen from the following. Assume annual sales of $100,000, with an average inventory of $25,000 on hand at all times (an inventory turnover of four times). If the interest cost on this inventory is computed at six per cent per year, it would be $1,500. If this inventory turnover can be increased to ten by decreasing the average inventory to $10,000, the interest cost declines to $600, a savings of $900.

There are many advantages and disadvantages to increasing merchandise turnover, but the sole purpose here is to indicate that as inventory turnover increases (assuming that sales remain constant), the average size of shipment tends to decrease. The effect is smaller, more frequent orders than would be the case with the higher inventory, and an increase in the performance of break-bulk and reassembly would ensue.[12]

THE DISPERSION SYSTEM COMPROMISE

From the producer's point of view, the ideal dispersion situation would be a straight line (or a circle), with consumers placed at intervals along the line. This would be somewhat similar to a conveyor system, with the consumer placed at various points along the belt removing required items as they pass his particular station. All output placed on the conveyor would be removed, and subsequently consumed, by the time the end of the belt was reached. This method would allow a constant rate of production and an equal rate of consumption, assuming that the rate of consumption is constant and that the consumer cannot be at the point of production to obtain the desired goods. The water system serving householders most nearly approaches this model. Water is transported by pipes from the

---

[12] From retailers' and wholesalers' points of view, the advantages of a more rapid stock turnover are the following: a decrease in the amount of space required to do business; reduction in interest costs, insurance costs, and taxes; reduction in risks due to price change; reduction in depreciation and obsolescence of inventory. There are also limitations to a rapid stock turnover, however: lost sales through shortages of merchandise, cost of paper work on increased numbers of orders, losses of quantity discounts and savings on freight rates of volume shipments, and a possible increase in the cost of the buying function due to increased orders. For reference see T. N. Beckman and W. R. Davidson, *Marketing* (New York: Ronald Press, 1962), p. 398.

production unit directly to the consumer and is consumed as soon as it is obtained; thus, the need for the consumer to store any of the product is eliminated. After the pipeline is initially filled, the producer pumps into the system only that amount of water that has been consumed.

Dispersion is, in reality, a compromise between the desires or exigencies of the producer and those of the consumer. The producer would like the consumer to take possession of the item directly at the time and site of production. The consumer, on the other hand, would like the item brought directly to him in consumable quantities at approximately the time he would like to consume them. Obviously, neither one has sufficient power to impose completely his desires on the other. Hence, the dispersion system has evolved from interaction, competition, and compromise.

Institutions have come into existence as a dispersion bridge between the producer and the end consumer. Distribution channels for industrial goods include: (1) manufacturer-user; (2) manufacturer-industrial distributor-user; (3) manufacturer-agent middleman-user. Distribution channels for consumer goods include: (1) manufacturer-consumer; (2) manufacturer-retailer-consumer; (3) manufacturer-wholesaler-retailer-consumer; (4) manufacturer-agent middleman-wholesaler-retailer-consumer. These channels are commonly used for the job of demand creation and physical fulfillment of that demand. Although it is pointed out later that it is often a mistake to consider that both tasks must be performed by the same channel of distribution for a given market, it is convenient at this point to consider that these are the only channels available for dispersion.

Industrial goods are primarily sold direct from manufacturer to user, without the necessity for an institutional setup to perform the break-bulk and assembly in movement. The average amount per sale is much larger in industrial goods than in consumer goods. Because of larger average sales, the manufacturer can accumulate a large enough volume of goods for a single direct shipment to the customer without a break-bulk and reassembly point. From the demand creation point of view, manufacturers apparently prefer this channel of distribution because of the highly rational and qualified buyers in the industrial market. Manufacturers feel that highly technically trained salesmen are required. Many of them feel that the industrial distributor, since he must by his very nature handle several lines, does not have the technical competence in each line to represent them adequately. In any case, the typical physical movement is direct from the manufacturer to the customer, in sharp contrast to the rather elaborate structure for dispersion of consumer goods.

In order that one may understand the dispersion system for consumer goods from a physical movement point of view, it is first necessary to investigate the nature of the retail structure. Phillips and Duncan classify retailing into four distinct methods:

"The first and most important of these is through the retail store to which the customer comes to make selections or from which he orders by telephone or by mail. The authors estimate that about 97 percent of all retail sales are made in this manner. The second method is retailing by mail, in which orders are solicited by catalogues, advertising in publications and correspondence with shipments by mail, express, or freight. This method is illustrated by the mail order house, and it accounts for nearly 1 percent of all retail sales. House to house selling, the third method of selling at retail, is responsible for about 1.3 percent of total retail sales. Finally, about 1 percent of all retail sales is handled through automatic vending machines.[13]

Thus, nearly all retail scales are at locations where the customer comes to make selections. There is, however, a considerable range of distances traveled and sizes of purchases which depend upon the individual, the type of goods desired, and the type of location to which he travels.

If the retailer's volume of business justifies volume shipments direct from the producer, these may take place. However, many thousands of retailers and/or producers do a volume of business so small, with consequent small single shipments, that such volume shipments are not economically feasible. From the physical movement point of view, this justifies the wholesale structure. The nature of this physical function is shown in Figures 2-3 and 2-4.

Producers ship volume quantities to a warehouse, as indicated in Figure 2-3, and then shipments of less than volume quantities are made to the retailer. The reassembly operation is demonstrated in Figure 2-4. On the inbound side of the warehouse, either a rail siding or a truck dock handles inbound truckloads or carloads of particular kinds of commodities. These goods are then unloaded from the rail car or truck and placed in storage in the warehouse, as indicated by the arrows in the chart. A particular retailer's order might consist

[13] F. Phillips and D. J. Duncan, *Marketing Principles and Methods* (Homewood, Ill.: Richard D. Irwin, Inc., 1964), pp. 134–135.

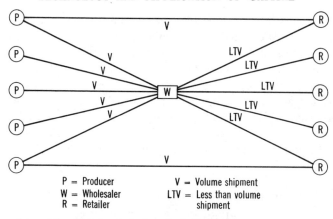

P = Producer   V = Volume shipment
W = Wholesaler   LTV = Less than volume
R = Retailer   shipment

Figure 2-3. *The Wholesaler's Break-Bulk Process.*

of five cases of pears, three cases of peaches, four cartons of orange juice, and three cartons of coffee. An order picker will then take these quantities from storage and reassemble them on the outbound dock as a single shipment for delivery to the retailer. Many times these so-called order picking lines are mechanized, in an attempt to modify or lower the reassembly cost in the warehouse.

Authors in the marketing area usually consider the wholesale structure to consist of the following: merchant wholesalers, manu-

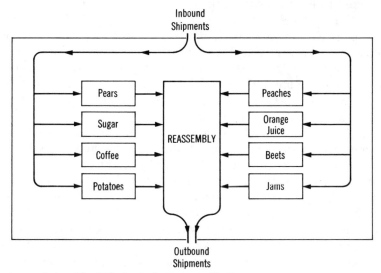

Figure 2-4. *The Wholesaler's Reassembly Process.*

facturers' sales branches, petroleum bulk tank stations, retailer owned wholesale operations agents and brokers, and assemblers. The break-bulk and reassembly operation is normally performed by all of the first four. Agent middlemen do not normally perform physical break-bulk. Many large manufacturers and retailers perform their own break-bulk and reassembly operation, either in their own warehouses or in rented spaces. These branch warehouses might also be called part of the wholesale structure, since essentially the same physical operations would be performed in them as by an independent wholesaler.

THE EFFECT OF CUSTOMER REQUIREMENTS ON FIXED COSTS IN DISPERSION

All carriers, both on the concentration and dispersion sides, want to apply capital, in the form of transport equipment, to movement in order to obtain declining unit costs. However, as noted above, since the consumer usually travels a very limited distance to make a purchase and purchases small quantities at any one time, large volume shipments direct from the producer to the consumer are considerably less feasible on the dispersion side. Therefore, as we found earlier, the retail and wholesale structures have developed to fulfill the needs of the dispersion system for break-bulk and reassembly points between volume and less than volume shipments.

Quicker times in transit are demanded in dispersion for a variety of reasons. One of the more important is the added value of the goods after processing. Any delays in getting the goods from the producer to the consumer will increase the amount of interest expense on inventory while the goods are in this pipeline. Therefore, it is desirable to consider inventory interest cost, then to select the means of movement which will keep this at a minimum.

Faster transit time between producer and consumer usually will require smaller shipments; consequently, the application of capital to the movement process will not be as feasible. Thus, there is a very clear need on the dispersion side of movement for a qualified service for smaller quantities per shipment, a capable performance of the transfer operation, and faster times in transit. This means a smaller number of movement units per power unit. There is, correspondingly, less opportunity for the cost curve of movement to be a declining unit cost curve. In fact, dispersion movement tends to approach a constant unit cost curve because of the high proportion of variable costs in the operation.

SUMMARY OF APPLICABILITY OF CAPITAL TO MOVEMENT

Capital application will be within the framework of movement units per power unit and the characteristics of the concentration and dispersion movements, as described in earlier portions of the chapter. The applicability of capital is determined by total volume available through a given period of time, quantity per shipment, repetitive operations (both transfer and line-haul), speed in transit, and the nature of the commodity. The influence of these factors is summarized in Table 2-1.

TABLE 2-1. *Applicability of Capital to Movement in the Various Transportation Agencies*

	RAIL		MOTOR		WATER		PIPELINE		AIR	
	C	D	C	D	C	D	C	D	C	D
1. Volume										
a. Total volume available through a given period of time.	F	U	U	F	F	U	F	F	U	F
b. Quantity per shipment.	F	U	U	F	F	U	F	F	U	F
2. Nature of the commodity	F	U	U	F	F	U	F	F	U	F
3. Repetitive operations										
a. Transfer	F	U	U	F	F	U	F	F	U	U
b. Line-haul	F	F	U	F	F	U	F	F	U	F
4. Speed in transit	U	U	F	F	U	U	U	U	F	F

Key: C—Concentration
    D—Dispersion
    F—Favorable to the application of capital to movement in the form of more movement units per power unit and larger power units.
    U—Unfavorable to the application of capital to movement in the form of more movement units per power unit and larger power units.

RAIL MOVEMENTS

Capital is best applied to railroad movement on the concentration side. As noted earlier, the rail operation adds more movement units to the power unit on the concentration side. The quantity per shipment is large, and the commodity basically consists of bulk, unpackaged raw materials. Since raw materials are more easily handled by mechanical means in the transfer operation than are packaged goods, application of capital on the concentration side is advantageous. The comparative speed of rail movement is slow, but the cost advantages from capital application overcome this disadvantage.

On the dispersion side, railroads are unable to meet the demand of the customer for the movement of manufactured commodities. This does not mean that the railroads do not handle volumes of manufactured goods, but the demands for speed in transit, ease of transfer, and smaller quantities per shipment all combine to favor other forms of transportation in their movement. However, this does not consider the improvement in service brought about by increased use of "piggybacks," trailers or containers on flat cars.

Thus, the railroad industry can better apply capital to its concentration side than to its dispersion side. Evidence of this may be seen in Table 2-2, which shows the ratio of empty car-miles to loaded car-miles by type of equipment. In the eastern district, for example, the ratio is 38 per cent for boxcars, 72 per cent for gondola and hopper cars, 97 per cent for tank cars, 75 per cent for refrigerator cars, 102 per cent for stock cars, and 48 per cent for flat cars.

TABLE 2-2. *Ratio of Empty to Loaded Car-Miles of Type of Equipment*

TERRITORY	BOX CARS		GON-DOLA	TANK CARS	REFRIG-ERATOR CARS	STOCK CARS	FLAT (T OF C) CARS
	Total	Car-load					
Eastern district	.45	.47	.74	1.02	.79	1.02	.20
Pocahontas region	.57	.59	1.06	1.07	.76	1.93	.21
Southern region	.42	.44	.88	1.03	.82	.97	.36
Western district	.41	.42	.89	1.02	.52	.82	.29

Source: *Rail Carload Cost Scales by Territories for the Year 1961*, Interstate Commerce Commission, Bureau of Accounts, Cost Finding and Valuation, Washington, D.C., February, 1963.

WATER TRANSPORTATION

Water carriers on the inland waterways usually move multiple movement units with a single power unit, and are most amenable to the application of capital on the concentration side. Forty barges with one tug on the lower Mississippi River can move the equivalent of several trainloads of raw materials. The combined factors of multiple units with a single power unit and the buoyancy of water make possible the hauling of large volumes. Although the speed of barges compared to motor and air transportation is relatively slow, the large volumes and ease of transfer and line-haul operations overcome the unfavorable slow transit time. It is relatively easy to perform the transfer operation for bulk commodities moved by water, but more difficult to do this for packaged freight. Water transport on the inland waterways is mainly in the form of raw materials.

MOTOR TRANSPORTATION

The application of capital in motor transportation is most favorable on the dispersion side of movement. Since the motor carriers are single movement units with single power unit operation, they cannot compete successfully, on a cost basis, with the railroads and water carriers in the concentration process except over short distances and under special circumstances. A modification of this occurs when there are two trailers per power unit.

Motor carriers are better suited for handling smaller quantities per shipment. It was pointed out that, in the dispersion process, the quantities per shipment become smaller as they approach the ultimate consumer. In the transfer operation, the problem of break-bulk and reassembly looms large on the dispersion side. This operation is primarily concerned with packaged freight, which is more difficult to transfer mechanically than is bulk freight. For this reason, the motor carrier, with its lower terminal costs, is more economically justified in performing the transfer operation on the dispersion side than are railroad and water transportation. The operating ratio (or proportion of total operating expense to total operating revenues) of the motor carriers is much higher than that of the railroads. However, this is compensated for by the higher capital turnover, or higher ratio of annual gross operating revenue to investment in operating assets, of the motor carriers.

Motor transportation's over-all speed, as compared to water and rail transport, is somewhat greater. Although the line-haul speed of the motor and rail carrier may in some cases be approximately equal, the over-all speed of the motor carrier seems to be somewhat faster from consignor to consignee. Thus, capital in the motor carrier industry seems best applied to the dispersion side.

PIPELINES

Pipelines are unique in that conditions for the application of capital are favorable on both sides of the movement process. However, the same pipe is rarely used for both concentration and dispersion. Rather, one pipe carries the crude oil from the oil wells to the refinery, and another set of pipes carries the finished products from the refinery to the markets.

The pipes used in concentration are generally larger than those used in dispersion. The pipes are smallest at the producing wells, becoming larger in diameter as the shipments are concentrated into larger quantities for shipment to the refinery. The dispersion pipelines are largest at the refinery, becoming progressively smaller as break-bulk points near the markets are reached. The liquid nature of the product makes it relatively easy to perform the transfer operation. The line-haul speed of pipelines is roughly comparable to that of inland water transportation.

AIR TRANSPORTATION

The application of capital to movement by air is most favorable on the dispersion side, particularly for those shipments that are moved long distances and for which high speed is desired. Goods moved by air are mostly packaged goods of sufficiently high unit value to bear the additional cost of the high speed movement. Present movement costs limit the volume of goods that can be moved per shipment, and these are restricted to those necessitating speed. Future technological improvements may make it possible to have multiple movement units with a single power unit and, thereby, increase the volume of goods moving by air.

TABLE 2-3. *Selected Comparative Characteristics of the Various Agencies of Transportation*

	RAIL MULTI-MOVEMENT UNITS		MOTOR SINGLE MOVEMENT UNITS		WATER MULTI-MOVEMENT UNITS		PIPELINE		AIR SINGLE MOVEMENT UNITS	
	C	D	C	D	C	D	C	D	C	D
1. Comparative Cost										
a. Long haul	Low	—	—	Medium	Low	—	Low	Medium	—	High
b. Short haul	Low	—	—	Medium	Low	—	Low	Medium	—	—
2. Speed in transit										
a. Over-all	Medium	—	—	Medium	Slow	—	Medium	Medium	—	Fast
b. Terminal time	Slow	—	—	Fast	Medium	—	Fast	Fast	—	Medium
c. Line-haul	Medium	—	—	Medium	Slow	—	Medium	Medium	—	Fast
3. Loss and damage	Low	—	—	Medium	N.A.		N.A.		—	N.A.
4. Packing requirements	Low	—	—	Low	Low	—	None	None	—	Low
5. Interchange of equipment within the form	Nearly All	—	—	Some	Nearly All	—	All	All	—	Some
6. Unit value of goods generally shipped	Low	—	—	Medium to High	Low	—	Low to Medium	Medium to High	—	High
7. Effect of weather/climate	Very Little	—	—	Some	Some	—	None	None	—	Some
8. Turnover of capital	Slow	—	—	Fast	Medium	—	Slow	Slow	—	Medium
9. Flexibility in meeting changing traffic patterns	Inflexible	—	—	Flexible	Flexible	—	Inflexible	Inflexible	—	Flexible

Appendix to Chapter Two

Methods of Cost Determination

Companies involved in distribution need reasonably accurate information on the cost of furnishing particular services in order to be able to plan and control properly.[14] The control department should primarily report and analyze for management the results of efforts by involved departments to meet the costs upon which the sales price is predicated.

Much of the difficulty in cost accounting originates with the way the account books are maintained. When managers first realized the necessity for keeping data on the operations of the business, their first concern was to establish accounts which would reflect the status of the business at a particular time. These accounts came to be known as balance sheet accounts, reflecting the assets and equities of the business on a certain date. Gradually, managers began to feel the need for flow information which would reflect the income and expense of the enterprise. Such accounts came to be known as statement of profit and loss accounts, and were usually kept on a functional basis in order to summarize the over-all costs of performing a particular function or service.

Records of this sort may well serve the needs for financial control of the business enterprise, but they are inadequate for the application of management planning and control to particular segments. For example, if the manufacturer wished to obtain the cost of manufacturing a particular product, he would have to allocate parts of the various functional accounts to the production costs of the job concerned. Much progress has been made by industrial and public utility cost accountants in developing methods of allocation for determining

---

[14] Perhaps the prime managerial purpose of cost analysis should be to evaluate the cost of performing the service in any one of a number of alternative methods in order to properly meet or beat a competitor's price in a given market.

and planning costs of production and/or service.[15] Some of this technology will be described in this chapter.

CLASSIFICATIONS OF COST

Four categories of cost need to be defined before discussing the methods of determining costs. These include *variable costs, fixed costs, joint costs,* and *common costs.*

Variable costs are those expenses that vary with changes in volume of output; these are usually considered as cost which will increase as volume increases. *Fixed costs* are those expenses which do not vary with changes in volume of output, but are related to time and plant capacity. Since, in the long run, nearly all costs are variable to some degree with changes in their level of output, the element of time is important in defining fixed costs. For example, depreciation on equipment might be considered a fixed cost (assuming use of the straight line depreciation method) if the expense period were one year or less; however, it could be considered a variable expense if the period of time were long enough to provide for replacement. Fixed costs are related to capacity in the sense that they will increase or decrease as the capacity of the plant is increased or decreased. They are the expenses of providing capacity in the distribution system.

Joint costs are those costs incurred when the production of one commodity or service creates another at the same time. *Common costs* are those costs incurred in providing a service for a range of products. An example of a common cost is the expense of the power unit for

[15] In 1914, the Interstate Commerce Commission prescribed a uniform system of accounts to be used by all reporting railroads. This same system was later adapted for use in the motor common carrier industry and for other agencies regulated by the Interstate Commerce Commission. Similar systems have been devised for the airline industry by the Civil Aeronautics Board. Unfortunately, in attempting to determine movement costs, one must work the functional accounts as they are defined for each of the movement agencies by the respective regulatory body.

The Interstate Commerce Commission periodically publishes a summarization of railroad carload and less-than-carload costs. Similar studies are also published for the motor carriers. The studies are usually for a particular geographic region and are brought up to date by adjusting for changes in wages and prices since the previous study. They represented a pioneering effort in transportation cost accounting, but the techniques need modification to determine more accurately costs in today's highly competitive market.

line-haul movement of several railroad cars as a single train load; the expense of the power unit must be borne commonly by all of the cars in the train. Up to a point, common costs and joint costs are alike in that they are not divisible or apportionable to the products for which the costs were incurred. The distinguishing feature of joint costs of commodities is that an increase in the production of one commodity or service means an increase in the production of the other. One of the best examples of joint costs is the situation in which the movement from a terminal by a carrier brings about the necessity, at least theoretically and often actually, of a return movement to the original terminal. Round-trip total costs, therefore, are true joint costs.

We might say that all joint costs are common costs, but that common costs are not necessarily joint costs. For example, if a train of one hundred cars moved from A to B, fully loaded, and returned empty from B to A, the expense of their return (a joint cost) would have to be borne jointly by all of the one hundred cars fully loaded from A to B. However, train operating costs are incurred in common for a number of commodities or services, and are not joint costs. The allocation of either joint or common costs to particular products is very difficult and, in many cases, is done arbitrarily to determine costs of service.

In spite of the difficulties encountered in assigning common and joint costs, distribution managements must attempt to determine them in some manner, in order that they may exercise properly their planning and control functions. Industrial cost accountants have long segregated the functional accounts into cost centers and then attempted to determine the behavior of costs within each of these cost (or profit) centers. These centers are normally the principal activities of the business enterprise, and normally there should be a measurable output from the center, regardless of whether or not the particular activity retains its specific identity in the finished product or service.

The Interstate Commerce Commission, in studies of railway operating costs,[16] utilized the following cost centers:

1. *Running service* (all line-haul or road operations but excluding train switching).

[16] Bureau of Accounts, Cost Finding Section, Interstate Commerce Commission, *Explanation of Rail Cost Finding Procedures and Principles Relating to the Use of Costs* (Washington, D.C., November, 1963, Statement No. 7-63), pp. 94–95. Also Bureau of Accounts, Cost Finding Section, Interstate Commerce Commission, *Formula for Use in Determining Rail Freight Service Costs* (Washington, D.C., November, 1963, Statement No. 6-63).

2. *Switching service* (all switching operations, whether yard or train switching).
3. *Station platform service* (all platform work for carload and less-than-carload shipments).
4. *Station clerical service* (all freight station operations, excluding only the platform work and such train work as dispatching train orders, and so forth).
5. *Special services* (cleaning cars, furnishing grain doors, bidding livestock, and so forth).
6. *Less-than-carload pickup and delivery.*
7. *Loss and damage.*
8. *Coal and ore wharves.*

The Commission has a cost formula for the separation of freight and passenger costs. A similar classification for common motor carriers might include line-haul expense, dock expense, pickup-and-delivery expense, shipment clerical expense, and general overhead.[17]

The cost formulas of the Interstate Commerce Commission attempt to allocate joint and common costs by determining the variability within each of the cost centers with changes in volume of traffic. Constant expenses in each category are determined by relating dollars of expense per mile of road to thousands of gross ton-miles per mile of road. This shows the variability of the expense category with changes in traffic density; the intercept of the line of best fit with the vertical axis indicates the level of constant expenses within that particular expense category.

Various service units are used to proportion the cost from the cost centers to the factors which cause cost differences in freight transportation. The factors selected by the Interstate Commerce Commission were weight, weight density, and distance. These assignments were made on an average basis, the average being a result of the division of the total expense in the respective cost centers by the total number of service units for that particular cost center. Constant costs in each cost center were assigned to the appropriate category of weight, weight density, and/or distance. The result was a summation of costs by distance groups which showed the effects of weight and weight density within each distance block.

---

[17] Bureau of Accounts, Interstate Commerce Commission, *Simplified Procedure for Determining Cost of Handling Freight by Motor Carriers* (Washington, D.C., July, 1962, Highway Form B, Statement No. 5-62). Also, Bureau of Accounts, Cost Finding and Valuation, Interstate Commerce Commission, *Formula for the Determination of the Costs of Motor Carriers of Property* (Washington, D.C., August 1955, Highway Form A, Statement No. 8-55).

AN ILLUSTRATION OF A COST STUDY

In order to illustrate the techniques that can be utilized in solving the problem of common and joint costs, a study is presented involving regular common motor carriers in the following section. This study, conducted by the A. T. Kearney Company for the Michigan Public Service Commission, investigated costs of common motor carriers operating in Michigan.

The transporting of general freight by a motor carrier involves the following main elements: (1) picking up the shipment from the shipper in the originating city; (2) if it is a less than volume shipment, handling the shipment across the dock in the originating city; (3) transporting the shipment inter-city (the line-haul operation); (4) if it is a less than volume shipment, handling the shipment across the dock in the destination city; and (5) delivering the shipment to the consumer in the destination city. In addition, under certain conditions, the transfer of a less than volume shipment across the dock may be necessary at an intermediate break-bulk terminal. Also, shipments are sometimes interlined or transferred between carriers.

Nine factors causing cost difference were used in determining the cost of transporting general freight. These included: length of line-haul trip; balance or flow of traffic; load factor; size, congestion, and other characteristics within the pickup-and-delivery cities; number of pieces in the shipment; density; weight; abnormal shape or size of the shipment; and susceptibility to loss or damage. The costing of a freight shipment requires a determination of the effect of each factor on costs at the various centers of work activity. Since each factor is involved in several work centers, its over-all effect may be treated more logically by building up costs by work centers and summarizing the results in tables.

The development of cost by work centers is discussed under the headings of Dock Handling Costs, Pickup-and-Delivery Costs, Terminal Clerical Cost, Overhead Costs, Transfer or Break-Bulk Costs, Interline Costs, Claims Costs, and Line-Haul Costs.[18] Alloca-

---

[18] All operating costs were analyzed and allocated to the following centers: line-haul costs (equipment costs, wages, and overhead costs), pickup-and-delivery costs (equipment costs, wages, and overhead costs), dock costs (wages and overhead costs), terminal facility costs, other terminal costs (clerical costs and general overhead costs), and general and administrative costs (clerical base costs and general base costs).

tion of these groups of expenses, while not complex, relied on detailed accounting analyses. This involved not only collections of varied expense pools, but also varied methods of distribution involving different base units. Typical base units used for this purpose were: line-haul miles, pickup-and-delivery miles, pickup-and-delivery hours, dock pounds, pickup-and-delivery pounds, freight bills, revenue, and tonnage.

DOCK HANDLING COSTS

In determining the direct labor cost of handling freight on any dock, three basic factors must be considered: (1) physical characteristics of the dock; (2) physical characteristics of the freight handled; and (3) type of handling system used. Once this information has been determined, through actual or statistical analysis, labor standards (based on time study or methods of time measurement) can be applied to produce elemental time values applicable to each stage of the operation for the various types and combinations of handling systems. These, in turn, can be compared with actual dock man-hours to establish productivity levels. Current labor rates may then be applied to arrive at dock handling cost.

With time elements established and labor cost per hour and overhead unit costs determined, the final dock cost figures could be developed for weight, pieces and density, as shown in Table 2-4.

TABLE 2-4. *Dock Handling Costs for Detroit and Pontiac**

	PER SHIPMENT	PER POUND	PER PIECE	PER CUBIC FOOT
Dock Time (Hours)	0.125025	0.000042	0.006380	0.000554
Cost Per Hour	$3.2034	$3.2034	$3.2034	$3.2034
Subtotal	0.40052	0.00013	0.02044	0.00176
Dock Overhead	0.09576	0.00003	0.00489	0.00042
TOTAL COST	$0.49628	$0.00016	$0.02533	$0.00218

Additives: $0.007 per piece for shipments with one to ten pieces.
$0.002 per piece for each additional piece over ten in a shipment.
$0.379 per shipment for every 40 cubic feet beyond the initial 40 cubic feet which is covered in the per-shipment constant.

* *State of Michigan, Intrastate Motor Carrier Cost Study, General Commodities* (Chicago: A. T. Kearney & Co., April 1961), p. 11–23.

PICKUP-AND-DELIVERY COSTS

As in the analysis of the dock handling operation, certain basic data had to be determined for comparative purposes. The two major cost factors in pickup-and-delivery are time and distance. The time factors established were: (1) terminal time spent by the driver at the start and at the end of each dispatch, (2) driving time, both stem[19] and that within the delivery or pickup zone, and (3) stop time.

Volume and less than volume shipments were analyzed separately. The break point between volume and less than volume was adhered to in order to establish, insofar as possible, the conditions which are inherent in handling shipments of various sizes. Less than volume shipments are those that are dock handled, while volume shipments are not handled across the dock. Volume shipments were subdivided into shipments that were worked by the driver and those that were loaded or unloaded by non-carrier personnel.[20]

A separate analysis was made for the pickup-and-delivery operations. However, the analysis resulted in only a four per cent difference in the less than volume operation and a two per cent difference in the volume operation. In both cases, the delivery was more costly than the pickup. Because of this relatively minor cost differential, and because every shipment involves both a pickup and a delivery, these two items were combined for an average cost of both pickup and delivery.

The effect of number of shipments per stop on the stop cost per shipment also had to be determined. The cost per stop was approximately the same, regardless of the number of shipments picked up or delivered. The number of shipments per stop was developed independently for each location, so that the cost influence would be reflected by locations. No significant correlation between size of shipment and number of shipments per stop was determined. It was also necessary to determine the additional cost of the trailer used in spotting a volume load at a customer's dock. This cost was used in the buildup of the total cost of handling volume loads to the extent that each weight bracket consisted of spotted freight.

Separate pickup-and-delivery costs were established for less than

---

[19] Stem refers to driving to and from the delivery or pickup zone.

[20] Special considerations with respect to the buildup of the cost tables included the separation of pickup from delivery and the effect of the multiple shipment stops and trailer spotting costs.

volume shipments, volume shipments worked at the customer's dock, and volume shipments spotted at the customer's dock. The variables that had to be established for each type of pickup-and-delivery operation were:

1. Driver labor costs:
   a. at the terminal before and after each dispatch
   b. en route (driving time)
   c. stop time (material handling and other elements related to the stop)
   d. overhead costs
2. Equipment costs:
   a. at the terminal
   b. en route
   c. at the stop
   d. trailer cost of shipment if shipment were spotted

An overhead per cent was calculated from an analysis of the cost figures and reflected welfare, social security, state unemployment tax, dispatcher salaries, etc. The time values and unit cost for wages and overhead were established; it was then possible to cost out a pickup-and-delivery portion of the terminal activity. The shipment cost is specifically calculated, but the material handling portion is shown as unit costs summarized by labor, equipment, and overhead by pounds, density, and pieces.

TERMINAL CLERICAL COSTS

A clerical cost per shipment was calculated in order to spread the cost of clerical activity to both the originating and destination terminals. These costs include all office costs at the terminal level. The total costs were divided by double the number of bills issued, counting each bill as both inbound and outbound.

OVERHEAD COSTS

General overhead costs were computed for the following cost centers: terminal facility costs, terminal overhead costs, and general and administrative overhead costs. The cost for terminal facilities represents rent, building depreciation, and property taxes. A portion of these costs is related to weight, and a portion to shipments. This relationship mainly reflects the use of the dock to handle less than volume shipments and, therefore, a higher percentage of facility costs involved in handling this type of freight, compared to volume shipments. Terminal overhead costs are all terminal costs of a general nature. The basis of distribution selected was a percentage of all other terminal costs.

General and administrative costs are general costs at the home-office level. They include, primarily, expenses of administrative activity, but also some general sales and advertising costs. These costs fall in two categories: those that may pertain to the handling of freight bills, and those that pertain to the total operation. For this reason, total general and administrative costs were distributed partly as a per cent of all other costs and partly as a cost per freight bill.

TRANSFER OR BREAK-BULK COSTS

In the normal operation of a truck line, line-haul loads can often be improved by loading freight through intermediate terminals. To do this, the less than volume freight must be handled across the dock of the intermediate location. This transfer, or break-bulk operation, adds to the terminal costs and partially offsets the savings gained in the line-haul operation.

To apply this additional cost to a specific move, the percentage of transfer or break-bulk freight, point to point, for the cities in the study, or the average for all of the points, must be known. In any movement where 100 per cent of the freight is handled through a break-bulk terminal, the entire additional cost per hundredweight would be added. When less than 100 per cent of the freight was transferred, the proportionately smaller per cent should be added.

INTERLINE COSTS

As in break-bulk operation within one company, there are instances in the handling of a shipment where transfer occurs between carriers. This interline operation adds to the cost of handling, and, in such cases, additional cost factors will have to be included. For less than volume shipments, there will be two additional dock handlings and one additional delivery; for volume shipments, there will be one additional delivery. The average percentage of interline freight and the intended cost were determined for such movements. Such costs were added to other costs in proportion to the amount of such freight moving through the terminal.

CLAIMS COSTS

Included as a cost of handling a freight shipment is the cost of loss and damage to the cargo. This cost was distributed through the terminal cost factor on the basis of a cost per shipment. To consider this as applicable equally to all shipments is not sound from a cost accounting standpoint. Each shipment provides an opportunity for error, and the rules of chance govern which piece of freight may be lost or damaged. The two most important aspects of claims costs are susceptibility of the item to loss or damage and value of the merchandise. Such claims are normally applied on an over-all basis. A special study was made, however, to indicate the extent of necessity adjustments to cost based on the experience of a particular commodity with loss and damage claims. A similar study is needed to determine the increase in carriers' rates necessitated by their increase in liability in the transportation of shipments of extraordinary value.

LINE-HAUL COSTS

Line-haul costs relate to the over-the-road operation between terminal locations. Each of the individual cost items, except "driving" wages, was put into one of four groups of cost and then converted to the formula, involving the following: equipment cost per mile, extra trailer cost per day, overhead on driver wages, additional overhead on driver wages. Since the basis of application for this formula is driving wages, it was necessary to develop the driving wage cost per mile under existing operation conditions. This labor unit cost per mile and the four elements in the line-haul cost formula became the basis for the development of the line-haul cost per trip by mileage brackets. It was determined in the study that, in normal operations, a full day's use of the line-haul trailer is required in all line-haul operations, irrespective of distance. Therefore, the full daily cost of trailer was included in the cost of each line-haul move. Using the driving cost per mile and the line-haul cost formula, the total line-haul cost for each mileage bracket was computed.

Since only negligible cost differences exist between the movements of an empty and a fully loaded trailer, the total cost of the line-haul was regarded as constant. The line-haul cost per hundredweight, then, depends entirely on the amount of weight being carried. The constant cost of the line-haul move for all mileage brackets was divided by load weights to determine line-haul costs in terms of hundredweight.

In order to assess properly line-haul costs to a freight movement on a point-to-point basis, it is necessary to have information on the average-line-haul load factors between various points.

The proper costing of a line-haul movement was treated in this study on a round-trip basis. Inbound load averages were calculated for this purpose. Once the inbound load averages, based on the origins of the trailers and the weight of the loads carried, were developed, a statistical average-inbound trailer was constructed for each inbound point in terms of miles traveled and weight carried inbound. The inbound average includes volume loads, combination loads, and empties, because the same inbound equipment is used for all loads outbound.

Once the statistical inbound trailer was determined, it then was combined with the point-to-point outbound load average on a weighted basis to determine the proper round-trip load factor used on point-to-point operations between the terminal cities.

Density of the product transported has an effect on the line-haul cost per hundredweight in those cases where the lack of density makes impossible full utilization of the actual weights permitted by law. In line-haul operation, since tonnage or service requirements are not available where full loads are not ordinarily handled over the road, the density of the product is not a cost-causing factor. Also, when the density of the product exceeds the requirements to fully utilize the weight limitations of the trailer, the limit is reached from the standpoint of its effect on cost. As the density increases beyond the requirement to meet the weight limit of the trailer, there is some opportunity to mix low density with heavy freight to provide full utilization of equipment. However, for the purpose of this study, the effect of density as a cost-causing element was limited to the range of densities below the point at which the full utilization of the weight capacity of the vehicle could be made.

A study of the fleets of the carriers to determine average trailer size showed maximum useful density from a line-haul standpoint to be approximately fifteen pounds per cubic foot. This calculation was based on an average trailer length of 35.6 feet and a load average weight limit, under existing law, for the average trailer of approximately thirty thousand pounds. The interior area of the average trailer was computed at two thousand cubic feet, which, equated to the thirty thousand pound average maximum load, equals an average density of fifteen pounds per cubic foot.

A study of the principal commodities moved by the carriers involved in the study was conducted, and the density determined for each of the major items. Once the average density was established, it was possible, since average cost would represent average density, to develop an adjustment table to increase or decrease line-haul cost as the density of specific products varied from the average density.

Since under some circumstances, due to operating conditions, actual point-to-point load factors are higher or lower than if a trailer were loaded completely with the product involved, an adjustment limit was established.

COMPARISON OF COST AND REVENUE

Several uses may be made of the results of cost studies of freight movements. Cost incurred and revenue obtained on various segments of traffic can be compared. Some results of the Michigan intrastate motor common carrier study are shown in Table 2-5. It is apparent that the motor carriers incurred operating losses on shipments under 800 pounds. At volumes over that amount, the carriers incurred an operating profit.

Such figures are somewhat misleading when taken as totals. It was possible, on individual shipments, to compute whether or not there was a profit or a loss. However, the calculation of arithmetical means and standard deviations within each weight group indicated a wide range in the percentage of cost to revenue. For example, in the weight group of 100 pounds the percentage of cost to revenue was 184.3, as shown in Table 2-5. The arithmetic mean was 247 and the standard deviation was 237. This indicated that while the industry was losing over-all on the 100 pound shipments, it nevertheless was earning money on some categories of shipments.

Therefore, it was necessary to search further for data which would guide management decisions on pricing. Tabulations of cost to revenue were calculated on the basis of mileage, classification rating, and classification commodity item number. Cross-classifications then made it possible to compute more accurately the segments of traffic where the carriers were making or losing money on freight movement.

The use of such data by both motor carriers and regulatory

TABLE 2-5. *Comparison of Cost and Revenue by Weight Group*

WEIGHT GROUP	NUMBER OF SHIPMENTS	TOTAL COSTS	TOTAL REVENUE	PERCENTAGE OF COST TO REVENUE
100	11108	$75710.36	$41069.59	184.3
300	2323	18818.78	11276.76	166.8
500	1124	10322.14	8059.71	128.0
800	923	10323.23	10395.30	99.3
900	740	8687.75	9137.20	95.1
1000	676	8141.32	9457.98	86.1
1500	2133	29488.62	38043.99	77.5
2000	1064	19900.25	26959.74	73.8
3000	532	14453.62	18394.59	78.6
4000	261	8807.58	12543.90	70.2
5000	202	7930.54	10399.52	76.2
10000	73	4615.44	5904.01	78.2
15000	69	5016.61	5349.49	93.8
20000	122	9361.05	9101.56	102.8
25000	21	1811.92	1957.82	92.5
30000	35	3060.89	3623.68	84.5
40000	23	2000.11	2491.47	80.2

Sources: Costs were computed from *State of Michigan, Intrastate Motor Carrier Cost Study, General Commodities* (Chicago: A. T. Kearney & Company, April, 1961). Revenues were computed from a one week waybill study.

agencies gives a much more rational basis to the pricing structure of the industry. Carriers can use it to make decisions on particular rates. Regulatory commissions can use such information as a test of the present rate structure, and for rate proposals in the future.

OTHER POSSIBLE USES FOR COST STUDIES

One use for cost studies is to provide carrier managements with the basis for establishing performance standards in particular segments of their operations. This is particularly true where the basis of cost allocation has been an engineering or statistical study to determine the behavior of cost. For example, if the standard for a hundredweight of freight moved across the terminal dock is a given figure, then variances from this figure can show management points where corrective action may be needed.

Considerable care needs to be taken, however, in the use of these figures for standards. They must be applied only to cost situations similar to the ones for which the performance standard was constructed. An example in the cost study just described is in the area of dock costs. The largest dock in the survey was 384 feet long, 70 feet wide, and had 70 doors; the smallest dock reported was 26 feet long, 20 feet wide, and had 3 doors. An average dock was constructed for the state, resulting in an average dock size of 179.4 feet in length and 50.6 feet in width. Considerable variance was also present in crewing practice, the use of handling systems, and movement patterns across the dock. Anyone using the figures as a basis for performance standards would have to be sure that the docks under consideration were reasonably close to the average.

Another possible use of cost figures is for regulatory purposes by various governmental agencies. Most federal and state regulation has, as one objective, the assurance that the rates charged by the carriers are just and reasonable. One criterion of just and reasonable is whether or not a particular commodity pays its appropriate share of the cost of moving freight. This question can only be answered adequately by the regulatory agency if it has available to it cost figures which make possible a determination of the cost of movement. Almost equally important is the desire and ability of responsible personnel to use the cost information in making decisions; otherwise, the determination of what is just and reasonable is made myopically or by sheer intuition.

CHAPTER THREE

PROCESSING CENTERS

AND THE SPATIAL EXTENT

OF DISTRIBUTION SYSTEMS

The place of the distribution system in the interaction of human wants, skills, and resources was discussed in Chapter 1. The applicability of capital in the various movement agencies was related in Chapter 2 to the market requirements for concentration and dispersion. This chapter considers processing characteristics and movement costs in determining levels of flow. Principally, weight loss or gain in processing and the type of production cost curve of the processing organization[1] determine the spatial extent of movement at the interregional, regional, and sub-regional levels.

UNBALANCED FLOW AND RATE DIFFERENCES

Normally, rates on raw materials and finished goods charged by the various transportation agencies differ. These differences make it desirable for processors to locate where their total movement cost from origin of materials to point of consumption will be minimized. If there were no difference between the inbound rate on the raw material and the outbound rate on the finished goods, the problem of industrial location would not be nearly as complex as it is.

---

[1] For the individual firm, of course, production costs would have to be computed and compared to applicable distribution costs.

70

It is germane at this point to explain why the rates on raw materials and finished goods differ.[2] It was pointed out in Chapter 2 that one of the transportation system's objectives is to apply power movement as quickly as possible, in order to achieve either a declining unit cost curve or a lower total cost curve. This may be accomplished by applying more movement units per power unit or greater payload in relation to the horsepower of the power unit itself. The job of concentration is performed as quickly as possible in order that power may be applied with a resulting movement in volume. This volume movement takes place as early as possible in the movement process, and continues through the distribution channel beyond the processing point until it reaches the point where break-bulk and reassembly occurs. After the initial break-bulk and reassembly, subsequent movements of individual shipments are lower in volume, and it becomes less and less possible to apply power to the movement process in terms of the relation of payload to the power unit.

UNBALANCED MOVEMENT

If the carriers had a balanced flow of movement directionally on each portion of the transportation system, and if population and raw material were equally distributed throughout the market area, it might be possible for the transportation agencies to follow a system of average pricing. The result, considering only weight and distance, would be an equal rate on the raw material and the finished goods. However, populations and raw materials are not located uniformly throughout the market place, and there are no uniform directional movements throughout the transportation system. Populations are clustered in certain geographic areas; raw materials are available only in certain locations. The consequent imbalance in the transportation system causes a difference in rates charged on commodities moved.[3]

---

[2] There often are cost reasons which result in different rates at different points in the transportation system. The effect of such transportation cost-causing differences as weight, weight-density, distance, and the number of pieces in the shipment was discussed in Chapter 2. However, temporarily abstracting from these cost-causing differences, the explanation of differences in raw material and finished-goods rates becomes considerably simpler.

[3] For an example of geographic imbalance in the rail industry, see Table 3-7.

EXCESS CAPACITY

Carriers, thus, have excess capacity in the transportation system from two points of view. Shippers who transport their own goods and are therefore considered private carriers have problems similar to those of the carriers. The fundamental cause of imbalance arises from unequal distribution of population and raw materials. The other cause, not necessarily resulting from the first, is that the transportation system may have excess capacity between points in time throughout the whole system.

A map illustrating the effect of the first cause shows that the major population centers are located in the Northeast quadrant of the country. Raw materials from the West are moved to these centers for processing. Much of the equipment is empty on the return journey to the West because the market for finished goods in the West does not provide full volume for the equipment on the return trip.

The alternatives available to the carrier are: (1) to make the raw materials move bear the entire cost of the round trip[4] or (2) to price the return trip low enough to attract additional traffic. The carrier must, of course, recover full cost, plus a reasonable profit for both segments of the trip. He therefore tends to charge more than the actual cost for moving raw materials and to price the return portion of the journey, with finished goods, below its full cost.

Therefore, directional excess capacity provides the mechanism for value-of-service pricing which, in turn, can lead to rate charges of more or less than the full costs of movement. Specific examples of directional excess capacity are: (1) raw material movements to the eastern part of the United States; (2) the high ratio of empty miles to loaded miles for specialized types of equipment such as tank cars, refrigerator cars, stock cars, and petroleum tank trucks; and (3) the unbalanced movements into automobile assembly centers, where the inbound move of parts may be by motor common carrier of general commodities and the return move by specialized automobile haulaway truck equipment. In each of these instances, the phenomenon of directional excess capacity lets the carrier, if he so desires, utilize

---

[4] The round trip is an excellent example of joint cost, since the return trip is necessary for the equipment to be returned to origin for additional movements of raw materials. An increase in one results in an increase in the other.

value-of-service pricing to promote traffic in the direction of light loadings.

Seasonal or cyclical fluctuations in demand are another aspect of excess capacity. A common carrier must be able to handle any reasonable demands by the shipper for transportation service (within the carrier's operating rights). He must be prepared to meet such variations in the sale of the shipper's products by having the necessary equipment on hand to move them. For example, in the automobile industry 7.92 million cars were produced in 1955, 4.26 million in 1958, and 7.64 million in 1963. Carriers had to provide enough transportation equipment to meet the fluctuating demand. Such an excess capacity, created by seasonal and cyclical fluctuations of shipper demand, tends to create value-of-service pricing to induce traffic to move.

CARRIER AND SELLER COMPETITION

In value-of-service pricing (through the mechanism of excess capacity), carrier competition and seller competition in common markets create a difference between raw materials rates and finished-goods rates. To illustrate, assume, as in Figure 3-1, that Carrier 1 has been

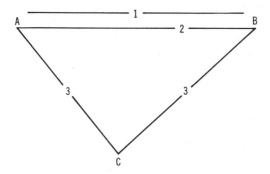

Figure 3-1. *Illustration of Carrier Competition.*

operating between points *A* and *B* and now faces competition with Carrier 2 between these two points. Further, assume complete freedom of competition within the field under consideration; there is: (1) no agreement between producers to restrict competition or production at any level, (2) no price agreement, (3) relative freedom of the companies' managements to utilize the factors of production, and (4) an elastic demand curve for the firms' services. Under such circumstances, the two carriers in the field must attempt to compete on a price and/or service basis to secure business from each other. Under conditions of pure competition, these two carriers would be willing to quote prices lower than the full cost of furnishing the service in order to take business from each other. However, it must never be overlooked that we have regulated, rather than pure, competition.

For further illustration, assume that a third carrier operates between points A and B via point C. In this instance, Carrier 3 would be a circuitous-route carrier, and would have to at least meet the price of Carriers 1 and 2 between points A and B. Carrier 3 may actually be in a fortuitous position, since it monopolizes traffic between points A and C and C and B, and therefore may be able to raise rates between these respective points in order to compete with Carriers 1 and 2 between points A and B.

Such situations may exist at various times under pure competition, regardless of the carrier's ability to obtain constant or variable costs. This is well illustrated by the rate wars of the railroads during the nineteenth century, and of the airlines and motor carriers before regulation by federal and state law. In an attempt to obtain business, carriers quite frequently lower their rates, not only below the level of their full costs of operation, but sometimes below the level of their variable costs. If such a competitive situation continues for a long period, one or more of four events is likely to occur: (1) the carriers may voluntarily agree to restrict competition on either a service or a rate basis; (2) there may be some business failures, resulting in less competition; (3) amalgamation, merger, or consolidation may occur among the carriers; or (4) restriction upon entrance into the transportation field may occur through outside control. Actually, all four have occurred in the field.

The significance of the relationship between excess capacity (directional and/or seasonal or cyclical) and carrier competition is that the former provides the mechanism for value-of-service pricing and the latter makes the carriers want to engage in this pricing practice. Beginning about 1900, railroads developed rate associations to minimize price competition among themselves. This practice has been followed by other forms of transportation, particularly those engaging in common carriage.

SHIPPER COMPETITION

In addition to the components creating value-of-service pricing, shipper competition also helps explain the differences between raw material and finished-goods rates. This will be treated in two phases: first, the competition of raw material shippers who are spatially separated from a given market; and, second, competition of processing plants to supply given markets from alternative plant locations.

Distant raw material shippers must compete with close sources for sales to a given market. Assume, as in Figure 3-2, that suppliers at

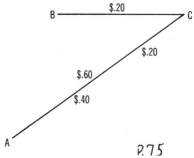

Figure 3-2. *Illustration of Shipper Competition.*

points *A* and *B* with raw material sources of equal grade are competing for sales of this raw material to a plant located in city *C*. Assume also that two different carriers are serving from *B* to *C* and from *A* to *C*. In this instance, it is obvious that if raw materials suppliers located in *A* are to compete with city *B*, they must absorb at least 40 cents per hundredweight in freight charges, the difference between the 60 cent *A*-to-*C* rate and 20 cent *B*-to-*C* rate. Only suppliers at *A* who can absorb this freight charge may attempt to compete in market *C*. However, a common result from such a competitive situation is that sellers pressure transportation companies to lower the rate in order to compete in the sellers' more distant markets.

The net result on the carrier's rate structure will be the same in terms of shipper pressure for depressed rates from geographically distant points to a common market whether raw materials or finished products are concerned. As was pointed out by J. H. von Thunen, and later by August Losch, with a single seller in a market place and a constant transportation rate per ton-mile, the market area for the product from a given plant will tend to be circular. Losch points out that as more producers enter the market place, each producer's market area becomes hexagonal. Introducing the concept of a decreasing unit cost curve (to be discussed in detail later in this chapter), the market patterns of spatially differentiated producers serving common markets will overlap at varying points in time. As presented later by Walter Isard, these hexagonal markets continuously overlap as producers competing in a common market constantly evaluate their unit costs of production, the costs of transport to the market, and the extent to which they can absorb freight into these common markets at any point.

As a result of these pressures from shippers of both raw material and finished products, the carriers have the dilemma of whether or not to lower the rate below full costs of movement to allow competition in a common market. These pressures, in the aggregate, force individual and competitive carriers to adjust their rate structure for maximum movement of goods (in keeping with revenue requirements to meet total costs of operation). This, in turn, leads to value-of-service pricing in order to maximize their total revenue.

In the railroad industry, evidence of value-of-service pricing is shown in Table 3-1. Mine products moved by the railroads had a destination value of $11.16 per ton and a rate charge of 28.13 per cent of that figure; value at destination of manufacturers' and miscellaneous products was $280.60 per ton, with a gross rate revenue at 4.06 per cent of that figure. The rate structure reflects the higher rate charge per ton for the manufactured products, which have a higher unit value. However, in proportion to the unit value of the product, rates are lower on manufacturers' products than for raw materials.

MOVEMENT COSTS OF RAW MATERIALS AND FINISHED GOODS

A final consideration in the difference between raw material and finished-goods rates is the previously discussed difference in carrier's handling costs for the two. This can easily be visualized in the case of coal. Coal cars are loaded directly from the coal tipple, and are unloaded (in the case of hopper cars) by gravity flow from the bottom of the car at the shipper's docks. Or in transferring coal from cars to lake vessel, the cars are simply turned upside down and dumped into

TABLE 3-1. *Freight Revenue and Value of Commodities Transported by Class I Line-Haul Railroads, 1959* *

PRODUCTS OF	REVENUE FREIGHT (000 TONS)	GROSS FREIGHT REVENUE		VALUE AT DESTINATION		PER CENT GROSS FREIGHT REVENUE OF VALUE AT DESTINATION
		Total (millions)	Per Ton	Total (millions)	Per Ton	
Agriculture	147,585	$1,226	$ 8.31	$ 14,592	$ 101.31	8.20
Animals and Products	10,217	243	23.80	6,145	601.44	3.96
Mines	629,128	1,975	3.10	7,023	11.16	28.13
Forests	85,939	707	8.24	4,981	57.97	14.21
Manufactures and Miscellaneous	365,339	4,160	11.39	102,515	280.60	4.06
Less-than-Carload Freight[1]	3,923	183	46.88	6,721	1,713.28	2.74

* Source: Bureau of Transport Economics and Statistics, Interstate Commerce Commission, *Freight Revenue and Wholesale Value at Destination of Commodities by Class I Line Haul Railroads, 1959* (Washington, D.C.: Interstate Commerce Commission, September, 1961), Appendix A. These figures are published every three years.

[1] All other figures in the table are for carload traffic.

the laker, which then hauls the coal to other lake ports for further transfer. Another example is wheat, which may be unloaded into a storage facility by gravity flow. The wheat is then moved into the storage elevator by conveyor belt and reloaded by gravity flow from a chute into the rail car.

At the other extreme, in the motor carrier terminal operation, a pickup unit gathers small discrete packages from the various shippers in the metropolitan area and brings the load into the terminal for reassembly into an outbound line-haul motor carrier movement unit. The individual packages must be hand moved from the shipper's dock onto the pickup truck, then unloaded, by hand, from the pickup truck onto the carrier's dock, then moved either by hand or mechanically to the other side of the dock to the appropriate line-haul unit. This process is reversed at the destination terminal. Obviously, there is a vast difference in the cost per hundredweight of handling raw materials and finished goods. These differences in handling costs add to the possibility of the carrier's pricing transportation to the shippers on a value-of-service basis.

EFFECT OF PROCESSING FACTORS

In the previous section, the factors which lead to differing raw material and finished-goods rates were discussed. Plant location analysis requires an understanding of these factors. In this section, a discussion of the weight loss or gain in processing and the type of processing cost curve as fundamental determinants of plant location is presented.

WEIGHT LOSS OR GAIN IN PROCESSING

Much has been written on the effect of weight loss or gain in processing upon the location of the processing plant. Generally, two kinds of industries locate at the point of production of the raw material: first, those industries where a high percentage of the raw material is lost in processing the material into a finished product; second, those industries where perishability of the raw material makes it necessary to locate the processing plant near its resource region.

In the forestry and mining industries, for example, there is a high proportion of weight loss in at least the initial stages of manufacture. Only one per cent of copper ore, as extracted from the ground, is commercially useful. Smelting plants are located near the mining area, and the other 99 per cent of the ore is extracted and dumped near the smelting plant before the refined copper is shipped on to other destinations. In the lumber industry, the logs are trimmed, cut, and sized into rough lumber near the production points. The lumber is then shipped from the mill to ultimate destinations, where it is transformed into various wood products in the market areas. In the beet industry, only a portion of the beet as it is dug from the ground is used for sugar purposes. Many fresh products, of course, are moved intact to the market without any processing.

Agricultural commodities such as cherries, asparagus, and tomatoes are other perishable goods processed near the production point. In such instances, the produce must be left in the field to ripen, then canned immediately, in order to maintain maximum palatability. If these products were shipped to the market either before or after reaching ripeness, they would deteriorate enough so that the canning plants must locate near where the agricultural products are grown.

Normally, products which gain weight in processing are market-oriented. From a transportation cost point of view, the material can be more economically added at the market than at an intermediate point or the point of raw material production. For example, in the soft drink industry, the basic syrups are shipped from raw material-producing points to the market place, where carbonated water is added. Such carbonation plants are usually located in the market in which the product is to be sold.

Weight loss or gain definitely affects transport requirements. Plants for weight-losing products are usually located near the raw material source, and the raw material will move a relatively short distance. On the other hand, the finished product tends to move at intra- and inter-regional levels, depending on the extent of the individual producer's market for the finished product. The raw materials of weight-gaining products may be shipped either inter- or intra-regionally, with the finished goods shipped sub-regionally. In other words, the transportation requirements for weight-losing and weight-gaining products are exact opposites. The transportation system must adapt to these requirements.

EFFECT OF SCALE ECONOMICS

Much economic theory concerns the effect of economies of scale on production costs of a firm. If a firm can realize economies of scale, the long run average cost curve will decrease over a wide range as output increases. This decrease means that successively larger scales of factor utilization are more efficient than smaller ones. Two of the greatest contributors to increasing efficiency and, hence, decreasing costs are (1) division and specialization of labor, and (2) larger and more efficient machines and/or advanced technological methods.

Not all increases in scale result in decreasing unit costs. Some firms have relatively constant costs, while others may have increasing costs. Constant cost firms do not realize substantial economies or diseconomies as they increase their output and, hence, can expand or contract their output with relatively little change in long run average total costs. Increasing cost firms, or "diseconomies of scale," mean that the long run average cost curve may first decline with an initial increase in output, but would reach its lowest point rapidly and continue with increasing costs over a wide range of output. Such diseconomies of scale can result from increasing prices in the firm's factor markets as it increases its demand, the hiring of labor which is progressively less efficient, or management's inability to control larger scale operations.

In normal economic usage, the term "production costs" and the average total cost curve would include the transportation costs of a firm. In the analysis which follows, the transportation costs of raw materials and finished goods have been removed from "production costs" and are shown separately. Thus the effects of transportation costs, as an input into the cost structure of a firm, can be considered separately. The three cases of decreasing, increasing and constant costs are shown in Figures 3-3, 3-4, 3-5. The lower solid LAPC line

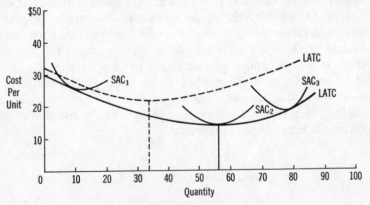

Figure 3-3. *Decreasing Unit Costs.*

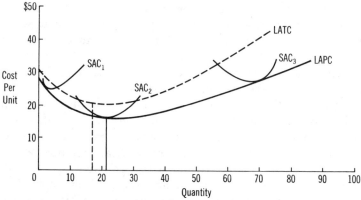

Figure 3-4. *Increasing Unit Costs.*

represents the long run average production costs (minus transportation costs), while the dotted LATC line above represents long run average total costs (production costs plus transportation costs). The smaller curves in each illustration represent three of the short run average production cost curves from which the long run curve was derived. Assuming a competitive product market and no transportation costs, the lowest point on the LAPC curve would be the optimum output for the firm, from a production cost point of view. Given the competitive product market, this is also the point of equilibrium for the firm. The space between the LAPC and LATC curves indicates the average transportation costs at any given level of output.

In analyzing transportation costs in relation to the level of output,

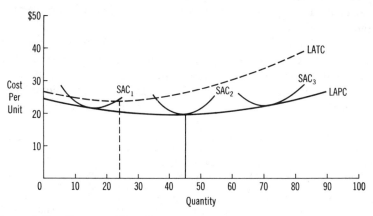

Figure 3-5. *Constant Unit Costs.*

three effects may occur. First, as output at a given location increases, it may require that raw materials be acquired at more distant sources. Second, expanding output may require the firm to either cultivate more intensively sales in its given market area or attempt extensive sales cultivation in markets more distant from the plant. Third, both of the above may occur as output expands.

In each of the illustrations, the transportation costs were assumed to be a constant cost per unit per mile, but the raw materials and finished goods both required longer shipments as output increased.[5] This increase in shipping distances causes the average transportation cost to increase with output. Herein lies the general case of the effect of transportation costs in relation to increasing levels of output. Transportation costs in a given location normally result in diseconomies of scale (increasing average transportation costs) due to the sheer activity of overcoming increases in space resulting from increases in the level of output.

The interrelationship between production costs and transportation costs to the location of a firm can be analyzed with the help of Figures 3-3, 3-4, and 3-5. As noted earlier, the optimum output and point of equilibrium in each case is the lowest point of the respective LAPC curves. Likewise, when transportation costs are added to the production costs and a competitive product market is assumed, the optimum output and point of equilibrium is the lowest point on the LATC curve. In each case this point, with transportation costs included, is at a lower output than the previous point. Therefore, in the general case (increasing average transportation costs) the effect on all three types of production costs firms is to cause the optimum output and equilibrium point to be at a lower level than if there were no transportation costs.

Thus, industries with declining average production costs tend to locate in or near their primary markets in order to minimize finished goods movement costs (since raw materials move at generally lower rates than finished products). Their raw materials move either regionally or inter-regionally, depending on the geographical separa-

---

[5] It should be recognized that there are many other cases than the one above which could cause the average transportation cost curve to take one of many possible shapes. The average transportation cost per mile is not only affected by the distance involved, but also by the size of shipments. Like other components of cost, an increase in the scale of transportation operations (the size of shipments) can result in increasing, decreasing or constant average costs. This is true since the same possibilities for using division and specialization of labor and larger and more efficient methods become available.

tion of raw materials sources and markets for the companies' products. Under such conditions, a firm with decreasing production costs tends to deliver its products to markets at a point of distance where the transportation cost increase approximately equals the production cost decrease.

Those firms with increasing production costs and a difference in raw material and finished goods rates will tend to orient themselves toward the primary markets in which they sell. Consequently, finished goods move relatively short distances in sub-regional markets. Raw materials (having the lower rates) move either intra- or inter-regionally, depending on their distance from such highly market-oriented plants. Thus, firms with increasing average production cost curves decentralize, whereas those firms with decreasing average production costs centralize and ship their finished products over a wider geographic area.

Those firms having relatively constant average production costs will have a degree of plant centralization between that of decreasing and increasing cost firms.

TRANSPORTATION AGENCY COST CHARACTERISTICS

Although the detailed cost characteristics of the various transportation agencies were presented in an earlier chapter, these characteristics are presented here in summary form in order to interrelate them with the transportation requirements presented in the above discussion. A summary is presented in tabular form (Table 3-2). The carriers have

TABLE 3-2. *Transportation Agency Cost Characteristics*

TYPES OF CARRIERS	INTER-REGIONAL (LONG DISTANCE)	INTRA-REGIONAL (MEDIUM DISTANCE)	SUB-REGIONAL (SHORT DISTANCE)
Declining unit cost			
High curve (air)	X		
Medium curve (rail, pipe)	X	X	
Low curve (inland barge)	X	X	
Constant unit cost			
Medium (motor)		X	X
Low (water)	X	X	

been grouped together as declining unit cost within the normal sphere of their operations. Based on their operational cost characteristics, the carriers are shown as participants in inter-, intra-, and sub-regional movements.

The transportation agencies with declining unit cost curves are divided into three groups: high, medium, and low cost curves. The terms high, medium and low cost curves refer to the level of origin of the cost curve being considered. This level is a function of the fixed investment required by a particular transportation medium to move a given volume of freight within a given geographical area and within a given span of time. The airlines, relative to the other forms of transportation, have a high cost curve with the bulk of their freight traffic at the inter-regional or long-distance levels. Railroads and pipelines have medium cost curves, and the bulk of their movements are at the inter- and intra-regional levels, with a relatively small amount moving at the sub-regional level. Because inland barge lines have relatively low unit cost curves, they move at all levels where the nature of the commodity and the availability of waterway facilities make barge movement practicable.

Agencies with constant unit cost curves are divided into medium-level and low-level cost agencies. Motor carriers have a medium level constant-unit-cost curve. As a result, the bulk of their traffic moves at the intra- and sub-regional levels. Although the table indicates that the motor carriers and inland barge carriers are the only agencies which share in sub-regional traffic, this is not absolute. It indicates only that the bulk of traffic at this level moves via these agencies, principally via motor transport, and that while other agencies may have some traffic at the sub-regional levels, the bulk of their traffic is at the intra- and inter-regional levels. Water carriers, other than barge operations, are a low constant unit-cost operation. Such carriers move traffic at the inter- and intra-regional levels, with only a relatively small volume at the sub-regional level.

INTERRELATION OF TRANSPORTATION REQUIREMENTS AND CARRIER COST CURVES

The purpose of this section is to interrelate the levels of transportation requirements to the cost curves of the various agencies of transport, as presented in Table 3-3.

Based upon a consideration of weight loss or gain and the type of production cost curve of the processor, the goods which move inter-regionally include finished goods from materials where there is a weight loss in processing and raw materials of products which

TABLE 3-3. *The Interrelationship of Transportation Requirements and Carrier Cost Curves*

	DECLINING UNIT COST			CONSTANT COST	
	High (Air)	Medium (Rail, Pipe)	Low (Inland Barge)	Medium (Motor)	Low (Water)
INTER-REGIONAL MOVES:					
Weight loss—finished goods	X	X			
Weight gain—raw materials		X	X		X
Type of prod. cost—finished goods					
Declining unit cost	X	X			
INTRA-REGIONAL MOVES:					
Weight loss—finished goods	X	X		X	
Weight gain—raw materials		X	X		
Type of prod. cost—finished goods					
Declining unit cost		X		X	
Constant unit cost		X		X	
SUB-REGIONAL MOVES:					
Weight loss—raw materials		X	X	X	X
Weight gain—finished goods				X	
Type of prod. cost—finished goods					
Declining unit cost				X	
Constant unit cost				X	
Increasing unit cost				X	

experience declining unit costs of production. Finished goods, where there is a weight loss, tend to move by air freight (where the unit value of the product or other factors justify the higher expense of air transport), by railroad, or by pipeline, depending upon the nature and unit value of the commodity. The raw materials of weight-gaining products tend to move by railroad, pipeline, or inland barge or other water transportation. Finished goods of declining unit cost producers tend to move by either airline or railroad and pipeline.

The commodities which move intra-regionally include: the finished goods from weight-losing materials, the raw material of weight-gaining products, and the finished goods of producers who experience decreasing and/or constant unit cost curves. The finished goods from weight-losing materials move by air, railroad or pipeline, and motor transportation. The raw materials of weight-gaining products move by railroad and pipeline, inland barge, and water transport other than barge movement. The finished goods of decreasing and constant unit cost producers move by railroad, pipeline, and motor transportation.

Those goods which move sub-regionally are: raw materials of weight-losing products, the finished goods from weight-gaining processes, and the finished goods of all producers, regardless of the type of production cost curve. The raw materials which involve weight loss in manufacture move by railroad, pipeline, motor transport, and water transport. The finished goods from processes involving weight gain move by motor transportation. The type of production cost curve has little, if any, effect on the choice of agency at the sub-regional level, since most goods will move via motor transportation at this level.

To ascertain properly market requirements for a distribution system, complete information on the flow of commodities between the various points is required. This information is readily available from the past sales records of an individual carrier which has been doing business in particular markets over a period of years. For the economy as a whole, however, its lack forms one of the major deficiencies in the field of distribution. Traffic flow data has been collected by the railroads and reported to the Interstate Commerce Commission since 1947. Similar information is available for the petroleum pipelines, but is notably lacking for motor carriers, inland waterways, and air freight.[6] National totals on each of the forms of transportation are available, but the real usefulness of traffic flow data is in establishing the nature of distribution requirements as a basis for establishing need for changes in the distribution system.[7] Therefore, in this analysis of

---

[6] It is available for the airline common carrier passenger service, through the Civil Aeronautics Board, but air freight information is available only as tonnages originating at selected cities.

[7] For several years, several transportation industry groups have requested

the regional character of traffic, principal reliance has been placed upon the traffic flow information in the railroad and petroleum pipeline industries.

In order to determine the spatial extent of movement, three levels of flow have been arbitrarily established: inter-regional, intra-regional, and sub-regional levels. The inter-regional traffic reflects long-distance movements, the intra-regional medium-distance movements, and the sub-regional short-haul movements. All figures, however, are for inter-city traffic, with no purely local traffic included.

Ten regions have been selected, principally on the basis of a classification developed by Jerome B. Pickard for the Urban Land Institute.[8] These regions were selected primarily for the population projections to be presented in Chapter 4, where some comments will be made about the increasing regionalization of our population, together with the resulting changes on transportation requirements. The ten regions include: Great Lakes, Atlantic, Southeast, Midwest, Mid-Southwest, West, Southwest, California, Florida, and Maine.[9] The regions used in tabulating railroad traffic flow do not exactly coincide with the dividing lines used by Pickard. Railroad traffic flow data is shown by state-to-state boundary lines, whereas the dividing lines used by Pickard are independent of state boundary lines.

As might be expected, traffic flow was heaviest in the areas of population concentration. More railroad traffic, accounting for 30.5 per cent, was generated in the Great Lakes region than in any other region. In the Atlantic metropolitan region, 12.6 per cent of the railroad traffic was generated; in the Southeast region, 17.4 per cent; and

a census of transportation. Pilot studies have been conducted with the expectation of conducting an adequate census. It is just as important for the transportation agencies to know flows of goods throughout the economic system as it is for manufacturers, wholesalers, and retailers to have market information as a basis for forecasting the sales of their commodities.

[8] Jerome B. Pickard, *Metropolitanization of the United States* (Washington, D.C.: Urban Land Institute, 1959), Research Monograph 2.

[9] The states included in the respective regions are as follows: Northeast region—Maine; Atlantic region—New Hampshire, Vermont, Massachusetts, Rhode Island, Connecticut, New York, New Jersey, Pennsylvania, Delaware, and Maryland; Great Lakes region—Ohio, West Virginia, Michigan, Illinois, Indiana, and Wisconsin; Southeast region—Virginia, North Carolina, South Carolina, Georgia, Alabama, Mississippi, Tennessee, and Kentucky; Florida region—Florida; Midwest region—Minnesota, Iowa, Missouri, North Dakota, South Dakota, Nebraska, and Kansas; Mid-Southwest region—Arkansas, Louisiana, Oklahoma, and Texas; Western region—Montana, Wyoming, Colorado, Idaho, Utah, Washington, Oregon, and Nevada; Southwest region—Arizona and New Mexico; California region—California.

TABLE 3-4. *Tons of Railway Traffic Originated, 1961, Shown by Level of Flow.*

REGION	INTER-REGIONAL[1]		INTRA-REGIONAL[2]		SUB-REGIONAL[3]		TOTAL	
	Tons	Per Cent of Total	Tons	Per Cent of Total	Tons	Per Cent of Total	Tons	Per Cent of Total
Great Lakes	1,452,811	40.89	834,438	23.48	1,265,966	35.63	3,553,215	30.50
Atlantic	359,297	24.48	546,200	37.22	562,156	38.30	1,467,653	12.60
Southeast	715,000	35.37	509,676	25.21	796,986	39.42	2,021,662	17.36
Mid-West	827,646	48.28	247,933	14.46	638,603	37.26	1,714,182	14.72
Mid-Southwest	281,723	28.11	155,273	15.49	565,235	56.40	1,002,231	8.60
West	324,883	40.55	141,650	17.68	334,658	41.77	801,191	6.88
Southwest	77,002	42.54	2,315	1.28	101,681	56.18	180,998	1.55
California	143,567	38.29			231,417	61.71	374,984	3.22
Florida	126,549	26.7			347,151	73.29	473,700	4.07
Maine	29,017	49.40			29,718	50.60	58,735	.50
TOTAL	4,337,495	37.24	2,437,485	20.92	4,873,571	41.84	11,648,551	100.

[1] Traffic having its origin in one region and its destination in another region.
[2] Traffic having both its origin and destination within the same region.
[3] Total of intra-state traffic within a region.

Source: *Carload Waybill Statistics 1961, State to State Distribution, All Commodities,* Interstate Commerce Commission (Washington, D.C., January 1963).

88

in the other regions: Midwest, 14.7 per cent; Mid-Southwest, 8.6 per cent; Western, 6.9 per cent; Southwest, 1.6 per cent; California, 3.2 per cent; Florida, 4.1 per cent; and Maine, .5 per cent.

One of the most striking observations is that the most important segment of the traffic is sub-regional. In 1961, sub-regional traffic (intra-state) for the United States as a whole was 41.84 per cent; inter-regional traffic was 37.24 per cent, and intra-regional was 20.92 per cent. Thus, the railroad's traffic pattern, from the standpoint of tons originated, was most importantly in the sub-regional and inter-regional markets.

In the Great Lakes region, sub- and intra-regional traffic accounted for 59.1 per cent of the total traffic of the region. The combined intra- and sub-regional traffic for each of the other regions was as follows: Atlantic, 75.5 per cent; Southeastern, 64.6 per cent; Midwestern, 51.7 per cent; Mid-Southwestern, 71.9 per cent; Western, 59.4 per cent; Southwestern, 57.5 per cent; California, 61.7 per cent; Florida, 73.3 per cent; and Maine, 50.6 per cent.

It should be emphasized that the figures presented in Table 3-4 are tonnages originated, and do not constitute ton-miles. The data, however, have been compared to show spatial differences in the amount

TABLE 3-5. *Tons of Railway Inter-Regional Traffic, 1961, Showing Outbound and Inbound Flows for Each Region*

REGION	TONS FROM REGION GIVEN TO OTHER REGIONS	PER CENT OF TOTAL	TONS FROM OTHER REGIONS TO REGION GIVEN	PER CENT OF TOTAL	TOTAL OUT-BOUND AND INBOUND TONS FOR REGION GIVEN
Great Lakes	1,452,811	50.4	1,430,177	49.6	2,882,988
Atlantic	359,297	26.9	976,930	73.1	1,336,227
Southeast	715,000	48.31	764,986	51.69	1,479,986
Mid-West	827,646	71.0	338,158	29.0	1,165,804
Mid-Southwest	281,723	47.3	313,943	52.7	595,666
West	324,883	72.5	123,186	27.5	448,069
Southwest	77,002	73.5	27,824	26.5	104,826
California	143,567	39.0	224,756	61.0	368,323
Florida	126,549	51.7	118,135	48.3	244,684
Maine	29,017	59.9	19,400	40.1	48,417

Source: *Carload Waybill Statistics 1961, State to State Distribution All Commodities,* Interstate Commerce Commission (Washington, D.C., January 1963).

of traffic moving, and indicate differences in levels of movement among the various regions. Intra-regional movements are considerably more important in the Atlantic region, but considerably less important in the Southwestern region. For the country as a whole, sub- and intra-regional traffic constitutes the basic part of railroad movement requirements.

In Table 3-5, the railway inter-regional flows are shown for both the tons shipped from a region to all others and the tons received by a region from all others. This was done to determine the balance of rail traffic between a region and all other regions. It is interesting to note that the regions differ widely in their balance of inbound and outbound inter-regional flows. The Great Lakes, Southeast, Mid-Southwest and Florida regions are extremely well balanced. The dominant portions of inter-regional traffic in the Atlantic and California regions are inbound movements. The Midwest, West, Southwest and Maine regions have predominantly outbound inter-regional flows. Thus, the geographic demand for railroad movement among the various regions is more often an unbalanced than a balanced demand.

LEVELS OF CRUDE PETROLEUM TRAFFIC

Among the flow levels (inter-regional, intra-regional, and sub-regional movements) of crude petroleum within the United States, the principal method of transportation is via pipeline (83 per cent). The small balance moves by boat, tank car, and truck. Therefore, the figures presented in Table 3-6 relate primarily to pipeline transportation, indicating the nature of crude petroleum flows.

The flow of crude petroleum traffic is primarily sub-regional (intra-state) with 55.3 per cent moving at this level. Intra-regional movements account for 12.3 per cent, and inter-regional movements for 32.4 per cent. The principal producing region of the United States is the Mid-Southwestern area, which accounted for 61 per cent of total crude petroleum flow, and, even within this region, 56 per cent of the flow was at the sub-regional level. In California, the other major producing area, 99 per cent of its movements are within the state.

When one considers the nature of raw material distribution and the market locations utilizing petroleum products, it seems fairly probable that inter-regional movements flow in large diameter pipelines and that sub-regional movements flow in smaller or gathering pipe-

TABLE 3-6. *Barrels of Crude Petroleum Traffic Originated January, 1961, Shown by Level of Flow*

REGION	INTER-REGIONAL		INTRA-REGIONAL		SUB-REGIONAL		TOTAL	
	Barrels (000)	Per Cent of Total	Barrels (000)	Per Cent of Total	Barrels (000)	Per Cent of Total	Barrels (000)	Per Cent of Total
Great Lakes	817	8.27	4,290	43.96	4,652	47.67	9,759	4.31
Atlantic			133	17.32	635	82.68	768	.34
Southeast	3,857	56.94	491	7.25	2,426	35.81	6,774	2.99
Mid-West	5,319	36.76	21	.14	9,130	63.10	14,470	6.39
Mid-Southwest	42,163	30.53	18,112	13.11	77,843	56.36	138,118	60.98
West	13,038	58.78	4,675	21.08	4,466	20.14	22,179	9.79
Southwest	8,271	91.94			725	8.06	8,996	3.97
California[1]	2	.01			25,437	99.99	25,439	11.23
TOTAL	73,467	32.41	27,722	12.25	125,314	55.34	226,503	100.

[1] Includes Nevada and Alaska.

Note: Later data is available, but this period of time was selected to make it comparable to the railroad flow data.

Source: Computed from *Monthly Petroleum Statement*, Bureau of Mines, U.S. Department of the Interior, April 10, 1961.

91

lines.[10] In any case, it seems to correspond with the figures on railroad flow in that the primary level of movement is sub-regional. Intra-regional and sub-regional figures account for approximately 68 per cent of the total, with inter-regional movements of lesser importance.

AVERAGE LENGTH OF HAUL

Since data are available only for rail and petroleum pipelines, the available lengths of haul for rail, pipeline, and motor transportation are compared. The figures presented in Table 3-7 are, of course, averages, and do not indicate extremes on either side.

TABLE 3-7. *Average Hauls per Ton for Rail, Motor, and Pipelines**

		CLASS I MOTOR CARRIERS		PIPELINES (OIL)	
YEAR	RAILROADS	Common	Contract	Crude	Products
1939	351	219	a	a	a
1946	415	195	198	258	270
1955	430	235	139	302	286
1960	442	272	184	315	271
1962	460	263	138	311	263

*Source: For 1939–1959, *Intercity Ton-miles, 1939–1959*, Statement No. 6103, and for 1960, 1961 and 1962 Parts 1, 6 and 7 of *Transport Statistics in the United States, 1962*. Table quoted from *Transport Economics*, December, 1963, p. 11.

In 1962 railroads experienced the longest average length of haul, 460 miles. This might be logically expected from the cost and operational characteristics described in earlier chapters. Crude petroleum pipelines averaged 311 miles, and finished product pipelines, 263 miles. The crude pipelines might be expected to have longer lengths of haul than finished products lines, since the former move raw material to market-oriented refineries and the latter move the finished products shorter distances to market areas.

[10] It would be interesting to compare the traffic flows of common and other-than-common carriers by commodity and by weight to determine the movement levels of these respective types. Unfortunately, adequate data are not available to do this, pointing up the need for a transportation census, which would make such comparisons possible.

Common motor carriers had an average haul of 263 miles, and contract motor carriers, 138 miles. Clearly contract motor haulers moved traffic shorter distances than common carriers. While both are basically single-movement-unit-per-power-unit types of operation, much of the contract hauler's business consists of volume loads and much of the common carrier's operations are in less than volume loads. The less than volume loads consist of those shipments which are moved through a terminal for regrouping into line-haul movement units; the element of terminal expense might account for part of the longer haul of the common motor carrier. Another factor causing a difference in length of haul is that contract haulers often utilize specialized equipment to move particular commodities. Specialized equipment means less chance for return loads, with the loaded move having to pay for the unloaded move of equipment; this unloaded return move tends to reduce the average length of haul.

The average length of haul figures do indicate that the railroads probably participate more in the inter-regional movement of goods than do the other forms of transport. Motor carriers probably participate most heavily in the sub-regional and intra-regional traffic, with common motor carriers moving goods shorter distances than the common motor carriers. An accurate appraisal of both motor and water carrier traffic flows must await more reliable information. The average length of haul for all carriers has been increasing over the last ten years, with the exception of finished-products petroleum pipelines. The particular level at which this increase has occurred is still a matter for conjecture.

Effect of Transit Privileges on Industrial Location and Length of Movement

A number of factors tend to offset the difference between finished goods and raw materials rates in relation to plant location. However, these do not destroy the fundamental importance of the differing raw material and finished goods rates on plant location. For example, although a number of processing in transit privileges have been granted to shippers in the past, the amount of traffic moved under these privileges is only a small proportion of the total amount of goods moved. The in-transit privileges to be discussed in this section include processing in transit, storage in transit, concentration in transit, stopoff in transit to complete loading or unloading, and grouping of points of origin and destination.

The processing in transit privilege extends to certain consignors or consignees of selected commodities the right to remove these commodities from the cars, fabricate or otherwise process them, warehouse them, and eventually return them to the carrier for completion of the journey. The two or more separate movements are considered a single forward movement. The transit rate ordinarily is "the local rate into the transit point, the finished or semi-finished product being re-forwarded on the basis of the balance of the through rate applicable on the finished product from the point of origin to ultimate destination." [11] Transit arrangements involving change in form or packaging are found infrequently in motor carrier services. Stopoffs in transit to complete loading or unloading are found as often in motor carriers as in rail carriers.

The finished-product rate is figured, not from the transit point, but from the actual origin to the ultimate destination, less the rate which has been paid for the raw material-transit point movement. This is known as the revenue method of settlement. The balance remaining is paid at the time of reshipping or when the processed product arrives at final destination, depending on the terms of sale. Usually, the carriers establish the privilege of transit only on commodities where the rates on the raw or non-processed material approximately equal the rates after transit. If the raw material of the commodity which moves from the transit point is not recognizable, as on alcohol made from grain, the transit privilege is not usually granted.

Transit privileges emerged as a method of equalizing natural advantages. American railroads established early local and through rates, with the through rates being lower as a special bonus to the long-haul shipper. However, dispensations could not be granted to the shipper who wished to move his goods beyond route terminations. Frequently, then, such shippers were limited in their markets to the territories encompassed by these "rate-break" points, since they could not both pay the increased transportation charges of these outside limits and compete with the local manufacturers. "Rate-break" points thus became industrial centers, with the inherent advantage of being able to compete with adjoining territories as far as transportation charges were concerned. These points were usually along such natu-

[11] W. J. Knorst, *Transportation and Traffic Management* (Chicago: College of Advanced Traffic, 1957).

ral boundaries as major rivers or mountain ranges. Since no through rates existed at these places, no transits could be allowed. Rate breaks were primarily at points of origin or destination.

Other communities were quick to bargain for some other means of creating an advantage and bringing competitive equality. Out of this evolved the transit privilege, which helped build industries where they might not otherwise be. Consider the case of a producer who gathers his raw materials from areas remote from his producing point and major market. To obtain cheap transportation to his market, he naturally ships the raw materials all the way and fabricates them near his market, although perhaps cutting off potential customers along the way. To ship his finished goods back to them requires a double transportation charge. He is thus limited to the area immediately surrounding his plant. With the transit privilege, however, he may assemble his raw materials at one point, ship to another for fabrication, and sell at points all along the rest of the journey to his market.

A fictional illustration of a processing in transit privilege is presented in Table 3-8. Assume the raw material is produced at point A

TABLE 3-8. *Illustration of a Processing in Transit Privilege*

A	B	C
RAW MATERIAL POINT	MARKET	MARKET
Rate on raw material from A to B	—	$1.00 per cwt.
Rate on raw material from A to C	—	$1.75 per cwt.
Rate on finished good from C to B	—	$1.25 per cwt.

Assume processor desires to sell in both B and C. If plant is at C (and no transit privilege):

Raw material charges A to C	—	$1.75 per cwt.
Finished goods charges C to B	—	$1.25 per cwt.
TOTAL		$3.00 per cwt.

If plant is at B (and there is a transit privilege):

Raw material charges A to B	—	$1.00 per cwt.
Finished goods charges B to C (raw material rate)	—	$ .75 per cwt.
TOTAL		$1.75 per cwt.

Savings under transit privilege: ($3.00 − $1.75)	—	$1.25 per cwt.

and that point C is the primary market of the producer. Under the assumed conditions in the chart, if the producer places his plant at C and there are no transit privileges, his raw material charge from A to C is $1.75 per hundredweight. If he desires to sell in market B under these conditions, his raw material charge from A to C is still $1.75 per hundredweight but, in addition, he must pay $1.25 per hundredweight on the finished product back to point B, a total charge of $3.00/cwt. On the other hand, under the assumed conditions, if there is a transit privilege at B and it constitutes a market for his product, the producer may put up his plant at point B and sell in both B and C at a savings of $1.25/cwt. The illustration is oversimplified, but it demonstrates that producers may sometimes move back toward the original point of raw material movement to take advantage of markets between there and their primary markets.

Many communities owe their prominence to the transit privilege. For example, Kansas City was at one time the dividing point, or rate break, between the eastern and western railroad routes. Many grain elevators were located there, and grain was ground into flour for distribution in any direction. In later years, Chicago became that dividing point, and, had it not been for the transit privilege, Kansas City would have lost its importance in milling. Transits, however, allowed the existing elevator operators to remain and the shipments of grain to be unloaded, ground into flour, and sent to Chicago at little or no extra cost.

Other examples of processes having the transit privilege include: barreling; creosoting of lumber products; fabrication of such items as iron or steel bars by binding, drilling, and welding; grading, sacking, and cleaning of agricultural products; band sawing of lumber products; and finishing of wooden products.

The privilege of concentration in transit is sometimes extended to the shipper, and is usually employed in the dairy, cotton, or packing house industries. Under this privilege, several less-than-carload quantities may be shipped from different points of origin to a common point for assembly into carload quantity and movement to destination. The freight charges assessed are the applicable carload rates on each of the commodities from its point of origin to the final destination of the shipment, less the freight paid on the inbound movement to the concentration point; this is known as the reclaim method of settlement. These shipments might otherwise go as less-than-carload lot shipments, involving a higher rate. Obviously, the privilege would usually be granted only where the distances of moving the various component parts of the shipment in small volumes are a small proportion of the total movement distance of the goods. Many times, such privileges are granted for the performance of such accessory processing as weighing, grading, and sorting, preparatory for movement to primary markets. Perhaps in these instances the processors would tend to locate back toward the production point of the component raw materials, particularly if these were close together.

Carriers sometimes extend to shippers or consignees the privilege of stopping a car or truck in transit for partial unloading or for the completion of loading. The advantages of this depend on whether the indicated rate basis plus the charge for each stopoff is greater or less than the charge for making a direct less-than-carload shipment from origin than one from stopoff point to destination. The stopoff for completion of loading is usually at a point near the origin, and stopoff for partial unloading is near the destination. A typical shipment will help clarify this privilege.

Suppose a shipper in Philadelphia has 30,000 pounds for the Excelsior Manufacturing Company, Chicago, and 10,000 pounds for the Climax Distributing Company, Fort Wayne. He may ship the 40,000 pounds, consigned to the Excelsior Manufacturing Company, Chicago, with stopoff at Fort Wayne for partial unloading by the Climax Distributing Company. If the Excelsior Manufacturing Company had an order for 40,000 pounds of the product for the Monarch Hardware Company, Philadelphia, but found that 10,000 pounds had to be obtained from another shipper or its own branch at Fort Wayne, it would consign the car to the Monarch Hardware Company, Philadelphia, Pennsylvania, and stop off at Fort Wayne for completion of loading by the appliance company (possibly their own subsidiary). In either case, the rate to be applied would be the carload rate on 40,000 pounds (even though this amount was in the car for only a portion of the haul), plus the charge for the stopoff privilege. This privilege allows the producer and/or distributor a flexibility in plant or warehouse location, particularly when his raw materials and/or orders for finished goods are considerably under the minimum volume requirements.

Another point of flexibility offered to the producer in the location of his plant is the carrier practice of grouping points of origin together as a common point of origin, and points of destination in the same way. For example, on many shipments from New England and eastern New York to the West Coast, the entire area may be taken as a common point of origin, with the applicable rate on a shipment from Boston to Los Angeles the same as one from Albany to Los Angeles. On the same type of shipment, California, Oregon, and Washington might be considered a common destination point, with the same rate charged on a shipment from Boston to Seattle as from Boston to Spokane, Washington.

The reasons for grouping are as follows: (1) shipper pressure sometimes forces carriers to extend rate equalization to shippers who are distant from a given geographic market; (2) carriers with decreasing unit cost curves may find it quite feasible on long-distance shipments to treat a geographic area as a common destination (rather than single points), since their out-of-pocket costs to the more distant geographic point would not be substantially larger than to a nearer point within the common area; (3) such a practice simplifies rate construction and quotation to the shipper because of the smaller number of points to be covered.

Thus far in the discussion, the historical fact of a difference between the rates on raw materials and those on finished goods has been taken for granted. However, there is considerable evidence that today, and for the immediate future years, this differential is diminishing, and carriers in all forms of transportation are rapidly approaching an average-cost in moving raw materials and finished goods. The pricing gap, however, continues to exist and probably will continue to exist in future years. This difference can be lessened only as improved methods are found for handling finished goods in the transportation service. However, the evidence is so overwhelming that transportation agencies are, by one method or another, approaching average-cost pricing that it behooves us to investigate the permanence of the difference between raw material and finished-good rates.

That the various transportation agencies are moving from the historic value-of-service pricing, which more than amplifies the actual cost differences between moving raw materials and finished products, to a cost basis of pricing is evidenced by:

1. The tremendous shifts since World War II in the share of intercity transportation among the various agencies and, particularly, the growth of private and exempt motor transportation.
2. An increase in the number of volume or incentive rates such as multiple car and agreed rates.

3. The requirements of the Interstate Commerce Commission and various state public utility commissions for transportation cost information as a basis of making decisions in rate cases.
4. The efforts of the railroads, particularly since 1958, to make selective rate adjustments downward in order to regain traffic which they had lost to other forms of transportation.
5. The efforts of common motor carriers to determine their actual costs of transportation, and to translate these into rates.

The trend toward cost as a basis for pricing transportation service seems clear in today's competitive picture. The above factors show the growing importance of cost as a basis for the rate structure, leading to an abandonment of value-of-service pricing and a resultant narrowing of the difference between raw material and finished-good rates. The growth of private, contract, and exempt motor carrier transportation in the past few years evidences the persistence of many railroad and common motor carriers in value-of-service pricing, and this at least partially accounts for the growth of non-common motor carrier transportation. Nevertheless, it must be emphasized that value-of-service may not be discarded entirely as a rate-making factor, and that rate experimentation will continue to be used.

If the common motor carriers and/or railroads plan to hold this traffic, they must certainly be able to at least meet the costs at which a private shipper can perform the transportation service for himself. Evidence that the common carriers are readjusting their pricing patterns to meet this competition are the rate adjustments previously indicated. An increasing number of rates are being issued by the regulated carriers to meet nonregulated carrier competition. Recently, both the railroads and the common motor carriers have been actively attempting to determine their costs of transportation and, in many instances, using these costs as the basis for determining particular rates.

The Interstate Commerce Commission and the various state public utility commissions have required cost information from carriers who have come before them for rate adjustments based on changing cost conditions. This has been an additional impetus forcing cost into the rate-making picture.

The causes of the trend toward average-cost pricing in transportation, discussed in detail at other points in the book, are summarized to complete the picture of changing transport requirements and the ability of the system to meet these changes:

1. The competitive pressures on shippers selling in common markets to deliver products in these markets at a minimum cost. This is particularly important when the shipper is geographically separated from a particular market and is competing with a producer in that given market, perhaps forcing the more distant producer to absorb freight into the market.

2. The expanded amount of inter- and intra-agency competition in transportation, as evidenced by the shifts in the share of the market (described in an earlier chapter).

3. The possibility of shippers' starting their own motor carrier operation with a minimum of investment, giving them a device which acts as an effective brake on the carriers' desires to practice value-of-service pricing.

4. A lack of clarity in interstate motor carrier law to distinguish adequately among common, contract, private, and exempt motor carriers. Because of this inadequacy of definitions, much pseudo-common motor carriage has come into being and forced the common carriers' rates down toward the cost level, particularly for volume shipments. Part of the fault also lies with carriers and shippers who take advantage of this lack of clarity.

5. The lack of an effective Interstate Commerce Commission pricing policy as related to the "inherent advantage" of each of the transportation forms. In many instances, a transport agency has been prevented from lowering its rate to hold a given movement of traffic because such a rate might divert the traffic of a second agency. Such rulings have been made even though the first agency had an inherent cost advantage over the second. Such a policy hardly seems logical when the Commission is specifically charged with protecting the inherent advantages of each of the transportation forms. There is some evidence that the Commission's attitude has changed in recent years, and that the carriers will be encouraged to price their services more in line with the actual costs of transportation. Its earlier policy, however, encouraged the growth of non-regulated transportation, and ultimately forced the carriers toward cost pricing.

   Furthermore, the United States Supreme Court has ruled that before the Commission overrules a compensatory rate and applies the umbrella principle of rate-making "on the grounds that it is a destructive rate practice," it must be specific in its findings that compensatory rate-making violates the National Transportation Policy.

6. Adverse feeling between subsidized and non-subsidized segments of transportation. Competition with subsidized carriers has forced unsubsidized carriers to move toward cost pricing in order to hold their traffic. Subsidization of transport facilities is discussed in Chapter 7. It is a highly complicated subject involving the interrelationship of national transportation policy, public policy, and the other segments of the economy.

POSSIBLE RESULTS OF AVERAGE-UNIT-COST PRICING

As long as the causes mentioned above are present, carriers who furnish transportation service will be forced to continue the trend toward average-cost pricing. If this tendency continues, some conclusions may be posited about the effect of transportation costs on plant location and transportation requirements:

1. Plant location of industries where weight gain or loss in processing is the prime consideration would not be materially affected by the price of the transportation service. The producer's real consideration will be to eliminate freight on weight lost in the production process or weight which is added to the product at the market.

2. A change in the raw material-finished goods cost relationship would not materially affect the location of industries which presently possess processing in transit privileges. These industries tend to locate near the production point of the raw material, in order to sell in those markets between that point and the prime markets of the product. In this instance, the transit privilege minimizes the difference between the raw material and the finished-good rates. Thus, a change toward average-cost pricing has already been achieved.

3. Industries which experience decreasing unit costs of production may tend to locate plants near the raw material source in order to avail themselves of markets between the raw material point of production and primary markets. At present, if the added transport cost on the finished product is approximately equal to the decrease in production costs, such industries locate plants in primary markets and return the finished product to intermediate markets (between raw material and production sites). Such moves would be limited by, for example, availability of intermediate markets and diseconomies of scale from a larger plant constructed at the intermediate point. However, average-cost pricing, subject to these limitations, might lead to some plant relocation in industries with declining unit costs of production.

4. Industries experiencing increasing unit costs of production (and, to a lesser extent, those with constant costs of production) will apparently maintain their market orientation. By the nature of their production cost curves, any addition of transport cost to the finished product, without an offsetting decrease in production costs, acts to limit the market.

Although transport costs on both the raw material and the finished product would still have to be considered with respect to raw material sources and markets, as the carriers move toward average-cost pricing the importance of these costs to plant location is diminished. Labor costs, available power, taxes, and the aggregative influence of an industrial complex assume more importance between alternative sites.

EFFECT OF SHIPMENT SIZE ON TRANSPORT REQUIREMENTS

The average size of shipment, although not directly related to the differences between raw materials and finished goods, in combination with this vanishing differential tends to determine the nature of transport requirements. As discussed in Chapter 2, lower unit cost of movement is achieved by applying power to movement, thereby increasing the amount of payload in relationship to horsepower. This usually takes the form of more movement units per power unit and/or an expansion of the payload capacity of the unit. This process, called concentration in Chapter 2, is desirable from the standpoint of the transportation companies as far toward the ultimate consumer of the product as possible.

At the receiving end of the movement system, however, the users of the transportation service run into a counteracting force—the consumer buys most of his goods in quantities of considerably less than the standard movement unit of the carriers. This leads to the performance of break-bulk and reassembly at various points in the movement process. The retail store is a location to which the consumer will come and perform for himself break-bulk and reassembly (as in a supermarket). He goes to a supermarket, picks up a cart at the entrance, pushes this cart around to the various points in the store, assembles goods into a cartload, takes them to the checkout counter, and places them into his car for delivery to his home. In this sense, the consumer has purchased several items of less-than-cart quantity and reassembled them for the final completion of the movement system. Retail stores are essentially break-bulk and reassembly points where the opposing forces of agglomeration and deglomeration meet. They are the meeting point of the transportation system's desire to concentrate shipments and the customer's desire to buy in deglomerated lots.

Two factors have materially affected the average size of the shipment in recent years: first, increased inventory turnover within the distribution system; and, second, the increased emphasis on interest costs on inventory as a part of the cost of distributing goods. These two factors are interrelated as they affect the size of the shipment.

Inventory turnover is the ratio of turnover for any given period of sales to the average inventory on hand. A distributor wants to increase this ratio primarily to keep a minimum of capital tied up in inventory, thereby decreasing his interest costs of either his own or borrowed capital. Average merchandise turnover can be increased in three ways: average inventory can be held constant and sales increased, sales can be increased at a faster rate than average inventors, or sales can be held constant and average inventory decreased.[12]

Closely allied to the merchandising reasons for increasing turnover is the increasing capital cost of carrying inventory in recent years. Vendors at all levels in the various channels of distribution attempt to reduce the amount of interest cost on inventory, subject to the limits required by their customers.

Increasing the amount of turnover, particularly at the retail level, in an attempt to reduce interest costs on inventory has reduced the average size of shipments in the transportation system. Little factual information is available to substantiate the extent of change in size, but it is generally believed by distributors to have been significant.[13]

In terms of transport requirements, a decrease in the size of the shipment seems to have had the following effects: (1) there have been possible shifts of shipments below the volume minimums as now established in the various forms of transportation; (2) as a result of these shifts, there may have occurred shifts in traffic from one form of transportation to another; (3) the shipper has placed an increased premium on faster transit time in order to replenish inventories; and (4) there may be an increase in the performance of break-bulk and reassembly, although it is theoretically possible that there may be a decrease. Those factors influence the transportation media designated by the shipper or consignee.

The reason for hedging on the fourth point is that if the carriers

---

[12] From a cost point of view, the retailer or distributor must compare the larger quantity discounts and lower transportation rates via larger average sizes of shipment as opposed to the savings via lower capital costs with lower inventory and more frequent, but smaller, shipments.

[13] Another change affecting the size of the shipment is in the weight of the materials being shipped. Many carriers have noted that lighter-weight materials in use today have affected the average weight of the shipment. Unfortunately, it is difficult to back up a generalized statement with fact.

pursue average cost pricing, it may be possible to lower the transportation charges on some volume shipments to the point where these would offset the advantage of lower inventory costs. On the other hand, if the average size of shipment continues to decline, shippers may find it desirable to consolidate their warehouses and decrease the extent of break-bulk and reassembly.

Appendix to Chapter Three

Summary of Plant Location Theory

A theory of location must stand up as a general theory before it can be made to fit into the system of economic principles.[14] This may seem an insuperable task, since location factors vary from industry to industry. Furthermore, the explanation of plant locations must proceed within the framework of economic analysis, and rests upon the principle of substitution. This means that some reason must be given for a particular factor's importance to one industry and not to another, showing the extent to which one factor can be substituted for another. This is the basic problem in the selection of a plant site. This explanation is the purpose of location theory, and the objective is accomplished when the scarce means are best allocated among competing ends.[15]

SOME EARLY ATTEMPTS AT LOCATION THEORY

The origin of the theory of location may be attributed to three writers:

(a) Johann Heinrich von Thunen (1875).
(b) Wilhelm Launhardt (1885).
(c) Alfred Weber (1909).

VON THUNEN'S THEORY OF LOCATION

Von Thunen was concerned primarily with agricultural locations. Although his theory was designed to explain the type of crops that

---

[14] This appendix was written with Mr. Chunbong Kimm, Department of Advanced Products and Systems Development, Allis-Chalmers Company.

[15] George Stigler, *The Theory of Price* (New York: The Macmillan Company, 1950), p. 12.

would grow at various distances from the market, it is nevertheless applicable to manufacturing locations. Locational cost differences were considered to be due to land rent and transportation expenses. Thus, assume in Figure 3-6 that OA is the cost of producing a dol-

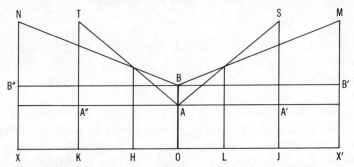

Figure 3-6. *A Graphic Representation of von Thunen's Theory.* Source: Melvin L. Greenhut, *Plant Location in Theory and in Practice* (Chapel Hill, N.C.: University of North Carolina Press, 1956), p. 254.

lar's worth of potatoes and $A'S$ (and $A''T$) the cost of transporting the potatoes over a distance of OJ (OK) miles. OB represents the cost of producing a dollar's worth of wheat, and the $B'M$ ($B''N$) lines therefore represent the freight rate over a distance of OX' (OX) miles, the freight rate being higher on potatoes than on wheat.

Von Thunen's assumption of a uniform homogeneous plane signifies that labor and capital are equal in unit rate and productivity at all locations, and that the cost of production (exclusive of transport cost) is everywhere the same. The land rent and the cost of transporting the goods are thus the co-determinants of location. The producers of potatoes will be found in the OL (OH) region, while wheat will be grown between LX' (and HX).

LAUNHARDT'S THEORY OF LOCATION

Launhardt explained the location of industry as resulting from the difference in cost and demand at alternative locations. He presented the first significant treatment of industrial location theory, distinguishing between determining the site of production within or at the corners of a locational polygon, where the corners represented raw material sources and a one-point consumption place, and supplying a consuming area from a given point of production. Although he handled both problems comprehensively for his time, he made no attempt to put them together. In fact, Launhardt's studies of industrial location and market areas treated a narrower set of circumstances than were encompassed in von Thunen's isolated state.

WEBER'S THEORY OF LOCATION

Weber's theory of location is procedurally the opposite of von Thunen's. Von Thunen assumes a homogeneous land surface and one consuming center, though his general discussions are framed in terms of a given buying point.

Weber's theory is based upon three general factors of location: transportation cost, labor cost, and agglomerating forces. Figure 3-7

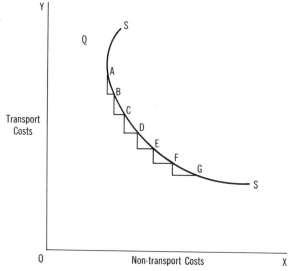

Figure 3-7. *Weber's Location Theory in Terms of Transport and Non-Transport Factors.* Source: Melvin L. Greenhut, *Plant Location in Theory and in Practice* (Chapel Hill, N.C.: University of North Carolina Press, 1956), p. 13.

illustrates Weber's theory of location in terms of the transport and non-transport factors. It combines, in one illustration, the general regional influences (transportation and labor) with the general local forces (agglomerating advantages). It depicts the cost substitutions which take place in the search for the least-cost site.

Transport costs include the cost of shipping and the different costs of fuel and raw materials at given sites, plus the agglomerating factors (proximity to auxiliary industries, marketing advantages). Non-transport costs include the cost of labor and the land costs (rental, police and fire protection, economies of size, etc.).

The curve of substitution SS is an isosale curve connecting a series of locations at which equal numbers of units may be sold. The isosale curve is less elastic from points D to A and more elastic from D to G. A movement from point B to A indicates a small saving in non-transport cost but a larger increase in transport cost. Point D on the curve of substitution is the least-cost location; it is the point of unitary elasticity. Therefore, the plant is located at D; the point represents the unique relationship between the transport cost factors and the non-transport cost factors, which minimize the total unit charges.

Weber's assumption of constant demand and omission of institutional factors left gaps which must be closed for a complete understanding of plant locations in a capitalistic economy.

The Size and Shape of the Market Area

Three individuals who have made substantial theoretical contributions to spatial relationships in size and shape of the market area are August Losch, Melvin Greenhut, and Walter Isard. The major contributions of each are considered in this section.

august losch's theory

August Losch, in his studies, goes beyond partial analysis and the mere recognition of the complex spatial interrelations of economic factors. He presents succinctly a highly simplified static model of a space economy operating under conditions of monopolistic competition.

Losch depicts the hexagon as the most nearly perfect market area shape; it is the shape which is required for locational equilibrium. Also, of all the regular polygons (hexagon, square, triangle) which will exhaust a given area, the hexagon deviates least from the circle form and, in consequence, minimizes the transport expenditures in supplying a given demand; expressed differently, it maximizes the demand of the population of a given area.

For each commodity, then, the plane is dissected into a honeycomb (a net of hexagons) of market areas. Losch next groups these honeycombs according to the size of their respective market units. And, in a manner consistent with the established criterion of minimum transport effort, he orders the resulting nets about a common, central production point to obtain his system of nets. Losch's equilibrium conditions are as follows: (1) the hexagon-shaped market areas are determined by a system of equations for which the initial condition is that each producer maximize his gains (MR = MC); (2) all extraordinary profits must disappear; (3) the area served by each individual is the smallest possible (to prevent profits from existing); and (4) any consumer on a boundary line is indifferent to the possible sources from which he can obtain a given commodity at minimum cost.

After establishing the hexagon as the ideal market shape and setting forth his equilibrium conditions, Losch views the trading area of various products as a net of such hexagons. By turning the nets around a common center, six sectors with most production centers and six with few are obtained. The coincidence of many of these centers concentrates the population, minimizes the freight burdens, and perforce enhances consumer demand by making possible diverse purchases from many local mills. This, then, is why Losch maintains that industry tends to agglomerate. These self-sufficient regions are considered ideal, economically.

While Losch's theory is highly informative, (1) he fails to include cost differentials, other than those attributable to agglomeration and transportation advantages, and (2) he consequently fails to combine an analysis of cost and demand factors in one model.

GREENHUT'S STUDY OF GENERAL THEORY OF LOCATION

Melvin Greenhut attempts to combine the Weber and Losch approaches. Weber abstracted from the area concepts, failing to consider adequately the problem of maximization of total effective demand. Losch abstracted from the influence of forces causing intra-industry locational interdependence, failing to appraise adequately the private capitalistic economy. Greenhut not only believes that a fusion of the two approaches is possible, but offers understanding of underlying location factors, and from such evaluation endeavors to formulate a general theory.

Greenhut mentions that location factors are divisible into three broad groups: demand, cost, and purely personal considerations. Location theory has been moving towards an emphasis of the site that offers the largest spread between charge and receipts.

The *demand factors* include:
1. The shape of the demand curve.
2. The location of competitors.
3. The competitiveness of the industry in location and price.
4. The significance of proximity, type and speed of service.
5. The extent of the market area.
6. The relationship between personal contacts and sales.

The *cost factors* include:
1. The cost of land.
2. The cost of labor and management.
3. The cost of materials and equipment.
4. The cost of transportation.

The *purely personal factors* include:
The extent to which the minimax principle outweighs the quest for maximum profits. This principle includes:
1. The importance of psychic income (size of plant).
2. Environmental preferences.
3. The security motive.

These factors are part of the system of plant location in a capitalistic economy, regardless of whether the particular focus be short-run or long-run, and possibly appear to be an entrée toward the understanding of the basic forces of location. In every site selection, a balancing is involved among the three groups of factors. In his final note, Greenhut emphasizes again that locational equilibrium exists when spent energy units equal received energy units. Adding psychic dissatisfactions to, or subtracting satisfaction from, the expenditures of energy units would completely generalize the theory of location.[16]

ISARD'S STUDY OF GENERAL THEORY OF LOCATION

Walter Isard's studies are much broader than Greenhut's. He attempts to improve the spatial and regional frameworks of the social science

---

[16] The authors particularly recommend to the avid student Chapters 5 and 6 in Melvin Greenhut, *Microeconomics and the Space Economy* (Fair Lawn, N.J.: Scott, Foresman and Company, 1963).

disciplines through the development of a more adequate theory of location and space-economy.

Isard demonstrates the utility of the concept of transport inputs in the determination of a firm's geographical position, and starts with the locational equilibrium of the firm when the problem of transport-orientation obtains. He presents the problem of transport-orientation quoted from Launhardt and Palander by a graphic explanation; in effect, he postulates (1) the absence of the various agglomeration economies and of geographic variations, and (2) uniform transport facilities.

Given M_1 as the only source of the first raw material and M_2 as the only source of the second raw material, at what point should production occur to serve consumers? Starting with the consumer at C, construct the locational triangle $CM_1 M_2$ and the corresponding weight triangle $OM_1 M_2$ erected upon the side $M_1 M_2$ of the locational triangle. O is one of Launhardt's poles, and circumscribes a circle around the weight triangle and connects the pole O with the point of consumption C by a straight line. P, the point of intersection of the pole line OC and the circumscribed circle, is the desired location, the transport optimal point, for serving the consumer at C.

Take another consumer at C_1. It shows that the relevant pole line OC_1 coincides with pole line OC. Since the point of intersection with the unchanged circumscribed circle remains the same, P is the logical production point to serve not only C but also C_1. Therefore,

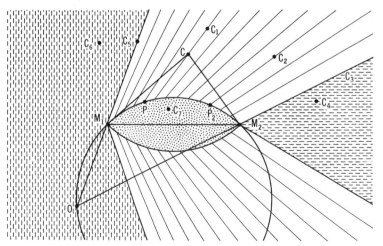

Figure 3-8. *The Launhardt-Palander Construction of Transport-Orientation.* Source: Walter Isard, *Location and Space Economy* (New York: John Wiley & Sons, Inc., 1956), p. 256.

it can be demonstrated that P is the optimal transport point for all consumers along the pole line OC_1 from P to C_1 and beyond.

Take another consumer at C_2. The locational triangle will be $C_2M_1M_2$, and the weight triangle erected upon side M_1M_2 would as before be OM_1M_2, since the relevant weights have not changed. The corresponding circumscribed circle therefore remains the same. The point P_2, intersection of the pole line OC_2 with the circumscribed circle, is the desired location.

For the consumer at C_3, the point M_2, intersection of the pole line OC_3 with the circumscribed circle, the source of the second raw material, is the logical production point for C_3. For the consumer at C_4, M_2 is the logical production point, too.

The consumers at C_5 and C_6 will be served by M_1, the source of the first raw material. If the consumer is located within the locational triangle, that very point will be the logical point of production.

In this way, we can obtain the distribution of logical production points, and the graphic presentation of transport-orientation, when a weight triangle generally exists, is extended to embrace an area of consumers. Also, the Launhardt-Palander construction can give insights into locational shifts, whether the changes are due to technological advance or to other forces.

Incorporation of labor into the Launhardt-Palander construction is obtainable, and it can be converted into a more generalized location problem which considers the pull of sites possessing advantages in factors other than transport and relative spatial position. Once again, Isard demonstrated that all such analysis can be embraced by a general substitution framework involving substitution among transport inputs and among outlays and revenues.

Isard treats economies of scale, localization economies, and urbanization economies as three subsets of agglomeration factors. Further, he adopts Losch's various other assumptions and conditions pertaining to his market area analysis. But unlike Losch, Isard locates major transport routes through the heart of city-rich and city-poor sectors, rather than at their boundaries. This catches more fully the significant scale (urbanization) economies in the use of modern transport media, and obtains a pattern of distorted hexagons which, in general, decrease in size as one approaches the central city. Isard also attempts a second contrasting path of integration, one that follows mathematical lines, to couple with the notion of a spatial transformation function the fusing of location theory and production theory.

CHAPTER FOUR

POPULATION CHANGE
AND DISTRIBUTION SYSTEMS

The level of economic activity in a society results from three inter-acting forces: the knowledge and skills of the population, wants and needs of the population, and the resources available to satisfy these wants and needs. The degree of interaction among these forces depends upon the extent to which the principle of comparative and/or absolute advantage can be practiced in the particular economic system. The development of transportation skills determines the geographic extent to which comparative and/or absolute advantage may be practiced. A change in any one of the three above factors may cause a change in the other two.

Determining the place of the various transportation forms in the economic system requires knowledge of cost patterns and flows of commodities between geographic areas. Since transformative skills are necessary to change resources into products, it is desirable to know the location of the points at which these transformative skills occur, in order to help determine the type of movement and the distance that each type of traffic will move. Weight loss or gain in processing and the type of production cost curve of the processor have been found to be important factors in determining the location of plants performing the transformation process. These factors, in combination with the operational cost characteristics of the various agencies of transportation, result in levels of flow for the various types of movement agencies.

Since the interaction of human needs and wants, technical knowledge and skills, and natural resource utilization takes place through people, an important part of the discussion of these interrelationships is the location of the people who constitute the economic system. Population distribution is in part decided by the locations of plants

113

and natural resources, but other factors also determine the place where an individual will live.

If man were always entirely rational, economic factors determining plant location and the utilization of resources might be the dominant factors in determining where a person would live. However, many noneconomic factors enter into such decisions, and, as a result, populations often are built up in regions with a minimum of plants and natural resources.

Individuals tend to cluster together for many purposes. Perhaps this tendency originally was for the purpose of self-protection, but in civilized times the tendency of people to group has been for other reasons. Population increases often suffice to allow an increase in the total gross product of an economy simply because size permits specialization of production and distribution skills.

GROWTH OF METROPOLITAN COMMUNITIES

The tendency of the population to agglomerate in central locations is readily observed from the figures in Table 4-1. The per cent of the population in urban centers was 56 per cent in 1930, remained steady at 57 per cent through 1940, increased rapidly between 1940 and 1950, and remained steady at 63 per cent in the 1960 census.

Demographers have speculated that the population of the United States will continue its expansion in total numbers in the future, and further predict that the tendency towards metropolitanization will continue. Since people generally continue to live where they were born, it would appear legitimate to make population and metropolitan area projections on a regional basis, providing the underlying assumptions of the projection are realized.[1]

Jerome B. Pickard made a population projection for the United States by region to the year 2000. His projections for the major metropolitan regions of the United States are presented in Table 4-2 for

---

[1] Census data for the years 1850–1950 show that approximately three-fourths of the population lived and died in the state where they were born. For the same period of time, approximately seven-eighths of the population lived and died within the census region where they were born. United States Department of Commerce, *Historical Statistics of the United States* (Washington, D.C.: U.S. Government Printing Office, 1960), p. 41.

TABLE 4-1. *Urban and Rural Population
of the United States, 1930–1960* *

	POPULATION (000's)[1]			PER CENT OF TOTAL	
YEAR	Total	Urban	Rural	Urban	Rural
1930	123,202	69,161	54,041	56	44
1940	132,165	74,705	57,460	57	43
1950	151,325	89,306	62,019	64	36
1960	179,323	112,056	66,267	63	37

* Source: U.S. Bureau of the Census, *Statistical Abstract of the United States: 1961* (Washington, D.C.: U.S. Government Printing Office), compiled from Table 12.

[1] According to the definition adopted for use in the 1960 census, the urban population comprises all persons living in (a) places of 2,500 inhabitants or more incorporated as cities, boroughs, villages, and towns (except towns in New England, New York, and Wisconsin); (b) the densely settled urban fringe, whether incorporated or unincorporated, of urbanized areas; (c) towns in New England and townships in New Jersey and Pennsylvania which contain no incorporated municipalities as subdivisions and have either 25,000 inhabitants or more or a population of 2,500 to 25,000 and a density of 1,500 persons or more per square mile; (d) counties in states other than the New England states, New Jersey, and Pennsylvania that have no incorporated municipalities within their boundaries and have a density of 1,500 persons or more per square mile; and (e) unincorporated places of 2,500 inhabitants or more.

the year 1956 and 2000.[2] The major metropolitan population was 45.6 per cent of the total in 1956, and it is estimated to grow to 65.9 per cent by the year 2000.[3]

As noted in Chapter 3, Pickard divided the United States into the Atlantic, Great Lakes-Midwest, California, Northeast, Southeast, Florida, Mid-Southwest, Midwest, West, and the Southwest regions.

[2] Many sociological and economic factors go into a determination of population size, including marriage rate, birth rate, death rate, immigration rate, productivity of the population, and level of economic development. These rates can change greatly from time to time, and result in considerably different estimates of the trends in population. The figures presented by Pickard are considered to be *projections* of the economy and not *predictions* of growth. See for reference Jerome B. Pickard, *Metropolitanization of the United States* (Washington, D.C.: Urban Land Institute, 1959), Research Monograph 2.

[3] The total population for the year 1956 was 167,000,000, and in 1960 was 179,000,000. The 1956 figures are used, however, in order to be compatible with the projections made by Pickard for the future.

TABLE 4-2. *Population by Major Metropolitan Regions of the United States, 1956 and 2000* *

	1956				2000			
	Major Metropolitan Population (000)		Total Population (000)	Per Cent of Total	Major Metropolitan Population (000)		Total Population (000)	Per Cent of Total
Atlantic	28,755	72.6	39,629	23.7	55,718	82.5	67,500	21.1
Great Lakes-Midwest	22,380	51.0	43,865	26.2	53,358	63.5	84,000	26.3
California	10,240	78.5	13,038	7.8	34,028	85.0	40,000	12.5
Northeast	—	—	745	.4	—	—	800	.2
Southeast	3,215	11.7	27,528	16.5	16,916	40.3	42,000	13.1
Florida	1,605	42.7	3,762	2.2	11,159	77.0	14,500	4.5
Mid-Southwest	4,000	29.5	13,561	8.1	17,897	73.0	24,500	7.7
West	2,760	29.2	9,461	5.7	8,771	42.8	20,500	6.4
Midwest	2,790	20.9	13,340	8.0	6,513	35.8	18,200	5.7
Southwest	460	19.7	2,330	1.4	6,448	80.6	8,000	2.5
TOTAL	76,205	45.6	167,259	100.0	210,808	65.9	320,000	100.0

* Jerome B. Pickard, *Metropolitanization of the United States* (Washington, D.C., Urban Land Institute, 1959), Research Monograph 2, pp. 15–33.

116

The metropolitan region of the United States at the time of the 1960 census extended approximately from Portland, Maine to Norfolk, Virginia and westward to St. Louis, Missouri and Davenport, Iowa. Within this densely populated and urbanized part of the country, the influence zones of the major metropolitan areas overlap continuously. This is the largest metropolitan region in the United States, and is divided into the Atlantic metropolitan and the Great Lakes-Midwest metropolitan areas. The former, having had an earlier start, is more highly metropolitanized. The third, and newest, of the three metropolitan regions of the United States is the California metropolitan region. Its metropolitan areas have the highest proportion of regional population of any region.

The increasing degree of population centralization is apparent in every region of the United States. Because of the aggregate size of the population in the Atlantic, Great Lakes-Midwest, and California metropolitan regions, future problems of transportation will probably be most acute in these areas. However, high concentration populations are also evident in certain sections of the Florida, Mid-Southwest, and Southwest regions.

THE CONCEPT OF A CITY

Let us examine the theoretical functions of cities in order to understand the metropolitan demands on distribution systems.

THE BASIC-NONBASIC CONCEPT

Basic functions are defined, in economic geography, as city-building activities, or "those activities which bring into the community purchasing power from the outside." [4] Nonbasic functions involve the exchange of money brought in through efforts of basic functions, and are those activities which serve local demand. The two functions can be seen in international trade, with the basic function being a nation's exports and the nonbasic function that portion of the national economy devoted to fulfilling national needs.

[4] Harold M. Mayer and Clyde F. Kohn (editors), *Readings in Urban Geography* (Chicago: University of Chicago Press, 1959), p. 87.

The basic function dictates the need for a city, and the size of that function determines the size of the population to be supported. The nonbasic function serves the needs of those employed in both basic and nonbasic activities. Without a basic function, a city could support the needs of only its own population. Unless the city were self-sufficient in all respects, it would soon develop an insurmountable deficit in its balance of payments to other areas, eventually becoming an economic ghost town. Cities must have enough basic activities to maintain economic growth. Transportation plays a vital part in making available the raw materials and in transporting the finished products of basic functions.

THE SUPPORT OF CITIES

Cities are supported, according to C. D. Harris and Edward L. Almond, in three ways.[5] There are central function cities, transport function cities, and specialized function cities. Central function cities perform services purely for a surrounding area. These services vary with the size of the city; the larger centers are much more complex than the smaller ones. Central function cities are especially prevalent in the nonindustrial regions of the country. They have imposing shopping centers or wholesale districts in proportion to their size, and are supported by the trade of the surrounding area. The eastern metropolitan centers, as a general rule, have larger populations than the agrarian portions of the country. Yet many of these metropolitan centers can support an economical size of plant, and these plants can devote their entire output to the local market. What may be a basic, or central, function in one metropolitan area may be a nonbasic, or noncentral, function in another.

Transport cities perform break-bulk and allied services along transport routes. These cities are supported by areas which may be remote in distance but close in connection because of the other's strategic location on transport routes. Cities of this nature tend to be arranged in linear patterns along railroad lines, waterways, and highways, or at coastal locations. But a city will not necessarily develop along a transport line unless that city performs break-bulk. A location where transfers occur between modes of transportation, such as a port, is ideal for a transport city.

[5] Harold M. Mayer and Clyde F. Kohn, *ibid.*, pp. 202–209, 278–279,

Specialized function cities perform one service such as mining, manufacturing, or recreation for large areas, including the tributary areas of many other centers. Their locations usually depend on natural resources used in manufacturing, water power, or other forms of flow energy sources, or recreational facilities such as a beach or lakes. Hence, these cities may occur singly or in clusters.

Most cities represent a combination of the three factors mentioned above, and each type of city has different transportation needs.

ECONOMIC ACTIVITIES WITHIN THE CITY

Cities are the result of population concentrations, and many occupations are required for the city to function. In order to describe the changes which have occurred in economic activities within metropolitan areas, the economic activities of the country are divided into primary, secondary, and tertiary. Primary activities are a result of the bounties of nature, e.g., farming, forestry, and other branches of agriculture. Secondary activities require at least one phase of manufacturing in the transformation process, e.g., mining, building, and manufacturing. Tertiary activities include the service industries, e.g., transportation, wholesale and retail trades, finance, service, and government.

In Table 4-3, these economic activities have been listed for the United States for the years 1920-1960. The percentages in each year are expressed as a percentage of the total for that year.

The farm population decreased from 33 per cent in 1920 to 9 per cent in 1960. Employment in secondary industries increased slightly, from 31 per cent to approximately 34 per cent. The tertiary industries increased significantly, from 36 per cent in 1920 to 57 per cent in 1960. Population employment has shifted dramatically from the agricultural industries to the service group industries. This latter group depends upon the city for its existence.

The growing importance of tertiary employment, coupled with growing metropolitanization, will place a heavy burden on the transportation system of the nation in future years. Although the percentage of individuals employed in transportation declined from 9.8 to 6.7 per cent between 1920 and 1960, innovation and adaptation will be needed even more in the future than in the past in order for the distribution system to adapt to the requirements of the market place.

TABLE 4-3. *Persons Employed in Specific Activities by Years
—Expressed as a Percentage of the Total
for Years Given*

ACTIVITY	1920	1930	1940	1950	1960	1961
PRIMARY						
Farm	32.7	30.0	25.5	17.6	9.4	9.2
SECONDARY						
Mining	3.0	2.4	2.1	1.6	1.2	1.1
Contract Construction	2.1	3.3	3.0	4.2	4.8	4.7
Manufacturing	26.0	22.6	25.0	27.4	27.9	27.3
TOTAL	31.1	28.3	30.2	33.2	33.9	33.1
TERTIARY						
Transport	9.8	8.8	7.0	7.3	6.7	6.6
Wholesale and Retail	11.4	14.6	16.1	17.6	19.0	19.1
Finance	2.7	3.4	3.3	3.3	4.5	4.6
Service and Miscellaneous	5.3	7.4	8.1	9.3	12.2	12.6
Government	6.4	7.6	9.8	11.0	14.2	14.8
TOTAL	35.6	41.8	44.3	48.5	56.6	57.7

* Source: Compiled from U.S. Bureau of the Census, *Statistical Abstract:
1961*, tables 271 and 292; and the *Historical Statistics of the United States,
Colonial Times to 1957*, tables D48–56.

DECENTRALIZATION WITHIN THE METROPOLITAN AREA

During the past century, a chief influence on the spread of our cities
has been the means of local transportation. Before 1880, even the
biggest city extended no further than approximately two miles from
its center. Cities were built without plan, with new communities being added as needed. Their streets and alleys were designed for the
slow-moving pedestrian and horse traffic; these same routes became,
with little change, the streets and highways of our present day cities,
with their tremendous traffic load.

The years between 1880 and 1910 were the "teen-age" of our
modern complex cities, presaging the manhood of the twentieth century. They were a transitional period which brought much larger
areas within living distance of the cities' central business districts.
The introduction of cable cars and early electric street cars rolled
back the perimeters of urban areas to about five miles from the city
centers. Within a few years cities grew much larger, expanding most
rapidly along the lines of available transportation.

The improved methods offered by the cable car and electric streetcar induced home owners to move farther out into newly opened suburbs to escape the encroaching business areas. Many former homes were converted into places of business. This phenomenon is known as decentralization. These years were also a period of inflation, firmly establishing the belief that centrally located business areas are gilt-edged investments. It was fixed so firmly, in fact, that even now it is often assumed that such properties are indubitably of high value, despite depreciation and obsolescence of buildings.

During this period of urban expansion, it would have been possible to extend transit lines beyond the five mile limit from the city center if travel time had not controlled route links to a major degree. People came to regard the five mile distance from the city hub as synonymous with thirty minute travel time, that being as much as they would spend commuting between home and work. Thus, the people themselves more or less arbitrarily created the city limits.

The changes before approximately 1910 were only preludes to the greater transitions about to take place. Automotive ingenuity and enterprise seized the spotlight just prior to World War I, changing the entire scheme of national existence and greatly stimulating city expansion. Concepts of transportation and travel were suddenly revolutionized by the millions of motor vehicles that began to roll over streets and highways.

Within a short time, an additional area was opened up for urban residents, and city limits stretched to many miles from the city's center. This decentralization gathered momentum in the late 1920's, slowed down during the depression years, and again hit full stride in the period just before World War II. The trend was slowed down somewhat during World War II because of lack of materials for construction and the rationing of automobiles, gasoline, and related parts. The momentum of the 1920's, however, has been surpassed since the end of World War II.

Decentralization of the city greatly affected the local transportation industry. Demands grew for faster, more expanded service to reduce travel time in the new outlying areas. In addition, there was much demand for connecting service between fairly distant points. Finally, there was increasing congestion in the city's central business district because of more automobiles and trucks.

Governing officials tried various solutions. Street widening projects, designation of certain routes as main traffic arteries, and the use of traffic signal systems were only partially successful in halting the deterioration of the central district. Vast expenditures of public finances on such projects over a period of years have not provided a technology capable of meeting the movement requirements of a decentralized urban population. This problem becomes even more acute when one envisions the population growth, metropolitanization, and decentralization for the years that lie ahead.

The internal structure of cities may be explained by the concentric zone, multiple nuclei, and sector theories, as shown in Figure 4-1.

In concentric zone theory, the pattern of city growth consists of five separate and distinct zones: (1) the central business district—

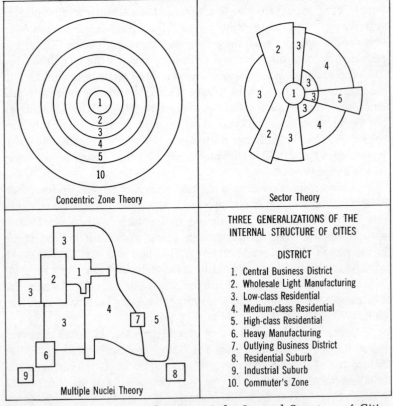

Concentric Zone Theory

Sector Theory

Multiple Nuclei Theory

THREE GENERALIZATIONS OF THE INTERNAL STRUCTURE OF CITIES

DISTRICT

1. Central Business District
2. Wholesale Light Manufacturing
3. Low-class Residential
4. Medium-class Residential
5. High-class Residential
6. Heavy Manufacturing
7. Outlying Business District
8. Residential Suburb
9. Industrial Suburb
10. Commuter's Zone

Figure 4-1. *Three Generalizations of the Internal Structure of Cities.* Reprinted from *Readings in Urban Geography* by H. Mayer and C. Kohn (editors) by permission of The University of Chicago Press. Copyright © 1959 by the University of Chicago.

the focus of commercial, social, and civic life; (2) the zone in transition—a zone of deteriorating rooming houses and tenements, usually the slum area of the city, with some business and light manufacturing; (3) the zone of independent working men's homes, inhabited by industrial workers who have escaped the zone of transition but desire to live near their working places; (4) the zone of better residential districts of single family dwellings and high class apartments; and (5) the commuter zone—a zone of spotty development of residential homes along routes of rapid transport, frequently outside of the city limits.

The concentric zone theory has found disfavor among some urban geographers because it was developed in Chicago, using only that city as a frame of reference. It is held that the concentric zones tend to develop in full circles, but that in many instances natural barriers tend to prevent the full development of these circles. These barriers do not destroy the theory, however, as the zones will develop where the topography allows.

The sector theory, developed by Homer Hoyt, considers the entire city as a circle, with sectors or areas radiating from its center. Similar neighborhoods originate near the center of the circle and move out toward its edge. The sector theory is a refinement of the theory of axial development, which claims that growth follows main transportation routes or lines of least resistance, forming a star-shaped city. In the sector theory, the zone continues out into the edge of the circle. A poor quality residential neighborhood located in one quadrant of the city will tend to grow out toward the edge in that same sector.

The multiple nuclei theory posits that cities develop around a group of centers, or nuclei, rather than around a single center. In some instances these nuclei develop as the city grows, while in others they exist from its inception. Nuclei develop because of one or more of the following factors. First, some activities require special areas. For example, port districts require waterfront areas with sufficient land to support the activities of the port; theatres and recreation facilities are located at a point which the population of a number of areas can reach. Second, certain activities tend to group together because they can profit from the cohesion. For example, service establishments and convenience goods stores may group together to attract the customer from further away. Third, certain unlike activities are detrimental to one another. Factories and residential sections are not particularly compatible, especially from the resident's point of view. Fourth, certain activities cannot afford the high land rents of choice locations, especially when they require a large land area. Petroleum tank farms are an example of these.

The rise of shopping centers and suburban housing developments indicates the growth of super cities in the pattern of multiple nuclei discussed above. Some of these centers and developments are outside of cities, but the outward growth of cities will eventually incorporate them. This multiple nuclei growth will place a heavy burden on the agencies of transportation performing distribution. The present congestion on urban thoroughfares, multiplied by expected growth of these urban centers, will make the task of distribution carriers increasingly difficult. This suggests the need for an integrated form of transport for carrying both passengers and freight and freeing the streets for strictly local use.

The growth of urban centers indicates the rise of regional metropolitan city-states. Their patterns of growth will probably follow those of the existing eastern urban centers. Economic activities within these rising metropolitan city-states will be increasingly internally oriented; they will depend less upon other centers for some of their requirements. It does not follow that these centers will be fully autonomous, since it is not economically practicable to apply unlimited amounts of capital to produce certain products simply to give one area economic independence. The flow of commodities between centers will probably use shorter average lengths of haul, particularly on the dispersion side, although there will be pressure upon interregional carriers to improve their technology to maintain present levels of traffic.

It is difficult to forecast the pattern of growth of the future. However, the following developments have some pertinency. First, in many areas development is occurring along the main automobile arteries, the interstitial areas being developed as good roads become available. Second, the movement of recreational and service facilities to the suburbs has not been zonal; these facilities have tended to jump over the intermediate areas, and have often been located on the outskirts of the city. Third, many manufacturing plants have begun to locate in areas where land is plentiful and expansion is possible. Fourth, minority groups are being absorbed into the fabric of society, and the old process of "invasion and succession" apparently does not have the force it formerly possessed. Fifth, the attainment of higher economic levels by minority groups has enabled them to become more powerful economically and acceptable socially; they are no longer satisfied with the reconditioned homes of their predecessors, and are able to move into new areas that will more closely fit their needs and desires.

Sixth, the mass movement of population since World War II into the suburbs has kept the central city (and often other parts of the city) from being utilized to capacity. The individuals who remain are forced to accept a greater tax burden, and seek to escape it by leaving. To overcome this problem, the cities have begun programs of internal redevelopment. The attractions are many, including access to shopping, recreation, employment, and other advantages. The programs of these cities are designed to entice those who were formerly moving to the distant suburbs. But, although it is difficult to project future city growth, apparently suburban development will not slow down materially in the future.

METROPOLITAN CITY-REGIONS AND DISTRIBUTION STRUCTURE

The suburbanization and projected rapid growth of the population in the years ahead have given rise to the growth of the metropolitan area and the development of an extended metropolitan complex. Although these two overlap in terms of geography, they represent two different levels of space utilization and, therefore, will be treated separately.

GROWTH OF THE METROPOLITAN AREA

The growth of the metropolitan area resulted in suburban development and, later on, in satellite communities. The suburban area is a "dormitory" area, with the population working in the central city; the satellite community is a developed suburb which offers job opportunities as well as living accommodations. As the population moved away from the central part of the city, retail institutions also moved into the newly developed areas to meet the demands of the market. The problem of optimum location of terminals, at retail and other levels, became more important. In many instances, the retailers have established larger retailing units, in order to attract the customer a longer distance and meet increased costs of operation.[6]

As suburbs grow and become satellite communities, it seems that more smaller break-bulk and reassembly warehouses, performing more specialized functions, will be needed to satisfy individual markets that abut one another. As the stores become more dispersed, it will become increasingly necessary to maintain the link between the mass movement per power unit kind of operation and the large volume retailer or wholesaler, or between the smaller volume retailer and the wholesaler. In this connection, the need for smaller terminals, with increased speed and efficiency within the terminal to reduce warehousing costs, and smaller, more efficient movement units becomes imperative. As the metropolitan area grows, roads become more congested, and the area to be served increases. As in Loschian hexagonal analysis, smaller hexagons develop as these new "trading areas" develop.

A counter-tendency is at work, however, on the part of retailers, to counteract continued decentralization. The regional shopping center and the freestanding large multi-line store are two variations on the same theme. They attempt to draw customers from wider areas by combining in one location many lines of convenience, shopping space, and, to a lesser extent, specialty goods. An attempt is made to reduce the number of retail stores (terminals) necessary to meet the customer demands by having the customer absorb the costs of transportation and storage. On the other hand, there are many who compare consumers' travel to the situation in large cities: people will buy necessities such as food once or twice a week from a relatively nearby store, but will shop in the regional shopping center less frequently because of distance and parking problems.[7]

Even with the retailer's attempts to offset decentralization, the conclusions regarding the size of terminal and the size of movement unit seem to be justified. As the projected smaller terminals are built,

---

[6] An interesting retailing development has been the practice of "scrambled" merchandising, in which the retailing institutions handle other than traditional lines in an effort to attract different classes of customers into the same retailing unit. For example, department stores have incorporated food supermarkets as departments. Many food supermarkets have retaliated by including nonfood products.

[7] For example, see David L. Huff, "A Topographical Model of Consumer Preferences," Regional Science Association, *Papers and Proceedings,* Volume VI, 1960. This paper deals with the factors that cause differences in spatial interaction.

automatic handling equipment contributes to "locking in" the system, making it less flexible. However, this very smaller size would be an advantage for the owner, as he would be able to meet new demands by moving the terminal or, if necessary, expanding it. Less capital would be tied up, and greater flexibility would be possible.

REGIONAL DEVELOPMENT AND MEGALOPOLIS

A distinctly different set of problems is faced by the distribution system when market change is viewed as a function of regional development. The megalopolis, or super city, is created when two or more cities and their suburbs become linked to one another. The filling up of the spaces between cities is made possible by the development of easily accessible systems of movement. Examples of megalopolises are the northeastern seaboard from Portland, Maine to Norfolk, Virginia; Madison-Chicago-Gary; Cheyenne-Denver-Colorado Springs; and the West Coast "city" which stretches from San Francisco through Los Angeles to San Diego.

As these region-cities develop, more productive facilities must be located near these markets to satisfy their needs and to supply the inhabitants with jobs. However, existing differences between regions are not easily overcome. The combination of diverse raw material locations and some production points possessing decreasing costs of production due to external economies of scale dictates that these regions will continue to dominate in certain types of production.

Yet it would appear that many of these areas will produce components of finished products, rather than the finished good itself. The assembly of the finished goods, particularly in consumer durables and semidurable lines, would probably be performed either within, or more likely at, the periphery of a given region-city. Then, from these points of assembly, trucks and/or short trains might be used to move the furnished products to terminals within the megalopolis. A great deal of planning would be needed to best move the traffic.

The most effective solution of region-city planning problems is the adoption of a comprehensive "master plan" for the entire area. The "master plan" is a form of blueprint which gives a program for future land use. It takes into consideration all the activities of the city concerned with land. Harold M. Lewis, of the American Institute of Planners, in examining the importance of movement and space utilization in region-city planning, describes the relationship as follows:

"The modern city is a complicated mechanism—the product of the industrial revolution. Like a great modern factory, it must be properly planned and arranged if it is to function effectively. Just as the machines and conveyors in a factory must be arranged so that materials will move to various processing points with minimum effort and lost motion, so must a city be arranged so that the flow of traffic —both men and materials—will be achieved with maximum efficiency and safety. Otherwise the modern city, like a poorly planned factory, becomes inefficient in performing the functions for which it exists.

The master plan of the city, however, presents far more complexities than does the plan for the factory. It must comprehend the needs of many industrial plants and of other types of business; and most important of all, the requirements for a satisfactory place to live, with proper housing, education, recreational and cultural facilities—all interrelated and coordinated into a living community. The great difference between plans for a factory and a city is that the one is designed primarily to service needs of machines whereas the other must service the needs of people without which the machines and factories themselves are but dead things.

So the master plan of a city must be based on the general concept that it is to provide a guide and a pattern for development of a better community in which to live and work. It must visualize the city as a dynamic mechanism, not as a mere static grouping of streets and buildings. This mechanism can function smoothly and effectively only as the daily flow of people and materials can take place with a minimum effort and delay.

The arteries of local travel perform a function in the community similar to that of the blood streams in the human body—all parts and activities of the community are dependent upon the flow of traffic for their life and development. Accordingly, the consideration given local travel needs determines whether the master plan adequately comprehends the dynamic nature of a modern city." [8]

A representative master plan should include provisions for future changes and improvements in streets, freeways, pedestrian and vehicular bridges and tunnels, parks and parkways, public building sites, building zone districts, and routes for railroads and public utilities, including surface transit lines. Proper correlation and interpretation of factors affecting movement and utilization of space involves a study of (1) trends and shifts in population; (2) adjustments in the land use pattern; (3) new developments and redevelopment projects; (4) zoning and subdivision advancement; (5) future riding

[8] Frank H. Mossman (ed.) *Principles of Urban Transportation* (Cleveland: The Western Reserve University Press, 1951), pp. 17–18.

habits and volume; (6) hourly, daily, and seasonal traffic fluctuations; (7) street improvements to relieve traffic congestion; (8) business activity and public works programs; (9) type of transit service to be rendered; (10) community action and attitude.

The working master plan must bring into proper balance the automobile, the motor truck, transit operations, and the pedestrian, all of which must be considered to obtain maximum usefulness for each. The master plan provides proper utilization of space by striking a balance among those who wish to utilize it. Such a balance is necessary in order that the growing region-cities may remain solvent and provide the job opportunities and attractions for modern living essential to their sound growth and development.

The problem of space utilization must also be faced when one views the region not as "cities" but as a group of urban and rural clusters. For purposes of control and planning, it is of utmost importance that regional analyses be undertaken in the following fields:

1. Physical resources—location, nature, extent and allocation
2. Population trends—location, growth rates, gross and net migrations, composition changes, urban-rural patterns
3. Labor force characteristics—composition, location, earnings, trends in real wages and spendable income
4. Transportation—facilities, cost, trends, relation between transportation changes and regional ecology, regional input-output analysis
5. Industrial characteristics—nature, distribution, facilities, sources of supply, nature and location of markets
6. Capital—sources, supply, and conditions and forces influencing its availability
7. Community development—the economic base, trends in regional economy, regional attitudes and their influences on rate and nature of change in business patterns, local government, and community organization[9]

Although such studies might be undertaken by individual firms, the expenditures necessary for such large scale studies would actually require public agencies or foundations to undertake them. The results could be utilized by distribution agencies as a basis for adjusting to changing market conditions and for ascertaining the effects of innovation upon other sectors of the economy.

[9] Randall T. Kemme, "Regional Analysis as a Business Tool," *Regional Science Association, Papers and Proceedings,* Vol. V, 1959, pp. 71–78.

COORDINATED SYSTEM DEVELOPMENT

It is necessary for regional studies to be undertaken to develop a better understanding of the character and nature of transport markets. Such studies would show that the various modes of transportation are not primarily competitors, but rather components in a total transportation system which offers various flexible alternatives to shippers. Increasingly, movement agencies will be called upon to offer their services on a cost-of-service basis. By so doing, the operator will be able to offer the shipper those services in keeping with his cost structure.

As the customers of transportation become more involved in the total marketing concept of operation, they become more concerned with developing total distribution systems to fit their needs. As their techniques of analysis become more refined, they will demand services which can be integrated with the system of terminals at all levels at the lowest possible total cost consistent with demand. Such developments help lower costs by allowing the dispersion and concentration agencies to combine their efforts to cut down on unbalanced movements.

By recognizing the necessary areas of development and effectively working toward a coordinated system, lower total costs of distribution can be achieved. The customer will be afforded more flexible alternatives, enabling him to have a wider choice of terminal locations. Coordination of the system should offer the customer a more efficient range of alternatives, contingent upon the price-quality relationship best for his total distribution system requirements.

PART TWO

TRANSPORTATION

REGULATION

AND POLICY

CHAPTER FIVE

THE REGULATION

OF TRANSPORTATION

The field of transportation as an integral part of the logistics of distribution systems offers so much of interest that merely selecting a particular segment for study poses the necessity of circumscribing the treatment as to time, media, area, content, and so on. Not the least of the areas of interest is that of regulation. One of the main difficulties here is to confine consideration to the salient aspects, foregoing undue descent to minutia in order not to broaden impossibly the task of absorbing the reason for and the nature of regulation, its facilities, its functioning, and its problems.

Someone from another country might think that laissez-faire principles govern our economy, but such is not the case. The hard core of the economics problem is to allocate resources so that goods and services are produced most efficiently. This is supposed to be effected through engendering and protecting competition, the regulator which compels producers—runs the classic argument—to be guided and governed by the free choice of the consumers. Free competition, however, does not exist here; our economy is governed by a regulated competition. The transportation business, like any other, is a matter of public concern; it must be regulated in the public welfare, to protect the honest from the dishonest. This holds true even though the advocates of a planned economy, by applying their credo, appear to be discarding the freedom of competition which they advocate.

In transportation, it is said that the "government has accepted monopoly as unavoidable and has substituted administrative regulation for competition as a method of control." [1] One basic economic control

---

[1] Clair Wilcox, *Public Policies Toward Business* (Homewood, Ill.: Richard D. Irwin, Inc., 1960), p. 17.

is that of entry into the field,[2] but limitation of entry to prevent an excess of transportation seems to encourage monopolistic situations. Control of entry is limitation of competition, to prevent revenues from descending to an unremunerative level, which would contribute to the demise of carriers unable to provide service of the character demanded by the public. The present wave of consolidations and mergers in all media indicates that the policies of our transportation administrative agencies under existing laws have only had a limited success, or the smaller carriers would not be hastening to escape the perils of competition in a cost-conscious transportation business of increasing complexity, scope, and financial requirements.

What, then, is the necessity for transportation regulation, how did it develop, what are the salient features of the controls which are applied in the public interest, and what are the merits and demerits of this application? That constitutes our approach.

TRANSPORTATION IN THE ECONOMY [3]

Transportation makes possible the physical transfer of persons and goods from one location to another. It makes production possible by bringing in raw materials and supplies, and it follows production in functioning in the distribution of the finished or semi-finished articles.

Transportation is not worthwhile unless, at the conclusion of the movement, there is a resultant profit, or unless the loss is minimized by the movement. Additional expenditures for transportation from a more distant point A with a lower cost of production are worthwhile if the difference between its production costs and those of a closer point with lower transportation costs is greater than the higher transportation charges from A.

There are those who say that we have enormous social wastes because we haul goods for long distances, particularly where cross-hauling is involved; i.e., shoes from Boston sold in the St. Louis

---

[2] The other principal ones are consolidation, securities, accounts and reports, service, and the level and structure of rates. When reference is made to certain carriers being regulated or not being regulated, the regulation in mind is economic regulation. All carriers, even private carriers, are subject to some varying measure of safety regulation.

[3] This section is based in part on an article by Newton Morton, "Transportation in the Economy," *Delta Nu Alphian*, Vol. XXII, No. 9, September, 1963, pp. 8–9, 14–15, 23. Used by permission of *Delta Nu Alphian*.

market and shoes from St. Louis sold in the Boston market. To disregard the advantages of large scale production, geographical division of labor and the location of industries at a favorable site, and advocate a return to decentralized production over a wide area, with local producers in control of a limited market, would tend to create the monopoly conditions against which economists inveigh.

TRANSPORTATION AND URBANIZATION

For many years, the standard comment concerning these two facets of our economic life has been that the growth of the large urban centers and areas has been both caused by and dependent on cheap and adequate transportation. This is true, but transportation also contributed to the so-called "flight to the suburbs" and, with the population explosion, to the creation of megalopolises. These have a whole new group of urban transportation problems, particularly concerning allocation of revenues to aid public transportation and limitation of private transportation to prevent stagnation, if not paralysis, of urban centers.

TRANSPORTATION AND PRODUCTION

Transportation affects production, and so aids in satisfying the needs of society. Industry provides what people want and can pay for, and they want what is available. Transportation provides this availability and facilitates distribution by effecting it at low costs. With economical transportation, goods can be secured from more distant points with less time and effort, since a reduction in transportation cost theoretically makes possible a reduction in delivered prices. Dispersed markets and greater specialization are possible, since the delivered cost from a more distant production point may be less than the delivered cost of the production performed at or near the point of consumption.

TRANSPORTATION AND WEALTH

Land, capital, and labor are the three economic factors which produce wealth.

Land is not valuable unless it is accessible to those who desire to use it. Transportation aids the production process by increasing the accessibility of land. Capital is the means by which wealth is made available. Its use provides a return called interest. Transportation improvements maximize investment opportunities, making possible wider markets and the use of more distant sources of supply. Investors will not make capital available if the enterprise seeking their assistance does not have fully adequate transportation to make more likely the proper return. Labor is the agency by which capital uses human effort. Labor receives an income known as wages. Real wages, the commodities and services which labor secures in return for its productive efforts, are greater where there is good transportation.

TRANSPORTATION AND GOVERNMENT

Transportation is so basically essential to the successful operation of the economic system that it is said to be "affected with the public interest." As the United States Supreme Court stated, in one noted early case:

> Whether the use of a railroad is a private one depends in no measure upon the question of who constructed it or who owns it. It has never been considered a matter of any importance that the road was built by the agency of a private corporation. No matter who is the agent, the function performed is that of the state. Though the ownership is private, the use is public.[4]

The carrier receives from the state or the federal government its authority to enter the transportation field and provide the vital service. In view of transportation's importance to the state, it should be regulated in order to make certain that, so far as possible, the state has available the benefits of such service. This is the *fundamental theory of transportation regulation*. It is no longer sufficient to say that any enterprise "affected with the public interest" is subject to regulation, for the decision in one leading case emphasized that "it is clear that there is no closed class or category of business affected with the public interest." [5] This means that the state can regulate any business which its legislature, reflecting public opinion, desires to regulate.

[4] Olcott v. The Supervisors, 16 Wallace 605.
[5] Nebbia v. New York, 291 U.S. 502 (1934).

Competition must be regulated, through control of minimum rates and right to entry into the field, in order to forestall damaging rate-cutting which would diminish the carrier's revenue and make it unable to provide the necessary public service. Equitable treatment for the shipper and the receiver, as well as for all modes of transportation, must, likewise, be guarded through the control of maximum rates and unduly discriminatory practices, although the development and expansion of various other carriers makes these controls less important today than when the railroads monopolized most of the transportation of the country. Maximum rate controls are only necessary where there is little competition, in order to prevent extortionate rates, while minimum rate controls are necessary where there is considerable competition, to prevent chaos on account of excessive rate cuts.

A transportation company may be given by the state the right of "eminent domain," the right to take private property for use after a fair payment.[6] The criterion for granting this right is outlined in the following ruling of the United States Supreme Court:

> The state would have no power to grant the right of expropriation unless the use to which the land was put was a public one. Taking land for railroad purposes is taking for a public purpose and the fact that it is taken for a public purpose is the sole justification for taking it at all.[7]

Transportation aids the unification of units of government. In Western Europe, an improved transportation system has tended to mitigate somewhat the intense racial, religious, political, and economic differences which have accumulated over so many centuries. Prior to the unifying influence of the railroads, these differences had resulted in small, separate countries. In large countries such as the United States, it would be difficult to maintain unity without the aid of modern transportation. Russia recognizes the importance of transportation, as evidenced by the emphasis it places on upgrading this service.

Transportation aids in national defense. Modern warfare, involving a tremendous logistics problem, would be impossible without the aid of all forms of transportation.

---

[6] The state itself exercises the right of eminent domain when it expropriates land for a turnpike or similar road development. The same right exists for smaller government units, such as counties or municipalities, or for the federal government.

[7] United States v. Joint Traffic Association, et al., 171 U.S. 505 (1897).

TRANSPORTATION AND MARKETING

Better time in transit enables a manufacturer or distributor to test the market for an article much more quickly, since the time from manufacture to final sale is shortened. Synchronization, much more effective utilization of transportation media, and better distribution practices generally will curtail warehousing costs, interest consumed in value of goods in transit or storage, and actual shipping costs. Many transportation privileges and services are vital in marketing particular commodities. Piggyback, container or trailer-on-flat-car services, stopoff in transit for partial unloading or completion of loading, fabrication in transit, milling in transit, storage in transit, pool cars, diversion and reconsignment are but a few of the carrier privileges without which many commodities could not be marketed quickly and economically. Special equipment, such as rack, damage free, roll-side cars or trucks, may make possible lower loading and unloading costs.

Transportation helps to stabilize prices at destination markets by making commodities available from other production areas when the supply for a particular production area is curtailed partially or completely. Good transportation also helps maintain the prices in other producing areas by siphoning off surpluses and permitting orderly marketing procedures and practices.

TRANSPORTATION, PLANT, AND MARKET LOCATION

An industry will locate where the aggregate of inbound and outbound charges is the least. This may be at the origin of the raw materials, at the source of fuel, at the main market area, or at any intermediate point. The layman is apt to think of proximity to market as being a matter of mileage, but it is more accurate to relate it to present or possible transportation costs. The higher the ratio of transportation to total costs, the greater will be the importance of transportation in influencing the location. Whether this location is nearer to the raw materials or to the market depends on the weight which is lost in the production process and the relationship of the rates on the basic material to those on the final product.

Where raw materials are found pretty generally in many parts of the country in volume sufficient to support local industry (i.e., the "ubiquitous" materials), production tends to locate near the market in order to minimize transportation charges to the point of production.

Grouping of rates tends to lessen the restrictions caused by distance. Where rates increase with distance, but not in proportion to distance, they are said to taper. This is a present day rate characteristic. This tends to influence industrial location to either end of the production process (raw materials or market), since the rate from origin to destination is ordinarily less than the combination of rates on the raw material to an intermediate point, plus the rate on the product from the intermediate point to final market.

Transit rates, such as those in milling in transit or other, similar services, result in equalizing through rates from origin of the raw material to the market, regardless of the location of the points of production on the same or different routes.

It is vital for the rails and other carriers to protect the interests of the shippers located on their lines in enabling them to secure business in competition with other producers. Unless they do this, the carriers' traffic will dry up. This continual and presently intensified competition for the markets may result in depressing rates to an unduly low level unless proper restraints are exercised by the Interstate Commerce Commission.

If we assume that two points of production, A and B, are X miles apart, and that the rates from A to an intermediate common market Y are on the same basis as those from B to the same market, the so-called "line of indifference" or, more accurately, zone of indifference, where A and B compete on a comparable basis, reflects the rate equality. The same thing is true where A through the intermediate point Y to B is not a relatively straight line, but both points are considered as the sides of a triangle with the common market the apex of the triangle. If the costs from B to any point are less than from A to the same point, B will secure the business and will merchandise over a larger market area than will A wherever the disparity is in its favor. Ability to compete is a matter of rates, not mileage; it is not proportionate to distance.

These assumed conditions may be modified by producers accepting a lesser margin of profit in order to compete, by absorbing a part of the freight, or by their quoting a delivered price over a wide area.

TRANSPORTATION AND PRICES

Improvements in transportation through reductions in the costs of handling between point of production and point of consumption may result in a reduction of the consumer's price. Goods will not normally be brought into a market if the cost of production plus transportation will not allow a margin of profit at destination. Another possible reduction in the price of the goods may come from reduction in the cost of assembling at the point of production the various raw and other materials. Conversely, an increase in transportation charges may dislocate established market relationships by forcing cessation of shipments from a more distant point of production with lower production costs.

It is difficult to predict the effect of a rate increase on market prices, for this, of course, is affected by the elasticity of supply and demand. Where the demand is not affected by price changes, an increase in transportation charges will tend to increase prices. If demand is influenced by changes in price (i.e., is elastic), there will be a tendency for rate increases to have less effect on market prices than when it is inelastic. Where the supply is elastic, rate increases may cause the market price to rise less than when the supply is inelastic, in view of the possible adjustment by increase in production.

Over a short term, "increases and decreases in rates may decrease and increase the profits of the producer and the middleman (jobber, etc.) for a while; but as long as competition remains in these lines of endeavor, the consumers will eventually bear the burden of increases and benefit by reduction in rates." [8]

Where a manufacturer quotes a uniform delivered price regardless of the location of his customer, his net income is less on shipments to more distant markets because he pays more freight to make the distant delivery. This is a type of differential pricing. It is similar in application to the carriers' use of commodity rates in meeting special competitive conditions. The return to the seller of a commodity or the seller of the transportation service (the carrier) is not the same. They receive varying returns from units of production as each strives to meet competition.

One basic characteristic of carrier pricing is that goods of varying values make varying contributions to constant costs. Rates should, of

[8] D. Philip Locklin, *Economics of Transportation* (Homewood, Ill.: Richard D. Irwin, Inc., 1960), p. 30.

course, and normally do, cover short-term or out-of-pocket costs and make some, although not necessarily an equivalent or "fully allocated," contribution to constant costs. Rates based on fully allocated or fully distributed costs result in average pricing, which would force cessation of shipments of low value. "Fully compensatory" rates are not the same as fully distributed rates. A rate can be fully compensatory in covering out-of-pocket costs and making some contribution to constant costs without bearing the same proportion of these constant costs as is involved in fully distributed costs or average pricing. A given rate increase is a greater part of the market price of a low-value commodity than of a high-priced commodity and, therefore, has a greater effect on whether this low-priced commodity continues to move. Since freight rates increase with distance, the ratio of freight charges to price is higher as the distance increases, although not in proportion to the increase in length of haul.

When the market value has been established, the one of two competitors who pays more freight (assuming production costs to be equal) may be forced to absorb the margin between his charges and those of a competing producer having lower freight charges.

In the marketing of agricultural commodities, the price is that at the primary market, less the inbound freight. This holds true where the supply is greater than the demand; when demand exceeds supply, the price is that at the more distant point of surplus plus the charges to the primary market.

It is sometimes said that absorption by the higher value commodity of a greater share of constant costs than is borne by the low-value commodity is a social subsidy which is unfair to the high-value commodity. However, if the impact of the freight rates stops the transportation of the low-value commodity, an even higher rate may have to be paid on the high-value commodity to make up for the revenue no longer available from the other commodity. Airplane parts, on which the ratio of transportation charges to value is only approximately one-quarter of one per cent, can absorb higher transportation charges than can gravel, on which such charges are over fifty per cent of the value.

TRANSPORTATION AND THE TERRITORIAL DIVISION OF LABOR

Each area specializes in the production of one or a limited number of commodities according to the principle of comparative advantage;

i.e., in goods whose costs reflect the greatest advantage. This may mean an actual cost difference in favor of the commodity, or, in some cases, production in which some other community has lower costs. In any case, production in any community or area concentrates on the products in which the cost situation is the most favorable. It is not possible to effect this territorial specialization unless cheap transportation is available, for markets are limited by the ability to compete on a delivered basis with other suppliers.

SUMMARY

Transportation has far-reaching influences on all parts of our economy —government, production, marketing, plant location, prices, and the territorial division of labor. It raises the standard of living. There will always be transportation problems, although their nature will change through the years. Transportation is so essential to our economy that it should be regulated equitably and effectively to be adequate for the public interest.

THE COMMERCE CLAUSE

The regulation of transportation in any organized society is based on the right of society to control the availability and proper functioning of any activity so necessary to its best interests. In the United States, the officially-stated authority for this control is the Commerce Clause, Article I, Section 8, Clause 3 of our Constitution. This disarmingly simple statement of the designated power states that "The Congress shall have the power . . . To regulate Commerce with foreign Nations, and among the several states and with Indian tribes." [9]

The importance of commerce in our colonial period is factual and highly interesting, both for the basic reasons for its founding and for its great current importance in our economic life. This importance may be gauged by the intensity of the resentment of the colonists against the restrictive measures of Great Britain in the post-1763 period, and the fact that in order to restore their former freedoms they were willing to restrict their vital commercial functioning by applying

[9] Capitalization employed herein follows that in the sources cited.

the Non-exportation and Non-importation agreements. It is an understatement to say that commercial entrepreneurs played a very important role in the chain of events which brought American independence.

In the period under the Articles of Confederation, a stronger central government was desired to protect the interests of men of property and to effectuate more harmonious and effective regulation of commerce. This latter necessity was very much in the forefront of the deliberations at the Constitutional Convention in Philadelphia in 1787, but there are substantial doubts that the far-seeing, astute founding fathers anticipated quite the present controls purportedly justified under the Commerce Clause.

In scanning the scope of these controls, it is in order to indicate the comments, judicial and otherwise, which delineate this. While the landmark case of *Gibbons v. Ogden*[10] stated in 1824 that "commerce is the only word which catches up in one single comprehensive term all activities affecting the wealth of the nation" and that "the power of Congress does not stop at the jurisdictional lines of the several states," consideration of other comments gives a clearer idea of the scope of these controls which have opened to question whether the federal government, with its amplified authority, has so derogated the authority of the states that a more realistic name for it would be the National Government.

No form of state activity can constitutionally thwart the regulatory power granted by the Commerce Clause to Congress.[11] This clause includes the power to restrain or prohibit commerce at all times for the welfare of the public, provided only that the specific limitations imposed upon Congress' powers, as in the due process clause of the Fifth Amendment, are not transgressed.[12] The Commerce Clause includes the power to reach and remove any obstacle or restriction upon interstate and foreign commerce from whatever source arising, whether it results from unfavorable conditions within the states, from state legislative policy, or both.[13] It also includes the instruments and agents by which commerce is carried on.[14] No enterprise which conducts its activities across state lines has been held to be wholly beyond the regulatory power of Congress under the Com-

[10] 9 Wheat. 1 (1824).
[11] United States v. Wrightwood Dairy Co., 315 U.S. 110 (1942).
[12] United States v. Carolene Products Co., 304 U.S. 144, 147 (1938).
[13] Second Employers Liability Cases, 223 U.S. 1, 47, 53 (1912).
[14] 9 Wheat. 1 (1824).

merce Clause.[15] In several cases,[16] even interruption of the transportation has been held not to constitute a removal of the processing from the commerce control under the "current of commerce" or "flow of commerce through a throat" concepts. In commenting on the *Darby* case,[17] Justice Roberts said that by placing wages and hours of persons employed throughout the United States under a single federal regulatory scheme, it completely superseded state exercise of police power in this field. Moreover, the Commerce Clause has been ruled an instrument for other purposes of general policy and interest.[18]

Today, commerce in the sense of the Constitution and hence interstate commerce when it is carried across state lines, covers every species of communications, every species of transmission of intelligence, every species of commercial negotiation that will sooner or later involve transportation across state lines.[19]

Interstate commerce has come in recent years practically to connote both those operations which precede as well as those which follow commercial intercourse itself, provided such operations are deemed by the Court to be capable of affecting such intercourse.[20]

Further, says Dr. Corwin, the commerce power can be used to sanction whatever standards "it may choose to lay down in any field of human action," [21] and that "the Federal System has shifted base in the direction of a consolidated national power . . . through, in part, the extension of the national legislative power, especially along the route of the commerce clause." [22]

State Taxation of Interstate Commerce

The control of Congress over commerce is exclusive in phases which require uniform regulation, but, outside of this, the states have a

[15] United States v. South-Eastern Underwriters Association, 322 U.S. 533 (1944).

[16] Swift & Co. v. United States, 196 U.S. 375 (1905). National Labor Relations Board v. Jones and Laughlin Steel Corporation, 301 U.S. 1 (1937).

[17] United States v. Darby, 312 U.S. 100 (1941).

[18] Brigantine William, 28. Fed. Cas. 16, 700 (1808).

[19] Edward C. Corwin (ed.), *The Constitution of the United States of America* (Washington, D.C.: U.S. Government Printing Office, 1953), pp. 119–120.

[20] *Ibid.,* p. 121.

[21] *Ibid.,* p. 165.

[22] *Ibid.,* pp. xxvii, xxviii.

concurrent power subject to the overriding power of Congress.[23] While the necessity of Congressional supervision to obtain uniformity is stressed by that dictum, the fact is that regulation by Congress need not be uniform, as the uniformity rule constitutes a test of the invalidity of state legislation affecting commerce, not a requirement that Congressional legislation regulating commerce need be uniform.[24] This is a rather strange discordance, reminiscent of the cliché, "Do as I say and not as I do."

Taxation is one salient area where state action may affect interstate commerce. Interpretations of the law as to whether this effect is more than incidental or indirect and, therefore, subject to the overriding power of Congress have produced some interesting rulings by the United States Supreme Court. These reflect a variance which is particularly perplexing when evidenced within a relatively short period.

The situation in imports and exports is not a problem area; the states cannot tax such business. But on domestic traffic involving interchange between and across the states, there is a confusing variance in interpretation of the laws. Because of economic and political realities, state taxation of interstate traffic is inevitable. The indications are that the Supreme Court will usually uphold these taxes as long as they are reasonable, not discriminatory, properly apportioned, and do not constitute a cumulative burden. Interstate traffic cannot be burdened unduly by the states, but it must contribute its proper share to state revenues.

This legalistic confusion of this area makes it a lawyer's paradise but a layman's nightmare. When the Supreme Court, with the highest official expertise in the land, evidences in split decisions (in many instances a sharp 5-4 division) differences of opinion and failure to agree on the applicable law, and where their official findings vary within a brief period in cases involving similar circumstances and situations, there is little hope of determining a reasonably fixed policy which will be applicable over a very long period. The members of the High Court and other levels of our judiciary have a great and complex responsibility. That does not minimize the problem for other than legal specialists. Consistency in rulings is desirable, but does not seem imminent.

[23] Cooley v. Board of Wardens of the Port of Philadelphia, 12 How. 299 (1851).
[24] Clark Distilling Co. v. W. M. R. Co., 242 U.S. 311, 327 (1917). Prudential Insurance Co. v. Benjamin, 328 U.S. 408 (1946).

THE INTERSTATE COMMERCE ACT AND THE
INTERSTATE COMMERCE COMMISSION

Since *Gibbons v. Ogden*[25] limned so clearly in 1824 the fundamental powers of the federal government under the Commerce Clause, it is rather strange that not until after the Civil War was there any federal economic regulation of interstate transportation under the Commerce Clause. This for several years was of a very fragmentary nature. The Garfield Act of 1866 [26] provided that any railroad company was authorized to connect with roads of another state to form continuous lines. Another act[27] that same year provided that states could not interfere with telegraph lines organized under the laws of another state. A third [28] provided that no livestock could be left in the cars for more than 28 consecutive hours, but had to be unloaded for food, rest, and water.

There were no additional laws on transportation until after 1880. The *Wabash* case[29] in 1886, which reversed the confirmation of the *Peik* case[30] as to the validity of the Granger legislation and, thereby, eliminated the only effective state controls then in existence came at about the same time as the report of the Cullom Committee recommending comprehensive federal regulation. The Act to Regulate Commerce became effective in 1887, with its name being changed to the Interstate Commerce Act by the Transportation Act of 1920.

The 1887 enactment created the Interstate Commerce Commission and established the broad lines of the regulation which this Commission was to administer. Moreover, the Act became the model for subsequent acts for other transportation media and other agencies, such as the Securities and Exchange Commission, Federal Trade Commission, and others.

The Act to Regulate Commerce applied, in the main, to the railroads, with some lesser application concerning water lines when their service was in connection with the railroads. In 1906, the Hepburn Act placed within the controls of the Interstate Commerce

[25] 9 Wheat. 1 (1824).
[26] 14 Stat. 66.
[27] 14 Stat. 221.
[28] R. S. Secs. 4386–4390 (1873).
[29] Wabash, St. Louis & Pacific R. R. Co. v. Illinois, 118 U.S. 557 (1886).
[30] Peik v. C & NW Railroad, 94 U.S. 164 (1873).

Commission express, petroleum pipeline,[31] and sleeping car companies, as well as spurs, switches, terminals, tracks, and all services in connection with the receipt, storage, handling, and delivery of property moving by railroad. In 1935, the Motor Carrier Act brought all except private transportation by motor vehicle under the Commission. However, not until the Transportation Act of 1940 was the Motor Carrier Act included within the Interstate Commerce Act. Regulation of the airlines came in 1938 under the Civil Aeronautics Act, presently the Federal Aviation Act (1958).

In 1940, the transportation under the Commission prior to 1935 was set up as Part I, and the Motor Carrier Act became Part II. The regulation of domestic water lines (coastal and intercoastal as well as the inland waterways, including the Great Lakes) was established as Part III, being removed at that time from the jurisdiction of the United States Maritime Commission.[32] In 1942, the Freight Forwarder Act (made Part IV) applied to such carriers regulation similar to that applied to others under the Interstate Commerce Act, although freight forwarders were not specifically designated as common carriers until 1950.

REGULATION UNDER THE INTERSTATE COMMERCE ACT

Each of the four parts of the Act regulates certain carriers. Some of the regulation is comparable under each of these parts. Some say that existing differences are due to differences in the nature of the carriers. Many feel not only that such differences are more fancied than real, but that simplification, streamlining, and elimination of duplicate and confusing verbiage are badly needed. Further, there is a feeling that the lack of a wholesale evaluation and correction of unwarranted differences in treatment is detracting from efficient allocation of resources and contributing to the confusion as to the real status of the regulation.

[31] Natural gas pipe lines have never been under the ICC. They were never regulated until 1938, at which time they were placed under the jurisdiction of the Federal Power Commission.

[32] The progression of water transportation controls involved the United States Shipping Board under the Shipping Act of 1916; the Shipping Boards Bureau of the Department of Commerce under Public Law 429, 1933; the United States Maritime Commission under the Merchant Marine Act of 1936 (with domestic water transportation being transferred to the ICC in 1940); the Federal Maritime Board and the Maritime Administration in 1950; with the newly-named Federal Maritime Commission taking over in October, 1961.

Step-by-step consideration of the various parts of the regulation, when they were enacted and why, and their significance would be extremely time-consuming and, while well worthwhile, is much beyond the scope of over-all coverage of the logistics of distribution systems. Unless restraint is exercised, the resultant treatment, while rewarding and interesting, might expand to separate courses in rail, highway, water, air, and urban transportation, procedure before the Interstate Commerce Commission, traffic management, and special consideration of carrier pricing (freight rates).

Some summarizations, nevertheless, are in order. Each part of the Act has some, although not exactly similar, provisions of the following nature:

> The carrier has a duty to furnish transportation of the proper standard.
> The ICC has the right to force carriers to establish through routes, rates and equitable divisions of revenue (except under Part IV). This was added in 1906 for the rail lines; it does not presently have the right to apply such regulation to the motor carriers of property.
> Rates, charges, and shipping rules must be just and reasonable.

Some special consideration, although inadequate, must be given briefly on this part of the regulation.

When the Act was passed in 1887, the Commission assumed, with reason, that when they were given the right to rule on rate reasonableness, they had the right to set the proper rates for the future. This was overruled by the *Alabama Midland* case[33] (the *Long-and-Short-Haul* case) and the *Maximum Rate* case.[34] These resulted in great restrictions to the functioning of the ICC, inaugurating a "doldrums period" in which the ICC was forced to abstain from effective regulation.

In the Hepburn Act (1906) restoration of the ICC's controls was begun. It was given the right to set maximum rates, after investigation, if someone else initiated the complaint. In the Mann-Elkins Act (1910),[35] the Commission was given the added right to set the

---

[33] ICC v. Alabama Midland R. R., 168 U.S. 144 (1897).

[34] ICC v. CNO & TP Ry. Co., 167 U.S. 479 (1897).

[35] This is not to be confused with the Elkins Act, which made tariff rates the *prima facie* standards of reasonableness; they had to be collected, and any connivance and collusion on the part of the shippers or carriers to apply lower-than-tariff rates was made subject to severe penalties under this Act, as well as under the Act to Regulate Commerce.

maximum rates based on investigations which they originated; another control was the suspension of filed rates before they became effective while they were being investigated as to reasonableness (I & S Procedure). The Transportation Act of 1920 gave the ICC the right to set minimum and specific rates.

The ICC controls new operations, extensions, and abandonments.

Undue or unreasonable preference or prejudice is prohibited.[36]

The ICC is given control of rules covering the payment of charges and the extension of credit.

Rates must be published in tariffs under rules specified by the ICC.

All carriers are to file copies of agreements with other carriers.

Penalties are provided for violations of the Act not covered by specific penalties; they vary as between different parts of the Act for the same offense.

The ICC must include in its reports specific findings as to its reasons for ruling that sections of the Act have been violated.

Unauthorized disclosure of information from the shippers is prohibited.

Shippers were given the right to receive compensation for furnishing transportation facilities within carriers' obligation to provide.

The Rule of Rate Making is included under each part.

Statutes of limitation of actions under each part is included.

Provision is made for service of process.

Commission is to receive copies of tariffs and annual reports.

Commission is to prescribe form in which carriers' accounts are to be kept.

The commodities clause, a provision against personal discrimination, specification of shipper's right to route, and procedure for valuation, is only included under Part I.

Long-and-short-haul and aggregate-of-intermediates provisions are under Parts I and III only.

Reparations provisions are only under Parts I and III.

IMPORTANCE OF REGULATED COMMON CARRIERS
AND THE ICC'S DUTY TO PROTECT THEM

The private carrier performs his own transportation when he has sufficient volume to do so profitably. The contract carrier is interested only in skimming the cream of the crop, with such special arrangements on

---

[36] Note that not all preference or prejudice is prohibited, only that which is undue or unreasonable.

such regular and sizeable shipments as justify these contracts. The smaller shipper, not having enough business to perform his own transportation or to interest the contract carrier in making a special arrangement, must depend on the common carrier. When the diversions of traffic by private carrier, contract carrier, and unregulated common carrier force regulated common carriers to raise their rates to recoup lost revenue, the small shipper is affected materially. This is one important reason for hoping and working for a healthy, regulated common carrier system.

> Most individuals will agree that the common carrier is an important member of our economic society. Each individual is, to a degree, dependent upon carriers that are obligated, as a condition of their franchise, to serve anyone who desires the services that they hold out to perform. Each individual is dependent upon the common carrier for the movement of raw materials they use in the performance of their jobs, the movement of their finished goods and the movement of the necessities and luxuries of life. There is no doubt but that our national economy is dependent upon the common carrier for the maintenance of our production system.[37]

ORGANIZATION OF THE INTERSTATE COMMERCE COMMISSION

When the Commission was first organized, following the enactment of the Act to Regulate Commerce in 1887, any actions by or before the Commission involved the entire body. In 1917, the Commissions Divisions Act permitted organization of the Commission into several divisions, each of which was to specialize in a particular type of case, subject to appellate action before the entire body. With the press of work from the growing number of actions, it was necessary once more to subdivide the administrative functioning. This was done in 1933 under the Delegation of Authority Act; the Commission was given the right to assign any part of its work to an individual commissioner or a board or bureau of its employees.

The most recent reorganization adopted by the Commission was in 1961. It is now divided into three purely functional divisions of three Commissioners each—Division 1, Motor Carrier Operating Rights (except rail), Division 2, Rates, Tariffs and Valuation, and

---

[37] Address by L. E. Galaspie, Director of Traffic, Reynolds Metals Company, "Some Pitfalls of Private Carriage," before the Regular Common Carrier Conference, American Trucking Associations, Inc., October 9, 1962.

Division 3, Finance, Safety and Service. The Bureau of Operating Rights, Highway, Water and Forwarder reports to Division 1; the Bureau of Rates and Practices reports to Division 2, and the Bureau of Finance to Division 3. Seven bureaus report to the new Vice Chairman through the Managing Director. The Commission sitting *en banc* hears only the most important cases.

CHAPTER SIX

NATIONAL TRANSPORTATION
POLICY—PART I

Transportation is so vital to the public demand for adequate service, both qualitatively and quantitatively, at reasonable and not unduly discriminatory rates, that each part of our economy is concerned with developing the most effective and equitable solution possible. This is our many-faceted transportation problem. While this is not controversial, the same cannot be said for the specific steps to be taken to solve the problem. Each group—shippers, carriers, regulatory and public authorities, and the general public—faced with its partial responsibility for solving the problem, tends to point in some other direction and say, "Who, me?"

Let us examine the developments and influences which have contributed to our present situation.

BACKGROUND OF THE NATIONAL TRANSPORTATION PROBLEM

Since the first settlements in this country, there has been a problem of providing adequate transportation. Until the Revolutionary War, the problem was admitted, but corrective treatment of the inadequacy of inland transportation necessarily took second place to the other problems of existing under frontier conditions and contending with friction with England. From this war until the end of the Civil War, the question of improving communications with the Pacific Coast was an intense issue in American politics.[1] Originally, this was based on

[1] Robert R. Russel, *Improvement of Communication with the Pacific Coast as an Issue in American Politics, 1783–1864* (Cedar Rapids, Iowa: The Torch Press, 1948).

a desire to improve our trade with Asia, but this was supplemented as a reason for a transcontinental railroad by other pressing questions such as our obligations to the Indians, policing the frontier, increasing trade with California and other coast points, and assimilating under our federal framework the numerous and widespread areas from Oregon to Florida acquired by the Louisiana Purchase, Mexican War, annexation of Texas, etc. Of course, there were also the long-standing needs of securing better transportation for many previously settled areas and extending the frontier.

The period prior to 1790 may be called one of unimproved transportation, but in the period 1790–1830, turnpikes, canals, steamboats, and the beginnings of railroads improved the system. Because railroads promised to help existing transportation, interest in their availability, planning, financing, construction and operations burned in all areas of the country, affecting all facets of economic life. The rapidly developing railroads not only made possible the more rapid settlement of our country, but diverted much of the tonnage from established carriers in the older areas and, naturally, secured substantial traffic from the newly opened and developed areas.

The restrictions of many railroad charters were largely removed by 1850, and the rails began a period of near-monopoly of national transportation, except for those fortunate communities located on or near coastal waterways or inland transportation. This brought about monopolistic practices, but it also generated an indifferent approach to the customer which persisted in the railroads after some admittedly improper conditions and practices were brought under control.

Congress found it advisable to initiate numerous investigations of these practices, such as those of the Windom Committee in 1874, the two Reagan Committees, and the Cullom Committee in 1886. The report of this latter committee in 1886, together with the famous *Wabash* case,[2] culminated in 1887, as we saw in Chapter 5, in the Act to Regulate Commerce. This act (with its name being changed in 1920 to the Interstate Commerce Act) created the Interstate Commerce Commission and provided the basic regulation which it was to administer in the public interest. Its function was not so much to limit earnings of the railroads as to restrain unfair practices. The objective of protecting the public from the improper practices of the railroads was not entirely successful, as is indicated by the frequent amendatory legislation.

---

[2] Wabash, St. Louis & Pacific R.R. Co. v. Illinois, 118 U.S. 557 (1886).

DECLINE OF RAILROAD PARTICIPATION
IN INTERCITY TON-MILES

During World War I, in order to relieve railroad congestion, the Highway Transport Committee instituted an arrangement whereby trucks built in Detroit for the French Army were loaded in transit to eastern ports with material for export. In 1917, the Goodyear Tire and Rubber Company, Akron, Ohio, in order to test their pneumatic truck tires, instituted their Wingfoot Express, which transported tires and tubes to New England and returned with tire cord. These two developments dramatically demonstrated the feasibility of regular and substantial motor carrier service for the general public.

After World War I, the railroads, concentrating on system rehabilitation, did not seem concerned by the growing diversion of their traffic by motor carriers. It was not until 1926 [3] that the ICC felt the need for the first federal investigation of motor carrier growth and the necessity for its regulation.

As a result of the depression following the stock market crash of 1929, motor carrier use accelerated tremendously. Various factors, such as unemployment, lessened manufacturing of equipment and consequent easy credit terms, inherent advantages of motor carriers, and the need of business firms to operate under diminished inventories combined to effect a new and significant appraisal of motor freight commodity movement. This transportation had "arrived," and offered advantages of speed and flexibility, as well as lower rates in some cases, which shippers of all sizes could use to their advantage.

The railroads' unconcern, if not complacence, gave way to a delayed but material concern with the competition which the motor carriers were providing. In 1939, the railroads carried 63.1 per cent of intercity ton-miles, while motor trucks carried only 9.8 per cent. During 1942 and 1943, the rail proportion climbed to over 70 per cent, with the motor carriers dropping to slightly over 5 per cent. In every year since that time, the rail proportion has declined and the motor carriers' portion has increased. In 1960, the rail share was 43.51 per cent, and motor carriers (including private carriers) obtained 22.5 per cent. The remaining share of 1960 business (33.99) was shared by water carriers (16.76 per cent), pipelines (17.18 per cent), and airlines (.05 per cent). Private automobiles secured 89.74

[3] Docket 18300, 140 ICC 685 (1928).

per cent of intercity passenger miles in 1960, rails 2.86 per cent, air-lines 4.5 per cent, bus lines 2.63 per cent, and water carriers .27 per cent.[4]

In less than twenty years, this trend, unless arrested, might mean a changed relationship, with the railroad proportion of intercity ton-miles decreasing to 35 per cent, which would be approximately equal to the share then transported by the motor carriers.

The railroads are a key element in the basic American economic tenet that mass production is completely dependent upon a mass market. Their future is tied up inextricably with the growth of the economy, as are other transportation media. Because of the differences in household buying preferences (e.g., instant coffee v. bean coffee), differences in production (such as decentralization because, of, in part, high transportation costs), use of substitute materials (such as lighter weight plastics for metals or increased use of higher iron content, imported ores), our economy requires relatively less ton-mile transportation. Transportation has risen more slowly than other components of our national income. Further, relatively less of what is transported now needs the economies of rail transportation in its predominantly advantageous area of mass tonnage movement. The railroad share of the required ton-mileage, then, is becoming less, while the share transported by other carriers is increasing.[5]

CONCERN FOR THE POSITION OF THE RAILROADS

The railroads are concerned with the availability of enough capital (on acceptable terms) to provide the service demanded by the public. This factor, together with energy, the desire to serve, and regulatory restrictions and obligations, determines railroads' performance and participation in traffic.

In 1921–1948, the average rate of return earned by the Class I line-haul carriers was 3.69 per cent, lower than for transportation as a whole, for utilities, or for industry. The full significance of this explains the further fact that in 1934–1948, no railroads were able to secure any equity capital for additions to and betterments of their plants. That is not to say that they did not provide these; it indicates

[4] "Passenger Subsidy Still Favored by ICC," *Railway Age,* Vol. 152, January 15, 1962, p. 94.

[5] Railway Progress Institute, *The Railroad Future* (Chicago, Ill., June, 1962), p. 6.

that their capital came from earnings or from fixed charge obligations.[6] The public saw so little profit in enterprise ownership of the rails that they would not subscribe to stock issues, for they felt that they could secure a greater return from their investment funds by owning utilities or industrials. The average rate of return for the Class I line-haul carriers has not progressed materially beyond that mentioned in the study of Sidney L. Miller and Virgil D. Cover; on the contrary, it has declined. In 1961, it had declined to 2.2 per cent.[7]

This country is still committed to the idea of private, although regulated, enterprise. The elements which advocate socialization are a distinct minority, so that any pressure towards nationalization of the railroads is most apt to develop, if it develops at all, because the railroads have failed to provide enough service to satisfy the public demands, rather than because of any shift in ideological principles. If the railroads are ever unable to provide this kind of service, it will not be because of a failure to admit or a lack of desire to fulfill their obligations, but because of a lack of capital brought about by their declining share of available traffic.

It will do no good to "make like an ostrich" and refuse to consider present tendencies toward nationalization. Certainly, the decline of the railroad share of intercity ton-miles, unless arrested, combined with an appreciably smaller rate of return for their investors, makes it a possibility. Considerable low-value traffic moves beyond a short-haul radius. General commodity motor carriers do not want this traffic, and follow the practice of "rate plugs" or "rate stops" which requires that such traffic, particularly for interline hauls, pay a higher rate than indicated in the basic classification and class rate pricing.

Many locations cannot invoke the advantages of water transportation to move traffic which the motor carriers do not want, except at a protected, minimum basis. It will have to move via the railroads. What will happen if the railroads are not able, because of deteriorated service, to move it properly? Conceivably, complaints from shippers and others could create an irresistible pressure on the federal government to subsidize the railroads or nationalize them entirely, which would mean an even greater contribution by the public treasury and taxes.

[6] Sidney L. Miller and Virgil D. Cover, *Rates of Return of Class I Line Haul Railways of the United States, 1921–1948* (Pittsburgh: University of Pittsburgh Press, 1950), pp. 2–3.
    [7] Statement of Net Income of Leading Corporations, First National City Bank of New York, April, 1962.

Should this happen, all transportation might be nationalized, as in Great Britain. This is not impossible, and motor carriers might be more concerned with this than they now admit. Moreover, nationalization might extend to other major industries. For one thing, the federal government would be greatly increasing the aggregate purchasing power which it would control, and would be in a position to impose on such industry any desired controls as conditions before it could even bid on and receive a contract for government-owned carriers' material and supplies.

Accordingly, industries and carriers other than railroads have reason to be concerned with nationalization. Should this occur, shippers would not have as effective choices in the event of deteriorating service by one carrier within a medium, or in weighing one medium against the others.

One way to solve the problem, short of all-out nationalization, would be for the United States Government to do the same as they have done for the airlines—provide the permanent roadway. This would involve buying the tracks and stations, then leasing them to the railroads, which would function as operating companies only. Another ameliorating action would be to free the railroads' rights of way from taxes. Airlines, water lines, and motor carriers pay no taxes on the roadways they use, which have been provided in whole or in part by government appropriations.

FACTORS CONTRIBUTING TO THE TRANSPORTATION PROBLEM

We must determine how we arrived at the present situation in order to ascertain the areas where changes in attitudes, actions, and regulations may help correct the transportation problem which faces us.

RAILROADS

At least a part of the problem is due to the railroads' own attitudes. In the past, too much aristocratic thinking that "we are the railroads" not only indicated their heritage of predominancy, but also promised sustained pre-eminence for the future. The Transportation Act of 1920 first evidenced concern by Congress for rail revenues which would be adequate to provide transportation service necessary for public interest. Current concern with areas which still need corrective action indicate that this concern was well taken.

Too often, in the past, the railroads seemed to feel that they were too big to worry about the diversion of any but the largest blocks of traffic. The situation at this time does not permit this attitude. In fact, rail management has long since abandoned it, but, in the meantime, diversion of traffic to other media for various reasons had resulted in the erosion of the railroads' share of intercity ton-miles from 63 per cent in 1939 to approximately 43 per cent today.

In the past, complaints have been most frequently registered against rude attitudes of railroad employees toward requests for information as to passenger fares, schedules and reservations. These responses are frequently compared with the airline personnel's courtesy, which has been one reason for increasing air travel. It is ironic that when the railroads have mended their ways and endeavored to develop better customer and public relations, they should be forced to contend with financial handicaps which offset the gains provided by their regeneration.

Right after World War I, rail management did not seem afraid that they would lose traffic through failure to provide door-to-door service on less-than-carload lots in competition with motor carrier services. It was not until 1931 that the railroads attempted, through the institution of pickup-and-delivery service, to cope with this inherent advantage of the motor carrier. At the present time, the rails' pickup-and-delivery arrangements are curtailed, at least so far as free service at the regular line-haul rate is concerned. Piggyback service was initiated in the late 1920's, but progressed slowly until its post-World War II renaissance began in 1953.

The motor carriers received a material impetus from the depression period, and had penetrated the rails' large-lot or volume business before the rails attempted to do much about it. In the early 1930's, before the airlines were subject to economic regulation, and before the Civil Aeronautics Board was created to confine expansion of air service to interests associated primarily with aviation, not with the rail carriers, the rails could participate in aviation development on other than a piecemeal basis. The depression of the same period, however, helped keep the railroads out of aviation activities.

The railroads were apparently slow to recognize the competition of these other media in both freight and passenger traffic. Let the railroads not make such a mistake again. In the competition for freight traffic, the profit-producing portion of their business, the motor carriers are the most active opposition. Their officials are usually earnestly devoted to the improvement of their service, recognizing that they will have to provide economic justification for it and sell it on its merits.

In the competition for passenger traffic, while planes have the speed and, in some cases, actual cost advantages, in some respects they do not compare so favorably. The airlines have a good selling point in free meals on flights around mealtime, but they are not served under such comfortable circumstances as rail dining car meals. (This is entirely aside from the high price of meals in a railroad diner.) An airline passenger gets wonderful views of the clouds, but for real scenery, one goes by rail. Railroads might emphasize these and other advantages instead of concentrating on a wailing-wall attitude.

Many people have catalogued and discussed the numerous sins of railroad operations in the free-wheeling, monopolistic period. However, to say that these sins are characteristic of the present rail management is no more just than to say that the present Congress is guilty of malfeasance because some of the members of Congress, during the rugged period, not only accepted bribes when offered, but actively looked for such loot.

THE PUBLIC

As new and improved means of transportation become available, it is difficult to question the right of the travelling and shipping public to use these to their own best advantage. If a person wants to ride buses or prefers to use his private automobile, he is entitled to his own opinion. Similarly, if he wants to use his private trucks or some type of for-hire motor carrier transportation to transport his goods, he has the right to do so.

When these diversionary influences have caused traffic on a branch line, or even a part of a main line, to decline to the point where it is no longer possible to make a profit, the rail carriers should have the right to curtail the service. The public has been saying, in effect, that the rails, in conformance to the requirements of their status as a common carrier, should maintain these stand-by facilities at their own expense for its convenience. This is not only inequitable, but it may be folly if it imperils the stability of the railroad service.

Rails will not necessarily continue to be available if operations continue to be unprofitable. Public service requirements should not be synonymous with continued absorption of losses over an extended period of time. How long can freight service continue to assume passenger deficits? Does the taxpayer want to pay if the railroads are unable to do so? In some cases, as is true in Boston and Philadelphia commuter traffic, the answer, strangely enough, is yes. but these instances do not indicate a general willingness to do so.

An industry having a plant which is not paying its way, with no apparent prospect of effecting a change, does not have to hesitate unduly before it decides to discontinue the unprofitable operation. It discontinues the plant, placing it on the market for sale and consolidating with other facilities those operations which are not discontinued. The rails should be allowed comparable rights.

Prior to the Transportation Act of 1958, the ICC had no jurisdiction over any service curtailments short of abandoning branch or main line service. Consequently, those who wished the rails to maintain stand-by facilities could exercise their delaying or preventive action more effectively, since rails had to act before the various state public service or public utilities commissions. The 1958 enactment took such service curtailment applications from such commissions where these had been delaying disposition unduly, or where state statutes or constitutions limited railroad discretion as to discontinuance of service. Under the new law the ICC could take jurisdiction in the interests of fair treatment for interstate carriers. Shortly after the enactment, efforts began to restore these rights to the states. This should not be allowed, and efforts to negate the provisions of the Transportation Act of 1958 should be defeated.

The fact that so much of the discussion as to transportation needs and problems and the proper national transportation policy involves the railroads indicates their fundamental position in our economy. Because of this importance, it is right that they be regulated in the public interest.

> The objective of public regulation in the transportation field is generally accepted to be the satisfaction of the transportation requirements in the economy with a minimum use of economic resources.[8]

The growth of transport media competing with the rails (highway carriers, airlines, and water lines) means a large and increasing use of unrenewable resources, such as minerals, leading ultimately to

---

[8] *The Railroad Future, op. cit.,* p. 20.

their depletion. The public should be concerned with the desirability of employing railroad fuel economy and conserving these fuels to increase the time available for adjusting to the inevitable use of nuclear fuel. If investment decisions employed resource use as a criterion, railroads would frequently have a cost advantage, since their use often incurs little expenditure of capital resources.[9]

Another part of the growing public concern with adequate transportation facilities and the most economical allocation of resources concerns urban and metropolitan traffic congestion. Taxpayers are acquainted with this problem through their own travelling, including commuting, shopping expeditions, and vacation trips. The fact that all recent transportation studies have referred to this underlines the point that public transportation must provide a part of the solution to obviate further traffic delays by further substantial investment in the construction of highways, cloverleafs, bypasses, etc. These seem to generate more traffic, which makes additional investment necessary, and so on.

The idea that highways could not relieve metropolitan traffic congestion, now receiving increased acceptance, originated within the last two decades. There was a growing realization that the financial demands of purported solutions solely reliant on highways would exceed municipal capabilities, even when buttressed with large state and federal grants. Therefore, decision-makers in state and local governments have taken the lead toward rail solutions. These have been motivated by the need for a rational distribution of the resources available to them. In other words, it is considered cheaper to relieve congestion through subsidizing railroad suburban traffic than to spend more on the highway program. Individual communities have learned to strike a balance between transportation and competing needs for schools, hospitals, sanitation, parks, playgrounds, police, slum clearance, urban development, and other local requirements.[10]

THE NATIONAL TRANSPORTATION POLICY

The importance of a national transportation policy lies in the fact that it helps to guide[11] all parties interested in transportation. Since

---

[9] *Ibid.*, pp. 20–21.

[10] *Ibid.*, pp. 21–22.

[11] It must be appreciated that the National Transportation Policy is a general statement of objectives, and it is extremely difficult to apply its terms with precision or consistency.

the power to regulate interstate commerce is specifically given to the federal government by the Constitution, Congress has the power to determine national transportation policy. Thus, in theory, knowing the intent of Congress through its expression of policy, regulatory agencies are better able to administer the various transportation laws.

This would imply that the expression of intent was so definite that the functioning of the administrative agencies is primarily a policing action. The criteria are subject to such material change through interpretation, however, that the agencies themselves actually determine the policy. The bare bones of the policy are phrased so broadly that they necessitate very considerable latitude. A further question is whether it is possible for Congress to phrase its intent so that the administrative agencies have a more precise awareness of what Congress did intend, instead of leaving so much to the discretion of these agencies.

CONGRESSIONAL ENACTMENTS ON NATIONAL TRANSPORTATION POLICY

Prior to 1935, the only substantive provisions of transportation policy were in the Transportation Act of 1920, which stated that both rail and water transportation were to be preserved in full vigor. The Motor Carrier Act of 1935, which became Part II of the Act by the Transportation Act of 1940, contained a more detailed statement of policy objectives, although then, as now, the methods by which these could be attained were not stated. In Section 2 of the Civil Aeronautics Act of 1938, Congress established for aviation substantially the same provisions that had been included in the 1935 Act. These 1935 and 1938 statements of policy concerned the development of motor carriers and air transportation, respectively, and gave no recognition to the needs of other forms of transportation. Nor did they give attention to the desirability of integration or coordination of transportation, or to methods by which these could be effected.

The 1940 law established the National Transportation Policy to apply to the carriers under each of the three parts of the Act which existed at the passage of that legislation. Part I applied to rails, express, petroleum pipelines, industrial railroads, sleeping cars, etc., Part II to motor carriers, and Part III to domestic water carriers. When the Freight Forwarders Act became Part IV of the Act in 1942, the National Transportation Policy was also included, as applicable to it.

Since there is a considerable interest in strengthening our National Transportation Policy, the present provisions are quoted substantially below:

It is hereby declared to be the National Transportation Policy of the Congress to provide for fair and impartial regulation of all modes of transportation subject to the provisions of this Act so administered as to

1. Recognize and preserve the inherent advantages of each;
2. Promote safe, adequate, economical and efficient service and foster sound economic conditions in transportation and among the several carriers;
3. Encourage the establishment and maintenance of reasonable charges for transportation services, without unjust discrimination, undue preference or advantages, or unfair destructive practices;
4. Cooperate with the several states and the duly authorized officials thereof;
5. Encourage fair wages and equitable working conditions;

all to the end of developing, coordinating and preserving a national transportation system by water, highway and rail, as well as by other means,[12] adequate to meet the needs of commerce of the United States, of the Postal Service, and the national defense. All of the provisions of this Act shall be administered and endorsed with a view to carrying out the above declaration of policy.

A similar policy is contained in the Federal Aviation Act to guide the Civil Aeronautics Board. The Merchant Marine Act of 1936 includes a declaration of policy for the guidance of the Federal Maritime Commission, concerning the export-import trade and other shipping under that body.

DIFFICULTIES OF EFFECTUATING THE NATIONAL TRANSPORTATION POLICY

Even a brief consideration will disclose many difficulties in effectuating, under this policy, a well-coordinated and smoothly functioning system in which each transportation medium furnishes the transportation which it can best perform. The Commission seems to be help-

[12] Even the ICC itself cannot state what is involved here. The only apparent type of transportation which could be involved is petroleum pipelines. It cannot include natural gas pipelines, which have been under the Federal Power Commission since 1938. It cannot be said to include space travel, which was a matter of rare extrapolation in 1940. It cannot include airlines, which are under the CAB and have a Declaration of Policy of their own.

ing water transportation in the territory accessible to rail-barge rates by forcing differentials in favor of the water route, even though a fair allocation of total costs in some instances would make such rates higher than all-rail rates between the same points.

If a carrier with lower costs files a rate which covers the cost of providing service and makes some, although not an equivalent, contribution to overhead, is it the function of the ICC to allocate the traffic by disregarding the Rule of Rate Making and ruling that this constitutes a violation of the destructive rate practices provisions of the National Transportation Policy, especially when in so doing the ICC itself appears to be disregarding the inherent advantages provisions of the same policy?

If a transportation economist concludes that rail carrier service is cheaper on long hauls and that long-haul service via motor carriers does not conform to principles of classical economics, a motor carrier who is already making money on hauls from San Francisco to Chicago or Boston, or other hauls of similar length, is not likely to accept willingly any limitation of his right to haul such traffic.

The ICC has a duty under the National Transportation Policy to encourage fair wages and working conditions. This means that the carriers must have a revenue adequate to support such conditions. This poses considerable difficulties for the ICC, since it has no direct control over the rate of return which transportation labor receives. The various unions and brotherhoods bargain with the carriers over contract terms, with the awards being made by the National Mediation Board, the National Railway Adjustment Board, and other arbitration machinery. The ICC does not participate in these awards, but it must try to rationalize their effect on rising transportation costs.

The ICC has no jurisdiction over how many and what type of roads are built and whether, in view of existing transportation, they are necessary in the first place, yet carriers under their control are affected by the competition accelerated by such roads and, because of this, may have to approach the ICC for rate increases. The ICC, likewise, does not determine the need for waterways improvements, yet the carriers under them are affected by such government-aided competition.

The lack of a coherent national transportation policy has clearly contributed to the excess of transportation facilities in the United States today. The historical fact that the Interstate Commerce Commission was established to regulate and restrain an already matured railroad system, while the Corps of Engineers, the Bureau of Public

Roads, the Federal Aviation Agency and the Civil Aeronautics Board are under statutory mandates to foster and promote water, highway and air transportation, and that each of these proceeds to its appointed task without reference to a common goal, can hardly have failed to have an unbalancing effect. . . . By whatever causes stimulated, the magnitudes of public investment, at the state and local levels as well as federally, in transport since World War II have approached astronomical proportions.[13]

Any transportation regulatory agency, whether it be the ICC, the Federal Maritime Commission, the Civil Aeronautics Board, or the Federal Power Commission, has basic duties—the promotion of transportation adequate to meet the public needs and the regulation of existing transportation under its jurisdiction. To the extent that it fulfills the promotion responsibilities, it complicates its regulatory responsibilities by creating transportation to regulate.

REPORTS ON THE NEEDS OF TRANSPORTATION REGULATION

BRICKER REPORT

The 82nd Congress, in Senate Resolution No. 50, authorized the formation of a special subcommittee on the Senate Interstate and Foreign Commerce Committee to make a thorough investigation to determine the needs of the country for changes in regulation and improvement of transportation. Again, we have an instance of the perpetual transportation problem. The recommendations of this subcommittee were released in October, 1951, as the Bricker Report.

Among their recommendations were that increased emphasis be placed on affording carriers an adequate over-all rate of return on their capital investments and that the agricultural commodity exemptions in Part II be clarified and rewritten. Some of the changes suggested were enacted in specific bills. However, in one so-called "one-shot" or "package" bill, Senate 1889, an attempt was made to incorporate every change suggested in the Bricker Report. Because these numerous measures caused the united opposition of each interest which would be affected by any one of the special measures, this bill failed. While some of the provisions of this bill were debatable, its general objectives were excellent, particularly the long-overdue general streamlining of the Act. This has not yet been effectuated.

[13] *The Railroad Future, op. cit.,* pp. 15–16.

REPORT OF THE PRESIDENTIAL ADVISORY COMMITTEE
ON TRANSPORTATION POLICY AND REGULATION

Another attempt to cope with the transportation problem came with President Dwight D. Eisenhower's release on April 18, 1955 of the above report. This was popularly known as the *Weeks* or *Cabinet Report*, since the chairman of the committee was Secretary of Commerce Sinclair Weeks and several of its members, either permanent or *ad hoc,* were of cabinet rank. However, a so-called task force of practical traffic men prepared a substantial part of the report.

The report emphasized that conditions at the time of submittal were materially different than when regulation was applied first to the railroads and, partially, to the water lines. The former monopoly position of the railroads had changed to one where the shippers had considerably greater options as to the available media, and much of this was due to the provision, by government appropriations of facilities, for competing media. Continuance of the outmoded regulation was not justified, particularly, said the report, because in many respects government policy prevents or limits severely the most economical use of our transportation plant.

The two main points stressed by the committee were (1) the essentiality of a modernized and financially strong system of common carrier transportation, both for peacetime and for defense requirements, and (2) increased reliance on competition in transportation in rate-making. With the use of the term "dynamic competition" in order to determine the abilities of each form of transport to compete in the market "in accord with shippers' judgments of the utility to them in terms of cost and service," there came strong opposition of other carriers, particularly the motor carriers. The latter feared that the recommendation that "rates be allowed to reflect cost advantages whenever they exist and to the full extent" meant that the motor carriers would be prejudiced through the impact of lower freight rates, which, on many commodities, would be lower than they could meet.

In place of the present National Transportation Policy, the Cabinet Report suggested the adoption of an almost entirely new one, in which the rate controls were substantially the same as at present, with the exception that it made no provision for the ICC's continued right to set specific rates.

SMATHERS REPORT

Early in 1958, a special subcommittee of the Senate Foreign and Domestic Commerce Committee, under Senator George Smathers of Florida, considered the national concern over what the report referred to as the deteriorating railroad situation. Several of this committee's suggestions were adopted later in the year as the provisions of the Transportation Act of 1958.

DEPARTMENT OF COMMERCE (MUELLER) REPORT

The number of reports through the years on what is wrong with our transportation system and the proper ways to correct it might lead the uninitiated to feel that the proper corrective measures might well have been taken, but such has not been the case. Another in the seemingly interminable series of reports was transmitted to President Eisenhower by Secretary of Commerce Frederick A. Mueller on March 3, 1960, after having been compiled by a study staff under Ernest W. Williams.[14]

The report submitted 78 recommendations. Among these were those which advocated that Congress take the following steps:

1. Eliminate motor carrier certificate restrictions on a time-phased program.
2. Set a floor for competitive pricing by amending the National Transportation Policy to define "unfair and destructive competitive practices" to include only rates below the long-run marginal costs of the carrier making the rates.
3. Tighten Section 22 procedures.
4. Facilitate collection of complete and consistent cost and statistical information about all modes of transportation and apply modern mathematical and electronic techniques as a basis for improved cost finding to be used as a basis for evaluating the propriety of rates.
5. Provide for a general census of transportation as soon as possible.
6. Develop and use techniques for measuring and forecasting total

[14] In addition, there were a Commerce Transportation Staff, the Transportation Council, and an *ad hoc* Transportation Committee of the Business Advisory Council.

transportation needs in the economy in the aggregate and by mode of transportation, correlating the development programs presently progressed by various agencies.

7. Establish a system of waterways and aviation user charges.
8. Determine the readiness of our entire transportation system for any situation of national emergency.
9. Ascertain how this country can have a merchant marine adequate to handle wartime requirements and peacetime commercial and strategic needs, at reasonable cost to the government.
10. Investigate passenger service deficits, railroad consolidations, inequities in taxation and other railroad problems.

THE DOYLE REPORT

On December 29, 1960, a transportation study group under the direction of Air Force Major General John P. Doyle, with a task force under Marvin Fair, transmitted to Senator Warren Magnuson, Chairman of the Senate Interstate and Foreign Commerce Committee, an outstanding example in the procession of reports on the subject of the needs and problems of transportation. The official designation of this report was "Report Prepared for the Committee on Interstate and Foreign Commerce, United States Senate, by the Special Study Group on Transportation Policies in the United States."

This report recommended:

1. Reconstructing transportation law to eliminate inconsistencies, duplications and other weaknesses. Consolidating all transportation laws into one Federal Transportation Act.
2. A brief, clear-cut and all-embracing statement of transportation policy to replace that which we now have in the Interstate Commerce Act.
3. A Federal Transport Commission to assume the major functions of economic regulation and closely related activities; this includes operating rights, rates and services, safety regulations, enforcement responsibility, coordination of transportation research and statistical programs. This commission should be responsible to Congress and all major functions of the Civil Aeronautics Board, Federal Maritime Commission and Interstate Commerce Commission not assigned to the Federal Transport Commission would be transferred to a new Executive Department of Transportation.
4. Charging the new Department of Transportation with continuing research and review of transportation trends, as well as serving as central coordinating and planning agent. It would contain the Bureau of Public Roads, Defense Air Transportation Administration, Federal Aviation Agency, Maritime Administration, and

some other agencies, such as the rivers and harbors work of the Corps of Engineers and parts of the work of the Coast Guard, Weather Bureau, and Coast and Geodetic Survey. It would also include inspections required by economic regulations, administration of airmail subsidy, and operating and construction differential subsidy programs.

5. Giving transportation Circuit Court of Appeals exclusive appellate jurisdiction in the judicial review of decisions of the transportation regulatory agency.

6. A national railroad passenger service corporation for intercity business. It would not offer commuter service or have control of train dispatch.

7. Coordinating of federal facility and redevelopment programs by the Executive Office under the President in order to aid metropolitan transportation. Creating metropolitan transit authorities.

8. Direct loan of Federal funds by the ICC for suburban railroad capital improvement in order to aid urban transportation; income tax aid through federal, state and local adjustments for the same objective.

9. Establishing a Joint Committee on Transportation to conduct continuous studies of transportation policy, problems and issues and to serve as a consulting group to other committees.

10. Measures to protect reasonable rates by preventing rates below long-run marginal costs and forbidding in substance the application of the umbrella principle of rate making.

11. Correcting inequities in Investigation and Suspension Procedure.

12. Tightening of provisions applying to long-and-short-haul rates.

13. Tightening of Section 22 procedure whereby the Government secures preferential rates.

14. Preventing illegal private carrier transportation.

15. Instituting a system of user charges for airlines, water lines, and highway carriers.

16. Creating a temporary agency to work with the railroad industry in the development and execution of consolidation plans.

17. Providing measures to police operations of transportation companies (common ownership). Provision for forced, inter-media exchange of shipments and joint through rates applicable thereto.

18. Correcting of inequities in taxation of transportation companies.

19. Federal jurisdiction over maximum desirable dimensions and weights of vehicles operated on the federal aid highway systems.

20. Eliminating the problem of fragmented motor certification.

21. Strengthening federal power on provision of transportation labor work rules and solution of labor conflicts.

22. Reviewing agricultural and bulk commodity exemptions.

CHAPTER SEVEN

NATIONAL TRANSPORTATION

POLICY—PART II

The previous chapter discussed the background of the present national transportation situation, the National Transportation Policy, which was introduced into the Interstate Commerce Act to provide objective criteria for solving this problem, and several of the more important investigations treating further needs in the area of bringing about a more equitable and effective transportation system and regulating it in the public interest. The present chapter will give more specific consideration to some of the more important problems demanding increased consideration and corrective action.

Public Interest and Railroad Consolidation

In the period prior to World War I, railroad consolidations originated more because of the desires of railroad entrepreneurs of the Hill, Morgan, Harriman, Vanderbilt, and Tom Scott type to maximize their control of lines and profits than because of inadequate revenues. As the end of World War I approached, a combination of factors caused justifiable concern for the ability of the railroads of the country to provide transportation service adequate for our economy. These included deferred maintenance, exhaustion of natural resources on which the traffic of the smaller roads had depended (in fact, which had been the main reason for these roads' being built), and the completion of the railroad net which was more than sufficient for our transportation needs; this is evidenced by the fact that the high point

170

in route miles in service came in 1916. There was much concern as to the solution of "the weak road problem."

The Transportation Act of 1920 included provisions for the formation of a limited number of railroads under a plan developed by William Z. Ripley of Harvard University. As the bill was passed, the Interstate Commerce Commission was not given the right to force the consolidation as outlined. If any railroad wanted to effect consolidations, it had to be in accord with the officially approved plan, and the ICC could designate inclusion of weak roads as a condition of approval of the main consolidation plan. A temporary plan was announced in 1921 (with 19 systems) and what was intended to be the permanent plan came out in 1929 (with 21 systems). During the Great Depression of 1929, consolidation lost its attractiveness; the new magic device was the acquisition of control through the formation of holding companies. While the ICC brought holding companies under control by the Emergency Transportation Act of 1933, the necessity for carriers desiring to consolidate to conform to the official plan was modified, so that approval of the desired acquisition of control might be secured if the planned action conformed in general to this plan. The Transportation Act of 1940 eliminated any necessity of conformance to any formal government plan.

As Justice Frankfurter stated in the *Schwabacher* case:[1]

> By 1940, it was becoming apparent that an ambitious nationwide plan of consolidation was not bearing fruit. . . . Studies revealed that the best was an enemy of the good, and waiting for the perfect official plan was defeating or postponing plans less ambitious but more obtainable voluntarily.

Under the Ripley program, the situation since 1940 has been that the ICC cannot, under the law, force carriers to institute and carry out any particular plan, regardless of how desirable they deem it to be.

Since the end of World War II, there has been an increased interest in railroad consolidations, the primary incentive in most cases being a desire to regain the revenue lost to motor carriers and water carriers in property transportation, and to private automobiles and the airlines in passenger transportation. The carriers, in other words, want to assure their continued functioning; the impetus toward con-

[1] Schwabacher v. United States, 334 U.S. 182 (1948).

solidation came, in most cases, from weakness rather than from strength, as was true in the pre-World War I period. In the 1950's, this trend toward consolidation accelerated.

As additional carriers announced or hinted at consolidation plans, the significance of the effect on many communities began to be realized. Belated attempts were made to defer consummation of the plans while searches were carried on for some means of warding off the effects of curtailment of service and loss of taxes and employment. Congress hearkened to its constituents and early in 1963, under the sponsorship of the late Senator Estes Kefauver, endeavored to move that all consolidations be deferred until a Congressional agency had had an opportunity to make an over-all, definitive study of the effects of the whole idea of consolidation. The piecemeal approach was not enough. This effort failed.

Congress had discarded in 1940 the idea of the necessity of conformance to any set plan and, in the interim, had had sufficient opportunity to become aware of the need for such a comprehensive plan, but had not done so until the plans of numerous roads were well advanced. If it should be decided to have other than a single system approach, joint hearings on separately filed actions would seem better than waiting interminably for an ideal plan obtained by a one-shot approach, while the conditions which caused consolidation fever continued unchecked. Some contend vigorously that the railroads are not in as bad shape as the carriers allege, but this contention does not yet appear to have countervailed the evidence which the roads filed with the ICC in the consolidations which that body has approved.

WHAT DOES THE PUBLIC INTEREST DEMAND?

Possibly the best take-off point for the discussion of many of the problems of railroad consolidation is the account of the basic principles governing merger criteria, released on March 6, 1963 by President John F. Kennedy's Interagency Committee on Transport Mergers.[2]

---

[2] While most of the treatment here concerns the railroads, it should be appreciated that pressure toward consolidation is touching other media, particularly the motor carriers and airlines. See Newton Morton, "Carrier Consolidation," *ICC Practitioners' Journal,* January, 1963, pp. 425–448.

1. Will the proposed merger restrict competition in the provision of transportation services in the areas affected?

The committee seems to have considered this point from the standpoint of classical economics in holding that "reduction of competition may result in reduced benefits to users and the possibility of this must be considered in evaluating a proposed merger."

It does not necessarily violate the National Transportation Policy for the Interstate Commerce Commission to permit intramodal mergers which lessen wasteful competition. In the Seaboard Air Line Railroad Company-Atlantic Coast Line Railroad Company Merger— Reply of Applicants to Exceptions of Interveners to Examiner's Report and Recommended Order,[3] Examiner Blond said, "Under such conditional restrictions, the benefits which would follow consummation of the transaction herein would far outweigh and overbalance the accompanying injuries." The applicants themselves had presented evidence that the proposed merger would tend to reduce competition (19.8 per cent) in their territory, but the record also showed that such reduction was only of slight significance to the public interest when the vigorous competition evidenced by transportation as a whole in the area and the fact that the proposed merger so plainly advanced the objectives of the National Transportation Policy were considered. In other words, the end result is more important than the immediate result.

In this case, the Department of Justice contended that a merger would create a monopoly, that intramodal competition is insufficient, that shippers need competition between railroads, and that this competition would be eliminated substantially. The findings of the examiner did not support these contentions.

Another pertinent comment was that:

> The evidence was clear that neither type of commodity nor distance any longer shuts out a movement by truck, although the effect of the truck on the movement of higher rated commodities has, of course, been greater and lower rated commodities appear to be handled by truck over the shorter distances.[4]

The weight of the evidence from the shippers in this *Seaboard-Coast Line* case was in favor of the proposed merger. Much was pre-

---

[3] ICC Finance Docket No. 21215, January 28, 1963. This will serve as a focal point for discussion of several of the issues involved in railroad consolidation.

[4] *Ibid.,* p. 51.

sented along the line that the old idea of shippers' requirements for at least two competitive rail carriers was the outgrowth of tradition, a heritage from the past before the time when truck and barge developments grew as big as they are today, and that the new competition lessened the validity of this principle. This does not eliminate intramodal competition entirely, but the growth of these other media has lessened dependence on it. The same is true today in every section of the country.

2. *Will the proposed merger permit more efficient allocation of resources through fuller utilization of plant and equipment and reduction in costs per unit of output?*

The mergers under consideration at the time seemed to promise such benefits, since they indicated lower short-term variable costs per unit as the load factor increased, lower long-term variable or constant costs as surplus facilities were eliminated, lower selling costs, and lower service costs—all of which should bring lower rates. The public would expect that these benefits might well flow from the planned corporate concentrations, but would also hold that continued availability of the railroads is important to provide the transportation on hauls on which it would have an inherent advantage.

In these consolidation-merger cases, at least in the *Seaboard-Coast Line* case, it seemed that the main concern of competing railroads was the maintenance of their strategic position of present available routings, which would do nothing to lower unit costs of the merging carriers, even though it protects intramodal participation.

One of the available means by which the ICC protects the public interest is the power to impose reasonable conditions in order to make the transactions conform to the requirements of that interest,[5] although the Department of Justice may allege, as it did in that case, that these conditions were insufficient. Examiner Blond did prescribe measures for the preservation of existing routes and channels of trade in terms reading:

> On a *reciprocal basis* with all connecting railroads requesting such arrangements and willing to afford equal privileges to the merged company, Seaboard Coast Line Railroad Company shall publish and

[5] County of Marin v. United States, 356 U.S. 412–418 (1958). Atlantic Coast Line Railroad Company v. United States, 284 U.S. 288, 295 (1932).
    Roy Brothers Transportation Company, Inc.-Purchase-Maliar, 65 M.C.C. 339, 345 (1955).

file appropriate tariffs and routing schedules . . . providing the following:

(a) Opening of the junctions and gateways of Seaboard Coast Line Railroad Company as to all its traffic moving through *each* such gateway, at the lowest applicable rate available through *any other* junction and gateway of the merged company; and

(b) *New* routes with applicable, competitive joint rates and just and reasonable divisions thereof, on the traffic handled by the said merged company in connection with other railroads via available junctions and gateways, moving to and from the stations of the merged company on the one hand, and, on the other, points and stations on or beyond the lines of the aforesaid connecting railroad or railroads.[6]   (Emphasis supplied.)

The public interest would seem to be preserved by the fact that the routes via the old junctions not only were continued, in effect, in the tariffs, but these rates were made available via those carriers through all junctions, and were also added for application to other lines not participating previously in much of the traffic moving via the companies merging.

Much of this whole question seemed to show opposing general staffs preparing for lines of battle, almost entirely overlooking that it is the "shippers who will continue to exercise the right to route their traffic in the manner they desire," preventing any company from "dominating the situation to the extent that continued, adequate transportation service to the public by other railroads would be seriously affected." [7] Aside from adequate service at reasonable rates, the shipper, in reaching his routing decision, considers reciprocity in company purchases, rate negotiations, claim payments, personal relations, and many other factors. The merged or non-merging carriers must, in any case, still induce the persons responsible for routing the most desirable traffic to designate the specific routes most favorable to the soliciting railroad. So said Examiner Blond on page 153 of his report of August 24, 1962, while pointing out that the exceptions of the Department of Justice "ignored the facts of life in the railroad industry."

Further protective measures taken by the examiner were that

[6] ICC Finance Docket No. 21215, *op. cit.,* p. 96.
[7] Spokane International R. Co. Control, 295 ICC 425, 435–436 (1956). Also see Detroit, Toledo and Ironton Railroad Company Control, 275 ICC 455, 490, 491–492 (1950).

the merged roads were to maintain cutoff times with their connections at interchange points and were to protect other aspects of scheduling and maintenance of special arrangements (such as trackage rights). In addition, there was a requirement for the incorporation of the inclusion and coordination condition that the ICC retain jurisdiction, for up to five years after the date of consummation of the proposed merger, in order to consider petitions which might be filed by railroad interveners.

3. *Can the proper economies be secured through leases, trackage rights, joint operation of various facilities, or similar measures short of consolidation-merger?*

These things are matters for determination by engineers, accountants, and other specialists, and no blanket statement by a nonspecialist would be valid.

4. *The shippers want rates as low as possible consistent with the necessary requirements for the service.*

The shipper does want a choice of services intermodally and possibly intramodally, and is apt to feel that admitted inferiorities of service via a particular route should be allowed to be compensated for by lower rates on such routes.

5. *What will be the effect of the proposed concentration on other carriers (intramodal or intermodal) in the industry?*

Motor carriers and inland water lines say that this concentration of power which a large scale railroad merger would bring would enable the new enterprise to throttle competition, which is not to be condoned. This, they say, is particularly true if coupled with the highly controversial proposal to eliminate the right of the ICC to specify minimum rates on exempt agricultural commodities (which motor carriers may now transport without restrictions) or commodities in bulk (which water carriers may transport free of economic controls). The rails ask for these same rights, since they will effect comparable, competitive conditions; the motor lines and the water lines cry murder, and ask that matters be equalized by placing this traffic under regulation, or at least under Sherman Antitrust Act provisions. Some of the rails are agreeable to the application of the Sherman Act.

H.R. 4700, introduced early in 1963 by Representative Oren

Harris, to add a new Section 23 to Part I of the Interstate Commerce Act under which

> Notwithstanding any other provision of this Act . . . the Commission shall have no authority to determine that such a rate, fare or charge is lower than a reasonable minimum rate, fare or charge. . . . The Commission, however, shall retain all currently effective authority and power to determine that such a rate . . . is in violation of applicable provisions, etc. . . .

is not the effectuation of the final settlement of this troublesome question. The power of the ICC to set the specific rates which are proper was added to Section 15 in 1920, along with its right to set the minimum rates, which is the subject of H.R. 4700; this right to set specific rates is not disturbed, as a close examination will disclose. At the same time, there appears to be an area of imminent conflict should H.R. 4700 or a similar bill pass. But it is not a good policy to attempt to determine in advance of settlement through a test case or cases the extent to which the "notwithstanding any other provisions of the Act" specified in the proposed Section 23 takes precedence over the same bill's provision that the "Commission shall retain all currently effective authority," in respect to reasonableness, undue discrimination, etc., or the extent to which Section 23 would affect Section 15.

While the Clayton Act does not apply to railroad mergers, particularly since the 1950 amendment to Section 7 of that Act and the ruling of the High Court in cases such as *Minneapolis and St. Louis R. Co. v. United States,*[8] its application to rates is not clear. However, Section 11 of the Clayton Act appears to substantiate ICC functioning where Section 5 of the Interstate Commerce Act is not involved. While the proposed Section 23 seems to invoke the Clayton Act, there is no provision in this section to amend the Clayton Act to treat this specifically, as amendments were added to the Shipping Act and the Federal Aviation Act to clarify them.

6. *Is the proposed move a short-term crisis approach or would it be in accord with the long-term interests of the public?*
7. *Is the move proposed because of the imminent failure of one or more of the merging carriers?*

Bankruptcy, or even the *failing business doctrine,* that consolidations are to be permitted when some of the carriers involved are in imminent danger of bankruptcy, is not a condition precedent to the

[8] 361 U.S. 173, 187 (1959).

right of two or more railroads to merge or consolidate. Section 5(2)(c) of the Interstate Commerce Act lists the factors which the ICC, in the public interest, must consider with respect to a proposed consolidation or merger; it does not anywhere impose a requirement that the carriers be insolvent, or on the verge of insolvency, before the proposal is approved.[9]

Certainly, the ICC must consider the weakened condition of some of the parties in any consolidation-merger, but that is only one factor. In the case of the *Norfolk and Western Railway Company Merger, Virginia Railway Company*,[10] the ICC stated that the merger of these two financially sound lines "will plainly result in a larger, stronger company, better able to meet the challenge faced by the railroad industry and better able to attract competent management personnel. Such is obviously in the public interest."

8. *Are the interests of the existing creditors and equity holders of the merging carriers protected adequately?*

There is a difference between the financial holdings of the owners and/or executives of a company and what we have in mind when we say "the shippers" or "the shipping public." Many shippers have no investments of consequence in carriers, yet have a very close, continuing, and pervasive interest in adequate transportation facilities at reasonable rates. The question of whether the protection of these interests provided by a proposed plan is adequate or whether some other plan is better should be based largely on the expertise of the ICC. The merits of this question are difficult to evaluate. It is recognized quite readily that this is a problem area and, here again, each case must be decided on its own merits.

9. *Does the merger provide adequate protection and assistance to affected employees and take into account community employment effects?*

In 1933, a provision of the Emergency Transportation Act stated that in the event of a railroad consolidation the status of rail-

[9] Brown Shoe Company v. United States, 370 U.S. 294 (1962), where the court rejected the request of the Federal Trade Commission for the application of other remedial measures on the grounds that the alternatives were lying wholly within the realm of speculation and that sale to a competitor did not substantially lessen competition or restrain commerce within the intent of the Clayton Act.

[10] 307 ICC 401 (1959).

road employees who would otherwise be affected could not be made worse, but no applicable period for this protection was specified. In the Harrington Amendment to the Transportation Act of 1940, it was specified as extending for four years. In addition, the carriers can bargain with their employees who would be affected by such consolidations, and may decide to give more favorable terms. The Oklahoma Conditions and the New Orleans Conditions are examples of this sort of agreement. They certainly seem to protect the rights of railroad labor, at least more definitely than motor carrier employees affected by consolidations are protected.

Certain aspects of the *Consolidated Freightways* case (MC-F-6135, MC-F-6276 and MC-F-6278 and others) in 1960 indicated that the ICC's responsibilities under Section 5(2) with regard to motor carriers are much less definite than the provisions for the protection of railroad labor. Once having made a general obeisance under the requirement that they "consider" the interest of the carrier employees affected, they are under no obligation to attach specific protective measures if the motor carrier employees do not intervene in their own behalf or have counsel do so.

In the *United-Capital Merger* case,[11] the CAB attached labor protective provisions based on the Washington Agreement. This, however, seems to be more a case of adopted procedure than the desired specificity which the Harrington Amendment provides. Congress should consider the advisability of placing in Part II of the Act, and in the Federal Aviation Act, provisions similar to the Harrington Amendment.

It is only being factual to question whether any community is justified in advancing the question of hardship of unemployment, as important as it is, as finally determining the merits, in the public interest, of disallowing a consolidation-merger. The public, whose interests are to be guarded, makes its decisions as to what transportation it wants to use, to transport itself (with approximately 85-90 per cent of intercity passenger miles being by private automobile) or its commodities. Then the carrier affected sufficiently by the loss of business has to decide which facilities he must contract. As regrettable as it would be, the community affected would have to use any cushion period afforded to it to attract other businesses. Who, other than the ICC, should make the final decision of the extent, in terms of time and money, to which the particular carrier is to continue to conduct operations at a loss?

[11] Docket 11699, April 3, 1961.

10. Will the proposed merger serve the objectives of public policy in the maintenance of a common carrier system, the protection of national security, and the protection of the public health and safety?

The common carrier is currently receiving increasing recognition as being vitally necessary for our economy. The small shipper does not have sufficient traffic to haul his own goods beyond a short-haul range; neither does he have sufficient tonnage to make it attractive to a contract carrier to give him special terms. The small shipper must therefore depend on the regulated common carriers for the greater part of his transportation needs, and any diversion of traffic by contract carriers, private carriers (legitimate or illegitimate) or unregulated common cariers tends to increase the regulated common carriers' rates. This is not to say that other legitimate carriers are not necessary.

The ICC, in deciding on the adequacy of the transportation in a particular territory following the presumptive approval of a consolidation-merger, determines whether the service will be adequate in the public interest. Similar factors affect the rulings of the CAB. Neither the ICC nor the CAB has seemed concerned about the effect of its decisions on the carriers under the jurisdiction of the other, although there are presently some indications of a concord of action through establishment of joint principles.

It is impossible to escape consideration of the application of the Sherman Antitrust Act to consolidations and mergers, etc. Once the conditions imposed under Section 5 of the Interstate Commerce Act are complied with, the ICC-approved transaction goes into effect. The ICC cannot ignore the antitrust laws, but when, after considering:[12]

> . . . competition, national antitrust policy, monopoly and all other factors that otherwise would offend the antitrust laws if the Interstate Commerce Commission and the Interstate Commerce Act were non-existent; . . . and the objectives of the National Trans-

[12] Phil C. Beverly, "The Consideration of Antitrust Policy in Determination of Mergers and Consolidations of Railroads under Section 5 of the Interstate Commerce Act," *ICC Practitioners' Journal,* November, 1961, p. 10. Used by permission. [In England during the 17th century, the courts denounced as illegal grants of monopoly by the Crown; the courts for two hundred years previously had refused to enforce the contracts which were deemed to be in restraint of trade.]

portation Policy and its findings, and the conclusions are adequately supported by the evidence of record, then *the Commission is free to make its decision without restraint from the antitrust statutes.* (Emphasis supplied.)

CONNOTATIONS OF THE PRESENT RATE
OF RETURN FOR THE RAILROADS

The Miller and Cover study has indicated the inadequacy of the railroad rate of return in the 1921–1948 period.[13] Figures for a later period continue to show an alarming trend. From 1956 to 1961, the rate of return on net property investment for Class I railroads was 3.95, 3.36, 2.76, 2.72, 2.13, and 1.97 per cent; during this period, the rate of return on total property investment ranged from 3.09 in 1956 down through 2.62, 2.13, 2.09, 1.62, to 1.49 per cent in 1961.[14] The inadequacy of these rates is evident.

President William Rice of the Atlantic Coast Line Railroad has stated that the "net return for the railroad industry for 1960 reached a twenty-year low of 2.14 per cent (see 2.13 per cent mentioned above), although the airlines' 3.22 per cent and the water carriers' 4.07 per cent were not much better." [15] The 5.37 per cent return of Class I motor carriers was also unsatisfactory, but it was considerably higher than that for Class I railroads.[16]

The rates of return for other industries which correspond to the rate of 2.14 for the rails and 5.37 for the motor carriers in 1960 (as mentioned by President Rice) are: private electric utilities, 6.18 per cent; natural gas pipelines, 6.48 per cent; telephone companies (Class A), 6.85 per cent; oil pipelines, 9.16 per cent; and motor carriers of passengers, 22 per cent. "Thus, the railroads are not only low on the

---

[13] Miller and Cover, *op. cit.,* pp. 2–3.

[14] *Statistical Record—1921–1961,* Bureau of Railway Economics, Association of American Railroads, Washington, D.C., 1962, p. 14.

[15] *Annals of the American Academy of Political and Social Science,* January, 1963, p. 104.

[16] *Ibid.* This brings up a point which has puzzled many; how the motor carriers could continue to operate when their operating ratio (ratio of operating expenses to gross operating revenue) was so much higher, roughly 93–95 per cent, compared to that of the railroads' approximately 80 per cent. The answer is, of course, found in their more rapid rate of turnover, or ratio of operating revenue to capital assets.

TABLE 7-1. *Investment Returns for Various Modes of Transportation*

	INVESTMENT TURNOVER[17]	
	Times Turned Over per Year	Years Required to Turn
Class I Railroads	.36	2.80
Motor Carriers of Property (Class I)	4.29	.23
Class I Motor Carriers of Passengers	1.80	.56
Water Carriers (Classes A and B)	1.15	.87
Oil Pipelines	.38	2.65
Airlines (excluding Federal Subsidy)	1.52	.66

totem pole in the transportation field, but they are extremely so when compared to other regulated industries." [18]

On page 4 of *Transport Topics,* issue of March 11, 1963, Clinton L. Sanders, President, American Trucking Associations, Inc., was quoted as saying that the railroads in the past ten years "have enjoyed a return on investment of 7.19 per cent as compared with, for example, 5.62 per cent by General Electric Company." Further, said Mr. Sanders, "most trucking companies would enjoy a profit situation such as that enjoyed by the average railroad." However, Mr. Sanders stated[19] that he was misquoted and that this should have read that the railroads "enjoyed a return on sales of 7.19 per cent" and that the "percentage of net revenue to sales in the trucking industry has ranged between 2.4 and 4.2 for the past ten years; this is before income taxes, the rail figure is after such taxes." This contrasts with the picture as found in the preceding figures and in the following figures.

The First National City Bank of New York statement of the Net Income of Leading Corporations for April, 1962, shows that for 1960 and 1961, the percentage return on net assets was as shown in Table 7-2:

The Interstate Commerce Commission[20] shows a return of 2.23

---

[17] Statement, Burton N. Behling, AAR, before Senate Committee on Interstate and Foreign Commerce, June 28, 1961, Table 7.

[18] Statement, March 8, 1963 from Bureau of Railway Economics, Association of American Railroads. The rate of return for the rails in 1962 is now estimated at 2.67 per cent, compared to 1.97 per cent in 1961; the increase in large measure was due to increased depreciation allowances.

[19] Letter of March 18, 1963 to Newton Morton.

[20] Letter of March 22, 1963, from Edward Margolin, Director, Bureau of Transport Economics and Statistics to Newton Morton.

TABLE 7-2. *Percentage Return on Net Assets*

	1960	1961
Class I Railroads	2.6	2.2
Common Carrier Trucking	6.3	11.4
Shipping	4.5	4.4
Air Transport	4.1	—
Miscellaneous Transportation	9.1	8.1

per cent for Class I railroads in 1960; this is more than shown in the AAR figures and less than shown in the First National City Bank figures. The ICC adds:[21]

> The accounts and records of the carriers are examined by the Commission staff in order to ensure compliance with the uniform accounting regulations. If the railways or others elect to adjust the published data to serve their own purposes, the Commission does not attempt informally to correct such use.

While it is not possible to reconcile all the differences in the statistics shown, it appears proper, as a generalization, to say that the public interest requires favorable consideration by the ICC of consolidation proposals, subject to the attachment of certain conditions for their granting. Disregarding instances of better returns for individual roads, particularly in areas other than the Eastern (Official) Territory, the figures shown indicate that the railroads, as an industry, need to better their financial status.

CONTROL OF GRAY AREA TRANSPORTATION

"Gray area" transportation is one excellent instance of a diversionary influence which results in carriers in competing modes of transportation uniting to wage a common battle. Gray area transportation intends to profit from doing a transportation business without assuming the obligations and the costs of regulation; it is unsanctioned transportation masquerading as legitimate enterprise. Here are several varieties:

[21] *Ibid.*

1. A shipper who buys in the open market at a destination where, as a private carrier, he has delivered a load of industry products, and transports back to or near the original point of origin, where the commodities are sold to anyone who will buy them. This is to curtail the round trip or joint costs.

2. A pseudo-common carrier who offers his brand of "buy-and-sell" transportation by engaging in a rigged transaction where he ostensibly buys from the shipper, agreeing to sell to his shipper's customers at invoice price less the cost of transportation. This attempt to escape the responsibilities and costs of regulated transport through pretending to be a private carrier during the course of transportation is a drain on traffic available to motor common carriers, the railroads, or both.

3. A group of men who decide to do a common carrier business in serving the general public without authorization, endeavoring to escape regulation and its obligations by claiming falsely that they are "shippers' associations" and, therefore, exempt from regulations under Part IV.

The ICC breakdown on the frequency of these illegal practices shows that shipper leases of vehicles with drivers amount to 45 per cent of the total; buy and sell operations of illegal truck operators amount to 21 per cent; and unlawful operations by carriers exempt from ICC economic regulations reach 12 per cent, with other types of operations of questionable legality amounting to 22 per cent.[22] The "buy-and-sell"[23] operations are employed extensively on hauls of goods which have a ready market.

[22] Release of Committee Against Unauthorized Transportation (prepared by the Transportation Association of America), January, 1962.

In addition to those mentioned above, the following are considered illegal transportation:

1. A "gypsy" for-hire operator transporting regulated commodities without a certificate or permit.

2. A shipper leasing a vehicle and driver from one entity, provided the shipper does not have complete control of the transportation involved, or leasing a vehicle and driver from separate entities which are in concert with each other for the purpose of performing a transportation service for the shipper.

3. Unlawful operations by carriers exempt from regulations such as hauling exempt agricultural commodities one way and nonexempt commodities on the return.

4. Intercity haulers operating beyond their territory and local cartage concerns operating beyond a specified metropolitan area.

5. So-called brokers participating in furnishing loads to carriers under illegal arrangements.

[23] As used under (2) above, a carrier doing business with the general public tries to escape regulation by saying to a shipper, "You sell me your shipment. During transit, it is mine technically, and, therefore, as private transportation is exempt from regulation. On arrival at destination, I will sell to

A for-hire carrier with legitimate operating rights in one direction of a haul may operate illegally on the return haul to correct his imbalance; a private carrier may resort to such practices for a similar reason. Some truckers practice this unlawful transportation because of lack of knowledge of the law, while others do so with deceitful intent. The practice enables the gray area carriers to quote spot rates and secure the traffic in competition with legitimate carriers. The skullduggery of this competition may make it necessary for otherwise law-abiding shippers and carriers to engage in illegal practices to protect themselves from unlawful competitors.

Since gray area transportation is not regulated or policed adequately, it is difficult to determine the share of intercity ton-miles which such transportation secures. In 1958, the ICC estimated that the diversions by gray area carriers amounted to 11.2 billion ton-miles, or approximately 4.5 per cent. At this time the total rail ton-miles decreased 4 per cent. While not all unregulated motor carrier transportation moves via gray area carriers, in the fifteen years ending with 1960, non-ICC truckers' tonnage increased 375 billion ton-miles, while that of the regulated carriers increased only 105 billion ton-miles.[24]

While the Transportation Act of 1958 attempted to check all aspects of gray area transportation by including a measure giving the ICC authority to police it, and the latter are doing so, there continue to be questions as to whether these controls are adequate. Legitimate, regulated carriers are supposed to live up to the rules and regulations of the ICC as well as the provisions of the Interstate Commerce Act. It is, therefore, only proper to force carriers doing a business with the general public and not coming under the benefits of exemptions to operate in accordance with the law. Appropriate provisions to strengthen enforcement of the law are advisable.

APPLICATION OF USER-CHARGES

Social, political, and economic consideration are important in determining whether or not facilities for transportation are to be made

---

your customer at your invoice price less my charge for transportation." The same term is applied to improper private carrier operations as treated under (1) above.

[24] Release of Committee Against Unauthorized Transportation, *op. cit.*

available at public expense. This was true in inaugurating the policy, starting in 1850, of land grants to assist the building of railroads and, thereby, the settlement of the West and the strengthening of its ties with the older sections of the country.

Nevertheless, for valid reasons, there is a substantial movement toward greater economic accountability for federal aids to particular forms of transportation, which means the application of the user-charge principle to the transportation system of the country. The user-charge principle is simply that those who have obtained the benefits of transportation improvements provided with government funds should repay these costs to the government. Of course, the user-charge principle applies properly to all fields, not merely transportation.

It may be advisable in some instances to consider any past construction cost as sunk costs, meaning that the improvements already constructed should not have their costs amortized by charges to the users, but maintenance and operating costs should be recovered and future improvements should be self-liquidating.

GOVERNMENT ATTITUDE ON USER-CHARGE APPLICATION

In the last decade, various Congressional committees, the Department of Commerce, the Bureau of the Budget, and even the President, as well as numerous private organizations such as the Transportation Association of America, have expressed themselves as being in favor of charging fees, tolls, or other such levies to recover the costs of aid to various transportation media.

While our interest is primarily in transportation, the user-charge has been utilized in other fields of government expenditure. In 1950, a special government report advocated that:

> Where the benefits of service accrue wholly to special interests which derive therefrom the means of financial success, the costs should be borne by the beneficiaries. Where there is a joint benefit to a particular beneficiary and to all the people, the costs should be divided equitably, but where there is doubt as to the degree of preponderance of benefit, there should be no fee.[25]

[25] U.S. Department of Commerce (Office of Transportation), "Charges for Private Use of Federal-Provided Transportation Services and Facilities" (Washington, D.C.: U.S. Government Printing Office, 1953), p. 12. This well-done user-charge study was prepared by Dr. Beatrice Aitchison.

Further, in 1952 another report in the same area provided:

> . . . it is the sense of the Congress that any work, service . . . certificate . . . or similar thing of value . . . performed, furnished, provided or issued by any federal agency . . . shall be *self-sustaining to the full extent possible* and the head of such federal agency is *authorized* by regulation to prescribe such fee, charge or price as he shall determine . . . to be fair and equitable . . .[26]

Some say that not applying the user-charge principle contributes to a socialist state. Those who oppose this view say that the money appropriated is paid by the people anyway. However, a distinction should be made between the limited good to the interests aided and the general good.

Any user-charge assessment must be for the general public benefit, the charge must not be unduly discriminatory or preferential, the money procured by the user-charges should not exceed the costs involved, and the charges must be reasonable and definite. Failure to collect such charges, where this is feasible, amounts to a subsidy.[27]

The arguments in favor of user-charges are that they will increase justice to the various transport agencies, to the users of transportation, and to the general taxpayers, from whose contributions the federal treasury provides the appropriations for transportation improvements. The arguments against their application are that they will result in discriminatory taxes (an argument difficult to accept), that new industries should have treatment equal to that accorded the railroads,[28] and that user-charges are impracticable[29] in view of the effect

---

[26] Independent Offices Appropriation Act of 1952, House Report No. 383, 82d Congress, April 27, 1952. (Emphasis supplied.)

[27] A direct subsidy is a payment made directly to a carrier or agency to enable its continued representation of service, while an indirect subsidy is a government appropriation to provide facilities which are used without payment of fees to recover the costs thereof. An example of a direct subsidy is a payment to a local service airline to enable it to stay in business, while money for the provision of airway and airport facilities without fees or other payments, wholly or partially, constitutes an indirect subsidy.

[28] The present aids to air and water lines do not include the principle of compensating advantages, or a *quid pro quo,* such as the concessions which the government-aided railroads gave to government property shipments (50 per cent) and personnel movements (80 per cent), until these were abolished in 1946.

[29] So far as the claim of impracticability is concerned, there is the view that this is advanced primarily by those special interests who have benefited from the non-application of user-charges in the past and who do not wish to have to pay them in the future.

on those who pay them, on international commerce, and on the Congressional intent[30] to aid and promote transportation on the waterways, on the airways, etc.

User-charges may be considered as being applied even when the revenue obtained thereby falls short of recovering full costs of the facility or service. Airport landing fees are a case in point.

THE NORTHWEST ORDINANCE AND USER-CHARGES

The Northwest Ordinance of 1787 provided that the waters of the Ohio-Mississippi River should be "forever free" of any toll, tax or fee. This is the ace in the hole on which the water lines rely to defeat the incipient application of user-charges. According to the Aitchison Study,[31] this refers to the right to use the waterway, and is not believed to apply to recovering the costs of improvements by fees or tolls. In fact, in the case of *Huse v. Clover*,[32] the United States Supreme Court stated that:

> The provision of the clause that the navigable streams should be highways without any tax, impost or duty, has reference to their navigation in their natural state. It did not contemplate that their navigation might not be improved by artificial means. . . . For outlays caused by such works, the State may exact reasonable tolls.

The same view was upheld in the case of *Sands v. Manistee River*[33] in the following year. That is not to say, however, that the application of user-charges would be upheld under this doctrine when the current advocacy of such charges results in their application and the initiation of a test case. Views change, both on the part of the public and on the part of the courts. The latter may decide that the *Huse v. Clover* view has outlived its usefulness as governing doctrine,

---

[30] The "inherent advantages of water transportation" which current Congressional policy is designed to protect are often conceived to be an artificially-conferred advantage rather than a natural advantage, in that the rates do not always encompass full costs. The current contention in regard to this, in water (and similarly in air transportation), is directed to the idea that Congressional intent should be changed.

[31] U.S. Department of Commerce Study, *op. cit.*, p. 61. Also, see *Report Prepared for the Committee on Interstate and Foreign Commerce, United States Senate, by the Special Study Group on Transportation Policies in the United States* (the famous Doyle Report), pp. 207–208.

[32] 119 U.S. 543 (1886).

[33] 123 U.S. 288 (1887).

but it is believed that if political pressure does not prevent the issue from coming down to a vote the omnipotence of the Commerce Clause alone will be sufficient to uphold the application of these charges.

INTERMODAL COORDINATION

Intermodal coordination is of vital importance if prospective transportation pricing developments and services are to best reflect public interest.

THE PUBLIC INTEREST

Probably nowhere has this term been pinpointed better than in the landmark cases of *Munn v. Illinois*[34] and *Nebbia v. New York*.[35] In the former case, the Supreme Court said:

> When, therefore, one devotes his property to a use in which the public has an interest, he, in effect, grants to the public an interest in that use and must submit to be controlled by the public for the common good.

In the latter case, the High Court said, in enlarging the old concept of a limited category of companies which were affected with a public interest:

> It is clear that there is no closed class or category of business affected with a public interest. The phrase, can, in the nature of things, mean no more than that an industry, for adequate reasons, is subject to control for the public good . . . So far as the requirement of due process is concerned . . . a state is free to adopt whatever economic policy may reasonably be deemed to permit public welfare . . . If the laws passed are to have a reasonable relation to a proper legislative purpose, and are neither arbitrary or discriminatory, the requirements of due process are satisfied.

The state, whether on a more restricted or a federal basis, may, with the above limitations, regulate not only industries, but any enterprise or activity where there is consistent support for such a move. If intermodal carriers concur in joint through rates, it is certainly

[34] 94 U.S. 113 (1876).
[35] 291 U.S. 502 (1934).

not entirely because of their public-spirited nature, but partly because of a selfish desire to maximize their participation in the transportation of available traffic. Nor is this necessarily objectionable or forbidden under our private enterprise system. It merely reflects the realities of human behavior.

The proposition is posed, therefore, that each carrier will only participate voluntarily in intermodal arrangements where he feels that this serves his best interest. What public interest requires in the way of added controls to force intermodal coordination is another story. The broadly-based powers mentioned previously may have to be invoked if it is made certain that intermodal coordination is necessary and the carriers of the different modes are reluctant to coordinate as deemed by Congress to be desirable in the public interest.

COMMON OBJECTIVES OF REGULATED COMMON CARRIERS

The carriers of the several modes may engage in united action against a common enemy, such as gray area carriers, but that is not quite a crusade in which the carriers of each mode march along vigorously toward a common objective—the common weal. Nevertheless, there are presently many more instances of such coordination than anyone would have dared to predict ten years ago.[36]

Another area of intermodal cooperation is the support by common carriers of any move to place labor unions under the antitrust laws; this would result in outlawing nationwide transportation strikes by groups such as the International Longshoremen's Union, the railroad brotherhoods, and the Teamsters Union. Common carriers in all modes would probably be sympathetic to a proposal to incorporate in the Interstate Commerce Act and the Federal Aviation Act, or elsewhere, provisions to outlaw make-work or featherbedding provisions in transportation labor contracts, even though they might not prove feasible to carry out.

THE CURRENT INTERMODAL ISSUE

As the rails in recent years surveyed the possibilities of increasing their revenue through acquiring facilities in other modes (such as joint rail

[36] One example is the increasing use of Plan V piggyback with joint through rates partly by rail and partly by motor carrier.

ownership of a barge line, single rail ownership of a pipeline, or amplified ownership of motor carriers), they began to stress, with the support of some shippers, the idea of "package," "department store," "integrated" transportation, or common ownership. Under this concept, whatever the needs of a shipper for a particular kind of transportation, the railroad-owned "transportation company" could provide it. This, of course, agitated other carriers. They contended that such rail ownership of facilities in other modes would enable the overpowering financial resources of the railroads to force rates down, forcing traditional carriers in other modes out of business; the railroads would then raise their rates. Further, said the other carriers (motor carriers, barge lines, etc.), such common ownership was not only against public policy, as being conducive to monopoly, but was also unnecessary, as the same participation could be brought about by intermodal coordination on a joint through rate basis. To the extent that modes of transportation other than railroads acquired facilities outside of their fields, common ownership would be constituted.

This is a continuing issue. To resolve it, it would be well to examine briefly the present ICC controls.

PRESENT ICC CONTROLS

By the Hepburn Act of 1906, the ICC was given the right to establish both through routes and joint through rates between rail carriers, and between rail carriers and water lines, as well as divisions of revenue which would apply if the carriers could not agree among themselves on revenue splits. This is carried currently in Section 1, Paragraph 4. Section 216(c) says that motor common carriers of property *may* establish such through routes and joint through rates with other such carriers, or with common carriers by railroad and/or express and/or water. Section 305(b) says that water carriers *shall* establish through routes and joint through rates with each other and with common carriers by railroad, and *may* establish such rates with common carriers by motor vehicle. Section 1003 of the Federal Aviation Act says that airlines *may* establish such through routes and joint through rates with other common carriers. There is no limitation as to the carriers with whom such airline arrangements may be made, except that air carriers not engaged directly in air transportation may not do so.

PROPOSED ICC CONTROLS

It was proposed in a bill submitted in the 88th Congress (H.R. 2088) that the ICC be authorized, after investigation and hearing, to require the establishment of through routes and joint through rates between motor common carriers of property, and between such carriers and common carriers by rail, express, and water. The bill seems consistent with the public interest. Nothing was said in the bill about such routes and rates with airlines.

The question naturally arises as to the railroads' reaction if H.R. 2088 or a similar bill is passed. Suppose the ICC told Railroad X that it could not have its entire haul as it formerly did from A to C. It was thought in the public interest to short-haul X so that it would receive only the haul from A to junction J, with motor carrier Y completing the intermodal transportation to point C. If the rail carrier X brought action in the courts to prevent this, how would the issue be resolved?

Section 15, Paragraph 4, of the Act states that the ICC cannot establish a through route requiring any railroad to embrace substantially less than its entire length of line, unless not doing so would make the route unreasonably long, or unless the through route proposed is needed to provide more adequate or efficient service. This means that whatever the ICC finds to be in the public interest, as justified under the National Transportation Policy, etc., would be upheld by the courts.[37] In the hypothetical case mentioned above, rail carrier X could not contend successfully against the intermodal short-haul. Comparable treatment would require that the ICC have similar controls over intermodal short-hauling of carriers in other modes.

There still appears to be no good reason for ruling out railroad ownership of facilities in other modes under proper ICC controls; this ownership is not incompatible with participation by the rails in intermodal rates under powers such as proposed under H.R. 2088. Consistency would also require that carriers in the other modes be able to acquire facilities under the same conditions as the railroads.

---

[37] D. A. Stickell & Sons, Inc. v. Alton Railroad Co., 255 ICC 333 (1943), affirmed in Pennsylvania Railroad v. United States, 323 U.S. 588 (1945).

OTHER TRANSPORTATION PROBLEM AREAS

The reports mentioned previously (the Bricker, Weeks, Smathers, Mueller and Doyle Reports) contain many specific suggestions for the improvement of our transportation system. The scope of our treatment does not permit examination in detail of the various points mentioned in those reports. There are, however, two problem areas which require special mention.

1. *Featherbedding.* There are almost as many definitions of featherbedding as there are examples of its presence in the several transportation media. The term signifies essentially make-work jobs forced on employers by organized labor. The practice at issue involves the railroads particularly. From the time that the railroad brotherhoods were organized in the latter part of the nineteenth century, they exercised considerable power. After World War I, railroad management negotiated, in 1919, an agreement as to work rules which was to apply for a forty year period. The standard working day was 150 miles for employees on passenger trains and 100 miles on freight trains, with extra pay for runs beyond that mileage. Yard crews could not do road work, and vice versa. Crews had the option of taking the mileage pay or securing the benefits of a scaled hourly basis, if that gave them more pay. Crews had to be changed when each division was reached.

When the agreement expired in 1959, protracted negotiations were entered into through the National Mediation Board, but these were not successful. The dispute then followed designated channels and was submitted to a Presidential emergency fact-finding board, whose suggestions were acceptable to rail management but not to labor. In 1963, rail management said they would put into effect the proposed new rules, which would eliminate many jobs, such as those of firemen on Diesel engines, and would curtail make-work practices characteristic of the previous rules. Labor threatened to strike; the Federal Government intervened with pleas to each side to be reasonable in the public interest. This seemed to signify that they wanted the railroad labor not to strike until the government could persuade the railroads to give labor what it wanted, which the carriers were not about to do.

After protracted negotiations and threats of widespread strikes, government intervention in 1964 forced a give-and-take on both labor and rail carrier management. While this did not eliminate entirely the threat of strikes, indications were that if they occurred at all they would be minimal in effect.

   2. *Relief of urban and metropolitan traffic congestion.* The Doyle Report, particularly, contained specific recommendations for alleviation of such congestion. The two contending camps involved subsidized rail transportation v. a bus system, with advocates of a monorail lurking on the outskirts of the dispute in an effort to advance their cause. The question of whether either of these, or some other type of transportation, will eventually be considered to have earned a superior rating as the remedy for urban and metropolitan transit ills remains unreconciled.

   There is seemingly a growing body of opinion that the long-held rights of labor to strike must give way in cases where the public interest is adversely affected, particularly in cases involving transportation, food supplies, and other public services.

PART THREE

LOGISTICS OF

MICRODISTRIBUTION

SYSTEMS

CHAPTER EIGHT

ADJUSTMENT OF THE MICRODISTRIBUTION SYSTEM TO CHANGE

A macroanalytical approach was used in the first two parts of the book to focus attention on the aggregative forces which affect the distribution system as a part of the economy. A microanalytical approach is used in this part of the book to analyze the various forces in subsegments of a given universe or macrosystem. As pointed out in the definitions in Chapter 1, the dividing line between macro- and microanalysis is difficult to discern in practice and, at best, usually results in a comparatively arbitrary division.

The dispersion system is the subsegment of the general system which will be given particular attention in this part of the book. It will be viewed primarily from the standpoint of the manufacturer or distributor of commodities. The concentration system will be mentioned at various points, but only as an adjunct to the performance of dispersion. The specific areas of coverage in this part of the book are the adjustment of microdistribution systems to change, logistics of terminal locations, and distribution system cost and revenue analysis.

The dispersion system of the manufacturer or distributor was selected for more detailed analysis because it is in this area that the most fruitful opportunities may be found for lowering distribution cost. The problems of distribution become much more complex as the shipment moves closer, in terms of both spatial proximity and transfer of physical possession, to the ultimate consumer. There is considerable evidence that distribution costs may increase more than proportionately to the decrease in shipment size.

The objectives in this study of a subsystem, as previously defined, are twofold: first, to develop a more thorough understanding of the various parts of the dispersion system; and, second, to develop tools which may be used for decision making in this system. Methods will be presented to analyze each of the segments, and also to combine each into a total system.

The starting point in this chapter is to view the changing life styles of the customer as these affect the firm's logistics system. Market planning and programming are then considered, with particular reference to distribution. This is followed by the presentation of a method for selecting distribution alternatives. A framework for change is presented at the close of the chapter.

CUSTOMER LIFE STYLES AFFECTING THE FIRM'S LOGISTICS SYSTEM

Since the early 1950's, literature in the area of demand creation and distribution has shown a strong orientation toward the consumer. Such phrases as the marketing concept, consumer orientation, target consumer, and veto power of the consumer have been used to show that a business firm must be adjustable, and that it is primarily in terms of its customers (both potential and actual) that it must adjust.

In Chapter 1, the triunal interaction model of an economy was presented. This model shows that there are three areas of adjustment for the firm. It must adjust to the needs and wants of consumers, the changes in knowledge and skills, and the changes in resources, at the same time recognizing that these are all interactive. For example, oil (such as there may be) underneath the ocean floor is not a resource available to the firms of our economy until knowledge and skills, and the resultant technology, are available at a competitive cost. If such technology were to become available, oil from the ocean floor would become an available competitive resource.

Similarly, changes in skills and knowledge which result in current resources' becoming available at a lower price can cause changes in the wants and needs of consumers. This type of interaction occurred when pipelines made natural gas and fuel oil competitively available for the home heating market. An example of change arising from needs and wants is the activity to develop the knowledge, skills, and special resources needed to place a man on the moon. Therefore, the initiating change can occur in any one of the three areas.

THE BUSINESS FIRM AS AN ADJUSTIVE SUBSYSTEM

The role of a firm within the above framework is to anticipate and adjust to change. Therefore, it is not surprising that the literature in the area of demand creation and distribution has taken the direction mentioned above, since, in a competitive economy, a firm's ability to adjust to the market place determines its fortunes. Only if the firm can provide a product and/or service which is perceived by consumers as being unique, different, and/or better can it hope to overcome

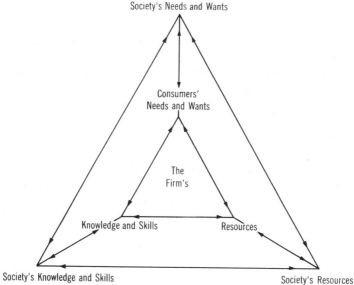

Figure 8-1. *The Interrelationship of a Firm to Society.*

the veto power of the consumer and be profitable. Specifically, a business firm wants to know who, where, when, why, and what size about all purchases, and what changes are likely to occur in any of these factors.

The triunal interaction model of the economy is the main system of which each business enterprise is a subsystem. In Figure 8-1, the firm is shown as a subsystem to the main system of the economy. The directional arrows show the interrelationships within the economy, as well as showing that the needs and wants of the firm's customers, its resources, and its knowledge and skills are derived from those of society while being capable of changing in these respective areas of society. Therefore, as a subsystem a business enterprise must adjust to changes in the main system while at the same time causing changes in it.

The adjustment to the main system, however, furnishes most business enterprises with their means of providing a profitable product or service. This is true primarily because it is normally easier to discover and move with a trend than to create one, both in terms of capital required and level of risk involved.

CHANGING CUSTOMER LIFE STYLES

The objective of this section is to identify and analyze some of the more important environmental trends occurring in the economy which affect the area of needs and wants. The trends selected for analysis include: time-consciousness, sociality, sedentarianism, affluence, mass transmission, and mobility. The perception and implementation of such market opportunities are discussed in the second portion of the chapter.

TIME-CONSCIOUSNESS.   *Time-consciousness* means that our society is clock-regulated, and that time becomes more compressed as the number of activities is increased. In the industrial society of the United States productivity has been emphasized, along with hard work, thrift, and competitive struggle. The belief is that material wealth must be obtained through work, but work takes time, and, as a result, is ever condensed.

One aspect of environmental time-consciousness is that the individual is expected to spend his free time visibly doing something for the betterment of himself or others. If a child is asked what he is doing, the reply is often "nothing." However, when the same question is asked of an adult, society has conditioned the individual to the unacceptability of doing "nothing." Even the leisure time activities of adults are conditioned by the customs and mores of their society.

The opportunities for marketing and distribution to capitalize on time-consciousness are limited only by the ingenuity of the managements in the individual firms. Some significant facts do stand out for the competitively market-oriented firm.

A firm's products and services will vie not only with competitors, but also for the time of the customer. Time-savers such as semi-automatic and automatic goods should increase in importance if they are very reliable, so that the consumer's time is not occupied with frequent maintenance problems caused by complicated or faulty operation. Although better transportation arteries are providing easier and faster travel, and enable the suburbanite to shop at the local shopping center or in the heart of a distant city, retail outlets would be wise to consider the time-pressed consumer before selecting the store site, size, method and hours of operation, in order to obtain the most promising customer-prospect mix. Telephone, mail order, and in-home shopping methods need to be re-explored. In addition, nighttime store operations as thorough as those in the daytime may be needed. Promotional techniques aimed at selling products to be used during one's leisure time, as defined earlier, may be off target for the immediate future.

SOCIALITY.   An important environmental living pattern developed in recent years is the increasing extent to which individuals consider the opinion of other persons in deciding their own personal behavior. This phenomenon is termed *sociality,* and signifies the overwhelming importance of group opinion in influencing individual personal behavior. It is particularly strong in the middle classes. The small group such as the neighborhood, is characterized by informal relationships, face-to-face communication, and multiple, instead of specialized, purposes. Individuals attempt to identify themselves with the group, and thereby lose a considerable amount of independence and privacy. In small groups, the slightest friction between members becomes a concern of all, and, in order to remain inside, the individual is forced to conform to the group's rules, often against his own beliefs. This indeed constitutes a hard choice between individuality and conformity.

The tendency towards homogenization of society has reflected itself, to some extent, in a homogeneity of purchase patterns. Such a situation cannot last indefinitely. Despite the overwhelming importance of homogeneous markets, the marginal differences in the products purchased do mean something to the individual consumer, who socially grades himself and others to a large extent on such minute differences. The producer, as well as the marketer, must always consider the fact that goods, especially durable goods, often constitute status symbols.

Market-oriented firms must be aware of the development of new status symbols which may be purchased by the innovators in a group and subsequently by the remainder of the group. New symbols are difficult to predict, but such items as luxurious boats or travel to distant lands are good examples.

The status symbol idea is by no means limited to the product itself. Package, brand, advertisement, and personal selling contact are equally important. Associational and indirect preference tests have proved that there is transference from the package to its contents in considering the advantages of a product over any one of its close substitutes in the market. The brand, the slogan, and the advertisement will limit the number of potential customers as a result of their aim to identify with the needs and values of specific groups in the population. The personal selling contact is no longer considered a mechanical presentation, but a technique varying with the particular needs and wants of each customer.

A tangible result of status consciousness is the so-called "package" of goods which is considered the minimum requirement to be socially accepted within a group. Such a package is carefully assembled by the persons who crave to "arrive," whereas those who are already at the top of the group do not care very much about the contents, being able to change and innovate on their own. Based on the assumptions that there will be continued increases in productivity in the economy and that there will continue to be consumer innovators who will lead a group, sociality will lead to increasing numbers of people trying to improve their social standing. This will create purchase patterns which affect distribution.

SEDENTARIANISM.   *Sedentarianism* characterizes individuals performing activities in sitting positions and living in a society requiring little exercise. The term includes people who can move about quickly, but who operate in a seemingly reclining position requiring little caloric expenditure. The process of inventing, operating, and maintaining machines increases sedentarianism. Ironing can be accomplished using specially designed boards adjusted to the sitting level. Lawn mowers are ridden, earth is moved, and roads are built by individuals sitting astride machinery.

Sedentarianism presents many opportunities for marketers. Sedentary passivity and its counterpart, physical exertion, make possible the sale of goods and services ranging from products designed for television lounging to reducing machines. There is the tremendously broad field of diet control, which has yet to be fully developed, not as a fad, but as a part of daily living for the sedentary worker. Another possibility is the development of in-home selling methods for comfort and convenience merchandise, provided cost factors can be held in favorable ratio to revenue. The growing interest in participation sports and the realization that youngsters should be included also presents a challenge for creating products and services to answer these needs and, in so doing, improve both the nation's health and its welfare.

AFFLUENCE. *Affluence* has been one of the marks of United States society since the end of World War II. Industrialization entails a division of labor and a specialization in the individual's activities. One of the fruits of such division is an increase in the knowledge and skills required in business activity. A result of this has been the development of "expertism," the desire of people to seek professional advice when dealing in matters outside their own fields of specialization or realms of activity. This desire for information has given added impetus to the quest for higher education, interest in the fine arts, and awareness of national and international affairs.

The development of affluence in the society leads to the presence of discretionary buying power which the population may use to satisfy its needs above the subsistence level. Added to this buying power is the consumer's practice of deficit spending or borrowing on tomorrow's prosperity. The thrift concept of the Protestant ethic appears to be on the wane, and the responsibility for credit buying is rationalized away because of commitments by government and/or business to provide security with welfare programs. It is probable that the practice will increase as the tendency towards guaranteed annual wages becomes more and more of an accomplished fact.

The success of industrialization creates the challenge of finding markets for an enormous production capacity. Although excess capacity in industry often leads to relative price stability, increased competition is also experienced by firms offering greater convenience, better service and quality, creation of a better product and company image, and community service.

Although in our affluent society the consumers have considerably increased the amount of income spent on services, it is likely that in future years durable goods will stage a comeback if economic conditions remain favorable. Family formations were at a low point during the early 1960's, but the post-World War II crop of babies will be of marriageable age in the mid-sixties. This segment of the population normally buys most of the durable goods.

The market for health and personal care fatigue-reducing products should increase as more women enter the labor market and as their life span increases. An affluent society is also likely to lead to a more sophisticated shopper who desires good quality merchandise and convenient shopping facilities such as in-home, telephone, mail order, Sunday, and night purchasing patterns.

MASS TRANSMISSION.   A significant environmental living pattern in our society is *mass transmission,* or the widespread dissemination of information through mass media. Much of this is done through one-way dissemination, and there is a lack of the discourse needed for group communication. Perhaps this pattern helps to explain the difficulty of assessing the effectiveness of advertising. The many individuals and organizations involved in surveys on motivational research attempt to remedy this absence of two-way communication.

Several media are available for mass transmission of messages from marketers to their actual and potential customers, including television, newspapers, weekly magazines, radio, and motion pictures. All of these are significant media and, with the exception of motion pictures, all are absorbed by the potential or actual customer in his own home. As an effect of the increasing popularity of television, many people stay at home for entertainment as well as for information.

The best example of personal exchange remaining in modern society of mass transmission occurs in suburban areas, where mouth-to-mouth communication is vital. In these areas the preponderant views about politics, economic perspectives, and fashions are developed by "opinion leaders" and spread throughout the whole group.

It is important that the firm create a good image in a group, particularly in the mind of the "opinion leader" who influences the group in its purchasing decisions. In planning advertising strategy, the firm should try to transfer the consumer's interest in a fashion already fulfilled by the firm towards its next functional alternative. The firm must also consider the importance of mouth-to-mouth communication in marketing to lower income groups where, perhaps because of insecurity and the fear of being cheated, recommendations by friends and relatives about quality and advantages of a product may well constitute the best source of advertising.

There is increasing evidence that the individual consumer is acquiring a greater degree of sophistication, probably partly because of increased education. To marketing management, this trend should suggest a different approach to advertising and promotional campaigns. Perhaps advertisers should realize that the customer desires to assert himself more and to increase his own self-esteem. By the extent that these needs are fulfilled, the failure or success of the product may be determined.

MOBILITY. Many young American families have moved to suburbia during recent years. The *mobility* of such families appears to be closely related to life cycles. The newly married couple normally lives in an apartment and then goes to suburbia. The family begins to move into bigger and better houses, which at the beginning are supposed to be permanent, but in actuality are temporary. At last, the family unit finds the lasting home, despite the fact that it will not be fully utilized as soon as the children begin to leave. When they do, the couple often decides to return to the city and live in an apartment.

The suburban society, in general, is characterized by homogeneity on the surface. Since in suburbia most people do not live permanently in one house, social or traditional differences as well as those in education and family background are blurring. Geographical mobility is also a way of social mobility, for the "only way to stay in the same place is to keep moving." [1]

Mobility can be upgrading for the new families arriving in suburbia, depending upon the immediate groups surrounding them. This aim, to improve household status, has been developed in the "life cycle suburb." Individuals living in suburbia also have different psychological needs, such as higher desire for achievement, power, variety, and novelty, than those not living in suburban areas.

The social position of an individual today is apparently mainly decided by only one traditional factor, status. The American of the nineteen-sixties has been defined as a "man with a status." [2] The remaining two factors, class and power, are not as important.

The word "status" has no clear-cut definition, and involves the interrelated factors of income, occupation, education, and social background. However, the traditional outward evidence of division among the different social groups has practically disappeared. Today it is

[1] D. Riesnan and H. Rosenborough, "Careers and Consumer Behavior," in Lincoln H. Clark (ed.), *Consumer Behavior,* Vol. 2: *Life Cycle and Consumer Behavior* (New York: Harper Brothers, 1958), p. 14.
[2] Editors of *Fortune, The Markets of the 60's* (New York: Harper Brothers, 1960), p. 11.

impossible to distinguish between a white and a blue collar worker by the suits they wear when they are not on their jobs. Moreover, the blue collar worker, who in the past was considered socially inferior to the white collar worker, often earns a higher income.

Education has historically been a means for men to move upwards to higher social and economic status, and has provided still higher levels of living for the population. As a consequence of the increasing amount of formal and informal education, the country is acquiring new tastes, particularly in literature, music, painting, and the performing arts. A better education is reflected in better taste and a wider range of choices, thus making production the agent, not of uniformity, but of constantly increasing variety. It also leads to increasing levels of sophistication in the quality of goods offered in the market place, as well as in the system of communication with the consumer.

Another interesting aspect of mobility is the growth of interurbia, where one suburb melts into another to form large metropolitan areas with no obvious political boundary lines dividing the area. While the growth of the population has played a large part in the growth of interurbia, geographic and social mobility have been more important than absolute numbers in expanding suburbia into interurbia.

The actual and future trend toward interurbia leads to changes in the marketing point of view, such as testing developments in the interurban strips rather than in an individual market and changing the geographical concept of sales distribution. Each interurban area will have to be considered a total sales opportunity, and marketing must be more selective because of more selective purchasing habits.

The trend towards interurbia has changed geographic shopping patterns considerably. Interurbia has shopping centers where there are branches of urban department stores as well as specialty stores. The consumer apparently has assumed some of the functions traditionally performed by the retailer in the past, particularly the performance of break-bulk and reassembly at the retail store level. The customer is traveling an increasing distance to meet the retailer, buying more per trip, and utilizing self-service equipment more than in previous years. The retail structure has attempted to adapt to meet these changing circumstances through larger retail stores, the construction of self-service establishments, and increased use of vending machines. It seems apparent that these trends will continue in the retail structure of interurbia.

MARKET PLANNING AND PROGRAMMING

Planning is the formulation of methods for accomplishing specific objectives, and has to be oriented toward the future. Programming is the advancement of the steps to carry out the plan. For a firm to capitalize upon a trend it visualizes in the market place, it must plan and program with the realization that its components act as systems, each interrelated and interacting with other enterprises and the ultimate consumer. A knowledge of environmental change leads to concrete, often measurable factors in broadly defining the markets in which the business will engage.

The objectives must be compatible with the firm's philosophy and closely tied to its resources of men, money, and material and the knowledge and skills it possesses. The components of the demand creation and distribution systems set forth their own specific compatible objectives which must be in tune with the trends in living and segmentation of society. The objectives will indicate the direction the firm should take in regard to the market it serves. Among the questions to be answered are the designation of persons to do the job, the most satisfactory way to accomplish the tasks, needed physical facilities and supervision, and optimum locations. Cost data must be compiled to show the cost of programs to be undertaken. Much of this information can be obtained from feedback from the sales force and the market research activity. If prohibitive costs are involved, modifications must be made.

A master marketing plan should be drawn from the plans and programs of the various components of the demand creation and distribution functions. The master plan would include a short range plan (perhaps one year), an intermediate range plan (perhaps two to four years), and a long range plan (five years or more), depending upon when or what management believes the required lead time is to make an impact on the market with its want satisfiers.

The master marketing plan represents a firm operating as a system, with its subsystems giving up certain advantages for the betterment of the total system. Proper research can identify the needs and wants of the customers, but the firm's demand creation and distribution plans and programs specify what can be sold feasibly and propitiously. Various demand creation and distribution mixes can be considered which will pinpoint interrelationships, call forth past data, and project future trends. The plans and programs of demand creation and distribution must be definite to be effective, yet there must be a climate of flexibility allowing responsible personnel freedom of operation to satisfy the affluent consumer.

SYSTEMS VIEW OF MARKET PLANNING AND PROGRAMMING

Throughout the text, the activities of demand creation and distribution have been discussed. When considering market planning and programming, these activities require a careful analysis. In many companies these activities are represented by separate departments, which may contain many specialized activities within each area. This is not surprising, since it has been recognized for some time (at least implicitly) that the channels used for demand creation need not be the same ones used for the actual physical movement of the goods. However, the potential danger in such a practice is that the specialists in each area may consider their area as separate rather than as part of a total interrelated marketing system. For example, it may be that a carton of soft drinks should contain fifteen bottles in order to minimize the "total cost" of distribution. However, no one would seriously advocate such a program unless there were sufficient demand for a fifteen bottle carton. Although the example above may appear obvious, the relationships between demand creation and distribution are not always so obvious. Therefore, marketing programming and planning must be accomplished through a systems approach which recognizes the pertinent variables which affect both demand creation and distribution and their interrelationship.

Figure 8-2 represents the systems view of market planning and programming. The arrow to market planning and programming from the needs and wants of the firm's customers shows that it is to the satisfaction of this area that the marketing effort is directed. The arrow from market planning and programming down to the next level of demand creation and distribution shows that these are the two main areas that must be provided for in planning and programming. The dotted arrow between the two shows that these two areas are interactive. The next level shows some of the variables which, once determined by the firm, constitute its demand creation and distribution systems. The dotted arrows show that these all interact with each other. Finally, the bottom level shows that it is in terms of the firm's

Figure 8-2. *The Systems Viewpoint of Market Planning and Programming.*

knowledge and skills and its resources that the inputs to the preceding level are obtained.

Therefore, it can be seen that optimum market planning and programming can only be obtained by solving a whole system of interacting variables, rather than solving each one separately as if it stood alone.

CHANGING EMPHASIS IN THE PERFORMANCE
OF THE DISTRIBUTION FUNCTION

The objective in logistics of microdistribution systems is to arrange the component parts so that differential gain can be created for the company. Since the parts often work at cross purposes, emphasis in computing distribution cost of a company should be on the total cost, rather than on each component element.

For example, if purchasing, warehousing, intercity movement, sales, and production control operate without coordination in a given combination of market circumstances, the result is a complete lack of coordinated company effort in serving that market. An industrial traffic man may buy the cheapest transportation but completely ignore the high cost of inventory resulting from larger unit shipments. The purchasing department may buy raw materials and supplies at the lowest mill price at the point of origin, but forget that there are transportation costs in movement to the buyer's site. The sales department may put in too many warehouses on the assumption that these are required to provide good service to the company's customers and, as a result, greatly increase the inventory, break-bulk, and reassembly expenses. Many other examples of a lack of coordination in the distribution efforts of the company could be quoted. The essential point is that the total cost approach is the only desirable one for a company to use in planning and controlling its distribution efforts.

The total cost approach in distribution is not necessarily a recent innovation in manufacturing and distributing companies. Some teachers and practitioners have for many years taught and practiced the desirability of coordinating distribution work within the company. However, the number of companies actually practicing the total cost approach was rather small until a few years ago. The increasing pressure of competition has forced nearly all companies to reinvestigate their geographic concepts of their markets. The result has been some version of the total cost approach to analyzing distribution systems.

COST ANALYSIS OF ALTERNATIVE DISTRIBUTION SYSTEMS

The traditional scientific approach to a problem is to define the problem, develop hypotheses and assumptions, and develop research techniques to test the validity of the assumptions. In the development of research techniques, a preliminary investigation usually precedes the full research project and has the objective of testing the validity of the approach to the problem (including the definition, hypotheses, assumptions, and research techniques) before going into a full research study. The use of preliminary investigations discussed in this section will be to narrow down the area of concentration so that the research effort can concentrate on a workable model.

COMPUTATION OF ALTERNATIVE TOTAL COSTS

In Table 8-1, four dispersion systems have been hypothesized to illustrate the computation of total costs under four alternatives for physical fulfillment of varying sales volumes. It is assumed that the shipments are being made from a given production point to a distri-

TABLE 8-1. *Assumed Inventory Requirements for Varying Movement Alternatives and Varying Sales Volumes*

ALTERNATIVE	ORDER PROCESS- ING TIME (DAYS)	TRANSIT TIME* (DAYS)	WARE- HOUSE TIME (DAYS)	RETAILER SHELF** TIME (DAYS)	TOTAL TIME (DAYS)	INVEN- TORY TURN- OVER PER YEAR
1. Air Freight to Retailer	5	1	0	0	6	60
2. Less Truck- load to Retailer	5	2	0	2	9	40
3. Truckload to Retailer	5	2	0	8	15	24
4. Carload to Warehouse to Retailer	5	4	4	11	24	15

* Assumes goods are priced at f.o.b. origin so that ownership in transit rests with the buyer.
** Retailer shelf time is the average amount of time that the goods would stay in the retailer's establishment until actually sold.

bution area. The four methods selected are air freight to retailer, less than truckload volume to retailer, truckload volume to retailer, and carload movement to warehouse and thence in smaller volumes to retail stores. The tools suggested refer to the dispersion system of a manufacturer or distributor, but they could also be adapted to the concentration system.

The following steps should be used as a preliminary cost analysis to compute total dispersion costs for the four alternative systems under consideration.

1. Estimate the sales of the area by period.
2. Calculate the inventory turnover necessary to maintain the estimated level of sales.[3]
3. Compute total costs for each of the alternative systems.
4. Select that system which will accomplish the desired objectives, e.g., minimization of costs, maximization of profits, or maximization of service.

A prerequisite condition to the entire process is a demarcation of the sales territory on a geographic or other basis. Since the analysis is concerned with a spatial movement system, the persons responsible for the demand creation and distribution systems must work together in establishing such boundaries. The specific sales forecast will normally be prepared by the market research section or some other statistical analysis unit within the sales department of the company.

The second step is to calculate the inventory turnover required to attain the estimated level of sales for the period. The calculation of inventory involves the determination of the following: time required for processing of the order, both at the origin and destination points; transit time required in the intercity movement; warehouse time, including delivery to the consignee; and retailer shelf time. Each of these steps can be subdivided into more detail, but this will suffice for illustrative purposes here.[4]

The order processing time for the four alternatives in the illustration is assumed to be five days. This will be treated as a constant amount of time, regardless of the method of movement; there is some justification for this assumption in that paperwork will not vary considerably with a change in the method of movement.

Intercity transit time varies considerably between the alternative modes. It is assumed here to be one day for air freight, two days for less than truckload, two days for truckload, and four days for rail carload. It has been assumed in the first three alternatives that shipments will be made directly to the retailer. The fourth alternative, however, assumes that the carload shipment will be made to a warehouse location and then broken down into smaller units for shipment to retailers; the assumption of six days for warehouse time has been made for the fourth alternative.

[3] In order to simplify the illustration, it is assumed that sales are made at the same daily rate throughout the year and that the inventory turnover is calculated on the basis of 360 days per year.
[4] For example, order processing expense and time could be subdivided into such activities as receipt of the order, checking the credit of the buyer, assembling the order for shipment, any necessary packaging or recrating assignable to the order, and cartage to the dock of the intercity carrier.

Since the goods will have to stay on the retailers' shelves for a given period of time, an assumed number of days has been added for this part of the distribution system. Air freight has been assigned zero days, less than truckload two days, truckload eight days, and rail carload eleven days. In each successive alternative, the amount of retail store shelf time has been increased to reflect the added volume per shipment, the additional amount required by the carrier to obtain the appropriate volume rate. A larger volume per shipment would normally require a relatively longer amount of retail store shelf time.

The inventory turnover figures that will be used in Table 8-2 are: 60 times per year via air freight, 40 times via less than truckload, 24 via truckload, and 15 via rail carload. These differences in the amount of total time required for distribution via the different systems accounts for the differences in the amount of inventory necessary.

TABLE 8-2. *Inventory Requirements for Selected Sales Volumes (in Dollars)*

REQUIRED INVENTORY LEVEL

SALES VOLUME	Turnover of 60	Turnover of 40	Turnover of 24	Turnover of 15
$40,000,000	$666,667	$1,000,000	$1,666,667	$2,666,667
30,000,000	500,000	750,000	1,250,000	2,000,000
25,000,000	416,667	625,000	1,041,667	1,666,667
12,500,000	204,333	312,500	520,817	833,333
5,000,000	83,333	125,000	208,333	333,333

For example, if the sales volume is $40,000,000 per year and the dispersion system is via air freight with a turnover rate of 60, then the required inventory level is $666,667. For the same sales volume and movement via rail carload, the required inventory is $2,666,667.

The computation of the total costs in the illustration is simplified to include only two elements: the interest on inventory and transportation charges. An annual interest charge of 10 per cent has been assumed. For a sales volume of $40,000,000, the resulting interest cost on inventory via the four alternatives would be air freight $66,667, less than truckload $100,000, truckload $166,667, and rail carload $266,667. Although the concern may not actually charge interest to itself in the statement of profit and loss as a direct addition to inventory cost, it is quite desirable to utilize a theoretical rate of return which one should realize from investment in inventory. Such an interest charge is a means of recognizing the cost of an opportunity lost. That is, if the money were not committed to inventory it could have been put to some other use which would yield a positive rate of return. The rate will vary between types of business, depending on capital turnover, merchandise turnover, sources of capital, and preferences of the management.

The transportation charges in this illustration decrease with volume. This assumption is made for each alternative and is in line with actual transportation pricing where larger volumes are given lower rates; these lower rates are in part due to economies of scale and in part to the wish to attract traffic. An inspection of each of the rates used in Table 8-3 illustrates this. Thus, for air freight (alternative 1) the rate goes from $6.56 per unit for a shipment of 10,000 units to $3.33 for a shipment of 80,000 units.[5] A differential is shown between the different alternatives to reflect the fact that there is a difference in transit time and cost structure that is shown in the rate structure.

The total cost of a given dispersion system is thus the combination of interest cost on inventory and the intercity transportation costs associated with that alternative. The total dispersion cost for an assumed sales level of $40,000,000 would be: $333,067 via air freight; $316,000 via less than truckload; $293,067 via truckload; and $281,867 via rail carload. If lowest cost were the desired objective in the assumed market circumstances, then clearly the dispersion system to use would be alternative 4, rail carload to warehouse to retailer.

The total cost lines for each of the four alternatives are plotted on Figure 8-3. Since both interest on investment and transportation are variable with volume, the lines still start at zero. The total cost curves intersect each other, and at these points it becomes advantageous to shift from one alternative to another. This is shown on Figure 8-3 where the total cost curve for air freight is intersected by

---

[5] In order to simplify the illustration, the size of inventory and size of shipment have been assumed to be the same. This assumption would have to be modified in practice. If a distributor in his calculations for alternative methods finds that the average shipment does not meet the carrier's volume requirements, he may have to move to another movement method. It has been the experience of many shippers that as the average size of the shipment has declined, they have been forced to utilize new methods of movement. For example, many shippers have moved from volume rail carload shipments to motor carrier truckload and from motor truckload to less than truckload volumes because they could not meet the minimum requirements for volume rates.

TABLE 8-3. *An Illustration of Total Movement Costs via Four Alternatives for Five Selected Sales Volumes**

		TRANSPORTATION CHARGES		
ALTERNATIVE	INTEREST ON INVENTORY	Unit Cost	Total Trans. Cost	TOTAL COST
		(Volume of 80,000 units = $40,000,000)		
1	$ 66,667	$3.33	$266,400	$333,067
2	100,000	2.70	216,000	316,000
3	166,667	1.58	126,400	293,067
4	266,667	0.19	15,200	281,867
		(Volume of 60,000 units = $30,000,000)		
1	50,000	4.10	246,000	296,000
2	75,000	3.31	198,600	273,600
3	125,000	2.34	140,400	265,400
4	200,000	1.14	68,400	268,400
		(Volume of 50,000 units = $25,000,000)		
1	41,667	4.54	227,000	268,667
2	62,500	3.65	182,500	245,000
3	104,167	2.83	141,500	245,667
4	166,667	1.74	87,000	253,667
		(Volume of 25,000 units = $12,500,000)		
1	20,433	5.65	141,250	161,683
2	31,250	5.37	134,250	165,500
3	52,082	5.13	128,250	180,332
4	83,333	4.09	102,250	185,583
		(Volume of 10,000 units = $5,000,000)		
1	8,333	6.56	65,600	73,933
2	12,500	7.65	76,500	89,000
3	20,833	8.67	86,700	107,533
4	33,333	8.57	85,700	119,033

* Assumptions: 1 unit equals $500; annual interest cost on inventory of 10 per cent; assumed inventory cycles from Table 8-1.

the cost curve for less than carload at approximately 28,000 units. Below this figure it is cheapest to use air freight, and above this it is more advantageous to use less than carload. The intersection between alternatives 2 and 3 occurs at approximately 50,000 units and between alternatives 3 and 4 at approximately 62,000 units.

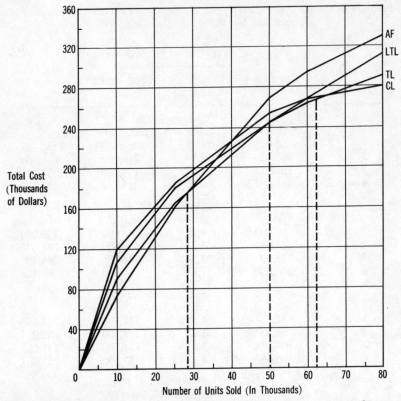

Figure 8-3. *An Illustration of Total Movement Costs via Four Alternatives for Five Selected Sales Volumes.*

The intersection is caused by the fact that the decrease in transportation costs more than offsets the increase in interest cost as one shifts from one volume to another. This is true both within an alternative and between alternatives. The increase in each of the total cost curves is at a decreasing rate, so that the curve is concave to the horizontal axis.

At the sales quantity indicated by the intersection between alternative systems, the manufacturer would have two possibilities available to him: first, the acceptance of the turnover figure and sales volume with the resultant conclusion as to the lowest cost system; or second, a decision as to whether or not the sales forecast needed revision in terms of the physical cost of serving the market. Such an alternative cost analysis gives a method for computing alternative total costs of movement under alternative distribution systems from a given point to a given market. The intersections serve as approximate points at which more detailed study should be made.

A REFINEMENT OF THE GRAPHIC METHOD
FOR DETERMINING COMPARATIVE TOTAL COST

On the graph of Figure 8-3, where total cost was plotted in relation to volume it was readily apparent that there were certain volumes where total costs could be lowered by switching from one distribution system to another. This was because differences in costs between the modes were more than offset by an attendant inventory cost increase. The graphic method is useful, and in simple cases may suffice. However, it would also be advantageous to be able to describe what is happening analytically by finding these intersecting points on the total cost curves.

The total cost is given by the equation:

$$TC = \frac{P(V)}{T} C + R(V) \quad \text{where}$$

TC = Total cost
P = Price per unit
V = Total volume
T = Turnover rate
C = Interest per cent
R = Transportation cost per unit

Assume that it is desired to find the point of intersection of the total cost curves for alternatives 1 and 2. This point occurs where TC_2 (total cost of alternative 2) and TC_1 (total cost of alternative 1) are equal. By considering the difference in total cost between alternative 1 and alternative 2, denoted ΔTC_{21}, the point of equality will be:

$$TC_2 - TC_1 = \Delta TC_{21} = 0$$

$$\Delta TC_{21} = \left(\frac{PV}{T_2} C + R_2 V\right) - \left(\frac{PV}{T_1} C + R_1 V\right)$$

$$= \left(\frac{PVC}{T_2} - \frac{PVC}{T_1}\right) + (R_2 V - R_1 V) = \Delta IC_{21} + \Delta TRC_{21}$$

where ΔIC_{21} = the difference in inventory cost between alternative 2 and alternative 1

and ΔTRC_{21} = the difference in transportation cost between alternative 2 and alternative 1.

As stated previously, the intersecting point in which we are interested occurs when $\Delta TC_{21} = 0$. Thus, equating the above to zero, we obtain

$$0 = \Delta IC_{21} + \Delta TRC_{21}$$

or

$$\Delta IC_{21} = -\Delta TRC_{21}$$

From above,

$$\Delta IC_{21} = \frac{PVC}{T_2} - \frac{PVC}{T_1}$$

and

$$\Delta TRC_{21} = R_2 V - R_1 V$$

Substituting,

$$\frac{PVC}{T_2} - \frac{PVC}{T_1} = -(R_2 V - R_1 V)$$

Dividing through by V,

$$\frac{PC}{T_2} - \frac{PC}{T_1} = -(R_2 - R_1)$$

Factoring out PC,

$$PC\left(\frac{1}{T_2} - \frac{1}{T_1}\right) = -(R_2 - R_1)$$

To eliminate the $(-)$ sign change R_2 and R_1. Thus,

$$PC\left(\frac{1}{T_2} - \frac{1}{T_1}\right) = R_1 - R_2$$

Although this last equation appears to be independent of volume, this is not the case, since R, the transportation rate per unit, is a function of volume. Thus, there will be a certain volume at which the equation will hold and this will be the point of intersection.

In order to find this volume, we need to know the relationship between R and V. However, in order to do this more assumptions are required than will be made in this section. The only other way, given the limited data used in the illustration, is to find when $|\Delta IC_{21}| = |\Delta TRC_{21}|$ but this requires graphing both ΔIC_{21} and ΔTRC_{21} and finding the intersection.

The preliminary analysis recognizes that insufficient data are available for a wholly analytical solution at this point. The graphical solution is an eliminating device to point up applicable quantities and alternatives where a detailed analysis should be made. Analytical

TABLE 8-4. *Values of* ΔTRC_{21} *and* ΔIC_{21} *for Selected Values of* V

V	ΔIC_{21}	ΔTRC_{21}
10,000	$ 4,167	$10,900*
25,000	10,417	7,000
50,000	20,833	44,500
60,000	25,000	47,400
80,000	33,333	50,400

* This is a negative value on the chart for a volume of 10,000 units. Since the graph is concerned only with the northeast quadrant of the Cartesian coordinates where both X and Y values are positive, the negative values on the graph have no relevancy to the problem here.

solutions are provided in Chapter 10. In Table 8-4 values of ΔIC_{21} and ΔTRC_{21} are presented for various volumes. In order to illustrate how the figures in the table were obtained, two calculations are shown.

$$|\Delta IC_{21}| = \left| \frac{PVC}{T_2} - \frac{PVC}{T_1} \right|$$

and $|\Delta TRC_{21}| = |R_1 V - R_2 V|$

Substituting the values from Tables 8-2 and 8-3 for a shipment of 10,000 units, we have

$$\Delta IC_{21} = \frac{500 \times 10,000 \times .10}{40} - \frac{500 \times 10,000 \times .10}{60}$$
$$= 12,500 - 8,333$$
$$= 4,167$$
$$-\Delta TRC_{21} = (6.56 \times 10,000) - (7.65 \times 10,000)$$
$$= 65,600 - 76,500$$
$$= -10,900$$

Similar substitutions for a shipment of 25,000 units gives

$$\Delta IC_{21} = \frac{500 \times 25,000 \times .10}{40} - \frac{500 \times 25,000 \times .10}{60}$$
$$= 31,250 - 20,833$$
$$= 10,417$$
$$-\Delta TRC_{21} = (5.65 \times 25,000) - (5.37 \times 25,000)$$
$$= 141,250 - 134,250$$
$$= 7,000$$

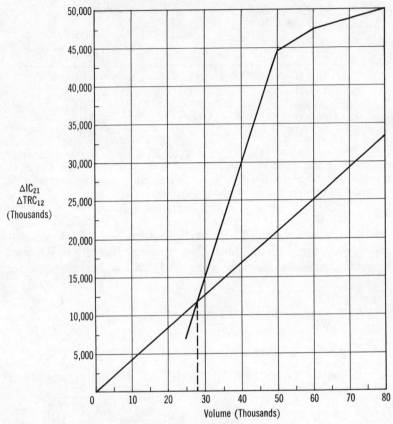

Figure 8-4. ΔIC_{21} and ΔTRC_{21} versus Volume.

These values are plotted against volume in Figure 8-4. As is evident from an inspection of the chart, the intersection point is at 28,000 units. In order to find the values of the other intersecting points, it would be necessary to graph ΔIC_{32} and ΔTRC_{32}, and ΔIC_{43} and ΔTRC_{43}. The methodology would be the same.

FRAMEWORK FOR CHANGE IN THE DISTRIBUTION SYSTEM

An individual firm for the most part does not cause short run change in the life styles of the market in which it operates. Its principal activities, therefore, will be to respond to the desires of the customer in such a way that the firm creates a differential position for itself in relation to other firms. The following four generalizations are advanced as a framework for thinking about change in the distribution system.

1. The utilization of alternative demand creation and distribution systems depends on both the demands of the firm's customers and the comparative cost characteristics of each of the alternative systems.

2. The comparative costs of each system depend on the technological characteristics of that system.

3. The relationship between the alternative systems is more readily visualized if one thinks of the distribution system as including all movement from the shipment of the raw material to its final resting point, consumption at the domicile of the consumer. In such an encompassing viewpoint, the distribution system would encompass not only intercity transportation agencies, but also the terminal points and terminal institutions at the various points.

4. If there is a change in the market's requirements for a given part of the firm's distribution system and the firm wishes to adapt to the market change, it must adapt its technology to the requirements of the new market. A good example of this may be observed within the intercity movement system. If the railroads contemplate attempting to serve the dispersion side of the market, their technology must be adapted to the requirements for dispersion. A railroad would have two options. First, it may attempt to lower its unit cost through a greater utilization of capacity through such practices as longer trains. Second, it may shift to the single-movement-per-power-unit kind of operation, in order to become more competitive with the motor carriers and airlines.[6] These two alternatives might be generalized into the following:

A. If a system contemplates a change from a less than volume operation to a volume operation, the sum of the volume line-haul unit costs plus the storage costs plus terminal costs must be less than the volume line-haul unit costs.

---

[6] Theoretically, of course, it may be more practical to combine these two technologically on a middle ground. For example, it is possible and practicable to design containers that can be interchanged between two or more agencies; this would minimize the transfer of lading, and perhaps enable one agency to shift competitively from one segment of the market to another with a minimum of technological change. In order to simplify the illustration here, only two alternatives are discussed, to differentiate the problems of serving different segments of the market.

B. If the system contemplates a shift from volume to less than volume operation, the less than volume line-haul unit cost must be lower than the sum of the volume line-haul unit cost plus storage costs plus terminal costs.[7]

Similar illustrations could be suggested for other parts of the distribution system, and different combinations may be effected for different segments of the market. The significant point is that the objective of the total system is to aid in differentiating the firm from its competitors, and thus to create differential gain. Understanding of environmental trends and knowledge of alternative technologies can be combined to attain this goal.

Organization of the System

Organization is necessary to put the plans and programs of demand creation and distribution into action. The system of action must be just as dynamic as the consumer it serves, incorporating as many change qualities as possible. In the past many systems have been centrally organized, and this is still effective for a small system serving a small market. Responsible persons under such a situation can maintain a direct relationship with the market and quickly adjust the system as the need arises.

As the market expands in geographic, product, and customer complexity, some provision must be made for decision- and policy-making at lower levels in the organization. This has been accomplished, in some instances, through decentralization of authority, and people in close contact with markets are able to act according to the needs of the local situation. However, a higher quality of personnel is needed at lower levels than under the centralized system. Optimum

---

[7] The comparison of volume and less than volume operations is between multiple- and single-movement-unit-per-power-unit operations. The storage costs refer to the expense of accumulating enough volume per shipment at assembly terminals to meet the volume requirements of the volume carrier; storage must also be provided at destination terminals of volume carriers until the goods can be absorbed into the distribution system by the less than volume carriers. Terminal expense is the cost of providing break-bulk, assembly, or a combination of these operations at any point in the movement system. Such a facility is necessary in a shift from volume to less than volume operations or vice versa.

demand creation and distribution systems would utilize all levels in the company as a team for policy and decision making. They would also include a research staff at top levels in order to provide information needed for action.

The following are some illustrations of the needs that must be provided organizationally within the demand creation system. The growing complexity of the market calls for an increasing amount of specialization in advertising. Consumers cannot be contacted individually, and advertising must increasingly be relied upon to inform the customer about the product. Since advertising is a one-way flow, the organization must include facilities for the return of information from the consumer.

Ways must also be found to improve the organization of advertising to respond to the improved education levels of the consumer. The problem is to utilize existing media to properly inform the customers that the product will satisfy his needs. The same problem exists with regard to the product image; as people change, so must the image change.

Sales forces must also be adapted to changes in the consumer. The organization of the demand creation system must properly provide for the training and administration of the sales force, if one is used. Marketing cost evaluation can be helpful in determining desired changes in the sales and advertising organization.

The distribution of the product must be organized to give optimum benefits to both the customer and the firm. With consumers becoming more time conscious, the system must be organized to give them most convenience. The consumer may not spend much time looking for a specific product; therefore, a product must be readily available or he will find a substitute. The system must provide the product and service when and where the customer wants it. The location and number of outlets must be determined and initiated on the basis of the consumer's location. As he changes and moves, the location program must keep up with him. These factors in combination call for a well-organized and changing distribution organization.

This change represents opportunities for management to create profits for their concerns. It also represents the possibility of loss. The responsibilities of management are to ascertain correctly the environmental changes occurring in the firm's market areas, to translate these into markets for the firm's products, and to combine the knowledge and skills of demand creation and distribution into one system that can create a profit. Obviously, in the more complex market situations the exercise of these responsibilities is through an organization structure of individuals having highly specialized skills. The top management of the firm must be able to lead these persons and meld the sub-systems into a general system that will provide for the survival and growth of the company.

CHAPTER NINE

TERMINAL LOCATION IN THE

MICRODISTRIBUTION SYSTEM

Terminal properties are important integral parts of the distribution system, and are necessary to equalize demand and supply considerations with respect to the size of shipment. Under this definition, retail stores and warehouses are considered to be terminals from a physical point of view, and their locations become important in terms of space preference of the consumers. The logistics objective of terminal location is to strike a balance between profitable store operation and consumer convenience.

The location of terminals at all levels of movement is clearly an important problem in the distribution system, as noted in Chapter 4. The location of dispersion retail and warehouse terminals has particular importance when linked to population expansion and decentralization. Population shifts initiate a whole series of secondary adjustments in the retail structure of the community. Many studies have indicated that the retail structure arranges itself so as to best serve the needs of the community. Probably the outstanding evidence of this has been the rapid growth of the suburban shopping center. Just as significant, though not as obvious, has been the growth of the retail structure along suburban streets and highways.

In taking the micro-approach to the study of distribution systems, it is not uncommon to encounter many cases of vertical integration, in which the entire distribution system is owned by one corporation. In such instances, terminal location would be a problem of real concern to the distribution organization. For the individual firm which is not vertically integrated, be it at the retail or plant levels, the location of such terminals would still be a problem. The manufacturer would have to consider what kinds of retail stores he would prefer to have handling his goods. To the independent retailer and/or warehouse operator, location may well be a matter of business life or death, insofar as attracting customers a given distance is concerned.

The retailer, in adjusting to the pressure towards large scale retailing and the move to the suburbs of great numbers of his customers, is faced with the problem of the type of store to build and where to locate it. These questions are probably more easily resolved for retailers of shopping and specialty goods than for those in convenience goods or services. Retail institutions selling shopping or specialty goods presumably would make fewer decisions, and would be more limited in alternatives, because of the nature of these types of retailing. Retailers of convenience goods, however, are faced with the problem of locating near their market. They usually serve small segments of the market, hence must develop good techniques for defining markets. These techniques assume major importance as the metropolitan area becomes saturated with convenience stores, leaving smaller and smaller segments open to development.

CONSUMER SPACE PREFERENCE

Production and distribution processes transform and transport the product to the point where the final consumer will purchase it. The retail terminal is the site at which the distribution system and the consumer meet. The basic problem is to devise methods which will allow a reasonably accurate estimate of the distance which the consumer will travel to make his purchase, and to select a site for the retail store terminal.

Since the consumer is spatially situated, and is faced with the task of satisfying his economic wants with an imperfect market,[1] he would probably arrange his travel pattern so as to receive the most utility for the time and effort expended. In order to understand the consumer's attitude towards optimization of utility, we must analyze the component elements of consumer movement and space.

[1] This imperfection is twofold; first, the consumer's spatial mobility in terms of time-distance movement rate is not equal in every direction, due to such factors as rivers, limited access freeways, and industrial developments; and, second, the consumer does not possess perfect knowledge of the market place. His knowledge may range from complete certainty about such factors as the available quantity, price, quality, performance characteristics, to complete uncertainty over the range of goods that one would normally purchase.

The basic factors to be considered include a demand base point, unit of travel, differentation of travel purpose, time period of reoccuring travel patterns, and quality of transport service.

For purposes of analysis in connection with the distribution system, the base point of demand is most commonly the residence of the individual. Therefore, the demands for transportation refer principally to the family, either as a unit, or, more commonly, as individuals.[2] If the home is used as a base point, the most logical unit of travel is the round trip.

The distance a person will travel must also be identified in terms of the time actually spent in travel and in terms of recurring travel patterns. The time spent in travel consists of both actual and psychological time (the impact of a given period of actual time on an individual), the most violent reaction occurring in the event of a delay. A five minute delay due to a traffic jam is much more frustrating, and seems considerably longer, to a driver than to a passenger; a similar delay in starting seems longer to someone waiting at a bus stop than it does to someone sitting in the bus. It is probable that the importance of actual time decreases as psychological time increases. Psychological time considerations may go a long way toward explaining the rapidly increasing preference shown in the New York metropolitan area for public transit.

Travel patterns tend to recur in daily, weekly, monthly, and yearly cycles. Most people have had the misfortune of observing the effects of the daily cycle on a first-hand basis in the form of the "rush hour," or daily peak time demand. In the United States the daily peak demand typically occurs from 7:00 to 9:00 in the morning and from 4:00 to 6:00 in the afternoon. The relationship between time demand and travel purpose is most clearly evident in daily demand at the beginning and end of the normal work day. Similar cycles can be established for travel patterns for different kinds of commodities in differing market combinations.

The relative quality of each transport alternative also helps determine how far a person will travel in order to make purchases. The quality of transportation includes the factors of speed, access, frequency, reliability, safety, comfort, convenience and cost. Changes

---

[2] The analysis here does not attempt to go into the ecological reasons for consumers' living in given locations. For a discussion of such factors as they affect decentralization of the population, see Amos H. Hawley, *Human Ecology, A Theory of Human Structure* (New York: Ronald Press Company, 1950).

in these factors will show some changes in the respective demands. The majority of these factors can be lumped into the general classification of comfort. If a passenger feels safe, and is traveling by a reliable, convenient and low cost vehicle, he feels more comfortable. In a sense, the factors are so closely interrelated with each other and with time, both actual and psychological, and purposes of travel, that to attempt to separate them often results in an artificial differentiation that has little or no meaning. However, in spite of the difficulty of establishing cause and effect relationships, retailers must make location decisions.

The source of demand is the difference between what is available at home and what is available away from home.[3] In any given time period, an absolute amount of time is allocated by a person to achieve maximum satisfaction. Some of this time is spent in travel. The traveler necessarily foregoes what is at home during his travel period. But in foregoing home satisfactions, the traveler gains the *total travel product*. This is defined as the result of travel; the *anticipated travel product* is defined as the reason for travel. These two products are frequently, but not necessarily, the same. The total travel product and the anticipated travel product both vary with the time absent from home. The traveler establishes some hierarchy of goals he expects to achieve. He will accomplish his most important goals first, then will attempt to accomplish his lesser goals. For maximum satisfaction, the traveler selects a time order of losses of satisfactions at home just as he selects a time order for travel satisfactions. To obtain the net travel product, the loss of at home satisfactions and the consideration of travel effort, both of which presumably increase with actual travel time, are subtracted from the total travel product. As time elapses, more home satisfactions are lost, and more time is spent in travel, the net travel product is reduced until zero is reached. After zero is reached, the traveler has to be paid to continue traveling. A good example of this payment is the use of premiums and special services in retail stores to attract the customer a longer distance. The retailer is, in a sense, paying the customer to travel.

The single most important factor in any consideration of passenger travel is time. Time is not only money; it is more important than money. The problem facing the decision maker on retail store locations is to establish the amount of time that customers will travel to a given site in order to purchase his commodities.

---

[3] Emery Troxel, *Economics of Transport* (New York: Rinehart, 1955).

Selection of the Retail Site

The objective of the retailer should be to locate where he offers the customer a maximum of utilities in order that, as a minimum, he attains a threshold level of sales. Beyond this level, he must select a site which will strike a balance between profitable store operation and consumer convenience. The individual retailer has an added burden in that he is required to make this decision in a competitive vacuum. At best, he can only guess what competitive action will be taken to counteract his decision, and a competitor, by appropriate location strategy, could disturb his balance. This section will be devoted to a discussion of the trading area surrounding a given retail site and the empirical methods utilized to determine the size of the trading area.

THE CONCEPT OF THE TRADING AREA

The term *trading area* has diverse meanings in different disciplines. The economist often considers it as a "perfect" selling zone, with its boundaries determined by plant location and transport costs. The individuals within the trading area are treated as not being subject to promotional or psychological pressures, and react in the best traditions of the "economic man" in their purchasing. The geographer views the trading area as a complex phenomenon, in which the geographical imperfections of the area determine the direction degree of travel of the inhabitants. A somewhat blurred perspective is presented in the marketing literature because of the common practice of accepting the customer as "spatially given." In marketing literature, the individual space preferences of the consumer are implicitly regarded as being determined by the product. Increasing suburbanization of the consumer and resulting retail decentralization have focused new attention on the usefulness of the trading area concept.[4]

The American Marketing Association defines a trading area as: "A district whose size is usually determined by the boundaries within

[4] For an excellent case study in the development of the trading area concept, see Bernard J. LaLonde, *Differentials in Super Market Drawing Power* (East Lansing, Michigan: Bureau of Business and Economic Research, Michigan State University, 1962). Major portions of this section of the chapter are from Professor LaLonde's study.

which it is economical in terms of volume and cost for a marketing unit or group to sell and deliver a good or service." [5] This definition is not operational, since it sets no objective criteria for evaluating the limits of a trading area. Others have offered as criteria drawing power, per capita sales, time the customer will travel, and population.

All of these criteria have certain weaknesses when applied to all retail units or groups. As stated by Applebaum and Cohen:

"As a broad definition, the authors suggest that the trading area is the area from which a store gets its business within a given span of time. This does not exclude the reality of overlap. It also emphasizes the trading area. People must come to a store from a specific area. If other stores offer equal attractions, then the trading area of a given store will be related to the store's distance and the convenience of access from the origin and destination of the potential." [6]

The individual retailing firm must choose a particular site in connection with its network expansion. Two objective measurements —drawing power and per capita sales—provide a useful framework for trading area analysis to meet these two objectives. Drawing power indicates the geographical nature of market coverage and, hence, is relevant to the problem of optimal network expansion. On the other hand, per capita sales provide a measurement of the quality of any individual site in terms of sales penetration. The two taken together provide a framework for decisions on site location and development planning.

Application of drawing power and per capita sales measurements is by no means a simple matter, and judgment must be employed in using these objective measurements. Distinct location profiles could be developed on the basis of past experience, if relevant variables could be isolated and integrated into the analysis of the proposed site. An example is the influence of population density or income on the drawing power and per capita sales of a store in a given size community. It is entirely possible that if enough observations are made, a reliable statistical relationship can be formulated.

Drawing power is the average distance traveled by a fixed percentage of the actual or potential customers of the store. *Per capita sales* are simply the dollars of sales per person within a

[5] Marketing Definition: *A Glossary of Marketing Terms* (Chicago: American Marketing Association, 1960), p. 22.

[6] William Applebaum and Saul B. Cohen, "The Dynamics of Store Trading Areas and Market Equilibrium," *The Annals of the American Association of Geographers,* Vol. 51, No. 1, March, 1961, pp. 73–101.

designated area. In order to calculate per capita sales in an area, three types of data must be available. First, the segment of the market must be clearly delineated for analysis so that both population totals and sales may come from the same reference point. Second, accurate population data must be available. Third, sales figures must be available for the market. The effects of store complexity and size on drawing power were investigated by Professor LaLonde for a selected sample of food supermarkets. He discovered that store complexity significantly affects drawing power, and that as the level of product offering at the retail site increases, drawing power increases, but not proportionately.[7] Although store size and store complexity are related to some degree, there was no systematic or reliable connection between store size and drawing power.

Store complex significantly influenced the amount of per capita sales, although the amount varied considerably at varying distances from store site for each type. There was no systematic or reliable connection between store size and per capita sales.

A concept of store complex can be useful in several ways in developing sound location policy. A supermarket chain has many types of stores within any metropolitan area. If these types are isolated and analyzed and their drawing power characteristics determined, an optimum network of distribution points can be established and maintained by adding or closing individual distribution points. New stores should be located so that the geographic limits of the market match a given store complex situation. Since consumers are always changing locations and travel habits, the retailer must keep up constant research to maintain an optimal network of distribution points.

DELINEATING RETAIL AREAS IN URBANIZED CENTERS

A site decision may be concerned with whether or not to place a store in an established shopping area or with the feasibility of store location in a commercially undeveloped area. In either type of location decision, a certain amount of inference and judgment will be required. However, the gathering of applicable data for a given site decision can aid considerably in improving retail store location decisions.

---

[7] There is considerable variance in the applicability of this statement to the different categories of stores investigated. The types studied included: urban strip, urban cluster, small town, neighborhood shopping center, and regional shopping center.

For either kind of site decision, two basic approaches may be used to collect data: the empirical approach and the gravitational approach.[8] The principal methods used in the empirical approach are customer interviews, automobile license plate analysis, prize contests, check cashing analysis, credit record analysis, newspaper circulation analysis, and area customer surveys. Each empirical method will be briefly discussed, and the principal advantage and disadvantage of each type pointed out.

Customer interviews may be made either on the site of the retail store or on an area basis. If they are made on a given site, a large amount of information may be obtained, but this is a rather costly method. Quite frequently, when the location decision concerns the establishment of a proposed site rather than an existing location, the customers of a potential trading area are interviewed in their own homes on a sample basis. Customer home surveys are accurate with respect to customer location; it is also costly to conduct this kind of interview, but it may be the only means available to evaluate a proposed site. Sometimes telephone interviews can reduce the cost of these surveys.

Automobile license plate, price contest, check cashing, and credit record analyses are designed primarily to determine the trading area of an existing retail location. Automobile license plate counts are sometimes made at a location, the addresses of the car owners obtained from the state license bureau, and these addresses then plotted on a map to delineate the trading area of the site. Prize contests also help establish the trading area by showing customers' addresses, while at the same time they boost sales. If a store does a considerable amount of its business either by check cashing or on a credit basis, an analysis of either one will tell the locations from which the store draws its business. All of these methods are very useful in establishing trading areas, but they should be used only by a skilled analyst who knows their advantages and limitations.

Gravitational models have also been devised to help define trading areas. In these models, the trading area is conceived as a mass which is structured according to certain principles. These principles are believed to govern, in an over-all fashion, the behavior of the individuals in the mass, acting both as constraining and initiating influences.

---

[8] For a good discussion of the principal empirical approaches, see Bernard J. LaLonde, *op. cit.*, pp. 150–166.

Gravitational models concern the interaction of many variables, much as the interaction of masses is viewed in the physical sciences. In the Stewart-Zipf hypotheses, three primary examples of gravitational models are presented. Stewart defines demographic force as a constant times the product of two masses divided by the square of the distance separating these masses. Where the population of cities I and J, designated Pi and Pj respectively, are taken as the relevant masses, demographic force F is:

$$F = \frac{GPiPj}{d^2ij}$$

where G is a constant corresponding to the gravitational constant. He defines gravitational energy (demographic energy where demographic energy is defined) as:

$$E = \frac{GPiPj}{d_{ij}}$$

Gravitational potential is demographic potential produced at point I by a mass at J, which may be designated iVj and defined as a constant times the mass at J, say Pj, divided by the intervening distance. That is:

$$_iV_j = \frac{GPj}{d_{ij}}$$

Although many problems arise in connection with the use of gravitational models, Isard feels that spatial interaction can best be analyzed through this approach.[9] Some of the more significant problems include the use of factors other than population as an index of mass, the selection of weights to be applied to the various masses, the selection of exponents for variables in both the potential and demographic concepts, and the connections that occur between constraining and initiating forces. Reilly proposes the following list of factors that influence the spatial size of a retail trading area:

1. Lines of transportation
2. Lines of communication

[9] For a general discussion of gravity models in regional analysis, see Walter Isard, *Methods of Regional Analysis* (New York: John Wiley & Sons, Inc., 1960).

3. Class of consumer in the territory surrounding the market
4. Density of population in the territory surrounding the market
5. Proximity of the market to a larger city market
6. Business attractions of the city
7. Social and amusement attractions of the city
8. Nature of the competition offered by smaller cities and towns in the surrounding territory
9. Population of the city
10. Distance which prospective customers must travel in order to reach the market, and the psychology of distance prevailing in that part of the country
11. Topographical and climatic conditions peculiar to the city and its surrounding territory
12. Kind of leadership offered by the owners and managers of various business interests of the city.[10]

In 1929 Reilly formulated a gravitational model in the statement that "under normal conditions two cities draw retail trade from a smaller intermediate city or town in direct proportion to some power of the population of these two large cities and in inverse proportion to some power of the distance of each of the cities from the smaller intermediate city."[11]

Various adaptations of Reilly's original formulation have been presented in the ensuing years. Two illustrations are presented here to show the use of such models and store location. P. D. Converse adapted Reilly's principle to predict the amount of fashion goods business that should be located in any town.[12] The formula was stated as:

$$\frac{Ba}{Bb} = \frac{(Pa)}{(Hb)} \quad \frac{(4)^2}{(d)}$$

where Ba = Proportion of trade going to the outside town
Bb = Proportion of trade retained by the home town
Pa = Population of the outside town
Hb = Population of the home town
d = Distance to the outside town
4 = Inertia factor

[10] William J. Reilly, "Method for the Study of Retail Relationships," *Research Monograph No. 4*, University of Texas Bulletin No. 2944 (Austin: University of Texas Press, 1929), pp. 21–22.
[11] William J. Reilly, *op. cit.*, p. 16.
[12] Paul D. Converse, "A New Application of the Law of Retail Gravitation," *Opinion and Comment*, Vol. XII (August, 1947), and Paul D. Converse, "New Laws of Retail Gravitation," *Journal of Marketing*, Vol. XIV (Oct., 1949), pp. 382–383.

An interesting formulation of the drawing power of shopping centers was made by Harry J. Casey, Jr.,[13] expressed as follows:

$$Bia = \frac{\dfrac{Fa}{(Dia)^2}}{\dfrac{Fa}{(Dia)^2} \dfrac{Fb}{(Dib)^2} \dfrac{Fc}{(Dic)^2} \dfrac{Fd}{(Did)^2} \dfrac{Fe}{(Die)^2} \text{ etc.}} \times B_1$$

where

B_1 = Buying power of neighborhood 1.

Bia = Purchases made by residents of neighborhood 1 in the shopping center A

Fa, Fb, Fc, etc. = The square feet of retail space in the shopping centers A, B, C, etc.

Dia, Dib, Dic, etc. = Driving time distances between neighborhood 1 and other retail centers

A high degree of judgment is called for in using the empirical or gravitational approach in selecting a retail location, and in defining the retail trading area of that site. If information is available on the factors affecting consumer travel, these approaches can be relied on. However, students of distribution must study thoroughly the reasons underlying a consumer's travel behavior. Considerable empirical and theoretical research still needs to be done on retail store location.

WAREHOUSE TERMINAL LOCATIONS

Terminals were defined in Chapter 2 as points in the distribution system at which the shipment size requirements of the market and the shipment size desires of the movement system are adjusted to each other. In that chapter, four types of terminals were described: dead storage, break-bulk, assembly, and break-bulk and reassembly operations.

LOCATIONAL ORIENTATION OF TERMINAL TYPES

Attention is called to Table 3-5, where transportation requirements are related to the various carrier cost curves. This reference puts in

[13] Harry J. Casey, Jr. *op. cit.*, p. 82.

perspective where the various kinds of terminal operations will tend to be placed. Inter-regional moves were largely performed by the carriers possessing declining unit cost curves, and subregional moves largely by the carriers having constant cost curves.[14]

In assembly, less than volume shipments are accumulated into volume quantity in order that power may be applied to the movement process as either multiple-movement-units-per-power-unit or more payload in relation to deadload. The assembly terminal allows a shift from less than volume to volume movement. Thus assembly terminals will tend to be located toward the origin point of shipments, near either the raw material or the producer-oriented locations. Assembly terminals might be located between the processing point and the market if there are multiple plants or sources from which volume shipments may be made. This is more often the case when nondistributional costs favor dead storage at a point midway between the processing point and the market.

A fundamental point in this discussion is the assumption of minimum distribution costs consistent with the requirements of the market place. Service and quick delivery or replacement of inventory are not considered cost elements. It is possible, however, to compute the costs of giving different levels of service and inventory replacement with terminal locations at various points in the distribution system.

Since break-bulk terminals are places to shift from volume to less than volume movements, such terminals will be oriented towards the markets in which they sell, although they may be between the processor and his primary markets. At a break-bulk and reassembly terminal, volume movements of single commodities are shifted to volume movements of mixed commodities. For example, individual carloads of separate commodities may come in from many separate origins and be placed in the terminal for temporary storage; they are then reassembled in smaller quantities, still as individual commodities, but each outbound shipment will constitute a volume move. There are many such warehouses. Break-bulk and reassembly terminals tend to be located toward the market and away from the processing points. The mixing point, of course, will be where the distribution cost of the products will be minimized.

---

[14] As discussed in Chapter 3, plant location was used to determine the nature of goods moving inter-regionally, intra-regionally, and subregionally through an analysis of the factors of weight loss or gain in manufacture, and the type of production cost curve of the processor.

If the customer's size of physical order and the volume requirements of the movement system are approximately the same, a volume shipment can be made direct from the processor to the customer without the necessity of a terminal operation. If the customer's physical requirements are smaller than the physical requirements of the movement system, a break-bulk operation may occur, in order to allow a less than volume shipment direct to the customer. However, if the customer's size of shipment requirements are lower than the less than volume requirements of the movement system, a break-bulk and reassembly terminal will probably have to be placed somewhere in the distribution system. The retail store is a break-bulk and reassembly terminal to which the customer comes to make his purchases.

As shown by Professor LaLonde, the larger the assortment of merchandise, either in an individual store or in a store complex, the farther the customer will travel to make his purchase. In order to fill the physical demands of the retail store where its purchases are below the volume requirements and, in some cases, the less than volume requirements of the movement system, break-bulk and reassembly warehouse points are inserted in the distribution system in order to allow the shift from volume to less than volume and back to volume movement to the retail store.

There is a distinct difference in the extent to which terminal operations are carried on in the industrial and consumer goods market. The amount per sale and the amount per shipment tends to be considerably higher in the industrial market. Therefore, on the dispersion side of distribution, the desires of the market and of the movement system are closer together in the industrial market than in the consumer goods market, and there is more need for the terminal function in the distribution of consumer goods.

MINIMIZING TRANSPORT COSTS IN TERMINAL LOCATION

The two primary jobs in transportation have been described as the concentration of raw materials and the dispersion of finished goods. For this section, it may be well to regroup these two operations into the following: first, assembly, in which the objective of the transport system is to concentrate goods into large volumes as quickly as possible for the purpose of applying capital to the movement process; second, volume shipment, in which the carrier moves volume shipments of raw materials to the processing points and volume ship-

ments of finished goods from the processing point to the initial distribution point; and, third, break-bulk and reassembly, in which the
goods are regrouped at a shipping point for distribution to retailers
and ultimate consumers.

The movement characteristics in the first and third situations
are different from those in the second. In assembly and break-bulk
operations, the shipments are smaller, moving in single-movement-
units-per-power-unit, and the carriers have a higher proportion of
variable costs to total costs. Assembly points are established as soon
as possible in order to accumulate larger volumes per shipment; dispersion points are established as late as possible in order to continue the principle of volume shipments in movement, but the force
of the consumer is soon encountered and the shipments must be
broken up or regrouped into smaller lots.[15]

The job of movement between assembly and dispersion points
is primarily one of volume shipments and volume operations. It is
very likely that more importance will be given to transportation
operating cost factors other than time cost. Time costs to both the
shipper and the carrier become more important as the shipment nears
the consumer, and often determine the choice of modes.[16] It is more
than likely, however, in the volume movements, that time costs will
not offset volume operating costs.

Since the rates on volume and less than volume shipments charged
the various transportation agencies differ, it is desirable for terminals
to locate at sites where movement costs will be minimized.[17] Theoretically, there are at least the following methods for minimizing movement costs, including:

1. Ton-center
2. Mile-center

[15] If the market will not support the volume shipment and is not near
another distribution point, shipment from production point may occur by a
nonvolume medium of transport.

[16] Time costs refer to the costs associated with such items as in-transit
time, order processing time and the resultant imputed interest cost on the level
of inventory required by the total lead time necessary to maintain a given
minimum level of inventory between shipments.

[17] The same methodology outlined in this section can be used for plant
location with respect to raw material and finished goods. The differences
between raw material and finished goods rates usually are found principally in
the volume operation between assembly and break-bulk points. If there were
no difference between the inbound rate on raw materials and the outbound
rate on finished goods, the minimization of transport costs would not be a
major problem in industrial location.

3. Ton-mile-center
4. Cost-ton-mile-center
5. Cost-time-ton-mile-center

Neither of the first two methods gives proper weight to the factors of both tonnage and distance combined. If distances were equal, Method 2 might be used. If the costs per ton mile on the inbound and outbound shipments are equal, Method 3 would suffice. However, costs usually are different on the inbound and outbound moves, and Method 4 would be recommended.[18]

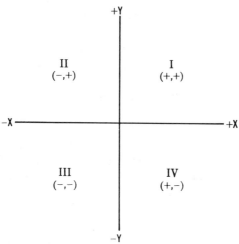

Figure 9-1. *Cartesian Coordinates.*

A Cartesian coordinate system will be utilized to determine the point at which the cost-ton-mile movement between given volume origins and less than volume destinations will be at a minimum. The Cartesian coordinates are traditionally represented by two axes, the vertical Y axis and the horizontal X axis. These are shown in Figure 9-1 to give the student an idea of the use of coordinates for X and Y values. As shown in Figure 9-1, there are both plus and minus

---

[18] If time is an important factor in the market requirements of the user of transportation, the method must include some element of time costs, as indicated in Method 5. Time becomes more important as one moves from volume shipments into the area of less than volume shipments, and many companies pay an increasing amount of attention to the amount of time costs as a part of the difference between raw material, finished goods, less than volume, and volume rates.

values for X and Y on either side of the zero point. Quadrant 1 will have plus values for both X and Y, Quadrants 2 and 4 will have both plus and minus values, and Quadrant 3 will have minus values for both X and Y. Therefore, in order to simplify the computations one may place all values within Quadrant 1 and have all plus values, rather than a combination of plus and minus values.

The basic steps in the use of the coordinates[19] are as follows: first, make sure that all points of origin and destination are included within the area being covered in Quadrant 1; second, assign mileage scales to both the X and Y axes; third, locate the points of origin and destination with respect to the zero value; fourth, indicate for each point the amount of tonnage to be shipped from or to that point; fifth, determine the applicable cost per ton-mile for movement; sixth, compute a weighted average of the cost-ton-mile forces for both the X and Y axes. The intersection of the coordinates erected for these weighted averages will indicate the point of least cost-ton-mile movement. Cost, tons, and miles may each be treated as independent variables and the terminal location (point of least cost-ton-mile movement) thought of as the dependent variable.

To illustrate the above steps, a hypothetical illustration has been set forth in Figure 9-2. The chart represents Quadrant 1 of a coordinate field, so that all values from zero will be plus for both the X and the Y axes. The mileages on both the X and Y axes represent the number of miles of each point from the basic reference point of zero; point A is twenty miles from zero on the X axis, and 580 miles from zero on the Y axis. Points A, B and C are volume shipment sources and points of origin for shipments; points D, E and F are markets to which less than volume shipments are made. To simplify the illustration, it has been assumed that 100 tons will be shipped from each origin point and 100 tons to each of the destination points.

In the illustration, the volume shipment cost is $.03 per ton mile and the less than volume cost is $.06 per ton mile. It is significant in the use of the coordinate method that the "cost" is a figure that is used in building up the rate. The indicated figure is not the rate in and of itself.[20]

[19] The method originally appeared in an article by E. W. Smykay, "Formula to Check for a Plant Site," *Distribution Age*, Vol. LVIII, January, 1959, pp. 32–34.

[20] As indicated in the chapter on comparative costs, the usual technique is for the carrier to determine its cost of performing transportation between two points and then to convert this into a cost per hundredweight. For example, if

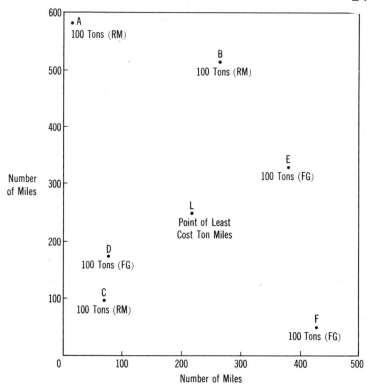

Figure 9-2. *Illustration of Data for Computation of Least Cost-Ton-Miles.*

In computing the weighted average, the object is to determine the coordinates for each of the X and Y axes. Each axis must be figured separately so that there will be a weighted average for the X axis and one for the Y axis. Thus, X equals the weighted average for the X axis and Y equals the weighted average for the Y axis.

the carrier determines that its cost for moving one hundred tons a distance of fifty miles is one hundred fifty dollars, then the cost would be $1.50 per ton, $.075 per hundred pounds, or $.03 per ton mile. The $.075 per hundred-weight figure is the one usually quoted to the shipper by the carrier (if the rates are based on cost). However, the figure that we are interested in here is the cost per ton mile used in constructing the rates.

$$X = \frac{\text{the sum of (cost} \times \text{weight} \times \text{miles)}}{\text{the sum of (cost} \times \text{weight)}}$$

$$= \frac{\text{the sum of cost weight miles}}{\text{the sum of cost weights}}$$

$$= \text{a weighted average in miles on the } X \text{ axis}$$

A similar computation would be made for a weighted average on the Y axis.

In the illustration shown in Figure 9-2, the respective values are substituted in the equation shown below:

$$X = \frac{\begin{array}{l}(.03 \times 100 \times 20) + (.03 \times 100 \times 300) + (.03 \times 100 \times 100) \\ + (.06 \times 100 \times 100) + (.06 \times 100 \times 450) + (.06 \times 100 \times 480)\end{array}}{\begin{array}{l}(.03 \times 100) + (.03 \times 100) + (.03 \times 100) \\ + (.06 \times 100) + (.06 \times 100) + (.06 \times 100)\end{array}}$$

$$X = \frac{60 + 900 + 300 + 600 + 2700 + 2880}{3 + 3 + 3 + 6 + 6 + 6} = \frac{7440}{27} = 275.6$$

$$Y = \frac{\begin{array}{l}(.03 \times 100 \times 580) + (.03 \times 100 \times 540) + (.03 \times 100 \times 100) \\ + (.06 \times 100 \times 200) + (.06 \times 100 \times 330) + (.06 \times 100 \times 20)\end{array}}{\begin{array}{l}(.03 \times 100) + (.03 \times 100) + (.03 \times 100) \\ + (.06 \times 100) + (.06 \times 100) + (.06 \times 100)\end{array}}$$

$$Y = \frac{1740 + 1620 + 300 + 1200 + 1980 + 120}{3 + 3 + 3 + 6 + 6 + 6} = \frac{6960}{27} = 257.8$$

For example, in computing the cost-ton-miles for A with respect to the X axis, the cost is $.03 per ton mile, the weight is 100 tons, the distance is 20 miles, and the product of these is shown as 60 (cost-ton-miles) in the computation. The computation for point B with respect to the X axis is .03 × 100 × 300, with a net product of 900 (cost-ton-miles) for the axis. This same procedure is utilized for points C, D, E and F in the numerator. The calculations in the denominator are simply the cost per ton mile times the tonnage shipped from or to the respective point. The weighted average for the X axis is 275.6 miles.

The computations for the Y axis are similar to those for the X axis. For example, in computing the cost-ton-miles for point A the figure would be the $.03 per ton mile times 100 times 580 miles for a product of 1740 (cost-ton-miles). The same computation is made for points B, C, D, E and F, and the sum of these products is then divided by the sum of the total cost tons in the denominator. The weighted average for the Y axis is 257.8 miles.

It was pointed out earlier that the independent variables are cost, tonnage, and mileage from the origin points and to the destination points. The dependent variable is the point of least cost-ton-miles. The point of least cost-ton-miles will be the intersection of the two coordinates erected from the X and Y axis, 275.6 and 257.8 miles respectively, resulting in point L on the chart. Point L is the location where movement costs will be minimized with respect to the cost per ton mile, the tonnages moved, and the mileages involved.[21]

Another possible approach to the location of the point of minimum cost movement is the use of linear programming. Transportation literature in recent years has often treated the terms linear programming, location, and distribution as almost synonymous. As stated by Donald Bowersox:

> When one speaks of a location problem, it is often assumed that linear programming offers the most efficient method of determining an optimum location solution. However, it is interesting to note, in current textbooks, the general lack of models to attack the market area location problem. Rather, given a series of locations, one finds models for optimizing equipment utilization or minimizing other objective functions. For example, the transportation model provides a comparatively simple method for determining which warehouse should supply which customer during the shipping period. Disregarding the multiple warehouse aspect, one prerequisite for programming this problem is the predetermined location of each warehouse point— precisely the dependent variable. . . .
>
> It is possible to determine the market area solution utilizing a modified version of the transportation or distribution model. This requires an assumption of an array of warehouse locations and isolation of the least cost location among that array. However, a possibility of error is involved in the selection of an array of alternative locations. The true least cost location could fall well outside the essential range of alternative locations. The analytic geometry method of Cartesian coordinates does not involve the same difficulty since the procedure for determining the location solution initially includes all potential alternatives.[22]

---

[21] As pointed out earlier, however, it may be desirable in the location of distribution points to consider the concepts of time because of the higher unit value of the goods involved and the higher cost of making deliveries to urban areas, where distribution points are usually located.

[22] Donald J. Bowersox, *Food Distribution Center Location: Technique and Procedure* (East Lansing, Michigan: Bureau of Business and Economic Research, Michigan State University, 1962), pp. 12–13. Major portions of this section of the chapter are from this study.

Some caution must be used in connection with the cost figures used in the coordinate method of solution. The point of least movement cost will be dependent on the relationship between inbound-outbound cost per ton miles, inbound-outbound tonnages, continuance or discontinuance of given sources of inventory or raw materials, and any changes which may take place in sales in the given markets. These input-output relationships can change either rapidly or slowly. It is part of management's responsibility for planning and control to ascertain present relationships and to prognosticate as accurately as possible the changes that may occur in the future.

As indicated in Chapter 1, the level of society's scale of living is a result of the interaction of the forces of human desires, human knowledge and skills, and the utilization of available natural resources. In much the same manner, the prosperity of the individual corporation rests upon its skills in transforming natural resources into products and services that will meet the wants and needs of the consumers. In a competitive society the individual company, region, and nation are bound to be in competition with one another, and all should strive to be able to adjust to change, as well as being capable of innovating change.

The distribution structure must be capable of reacting to change and, through innovations, causing change in the other areas of the economic system. Analysis of total costs and the coordinate method for minimizing transport costs are two methods which the individual company can utilize to minimize movement costs. Through these methods, management will have better information with which to exercise planning and control.

Appendix to Chapter Nine

A General Model for Computing

Elasticity of Demand for Service[23]

There are certain measurable characteristics of a market area which influence the success of any marketing effort. A combination of different marketing tools should be used in measuring, and the calculation of the optimum presumes that it can be measured.

The problem to be analyzed here is the best location of a warehouse.[24] The alternative locations are presumed to have measurable revenue producing characteristics as well as unique costs. This approach is to analyze factors which cause cost and revenue differences in alternative locations and thus discover the best marketing tools to be used in serving a given area, in this instance location of the warehouse.

THE MARKETING APPROACH

Classical economic theory, while presenting many important analytical tools, in some instances assumes away the very factors which must be considered by the marketer. While the classicist speaks of price, a more meaningful concept for marketers is the total of costs incurred by the customer in acquiring and using a product. The classical economist assumes costless, immediate transactions and distribution of

[23] This appendix was written with Mr. Mark Doty, Mr. Ward Fredericks, and Mr. Howard Tracy.

[24] The analysis developed here may be used whenever a firm faces the location problem with any of its terminal facilities, although it may require some modifications to consider all the factors causing cost and revenue differences.

products, yet the marketer must consider variations in cost and time, since they determine the profitability of a market area.

In many cases the customer must purchase amounts of goods in excess of his immediate needs. This is a rational decision for a number of reasons, such as an attempt to minimize clerical and ordering cost per unit of purchase. Since this decision necessitates the customer's holding inventories of one type or another, an addition must be made to traditional economic theory to account for this. The concept of elasticity of demand for service is an attempt to use the marketing approach to this problem.[25]

ELASTICITY OF DEMAND FOR SERVICE

A quasi-economic concept, *elasticity of demand for service,* is an important consideration when locating distribution facilities. In this analysis an improvement in service, measured as a diminution of time necessary for delivery, would cause a measurable increase in revenue from a group of customers.

As delivery time necessary to serve a demand center increases, the revenue produced by that area decreases, since the differential advantage of one supplier over another becomes smaller. Should one supplier, through an excellent location decision, achieve very short delivery times, his revenues would increase according to the relative service elasticity of the demand center.

The operation of this in the individual customer's thinking is roughly as follows: The customer must incur certain costs in buying and holding inventories. A reduction in delivery time needed to replenish stocks from a supplier will decrease his required inventory level. The reduction in inventory decreases the total cost to the customer of purchasing from one individual supplier. Therefore, the individual customer will have a rational reason for dealing with the supplier offering more rapid delivery. In the total market, the revenue-producing effect on all customers may be measured by a diagram such as Figure 9-3.

In the figure, DT is the total industry demand for the product. Of this total, the firm originally sells Q_o from demand curve D_i. By

---

[25] The term *service elasticity* is used frequently throughout this appendix as synonymous with elasticity of demand for service.

offering faster delivery, the effective price (cost) to customers is reduced to P_n and market penetration of the firm is increased to Q_n. In this way, the manipulation of delivery times causes revenue differences for the firm.

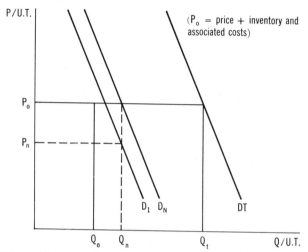

Figure 9-3. *Effect of Service on Demand.*

Given a measure of service elasticity in any market area, revenue differences can then be measured by establishing different delivery times. Since delivery times are made up of two major variables, distance from customer to warehouse and speed of the delivery conveyance, these factors must be included in the model. The fact that distance is an additional factor causing cost differences provides an interesting problem in constructing the model, as will be seen below.

TERMS USED IN CONSTRUCTING THE MODEL

Utilizing the service elasticity concept expressed earlier, a model of the market area was constructed. The following terms are used in the model: *demand center, distance, freight rate,* and *velocity.*

DEMAND CENTER. For purposes of this model, demand center is defined as the geographic center of a number of customers in close proximity to each other. The assumptions inherent in this formulation are: (1) the distance from the demand center to any customer is so small, in relation to the distance from the warehouse to the demand center, that it is considered negligible; (2) full truckloads shipped from the warehouse could well serve more than one customer within this geographic area and the time to travel from one customer to another is quite small compared to the road time from warehouse to demand center.

DISTANCE.   The distance is defined as the miles traveled from the proposed warehouse to the prospective, aggregate customer demand center. The symbol used for this in the model is small r, which is determined as a function of x and y Cartesian coordinates.

FREIGHT RATE.   The freight rate is the cost per ton that is associated with increasing distances or radii from the proposed warehouse site. Therefore, the freight rate will reflect the fact that customers more distant from the proposed warehouse will have an increased freight cost per unit.

VELOCITY.   The velocity, as defined in the model, is the average rate of speed in miles per minute that a delivery truck will travel from the warehouse site to the aggregate customer demand center. This velocity will take into account the interference of traffic and the accessibility of the aggregate demand center from the proposed warehouse site.

CONSTRUCTION OF THE MODEL

In order to illustrate the application of the preceding principle and to attempt to isolate and evaluate the variables causing cost and revenue differences, it will be helpful to construct an economic model.

ASSUMPTIONS

For added realism, this model will assume an undifferentiated oligopoly in which price competition would be highly disadvantageous. In this model, transportation and inventory size contribute appreciably to the customer's total cost. In order to avoid production stoppages, the customer must maintain a high level of inventory with attendant costs or must pay premium transportation on material to eliminate inventory shortages. It is assumed that product price is relatively low at the total market demand quantity, and price elasticity of demand is quite inelastic. The demand function for a demand center under these assumptions is shown by curve DT in Figure 9-3, with Q_t being the total quantity demanded and P_0 being the market price.

CRITERIA FOR SOLUTION

The optimal solution for this model will locate a warehouse in the market area in a position to afford maximum penetration of the market. Marketing research has determined that if a warehouse were located in a location where delivery time is no greater than currently being offered, a firm could expect to sell quantity q_o (Figure 9-3) at price P_o. Market research has also shown that delivery time is the most important single factor in serving customers in this market. By asking customers what influence slower delivery time would have on the quantity ordered, a function of the form below was developed, equating quantity to the negative delivery times.

(1) $$q = q_o{}^{-\alpha t/t_o}$$

where q = quantity ordered with delivery time t
      q_o = quantity ordered with delivery time t_o
      t_o = competitors' delivery times
      t = delivery time of new firm
      α = proportionality factor for specific demand area

SERVICE ELASTICITY OF DEMAND

The previous definition of service elasticity of demand arises from equation (1) as follows:

(2) $$\frac{dq}{dt} = -\frac{\alpha}{t_o} q_o{}^{-\alpha t/t_o} \log q_o$$

(3) $$\frac{dq}{dt} = -\frac{\alpha}{t_o} q \log q_o$$

(4) $$-\frac{t}{q}\frac{dq}{dt} = \alpha \frac{t}{t_o} \log q_o$$

Comparing the left side of (4) with the classical definition of price elasticity of demand

$$E = \frac{-P}{q} \frac{dq}{dP}$$

it is seen that service elasticity of demand

(5) $$E_s = \alpha \frac{t}{t_o} \log q_o$$

THE ANALYTICAL MODEL

As a condition for constructing the model, we will assume that factory costs are identical for all competitors in the market. Further, the selling price is composed of factory costs, margin, warehouse operating costs, and freight charges. Freight is assumed to be a linear function of distance to each demand center, and is not necessarily the same to each demand center. Under these further assumptions:

Cost to any one demand center from the warehouse (see Figure 9-4).

(6) $$C = qrf$$

where q = quantity shipped in tons
r = distance from warehouse to demand center in miles
f = freight in dollars per ton per mile

From Figure 9-4 with (X, Y) as warehouse coordinates and (x_i, y_i) coordinates of the i_{tn} demand center,

(7) $$r_i = [(X - x_i)^2 + (Y - y_i)^2]^{1/2}$$

Substituting (1) in (6)

(8) $$C_i = q_{oi}{}^{-\alpha_i t_i / t_{oi}} r_i f_i$$

is the cost of servicing the demand center from the warehouse.

In order to service the market, the warehouse must be supplied from a plant. The freight costs attendant to this inventory are given by

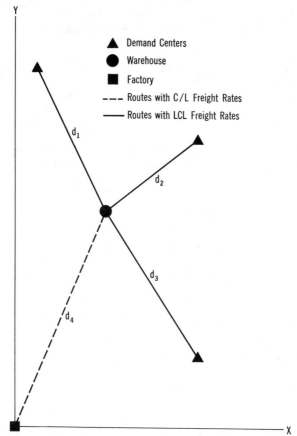

Figure 9-4. *Sales Territory Model.*

(9)
$$C_w = r'f' \sum_{i=1}^{i=n} q_i$$

where r' = distance from warehouse to plant
$\quad\quad f'$ = freight rate in dollars per ton per mile
$\quad\quad q_i$ = total quantity shipped to the ith demand centers

Summing up all costs to all demand centers, the total costs of serving the market will be given by

(10)
$$TC = \sum_{i=1}^{i=n} q_{oi}{}^{-\alpha_i t_i / t_{oi}} (r_i f_i + r'f')$$

For minimum total cost, the first partial derivatives of this function with respect to X and Y are set equal to zero, and the resulting system of simultaneous equations solved for X and Y. This will give the optimum location of the distribution warehouse.

$$(11) \quad \frac{dTC}{dx} = \sum_{i=1}^{i=n} q_{oi}^{-\alpha_i t_i/t_{oi}} \left[\frac{-\alpha_i}{t_{oi}} \frac{dt}{dx} + f_i \frac{dr_i}{dx} + f' \frac{dr'}{dx} \right] \log q_{oi} = 0$$

$$(12) \quad \frac{dTC}{dy} = \sum_{i=1}^{i=n} q_{oi}^{-\alpha_i t_i/t_{oi}} \left[\frac{-\alpha_i}{t_{oi}} \frac{dt}{dy} + f_i \frac{dr_i}{dy} + f' \frac{dr'}{dy} \right] \log q_{oi} = 0$$

Now t, the firm's delivery time, will be a function of distance r_i and the average velocity of the delivery vehicle V_i or:

$$(13) \quad t = \frac{r}{v}$$

$$(14) \quad \frac{dt_i}{dx} = \frac{1}{v_i} \frac{dr_i}{dx} = -\frac{(X - x_i)}{r_i v_i}$$

$$(15) \quad \frac{dt_i}{dy} = \frac{1}{v_i} \frac{dr_i}{dy} = -\frac{(Y - y_i)}{r_i v_i}$$

Substituting (14) and (15) in (11) and (12) gives

$$(16) \quad \frac{dTC}{dx} = \sum_{i=1}^{i=n} q_{oi}^{-\alpha_i t_i/t_{oi}} \left[\frac{\alpha_i (X - x_i)}{t_{oi} \; r_i v_i} - f_i \frac{(X - x_i)}{r_i} - \frac{f' X}{r'} \right] \log q_o = 0$$

$$(17) \quad \frac{dTC}{dy} = \sum_{i=1}^{i=n} q_{oi}^{-\alpha_i t_i/t_{oi}} \left[\frac{\alpha_i (Y - y_i)}{t_{oi} \; r_i v_i} - f_i \frac{(Y - y_i)}{r_i} - \frac{f' Y}{r'} \right] \log q_o = 0$$

Once these equations are solved for X and Y, the optimum location of the warehouse, the appropriate distances are computed and substituted in (10). We have them

$$(18) \quad TC = \sum_{i=1}^{i=n} q_{oi}^{-\epsilon_i/\log q_{oi}} \left[r_i f_i + r' f' \right]$$

or

$$(19) \quad TC = \sum_{i=1}^{i=n} q_{oi}^{-\alpha_i t_i/t_{oi}} \left[r_i f_i + r' f' \right]$$

or

$$(20) \quad TC = \sum_{i=1}^{i=n} q_{oi}^{-\alpha_i r_i/v_i t_{oi}} \left[r_i f_i + r' f' \right]$$

(18), (19) and (20) equate total costs to various causal factors and are all equivalent.

Service elasticity of demand has been defined in terms of delivery time by (5). It is entirely conceivable that other factors could affect this elasticity. At any one demand center, from (18)

$$(21) \qquad C = q_{oi}^{(-\epsilon_i/\log q_{oi})} [r_i f_i + r'f']$$

If we numerically classify this center as the first, we have

$$(22) \quad \frac{dTC}{d\epsilon_i}$$

$$= \log q_{oi} - \frac{\epsilon_1}{\log q_{oi}} q_{oi}^{(\epsilon_1/\log q_{oi})} [r_1 f_1 + r'f'] \sum_{i=2}^{n} q_{oi}^{(\epsilon_i/\log q_{oi})} [r_i f_i + r'f']$$

and this will give us an approximate measure of the influence on total cost of the elasticity of service.

There may be competitive retaliation in the form of improved delivery time by competitors. Under these conditions, the approximate change in revenues for our warehouse would be

$$(23) \qquad \Delta TR = \sum_{i=1}^{i=n} \frac{\alpha_i t_i}{t_{oi}^2} q_{oi}^{(-\alpha_i t_i/t_{oi})} [r_i f_i + r'f'] P_i$$

where P_i is the market price at the particular demand center under consideration.

If a decision involving changing delivery equipment is involved, where the choice is between a larger, slower vehicle and a smaller, faster vehicle, guidelines for decision may be formulated as follows:

Let V_m be the average velocity of larger vehicle and U_n be the average velocity of the smaller vehicle.

$$(24) \quad \text{then } \Delta TC = -\sum_{i=1}^{i=n} \frac{\alpha_i r_i}{v_i^2 t_{oi}} q_{oi}^{(\alpha_i r_i/v_i t_{oi})} \log q_{oi} [r_i f_i - r'f'](V_m - V_n)$$

(d) If, for some reason, a demand center should shift location, the influence of this shift on total costs may be given by

$$(25) \quad \Delta TC = -\left[\frac{\alpha_k}{v_k t_{ok}} q_{ok}^{(-\alpha_k r_k/v_k t_{ok})} (r_k f_k + r'f') - q_{ok}^{(-\alpha_k r_k/v_k t_{ok})} f_k \right] \Delta r_k$$

$$(26) \quad \Delta TC = q_{ok} \frac{-\alpha_k r_k}{v_k t_{ok}} \left[f_k - \frac{\alpha_k}{v_k t_{ok}} (r_k f_k + r'f') \right] \Delta r_k$$

DISCUSSION

In the model, the cost was outlined very specifically. For instance, in the model there are three factors which cause cost differences. Referring to equations (18), (19), and (20) showing the total cost function, it can be seen that distance (r), freight rate (f'), and velocity (v) are the factors. If there are various unique values for each aggregate customer demand center for these variables, then each absolute value of the amount of r, f', and v are gradations of three factors which cause a cost difference in serving any particular demand center. For each aggregate demand center, there are these physical differences in location and accessibility that cause different costs in different demand centers.

The importance of one factor over another can be determined by differentiating between the appropriate variables. We can examine the rate of change of one with respect to the total cost, then compare it with another factor, using the same method. This would also show how large the gradation or the steps in the level of gradations of the three factors causing cost differences would have to be in order to give significant differences.

So far cost is the only part of the marketing decision that has been examined. In any kind of business decision, some concept of a break-even analysis is used. A typical break-even analysis may be represented as in Figure 9-5:

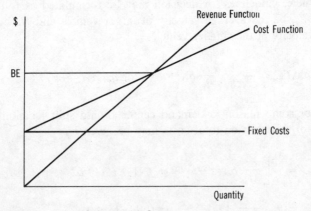

Figure 9-5. *A Break-Even Analysis.*

This graph shows cost and revenue as separate functions. In the preceding discussion, distance, freight rate, and velocity influenced the shape and the magnitude of cost. This is, of course, influenced by two factors: one, the initial penetration q_o; and, two, the service elasticity which displaces the demand curve to the right. One of the factors which causes a revenue difference in the model is *service elasticity*. This is the increase in quantity of goods demanded because of lessened service time to the customer. This effectively reduces the cost of the customer's inventory and other associated costs.

Another factor in the model which causes a revenue difference is the effect of competitive retaliation in the form of decreased delivery time. The effect of this can be accounted for by differentiating equation (23) with respect to time (t_o) to find the effect of a change in competitive delivery time.

The entire purpose of this model is to compare the revenue side with the cost in order to judge the profit potential of any new location. In the model, the revenue producing factors have to be contracted with the cost factors in total to make this kind of deduction. The total cost expression is given by equations (18), (19) and (20), but probably equation (20) is the easiest to use, so this will represent the cost function for considering the costs associated with distribution from the production site. The revenue function to be contrasted with this is composed of the total quantity of goods distributed. This is made up of the factors of q_o, the initial penetration into the market plus q_e, and the quantity increase due to more efficient distribution. The summation of these two factors times the price will yield the total revenue.

The total revenue less the total cost can then be used to determine the feasibility of the move. Of course, an arbitrary margin factor that reflects return on investment should be used as a yardstick to measure a positive difference between the revenue and cost functions.

One other very interesting use of the model is a decision as to what type of delivery fleet to use—whether to use a few large slow-moving vehicles or many small fast-moving vehicles. This can be accomplished by examining the change in total cost function with respect to a change in the average velocity of the delivery truck. (See equation (24)).

Another point is that the total cost function can be examined with respect to small changes in (r', r) the location of the warehouse from the demand centers and the warehouse from the production plant. This may be quite important because the optimum solution of equations (16) and (17) may not coincide with a real warehouse site. It may be necessary to shift the location slightly to fit the real situation—that is, to fit the availability of either a building site or warehouse space. This is illustrated by equations (25) and (26).

Conclusion

This model is widely applicable because of the very generalized nature of the assumptions about aggregate customer demand centers. These demand centers could be used in the aggregate sense, as in this model, or as single customers. The model could also be used in other applications outside of this immediate context.

The model is a method to quantify an operating decision through the use of mathematics and the computer. It should again be pointed out that this model would be very laborious to solve without the use of a computer because of the complex solution of equations (16) and (17). Also, as the number of aggregate customer demand centers increases the solution becomes virtually impossible by manual methods.

One last point is that any model must be viewed in the light of the real world once the solution has been developed. Therefore, in the final analysis the marketing manager must interpret the results and apply them using his own judgment.

CHAPTER TEN

DISTRIBUTION COST

AND REVENUE ANALYSIS

The interrelationship of the distribution system with the other parts of the economic system was analyzed in Part One of the book, and the distribution problems of the individual firm were presented in Chapters 8 and 9. This chapter presents a method of cost and revenue analysis which combines the demand creation and the distribution systems in such a way that the individual firm may more readily realize its objective of differential gain.

COMPETITIVE SYSTEMS COST AND REVENUE ANALYSIS

Systems costs discussed in this chapter are those concerned with demand creation and distribution.[1] Specifically, such systems costs include all those expenses of the enterprise having to do with all distribution movements, market delineation, purchase motivation, adjustment of the product to meet customer demands, communication of the seller's message to the customer, transaction, and the post-transaction period.

The purpose of cost accounting in the area of demand creation

---

[1] In the total competitive strategy of the firm, the transformation system costs would also have to be considered and interrelated with demand creation and distribution costs. Such costs are usually determined through production cost accounting techniques which have been well established for many years. Weight loss or gain in processing and the type of production costs curve were considered in Chapter 5, with respect to their effects on plant location and levels of flow in the distribution system.

257

and distribution has generally been to obtain cost information about particular parts of these activities in a company. For example, efforts are often made to determine the most profitable sizes of orders, the best allocations of sales territories, or the cost of a particular part of a sales operation such as delivery, order processing, or receiving routine. However, there is a need for the development of new competitive systems cost and revenue techniques which will furnish managements with reasonably accurate estimates of the costs of selling and distributing products and of the revenues obtainable from a given amount of such effort.

The normal techniques employed in cost accounting are as follows: first, definition of the purpose for which the cost study is to be made; second, selection of the applicable cost centers of the business enterprise and realignment of the natural accounts into these cost centers; third, allocation of accounts within the cost centers to achieve the objectives of the cost study; fourth, combining the allocations within the cost centers. The real difficulty is in the third step.

Traditional cost accounting for the sales and distributive systems follows the procedure of selecting a basis for allocation, which may result in an arbitrary allocation of cost to a particular product, but does not accurately reflect the differences in such costs between products or customers. Therefore, in the third step, when the resultant allocations of cost are made and combined in the fourth step, the result summation can only be as accurate as the basis of allocation selected in the third step. In order to determine with reasonable accuracy the differences in the costs of selling and distributing different kinds of products, perhaps another approach is necessary. The approach suggested in this chapter is the same in the traditional first and second steps, but differs in the third step.

We propose that the functional costs be allocated on the basis of the factors which cause cost differences in the demand creation and distribution systems for a given commodity, that gradations be established within each of these factors, and that the relationships between these factors be established. Summation of these costs should be the same in the fourth step as under traditional cost accounting methods.

Categories of Cost and Cost Allocation

One of the most difficult problems encountered by the cost analyst is the allocation of common and/or fixed costs to particular operations within the demand creation and distributive systems of the company.[2] In spite of the difficulties encountered, managements must attempt to determine these costs in order to carry out planning and control. There are four or more standard methods for the determination of fixed and variable costs; first, to approximate the proportions of fixed and variable costs at any two or more levels of production and to extrapolate costs beyond these points; second, to allocate costs arbitrarily, either by individual account or by aggregates; third, to determine by a study of individual accounts the extent of variation above and below a determined norm for that particular activity over a period of time; and fourth, to build up costs semi-independently of the individual accounts. The fourth method is recommended and analyzed in this chapter.

It is proposed that the natural accounts be allocated to the functional cost centers, as is the practice in traditional industrial or production cost accounting. The factors which cause cost differences in the demand creation and distribution of a particular commodity should then be determined, and gradations established within each one. The expenses within each of the functional cost centers would then be apportioned to each of the factors causing cost differences. The summation of these costs would be the same as in traditional cost accounting methods. If this can be accomplished, the commodity cost can be determined and fitted into the analytical structure of cost and revenue analysis.

The advantages of this method over the alternatives are the following: first, it provides a basis for allocation of cost to those factors which determine costs, thereby making possible the determination of the cost of demand creation and distribution for particular commodities under varying market conditions; second, it avoids much of the difficulty of assigning common or joint costs that would be present within alternative methods; and, third, if the allocation of costs from the functional cost centers to the factors causing cost differences is done accurately, it should cut down considerably on the proportion of common and fixed costs that will remain as an unassigned burden or overhead. The following examples illustrate this new approach to demand creation and distribution cost analysis.[3]

[2] An extensive discussion of each of the categories of costs was presented in the Appendix to Chapter 2.

[3] Major portions of this chapter appeared earlier in a monograph by Frank Mossman, *Differential Distribution Cost and Revenue Analysis: A New Approach* (East Lansing, Michigan: Bureau of Business and Economic Research, Michigan State University, 1962), pp. 8–30.

In the Kearney study of intra-state motor carriers in Michigan, presented in the Appendix to Chapter 2, functional cost centers were established for the following: dock handling, pickup-and-delivery, terminal clerical, overhead costs, transfer or break-bulk costs, interline costs, claims costs, and line-haul costs. All of the above categories, with the exception of line-haul costs, could be summarized as terminal costs of the motor carrier operation. Nine factors causing cost differences are given in that Appendix. When the functional cost centers were allocated to the factors causing differences in the costs of furnishing the transportation service, the summarized cost presented transport costs in terms of the different circumstances under which commodities move.

A brief illustration is presented in Table 10-1. In this table, the various functional cost centers which reflect terminal costs are sum-

TABLE 10-1.   *Illustration of Cost Factors for Motor Carrier Terminals (Dollars per 100 lbs.)*

		NUMBER OF PIECES IN SHIPMENT		
	601–700 lbs.	1	5	10
	0–4.9	.918	.941	.971
Density	5–9.9	.634	.658	.687
	10–19.9	.512	.535	.564
	701–800 lbs.			
	0–4.9	.857	.877	.897
Density	5–9.9	.558	.578	.598
	10–19.9	.494	.514	.534

Source: *Intrastate Motor Carrier Cost Study*, Truck Advisory Board, Michigan Public Service Commission, 1961, Exhibit 26. This study was prepared by the A. T. Kearney Company.

marized and presented according to the following factors causing cost differences: density of the product, weight of the product, weight of the shipment, and number of pieces in the shipment. For example, a shipment in the 600 to 700 pound category with a density of zero to 4.9 pounds per cubic foot would cost $.918 if there were one piece in the shipment, $.941 with five pieces in the shipment, and $.971 if there were ten pieces in the shipment.

The effect of density is also shown within the same weight category. For example, if the shipment consisted of only one piece in the shipment, the cost would be $.918 for a weight density of zero to 4.9 pounds per cubic foot, $.634 for 5 to 9.9 pounds per cubic foot, and $.512 for 10 to 19.9 pounds per cubic foot. The complete cost study allows the summation of costs according to the factors that cause cost differences in transportation. It is cited here simply to illustrate that there are instances in which natural accounts have been regrouped into functional cost centers and then reassigned to the factors which cause cost differences. The purpose of this chapter is to show that this can also be done in the fields of demand creation and distribution.

FUNCTIONAL COST CENTERS

Grouping natural accounts into the functional cost centers of the business enterprise aggregates expenses into those activities which are the principal efforts of the company. Since the object is to determine the expenses of demand creation and distribution, it would appear best to group the natural accounts into the functional cost centers which are the principal functional activities. These are:

1. Market delineation
2. Communications
3. Purchase motivation
4. Product adjustment
5. Physical distribution
6. Transactions
7. Post-transactions[4]

Market delineation is defined as the determination of potential purchasers and their identifying characteristics. Closely tied to this is the study of *purchase motivation,* which is the assessment of those direct and indirect factors which underlie, infringe upon, and influence purchasing behavior. These two activities constitute the framework within which the marketing effort of the firm must take place.

Communications consists of the transmitting of information and messages between buyer and seller so that the most favorable action

[4] Thomas A. Staudt, "The Managerial Functions of Marketing," in a book edited by Eugene J. Kelley and William Lazer, *Managerial Marketing: Perspectives and Viewpoints* (Homewood, Ill.: Richard D. Irwin, Inc., 1962), pp. 385–392.

climate for the seller is created in the market place. Finding the optimum combination of communication methods is a major responsibility of the marketer and typically consists of combinations of personal selling, advertising, publicity, and sales promotion.

Product adjustment includes those activities which are engaged in to match the product with the market in which it is to be sold, purchased, and consumed. Effective product adjustment depends in large part on how well the marketer has determined his market and ascertained the purchase motivations of the customers.

Physical distribution concerns the actual movement of goods from points of production to points of consumption. The prime concern in physical distribution is to transmit an optimum amount of goods for quick arrival to the consumer at a minimum of cost compatible with customer requirements. Such costs include the expense of intercity transportation, break-bulk and reassembly, and interest cost on inventory while the goods are in the pipeline from producer to the consumer.

Transaction includes those activities that must be performed between the time a meeting of minds occurs among the parties concerned and the actual transfer of ownership. *Post-transaction* consists of the activities which assure satisfaction with the product in use and the follow-through activities which provide feedback information for more effective continuing competition.

The primary items of expense in demand creation and distribution are communications, physical distribution, and transaction. Although market delineation, purchase motivation, product adjustment, and post-transaction are vital to the efficient performance of the firm, these do not compose a major part of expense in terms of dollars. Product adjustment may involve considerable expenditures, but these are chargeable mainly to the production division, not to sales or distribution. Post-transaction may likewise constitute a major item of expense, but it will depend to a great extent on the degree to which the concern furnishes warranties or provides service facilities.

A complete allocation of the natural accounts to the functional cost centers should include the complete list of these centers indicated in the previous paragraphs. However, in order to simplify the presentation, the list has been narrowed to the major items of expense: communications, physical distribution, and transactions. Post-transaction is included in transaction.

Communications has been broken down into advertising and personal selling. Physical distribution is divided into transportation, break-bulk and reassembly, and inventory level. Since most businesses have some element of overhead expense or burden that does not vary with the volume of business, an additional category of non-allocable overhead has been added. The functional cost centers thus will consist of the following:

1. Advertising
2. Personal selling
3. Transportation
4. Break-bulk and reassembly
5. Inventory level
6. Transaction
7. Non-allocable overhead

FACTORS CAUSING COST DIFFERENCES: GRADATIONS IN THESE FACTORS

The next step in the analysis of demand creation and distribution cost is to find the factors that cause cost differences for each of the cost centers. The objective of determining these factors is ultimately to spread the cost within the cost centers to each of them. The principal factors causing cost differences are: product knowledge, market density, average size of order, time element, servicing, distance, and volume. Since these factors are by no means all-inclusive, and since other factors may have a greater bearing upon the cost of selling and distributing a particular product, it may be desirable to change the above list. The number of factors selected, however, should be held to a minimum to avoid apportioning insignificant amounts of cost. A brief definition of each of the factors includes:

> *Product knowledge*—the knowledge of the product possessed by the customer within a given market.
> *Market density*—the number of customers within a given market area.
> *Average size of order*—the number of pieces in an order or a classification on the basis of dollar size of the order.
> *Time element*—the fashion or perishability inherent in a given product.
> *Servicing*—the number of services calls made prior or subsequent to the sale of the product.
> *Distance*—the number of miles the goods are to be shipped.
> *Volume*—the physical amount of dollar sales made during a given time period.

The objective of apportioning costs from the functional cost centers to the factors causing cost differences is to be able to combine the selling and distributing costs under varying conditions. The simplest concept of cost would be to utilize the average cost within each of the factors. For example, it might be possible to determine the cost of selling in a market of a given density based on an average number of customers within a designated market area. Since there are wide variations in each of the factors, the use of a simple average would not be too useful in making marketing decisions. Therefore, it seems appropriate to establish gradations within each factor causing cost differences for the purpose of apportioning cost to the degree of variance within each factor. As indicated, there are varying degrees of market knowledge.

It should be understood that the basis of establishing these gradations might vary with the product and the company. However, it is possible to determine the rationale for these gradations through market research, an analysis of historical records of the company, and industrial engineering studies.

The objective of the cost analysis will be to determine the unit cost of sales and distribution effort rather than the total cost. Since the price of the product is expressed in terms of unit price rather than total revenue, cost analysis could also be expressed in terms of units rather than total cost in order to make valid cost and revenue comparisons.

PRODUCT KNOWLEDGE

The gradations for product knowledge are based on the degree of knowledge the customer has about the product. The determination of the degree of product knowledge possessed by the customers would require the use of market research techniques, such as depth interviews and recall techniques. The suggested gradations are:

1. No consumer knowledge about the availability of a type of product
2. Knowledge that a given type of product is available on the market, but no brand identification of a given vendor's product
3. Some weak brand identification
4. Some differentiation of the product and a substantial brand identification
5. Complete brand identification

Two inherent difficulties in assessing the consumer's knowledge are the problems of setting quantitative limits on the knowledge of the individual and the measurement of such knowledge as related to action. It is extremely difficult to measure the knowledge a customer possesses or needs to buy a particular product unless he has actually purchased the item.[5] The second problem, the relationship of consumer knowledge to action, does not always show a positive correlation. The product manager, however, must attempt, through his advertising efforts, to effect this correlation.

The degree of customer knowledge is closely associated with the extent to which the product under consideration can be differentiated. Product variation refers to techniques which add variety and individuality to the goods in the market place. Some ways in which this is often done are: range of colors, variety of sizes and shapes, choice of materials, style changes guarantees or warranties, terms of payment, optional accessories, and packaging variations. How much product variations can expand demand depends upon their usefulness in satisfying consumers. Adrian Klaasen suggests that a combination of the following factors might be useful in measuring the sensitivity of consumer demand to product variation: susceptibility of the product to conspicuous consumption, susceptibility to superficial variation, actual usefulness of differentiation, growth stage of the industry.[6] The usefulness of these characteristics depends upon the extent to which they increase the customer's knowledge about the product and create product differentiation, so that the customer will desire a particular product on the market.

The degree of product knowledge will affect the type of advertising as well as the expense incurred for both advertising and personal selling. When a completely new product is to be introduced, advertising expenditure will be at its greatest. As the nature of the product, its use, and its brand identification become known, advertising may become directed more to demand creation and advice as to where the product may be obtained. Then advertising may be directed to differentiate the product from all others. A product manager always considers product knowledge in allocating his communication funds.

---

[5] Some individuals, however, have had outstanding success in determining quantity limits of consumer knowledge through depth interviews and recall techniques.

[6] Unpublished doctoral dissertation by Adrian J. Klaasen, *A Conceptual Framework for the Determination of Optimum Marketing Mix*, Michigan State University, 1961, pp. 84–90.

Klaasen suggests that the following criteria be used to establish the need for communication with respect to product differentiation: need for negotiation, sensitivity of the product to persuasion, effectiveness of demonstration, importance of identification, flexibility of primary demand, and the need for information. Each of these criteria should be evaluated in considering the market knowledge of the consumer.

MARKET DENSITY

The gradations for market density have been established on the basis of the number of actual customers in an area. The designated area may be sales territory, states, counties, etc. Whatever the area, there should be consistency in the selected space unit; in lieu of actual customers, potential customers or area population may be used. The following classification is suggested as an example:

1. 20 or fewer customers per square mile
2. 21 to 40 customers per square mile
3. 41 to 60 customers per square mile
4. 61 to 80 customers per square mile
5. over 80 customers per square mile

Market density would affect the costs of advertising, personal selling, transportation, and break-bulk and reassembly. As density increases, more customers may be reached per dollar of advertising costs, personal selling costs should decrease per unit because of a decreased traveling time, and transportation costs will decrease as because of more consolidated shipments and more carload and truckload movements. Break-bulk and reassembly costs might also be affected, since this operation would be carried on in the denser market areas, particularly where the average size of the order was small but the total volume of shipments was large enough to allow volume shipments to a break-bulk and reassembly point.

AVERAGE SIZE OF THE ORDER

The following gradations have been established for the average size of the order, on the assumption that a normal shipping pack has been established for a given category of customers. In this instance it has been assumed to be six units per pack. Similar gradations may be established whether the normal shipping pack contains a single unit, a dozen, two dozen, or a gross. The hypothetical gradations are:

1. 1 to 2 pieces
2. 3 to 5 pieces
3. 6 pieces
4. 7 to 8 pieces
5. 9 to 11 pieces
6. 12 or more pieces

Where the normal shipping pack is six units, an order of less than six units and one of seven to eleven units will require that the normal shipping unit be opened and the items removed and reassembled for shipment. Accordingly, the per unit cost of breaking bulk and reassembling the order is affected by the size of the order. The per unit cost of the transaction, similarly, will vary with the size of the order. A company should try to establish as few standard sizes as possible in order to minimize the break-bulk and reassembly function. In recent years, many companies have also made considerable efforts to reduce the amount of paperwork in handling transactions.

TIME ELEMENT

Time as a factor causing cost differences in marketing may be considered from several points of view, including: first, the presence of fashion; second, perishability; third, seasonal consumption and/or production; and, fourth. reluctance of the consumer to store. The presence of fashion in the marketing of a product generally tends to raise marketing costs; this is particularly true in a fad item where the product must be made available for sale to the consumer within a relatively short period because of rapid obsolescence.[7]

Perishability relates to a product's life expectancy. Some products, like cut flowers and fresh milk, have relatively short useful periods, whereas perishability is rather negligible in such items as steel and cement.

---

[7] Obsolescence of another kind, although not listed above, is technical obsolescence of the product, which is particularly important in the industrial market. Technical obsolescence would be important if a company were leasing its product, and had to insure that its investment in the leased equipment was recovered before new inventions made the equipment obsolete.

Seasonal consumption and/or production in any combination also affect the gradation of time chosen. In some respects, this is also affected by the extent to which the consumer will store an item when storage is necessary because of the seasonal consumption or production. For example, customers will not store the more expensive medicines, but will leave this to the druggist or other drug marketing institution. In many respects, the consumer has reversed the storage trend of recent years by taking storage out of the home and having it provided for commercially; however, the economy of buying in larger quantities has convinced some customers of the desirability of storing some commodities in their own homes, e.g., owning home freezers to store food products.

The gradations which have been established below concern the life expectancy of the product. The periods of time probably would be considerably shorter if they primarily included the fashion element, or some of the other elements mentioned as influencing gradations of time as causing cost differences. The illustrative gradations are:

1. less than 1 month
2. 1 month to one-half year
3. one-half year to 1 year
4. 1 year to 5 years
5. 5 years or more

The element of time would affect transportation costs and inventory costs. The shorter the life expectancy of the product, the more transportation expense will be incurred in getting the product to the market in time to meet demand. The life expectancy of the product will influence the length of time that inventory storage costs will be incurred and, to some extent, the level of inventory required.

SERVICING

Servicing costs are those necessary to insure customer satisfaction. Normally, these costs would be incurred subsequent to the sale, as in the case of warranty costs. Such costs may also include the services provided by salesmen in helping the customer to arrange his displays, control his inventory, or improve merchandising techniques. If the service is provided free of charge, then this must be considered as causing cost differences. However, if the customer is charged for the service and it is not included in the purchase price, this would not be a cause of cost differences.

DISTANCE

Gradations for distance are, of course, in terms of miles. The charge for transportation is usually quoted to the shipper as a given charge per 100 pounds or other unit of measurement. This charge per unit will increase as the distance increases, although the increment itself will probably decrease.

Selected gradations of distance for purposes of illustration are:

1. 0 to 49 miles
2. 50 to 99 miles
3. 100 to 149 miles
4. 150 to 199 miles
5. 200 miles and over

These distances will depend upon the individual market and the carrier under consideration. For example, there is a tendency for volume shipments (with lower per unit rates) to be made direct to the denser markets, and for these points to serve as break-bulk and reassembly points. There is also considerable variation in the per unit charge among the various forms of transportation for shipments of equal distance. Such variations in conditions can be determined, however, and a basis obtained for allocating transportation charges to the factor of distance.

VOLUME OF SALES

No gradations have been established for volume in cost differences, as they will vary considerably with the product and the company. The reason for including volume as a factor is that it will serve as the basis for spreading overhead costs over the range of sales volume.

ALLOCATING FUNCTIONAL COSTS TO FACTORS CAUSING COST DIFFERENCES

We are interested in the per unit cost within a given gradation of a factor causing cost differences. The reason for this is that the marketer, in planning a given market effort, must estimate the number of units of product that will be sold at a given price within this market. He must then compute his unit cost in order to see whether or not he can place the product successfully on sale in that market at a profit. The marketer will have a computation of total expenses and revenues in each category, but his planning must take place in terms of unit prices and costs.

The next step in systems cost analysis is to allocate the costs to the appropriate factors causing cost differences. This step, and the conversion of such expenses into unit costs, is one of the most difficult. It is difficult to generalize in this portion of the analysis, since the basis of allocation of the costs of functional centers to the factors causing cost differences will vary greatly with the product and the market. Some discussion was just given to the factors that would influence gradations within each factor causing cost differences. There is considerable strength to the argument that this same set of factors could be used to allocate the functional cost to the factors causing cost differences. For purposes of this discussion, the ability to accomplish this task will be granted and we will proceed to the next step.

The next step is to select those primary and secondary factors causing cost differences to which the functional cost centers will be assigned. A functional cost will be assigned to the gradations within the primary factor. Then within each gradation of the primary factors there will be gradations of the secondary factor. A tabulation of the primary and secondary factors for each functional cost center is presented in Table 10-2. It may be remembered from a previous table that the factors causing cost differences in motor carrier terminals were the number of pieces in the shipment, the density of the products in the shipment, and the weight of the shipment. These were combined in tabular form in Table 10-1 to show the variation of density and number of pieces within a given weight bracket. The same objective will be attempted in Table 10-2.

Since the prime objective of advertising is to increase the product knowledge of the customer about a given product, the degree of product knowledge will have the greatest influence on advertising costs; they are secondarily influenced by the number of customers for a given market area. Advertising expense is thus allocated primarily to the gradations established for the product knowledge of the customer, and within each gradation there will be an allowance for variation due to changes in market density. This is illustrated in Figure 10-1.

TABLE 10-2. *Allocation of Demand Creation and Distribution Costs to the Primary and Secondary Factors Causing Cost Differences (On a per Unit Cost Basis)*

FUNCTIONAL COST CENTERS

FACTORS CAUSING COST DIFFERENCES	Advertising	Personal Selling	Transportation	Break-Bulk and Reassembly	Inventory Level	Transactions[1]	Overhead[1]
Product Knowledge	1	2					
Market Density	2	1					
Average Size of Order				1		1	
Time Element			2		2		
Distance			1		1		
Volume							1

[1] No secondary factor is assigned.

Personal selling expense is the cost of keeping the salesman in the field, and the unit cost is inversely related to the density of the market. The primary factor, therefore, of personal selling expense is market density. The secondary factor is product knowledge, since the amount of time a salesman spends with a customer varies inversely with the customer knowledge of the product.

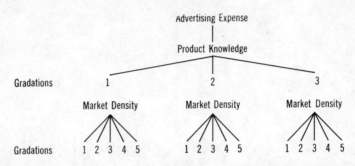

Figure 10-1. *Allocation of Advertising Funds.* Source: Frank H. Mossman, *Differential Distribution Cost and Revenue Analysis: A New Approach* (East Lansing, Mich.: Bureau of Business Research, Michigan State University, 1962), p. 21.

The cost of transporting the product depends primarily on the distance to the given market area. The selected secondary factor affecting transportation cost is time, since the greater the life expectancy (or other criteria referred to in the previous section on time) of a given product, the greater the opportunity for selecting optimum transportation mixes.

Performance of break-bulk and reassembly is primarily determined by the average size of the order: the greater the amount of physical handling involved, the greater will be the cost of the order. The secondary factor affecting break-bulk and reassembly is market density, since the number of customers per given market area, in combination with the average size of the order, will determine the extent to which break-bulk and reassembly is performed.

The expenses associated with inventory level are primarily determined by the amount of pipeline time involved in transit, and are a function of distance for purposes of the model here. The longer the distance, the greater will be the pipeline time, and the greater the expense attached to inventory level. The secondary factor affecting inventory level will be time, particularly where the commodity is perishable.[8]

Transaction expenses are primarily determined by the size of the order. Clerical and other facilitating functions are a constant cost per order and unit costs decline with an increase in the size of the order.

RELATIONSHIP BETWEEN THE FACTORS CAUSING COST DIFFERENCES AND AVERAGE TOTAL UNIT COST

At this point, it is possible to portray the characteristics of each of the factors causing cost differences in demand creation and distribution. In the following presentation, it is assumed that all of the factors except overhead costs are strictly variable in a linear fashion, and that as a unit cost they are not materially affected by changes in the volume of sales. There is considerable justification for this assumption, in practice, for a reasonable range of sales, based on the average for each factor. However, the exact shape of the curve would depend upon empirical observations obtained through market research, study of the historical records of the company, or industrial engineering techniques.

The allocation of the costs of functional centers to the primary and secondary factors causing cost differences was shown in summary in Table 10-2. Assumed unit costs for each of these factors are presented in Table 10-3 and, as stated in the previous paragraph, the assumption is made that the changes in unit costs with changes in gradation are linear. For example, it is assumed that in the assignment of break-bulk and reassembly costs to the factor of average size of order, the assignment of such costs will result in the average total unit cost figures of $.50 for Gradation 1, $.40 for Gradation 2, $.30 for Gradation 3, $.20 for Gradation 4, and $.10 for Gradation 5.

The following assumptions, which are generally in line with marketing experience, have been made with respect to the average unit cost (AUC) curves of the factors causing cost differences:

1. AUC tends to decrease as the average size of the order increases.
2. AUC tends to decrease as product knowledge increases.

[8] Another element of product buildup will be product permutations wanted by the customers. This aspect of inventory buildup has not yet been given much investigation. It deserves further study.

TABLE 10-3. *Assumed Unit Costs of Factors Causing Cost Differences by Gradation in Each Factor (Dollars per Unit)*

FACTORS CAUSING COST DIFFERENCES		Advertising	Personal Selling	Transportation	Break-Bulk and Reassembly	Inventory Level	Transactions
Product Knowledge Gradation	1	2.00					
	2	1.60					
	3	1.20					
	4	.80					
	5	.40					
Market Density Gradation	1		2.50				
	2		2.00				
	3		1.50				
	4		1.00				
	5		.50				
Average Size of Gradation	1				.50		1.00
	2				.40		.80
	3				.30		.60
	4				.20		.40
	5				.10		.20
Distance Gradation	1			1.00		.25	
	2			2.00		.50	
	3			3.00		.75	
	4			4.00		1.00	
	5			5.00		1.25	

FUNCTIONAL COST CENTERS

274

3. AUC tends to decrease as market density increases.
4. AUC tends to increase as distance increases.

In order to complicate allocation, both break-bulk and reassembly and transaction costs have been assumed to be assignable primarily to the average size of order. As shown in Table 10-3, the costs for this particular factor then would be a summation of the two columns, so that for Gradation 1 under average order size the AUC cost would be $1.50, $1.20 for Gradation 2, $.90 for Gradation 3, $.60 for Gradation 4, and $.30 for Gradation 5.

The figures shown in Table 10-3 are portrayed in Figure 10-2 for each of the five factors. The vertical axes on the figures are cost per unit, and the horizontal axes are gradations of the respective factors. The figures have not been combined to obtain an average total unit cost under each of the varying conditions, since the gradations have different meanings with respect to each of the factors causing cost differences.

TABLE 10-4. *Ranges of Assumed Costs for Factors Causing Cost Differences (Dollars per Unit)*

PRIMARY FACTOR (S)		SECONDARY FACTOR (S) GRADATIONS OF SECONDARY FACTOR				
		.1	.2	.3	.4	.5
Product	1	2.10	2.05	2.00	1.95	1.90
Knowledge	2	1.70	1.65	1.60	1.55	1.50
Gradation	3	1.30	1.25	1.20	1.15	1.10
	4	.90	.85	.80	.75	.70
	5	.50	.45	.40	.35	.30
Market	1	2.60	2.55	2.50	2.45	2.40
Density	2	2.10	2.05	2.00	1.95	1.90
Gradation	3	1.60	1.55	1.50	1.45	1.40
	4	1.10	1.05	1.00	.95	.90
	5	.60	.55	.50	.45	.40
Average	1	1.58	1.54	1.50	1.46	1.42
Size of	2	1.28	1.24	1.20	1.16	1.12
Order	3	.98	.94	.90	.86	.82
Gradation	4	.68	.64	.60	.56	.52
	5	.38	.34	.30	.26	.22
Distance	1	.85	1.05	1.25	1.45	1.55
Gradation	2	2.10	2.30	2.50	2.70	2.90
	3	3.35	3.55	3.75	3.95	4.15
	4	4.60	4.80	5.00	5.20	5.40
	5	5.85	6.05	6.25	6.45	6.65

In order to carry the illustrative figures presented in Table 10-3 one step further, an assumed set of unit costs is presented in Table 10-4 for the secondary factors as gradations of each of the primary factors. It will be recalled that, in the diagram for advertising expense, the cost of advertising was allocated primarily to product knowledge, and that within each of the gradations of product knowledge there was a secondary factor of market density.

To follow this example through in Table 10-4, the cost of advertising expense assignable to product knowledge was $2.00 for Gradation 1, $1.60 for Gradation 2, $1.20 for Gradation 3, $.80 for Gradation 4, and $.40 for Gradation 5. In Table 10-4 the range of gradations of the secondary factors is shown for each gradation of the primary factor. For example, in Gradation 1 of product knowledge, the range of costs for gradations of the second factor are $2.10 for Gradation 1, $2.05 for Gradation 2, $2.00 for Gradation 3, $1.95 for Gradation 4, and $1.90 for Gradation 5. Similar figures are assumed for each of the other gradations of the secondary factors within the gradations of the primary factors. The range of costs in each instance will appear as the dotted line shown for each of the respective factors in Figure 10-2.

Each of the lines in Figure 10-2 portrays the cost behavior of each of the factors which cause cost differences in the sale and distribution of a product. The solid lines represent the assignment of the functional cost centers to the primary factors that determine market costs. The dotted lines represent the range within each gradation from differences in cost caused by the secondary factors within each gradation.

Three illustrations in Table 10-5 show how the gradations can be used to compute average total unit costs in a marketing situation. The first illustration is composed of the following circumstances affecting marketing costs of the product in a particular market: product knowledge, Gradation 4.4 (primary gradation 4, secondary gradation 4), relatively good market knowledge about the product; market density, Gradation 5.1, relatively large number of customers in the market area; average size of order, Gradation 4.1, a relatively large order; and distance gradation 2.1, not shipped a very long distance. The summation of the unit costs assigned to each gradation in Table 10-4 are presented in Table 10-5, and in Illustration 1 the average total unit cost is $4.53 per unit.

Illustration 3 is the reverse of Illustration 1 in that there is very little product knowledge, there are relatively few customers in the

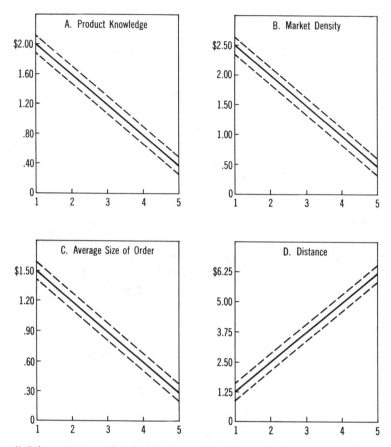

Vertical axes are cost per unit. Horizontal axes are gradations of the respective factors.

Figure 10-2. *Illustrations of Ranges for Factors Causing Cost Differences.* Source: Frank H. Mossman, *Differential Cost and Revenue Analysis: A New Approach* (East Lansing, Mich.: Bureau of Business Research, Michigan State University, 1962), p. 25.

market area, average size order is small, and the distance shipped is rather long. The average total unit costs in market circumstances number 3 are $11.80. In Illustration 2, a combination of factors somewhere between those of Illustrations 1 and 3 have been assumed, with a resulting average total unit cost for this combination of circumstances of $6.59.

The versatility of this procedure for planning purposes is quite evident. The product manager can assume certain changes taking

TABLE 10-5. *Illustrations of Average Total Unit Cost*

PRIMARY FACTOR	ILLUSTRATION 1		ILLUSTRATION 2		ILLUSTRATION 3	
	Gradation	Unit Cost	Gradation	Unit Cost	Gradation	Unit Cost
Product Knowledge	4.4	$ .75	2.4	$1.55	1.4	$ 1.95
Market Density	5.1	.60	3.5	1.40	2.1	2.10
Average Size of Order	4.1	.68	3.2	.94	1.3	1.50
Distance	2.3	2.50	2.4	2.70	5.3	6.25
AVERAGE TOTAL UNIT COST		$4.53		$6.59		$11.80

place for a particular product in some of the factors causing cost differences, and can determine the costs from the applicable figures. This information can be used in planning competitive strategy for the firm by analyzing each of the factors causing cost differences and then combining the individual cost to obtain the average total cost per unit.

RELATIONSHIP OF THIS APPROACH TO MARKET RESEARCH

The objective of market researchers is to apply scientific method to sales and distribution efforts. There are a large number of techniques available to the market researcher for obtaining the data needed to solve distribution problems. Too often, however, the data obtained for planning future marketing activities is in terms of aggregates, without an indication of unit costs or prices. Such aggregates are very useful to the sales and distribution executive in helping him to arrive at decisions on strategy, but leave large gaps in considering cost and revenue of a given product in particular markets.

Therefore, in an effort to narrow this gap, costs should be computed on the basis of the factors that cause cost differences in selling and distributing a product in a market. If the market researcher can obtain data on these same sets of factors with respect to the market place, a comparison of unit costs and revenue becomes possible. If these characteristics can be obtained for new markets, a considerable amount of the gap in decision making is eliminated, or at least considerably lessened.

TABLE 10-6. *Cost—Revenue per Unit[1] by Customers and by Types of Products*
(All Figures in Dollars per Unit)

TYPES OF CUSTOMERS

TYPES OF PRODUCTS	A Cost	A Revenue	A Gain or Loss	B Cost	B Revenue	B Gain or Loss	C Cost	C Revenue	C Gain or Loss
1	$ 4.28	$ 6.00	$1.72	$5.08	$6.00	$.92	$ 5.88	$ 6.00	$ .12
2	6.59	7.50	.91	6.74	6.50	−.24		no sales	
3	11.80	11.50	−.30		no sales		10.35	11.50	1.15

[1] Dollars in each instance are averages for this group. They could just as well be expressed as ranges, quantities, standard deviations, etc., for a product and/or category. Revenue figures come from sales records. Cost figures are computed on the basis of factors in Table 10-4.

The planning of demand creation and distribution programs demands the best in managements to create a reasonable profit is obtained from the company's products. As pointed out earlier, managements need scientific methods wherever possible to give them tangible data upon which to base decisions. This chapter has suggested a new approach to the analysis of costs and to demonstrate their use in making sales and distribution decisions. Here, a hypothetical example is posed to show one of the ways in which this particular data can be put to use.

In Table 10-6, cost and revenue per unit by types of customers are shown for each of the three kinds of products. Thus, for Product Type 1 the company made $1.72 per unit on Customer Type A, $.92 on Customer Type B, and $.12 per unit on Customer Type C.[9] Product Type 2 made a profit of $.91 per unit on Customer Type A, a loss of $.24 per unit on Customer Type B, and no sales to Customer Type C. The sales of Product Type 3 were at a net loss of $.30 per unit to Customer Type A, a profit of $1.15 per unit to Customer Type C, and no sales to Customer Type B.

At this point, the sales executive should look at the individual segments of the markets in order to get some basis for action in future sales and distribution efforts. A summary of the sales position of Product Type 2 with Customer Type A is presented in Table 10-7.

TABLE 10-7. *Product Type 2, Customer Type A*

	ANNUAL SALES AVERAGE FOR 5 YEARS	SALES FOR LAST 12 MONTHS	ESTIMATED SALES NEXT 12 MONTHS
Total Market	$120,000	$150,000	$175,000
Sales for Our Company	20,000	20,000	35,000
Our Company Share	$16\frac{2}{3}\%$	$13\frac{1}{3}\%$	20%

It is apparent that the company's position in the total market over the past five years has been approximately 16 per cent. However, during the last twelve months the company has slipped to approximately 13 per cent in the face of a growth in the market. Some action is needed. Therefore, in programming the sales executive may plan to expand

[9] The cost per unit figures are a result of the use of the three illustrations in Table 10-5. The variation between Customer Type A, B, and C was on the basis of market knowledge.

the position of the company to 20 per cent of the market for Product Type 2 in Customer Type A. Before he can do this, however, he must evaluate the alternatives available to him for expanding sales of this product in this customer type of market.

If the objective of increasing the company's share of the market to 20 per cent is to be realized, certain alternatives are open to the company under the assumed conditions of unit costs for Product Type 2 for Customer Type A. The assumed conditions were gradations of 2.4 for product knowledge, 3.5 for market density, 3.2 for average size of order, and 2.4 for distance. In this hypothetical situation, let us assume that the unit price is $7.50 and that this price will not change within the immediate future. In order to simplify the illustration, it may be best to stay with the primary factors causing cost differences, although the range of all alternatives will increase if the secondary factors are included. The range of alternatives then includes: first, an increase in the amount of expenditure devoted to the customers' knowledge about the products; second, an attempt to sell in a denser market; and, third, an increase in the average size of the order. The fourth alternative of shipping an added distance is not considered, since it would raise unit cost and reduce our margin in this market area. Actually, there are a great many possible alternatives to lower cost of shipment through utilization of such devices as transit privileges, consolidation of shipments into pool cars or mixed truck loads, and use of shippers' associations.

Two mentioned alternatives—selling in a denser market area and increasing the average size of the order—would decrease selling costs per unit, but the first alternative is not feasible, since the market area has presumably been defined. Increasing the average size of the order from 3.2 to 4.2 would lower this cost from $.94 to $.64 per unit, but would probably raise other costs. The remaining alternative of increasing the customers' knowledge about the product would presumably be done at the unit cost observed in Table 10-4. For example, if the knowledge of the customers were to be raised from gradation 2.4 to 1.4, the per unit cost would be increased from $1.55 to $1.95 per unit.

Both of the decisions on increasing the expenditures devoted to the customers' knowledge and trying to increase the average size of the order actually involve marketing decisions beyond the cost figures indicated in Table 10-4. At this point, market research would play a vital part in attempting to define the response of market A to price reductions due to decreased costs or to the increase in volume which might occur through increased advertising or other devices to increase the customers' product knowledge.

This information will guide management as to whether it wishes to go ahead and spend money in order to attempt to capture an additional share of the market, reduce prices to accomplish this same objective, or use a combination of the two. The figures do not tell the sales and distribution executive whether he will actually capture this share of the market, but these cost estimates, together with market analysis, provide him with a basis for decision making. In the last analysis, it is the product manager who must reconcile the considerations of cost with other demand creation and distribution factors.

PART FOUR

MICRODISTRIBUTION

SYSTEM POLICY

CHAPTER ELEVEN

DISTRIBUTION WAREHOUSING

In the discussion of macrodistribution systems, it was pointed out that their components include spatial inventories of raw materials, processing or value added in manufacture, retail sales, and total amounts moved via the various distribution agencies. There is relatively little information, however, on the spatial interrelationships between these various components.

The individual firm is much more fortunate in this regard. If it keeps its records properly, it should have available a great variety of data about flows of raw materials, processing points, and distribution points. The company should be interested in establishing a logistics system to help attain the goals of the enterprise. This system will consist of several subsystems, brought together in a coordinate relationship with the proper balance for each subsystem. A system using a distribution warehouse is one such possible subsystem.

A distribution warehouse is a point where one or more of the assembly, break-bulk, and/or break-bulk and reassembly functions are performed.[2] The possible desire for a distribution warehouse to serve given markets may be indicated through the use of the preliminary total cost analysis, presented in Chapter 9, which would narrow the available alternatives to a feasible number. If the distribution warehouse seems to be a possible alternative, a detailed analysis should be made of applicable costs; a procedure for determining such costs is suggested in this chapter.[3] Also discussed in this chapter are some considerations of distribution warehousing policy, particularly

[1] This chapter was written in conjunction with Mr. S. Richard Jones, Systems Analyst, Allis-Chalmers Manufacturing Company.

[2] Dead storage is not included in this discussion because it is not a function of the distribution warehouse. However, dead storage is vital in serving as an equalization point between demand and supply.

[3] Techniques for spatial location of the distribution warehouse are presented in Chapter 9.

with respect to expansion of the area to be served from an existing distribution warehouse. A brief consideration will also be given to centralization of distribution warehouse facilities because simulation techniques are necessary to adequately treat this subject; simulation is discussed in Chapter 12.

THE FUNCTION OF THE DISTRIBUTION WAREHOUSE

The distribution warehouse is the key point where large volume shipments of individual products are received from the manufacturer and blended into orders which meet the dictates of the individual retailer or other customer. This supply network is economical for both the retailer and the manufacturer. The buyer finds that consolidation of diverse products into single shipments from the warehouse avoids the necessity of large volume single commodity shipments from the manufacturer; the customer also may economically order slow moving items in smaller quantities. Manufacturers, particularly those with many plants and a complex product mix, have been able to reduce their own inventories through this central location. Storage and handling costs may be lessened while customer service is maximized. From the standpoint of transportation, the combination of diverse products into volume shipments has proven economically justifiable to the shipper. The distribution warehouse, then, is directly analogous to the retail outlet in relation to the consumer. In both places large shipments are broken down and customized for the individual.

SUBFUNCTIONS OF THE WAREHOUSE

As a cost center of the firm, distribution warehousing handles movement and storage. The most efficient distribution center would emphasize the former and minimize the latter. The more efficiently in terms of time movement is accomplished, the less time and space have to be devoted to storage.

Ideally, warehousing would be performed at lowest cost if the inbound products could be collected into an outbound unit en route to the shipping dock, thus eliminating all storage. However, this ideal situation is seldom attainable. Storage is necessary in varying degrees and is sandwiched between the four movement activities, which are:

1. Receiving
2. Circulation
3. Order picking
4. Shipping

Receiving is the inbound dock activity in which volume movements are unloaded and checked.[4] *Circulation* is the physical movement of the products to either stock shelves, for temporary storage, or to an area devoted to more permanent storage. *Order picking* is the keystone of distribution warehousing, with individual orders being customized and transferred for final processing. *Shipping* is represented by the outbound dock cost center; here orders receive a final check and are loaded in the outbound vehicles.

Temporary storage in varying degrees must be provided following circulation and prior to order picking. In most cases, goods will be conveyed to a safety stock area and integrated into the stock shelves as orders deplete the stock. However, in some instances goods will move directly to the bins, awaiting the order picker. Sometimes products will be removed from the active stream of inventory and transported into an area utilized for much more permanent storage.

MATERIALS HANDLING SYSTEMS

Warehousing is a distinct function within the firm. Each company will have individual warehousing needs to be satisfied. However, there are certain common underlying factors in warehousing, which may be grouped into production systems and materials handling systems.

Production systems are concerned primarily with plant layout and flow patterns which affect physical arrangements. Plant layout principles encompass the entire firm, and the different production method possibilities have an exacting influence upon the scale and layout of the warehouse.

Materials handling may be thought of as an element within two interrelated systems: first, the system of conveying materials throughout the entire network of the firm, from the initial handling as a raw material to the final phase of shipping the manufactured output; and second, the materials handling system operating entirely within the

---

[4] Implicit in this function is inspection of the goods received. Such inspection is for the purpose of filing a claim with the carrier and/or a protest with the vendor.

storage section. This second concept would construct boundaries enclosing the receiving, circulating, temporary storage, order picking, and shipping activities, and it is with this definition of materials handling that we are concerned in this portion of the chapter.

Improvements in materials handling systems for warehousing operations normally pursue one or more of the following courses of action: first, the reduction of distance transversed; second, reduction in handling; and third, increased equipment efficiency. Further analysis will show that all three of these classifications have time as a common denominator in measuring efficiency.

DETERMINING DISTRIBUTION WAREHOUSING COSTS

Warehousing costs have long been a neglected sector of business operations. Primary emphasis has been placed upon production costs, with only secondary stress on distribution costs. Distribution systems are receiving new attention, however, in competitive efforts to reduce operating costs. But even with this stimulant, warehousing costs have been comparatively ignored in both cost control and cost analysis.

Traditional methods of allocating costs of operating a warehouse have revolved around a distribution of the product according to the physical space it occupies.[5] In assigning these costs, all expenses (supervisor and worker salaries, payroll taxes, insurance, space costs, equipment depreciation, etc.,) are first totaled and then apportioned to individual products according to space occupied. One of the most common denominators is that of a "square feet occupied" proration.[6] This method has many shortcomings, and the "cubic-foot" assignment is sometimes used as a further refinement.[7]

These traditional methods of allocating warehousing costs, despite their current use, fail to recognize the primary function of distribution warehousing, which is movement. Figures which ignore receiving, circulating, order picking, and shipping costs lack the accuracy demanded in today's business operations. To achieve this ac-

[5] Donald R. Longman and Michael Schiff, *Practical Distribution Cost Analysis* (Homewood, Ill.: Richard D. Irwin, 1955), p. 73.
[6] Stephen B. Achter. "A Practical Way of Allocating and Controlling Warehousing Costs," *N.A.A. Bulletin,* February 1960, p. 77.
[7] *Ibid.,* pp. 78.

curacy, one must delve into the actual factors which cause differences in costs.

The costing of warehouse operations on the basis of space occupied implies that such costs vary with the physical size of the product, together with the number of units inventoried. Thus, 10 units occupying 2 cubic feet each would incur a higher proportion of total warehouse costs than would 15 items which individually occupy 1 cubic foot.

Example:

Product A = 10 @ 2 cubic feet

Product B = 15 @ 1 cubic feet

Total warehouse cost = $300,000

Total warehouse space = 100,000 cubic feet or $3 per cubic foot

Cost assigned A = $60

Cost assigned B = $45

This method of cost calculation is easy, but it totally disregards any differences in handling costs, distances and speed traveled, and turnover costs. Therefore, to refine and increase the accuracy of warehousing cost figures, one must consider the factors which cause cost differences.

HANDLING COSTS. In the warehouse, handling costs are those expenses associated with the actual order picking or selection of various products. This definition separates handling expenses from distance costs. Handling expenses can be categorized by three factors which may generate cost differences: physical characteristics, order combinations, and physical accessibility.

1. *Physical Characteristics.* As a broad generalization, most products are diverse in their physical characteristics. Different products may be packaged identically but may deviate in weight. Products equivalent in weight may differ in physical size. In reference to handling cost, it is a generally accepted principle that costs will increase

as the weight or size of the product increases. This fact is given credence in a study on motor carrier terminal costs.

>   The effect of the cube on the total handling time of a given weight package is related to the position of the center of gravity of the package which moves further out from the body as the piece gets larger. The greater the cube of the piece, the more difficult it is to carry and control it as compared to a denser smaller package of the same weight.
>   The greater the weight the more difficult it is to pick up the package and the more fatigue recovery time is necessary. These are reflected in the additives (cost) used.[8]

Weight and/or bulk also assume an important role in cost determination when the utilization of equipment capacity is considered. This is vital to ascertaining final warehousing costs.

2. *Order Combinations.* Costs are also influenced by the size of the orders (number of pieces comprising a load). If an order picker makes 20 selections for one load and ten for another, costs should be different for the two loads. The variance will not necessarily differ in proportion to the number of handlings, since each handling will be influenced by physical characteristics and accessibility.

3. *Physical Accessibility.* This concept considers the ease of handling, with reference to width, depth, and height. Height is discussed in comparative times of lifting and lowering; the horizontal moves are related to pallet arrangement. The ensuing discussion is related to pallet loads, but adaptations may be made for other methods.

The distance which a load must be lifted vertically has an effect upon handling time. This concept, as shown in Figure 11-1, shows that as the height is increased, the time spread between raising a full load and an empty one increases proportionately. It is also shown that lowering an empty fork-lift consumes more time than lowering a loaded one.

When considering the optimum stacking height in the warehouse, two limiting factors are the height that merchandise may be piled before its weight will cause damage to the bottom layers and the limit to which materials-handling equipment can be used effectively.[9]

---

[8] Michigan Public Service Commission, *Michigan Intra-State Motor Transporation Costs,* Report No. 2, 1961, exhibit 4, pp. 4–5. This was an extensive research report prepared by the A. T. Kearney Company of Chicago.

[9] *Ibid.,* pp. 8.

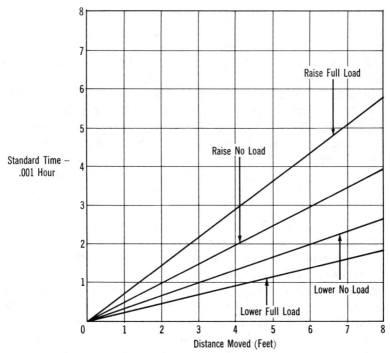

Figure 11-1. *Sample Fork Truck Lift and Lower Times.* Source: Ruddell Reed, Jr., *Plant Layout* (Homewood, Ill.: Richard D. Irwin, 1961), p. 165.

The physical positioning of the pallets also plays an important role in physical accessibility. This is closely interrelated with the distance traveled, as well as time necessary for handling. Pallets may be stacked squarely with the facings at 90 degree angles to the aisle or at some other angle. One authority says that the angles employed range from ten degrees to 45 degrees, with $26\frac{1}{2}$ degrees the most common.[10] If stacked at 45 degrees, the fork-lift truck need not complete a full turn to position the pallet load in front of the rack, but may make a direct approach. This can be accomplished without a full stop for the turn, and at a faster speed.[11] The simplicity of this approach is somewhat shrouded by the fact that space utilization is sacrificed to lower the handling costs. This fact was made apparent

[10] Smykay, Bowersox, and Mossman, *op. cit.,* p. 246.
[11] This entire discussion of physical arrangement has been a perplexing problem in a similar operation, parking lot design. Parking lot engineers are also forced to consider traffic flow and space utilization.

in one instance of a layout utilizing 1408 square feet; the 90 degree layout increased storage capacity by more than 15 per cent on the floor and provided 45 per cent more pallet facings.[12] From the above discussion, it is noted that physical position may cause cost differences, and the positioning alternatives must be weighed as to space utilization versus additional operating costs.

Throughout this section, it has been emphasized that differences in particular handlings cause differences in the behavior of warehousing costs. These cost differences, whether due to physical characteristics of the products, disparate order combinations, or physical accessibility of the merchandise, can be measured in terms of time expended.

DISTANCE COSTS. Physical location within the warehouse[13] also causes cost differences. Distance costs in the frame of reference are associated with both actual distance traveled and the time consumed in the operation. Physical distance covered can be described, in most instances, as units of time. Conversely, time could then be described as a function of distance. Flow patterns within the facility, however, distort the validity of the last statement. Certain conditions in the flow patterns established by the movements of handling equipment make time more a function of distance and speed. In selecting orders, the number of crosshauls, backtrackings, and turning maneuvers (corners) play an important part in time utilized in the order picking activity.

Load characteristics also affect the time consumed in travel. In a discussion concerning the rate of acceleration, braking rate, and cruising speed, one author asserts that all vary with the load handled.[14] This statement of load carried affecting distance and time is illustrated in Figure 11-2.

Implicit within the study of physical location is the fact that time must be consumed in travel to the selection site and to the shipping platform. The adding up of time in the handling and actual movement activities then will depict differences in cost behavior. However, the physical location of a product must be related to a discussion of volume as reflected in turnover costs.

[12] USDA, "Grocery Warehouse. . . .", *op. cit.*, p. 31.

[13] The use of the expression "distribution warehouse" seems to be declining, and its place is being taken by "service center."

[14] Ruddell Reed Jr., *Plant Layout, Factors, Principles, and Techniques* (Homewood, Ill.: Richard D. Irwin, 1961), p. 163.

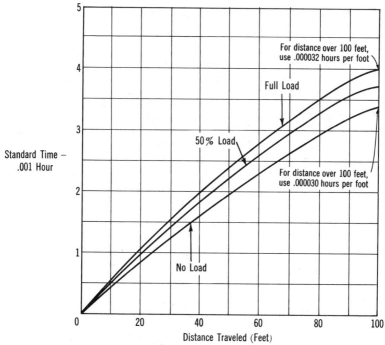

Figure 11-2. *Travel Time.* Source: Ruddell Reed, Jr., *Plant Layout* (Homewood, Ill.: Richard D. Irwin, 1961), p. 164.

TURNOVER COSTS. In this discussion, turnover costs are related to the positioning of particular stocks. In this capacity, it is desirable to conceive of stock velocity in terms of sales volume rather than strictly turnover. The sole use of stock turnover may be misleading, as is shown in Table 11-1.

TABLE 11-1. *Stock Velocity in Terms of Stock Turnover*

$$\text{Turnover} = \frac{\text{Sales}}{\text{Average Inventory}}$$

	PRODUCT A	PRODUCT B
Sales (units)	500	100
Average Inventory (units)	200	20
Turnover	2.5	5.0

For our particular use, the sales volume figure will be employed.

As previously stated, handling and distance costs may be designated as time costs, and distance costs are influenced by physical location. Therefore, placing most dynamic stocks at a point which would reduce distance costs would lessen total warehouse costs. This concept assumes a random flow operation in which the order picker need not complete an entire circuit within the shelves, but need only fill an order and return. This lessening of distance has been borne out by an actual operational overhaul.[15] In a warehouse where the merchandise layout was arranged according to commodity grouping, a particular thirty-five case order required 1,952 feet of travel for its assembling. After the selection line was arranged according to stock velocity, the same thirty-five case order required 1,231 feet for assembly, or nearly 59 per cent less travel distance (see Figure 11-3).

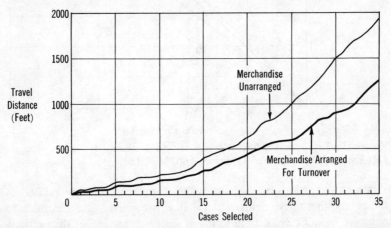

Figure 11-3. *Travel Distance Required to Assemble a 35-Case Order, Using An Unarranged Selection Line and A Line Arranged According to Sales Velocity.* Source: U.S. Department of Agriculture, *Grocery Warehouse Layout and Equipment for Maximum Productivity*, Marketing Research Report No. 348, p. 31.

To summarize handling and distance costs cause costs differences in distribution warehousing. These factors may be measured as time costs.

A PROCEDURE FOR QUANTIFYING WAREHOUSE COSTS

In attempting to add up warehouse handling costs, we must revert to the concept of two general variables which interact in any distribution warehouse activity: first, the diverse operational characteristics of the handling method employed; and, second, the many differences among individual products. Thus, any attempt to allocate costs may be successful only after certain aspects of these variables are further defined and quantified. The necessary ingredients for this success are figures on the operating costs of the method of handling (manual and mechanical), operational characteristics or the method of handling (speed, etc.), the distance the individual load must be transported, the physical characteristics of the product (weight, etc.), and the utilization of capacity for the given handling method.

The procedure normally followed in developing vehicle cost is to compute a standard set of costs which may be applied according to the dictates of the operation.[16] Vehicle operation costs can be divided into fixed ownership costs and variable operating costs. Thus, ownership costs consist of the depreciation, interest, insurance, and tax costs. Operating costs are composed of power costs, maintenance charges, and the wages of the operator. With these accounts determined, a utilization figure in terms of total hours must be established from either historical data or estimates. After settling on a utilization rate, a standard vehicle cost per hour can be established, and will be used in subsequent calculations.

The second element that must be arrived at is the two-way or total distance transversed. To be useful in the cost procedure, this figure should be in feet traveled and, as two-way suggests, include movement both loaded and unloaded.

The third step is to find the average speed at which the vehicle travels in performing the operation. Many components must be given quantitative definitions prior to arriving at a final figure for this factor. These elements are: time traveling at maximum speed, time accelerating and decelerating, any stop time, maneuvering time for loading and unloading, and time for actual loading and unloading.[17] Of these factors, certain ones may be standardized for particular aspects of the operation, thus simplifying calculation. With these factors defined, total trip time is then known (on a per hour base). Since the second step in this costing procedure gave the total distance traveled, the average speed in feet per hour is obtainable by dividing the distance by the operational time.

The fourth step is to derive a vehicle utilization rate which

---

[16] Though the vehicle in the illustration represents a fork-lift truck, the process formulated may be adapted to various handling methods.

[17] An excellent discussion on the determination of handling times is presented in Ruddell Reed, Jr., *op. cit.,* pp. 162–165.

relates the hours (or fractions of hours) allocated to the entire load-ing-unloading cycle of a particular trip. This rate is computed by dividing the actual total distance covered in the operation by the average speed in feet per hour of the vehicle. The result of this manipulation is a figure which discloses the number of hours utilized toward the completion of the job.

From the preceding steps, the vehicle operating cost per hour and the hours (or fraction thereof) of vehicle utilization for the specific job are now available. The multiplication of these two factors will result in a dollar value for that particular job. For some aspects of the business, this figure may be sufficient cost information. For the cost allocation to individual stocks, however, this figure will not suffice. The problem then is to apportion to each product its share of the internal warehousing cost.

Prior to delving into this issue, it should be noted that the individual vehicle has physical capacity limitations of weight and volume. A fork lift truck is used as an example. For this vehicle, the manufacturer always specifies the weight capacity of the particular model. The volume limitation is not so easily attained, but it can be computed, since there are physical limitations on the height, depth, and width of the cube which a particular truck may handle. Vertically, the limitations will most likely be the height at which the vision of the operator will be obstructed. The depth of the cube is governed by the load's center of gravity in relation to the front of the truck and the length of the fork extensions. Therefore, the longer the fork extends, the greater the cubic volume that may be transported. The width of the cube is confined to the width of the aisles and doors. Thus for any vehicle, the physical limitations may be calculated and an optimum load capacity designated.

Cost apportionment may be rather simple, as in the case of one product per load, or more complex, as in the case of more than one product in a load. The simplest assignment situation is that in which one product utilizes the entire vehicular capacity. Since the cost of the load is known, the entire amount may be assigned to this one product, without reference to weight or volume. Practically, however, distribution warehousing rarely presents this simplest of situations. In the order picking phase, many products are selected, usually varying in some degree in weight and/or volume.

The question posed, then, is how, for a given load, costs are allocated to products transported in that load, when the products differ in weight and/or volume. If prorated on weight, what about light, bulky items which occupy much more space than a heavy, compact product? If allocated on volume, what about the heavy, compact item that assumes more than its proportionate share of the weight capacity?

When cost calculations are completed for a load and the allocation must be made on the basis of the two variables, the allocation procedure becomes a moot point. Possible procedures include weight (every time), volume (every time), density, weight times volume. Table 11-2 typifies the perplexities encountered using one method, weight × volume.

TABLE 11-2. *Cost Allocation by Weight × Volume*

	WEIGHT (LBS.)	VOLUME (CU. FT.)
VEHICLE CAPACITY	2000	200
Product A	1200	50
Product B	300	40
Product C	500	110

Actual Utilization of Vehicle

	PER CENT OF WEIGHT CAPACITY	PER CENT OF VOLUME CAPACITY
Product A	60	25
Product B	15	20
Product C	25	55
	100%	100%

Cost Allocation if Assigned on Weight × Volume

	PER CENT OF TOTAL COST
Product A	47.2
Product B	9.5
Product C	43.3
	100.0

These figures show that this method would allocate only 9.5 per cent of the trip cost to a product that occupied 20 per cent of the space and accounted for 15 per cent of the weight.

When working with these variables, weight and volume, the cost allocation may have to be completed on an arbitrary basis. This is not to say that all movements will be costed on a weight proration (or a volume assignment). It is suggested here that the procedure is somewhat less arbitrary than this. The distribution will be made on one or the other, but will depend on the physical characteristics of the load in relation to the operating limitations of the vehicle.

As before, this method depends upon the calculation of the physical capacity of the vehicle. This, then, is step one. Next, the weight and cubic space occupied by the products must be determined. A comparison of the derived figures from these steps then must be made, and a ratio established. The allocation of cost will be based upon that variable which displays the highest ratio of utilized capacity. Table 11-3 shows this process in simplified form.

TABLE 11-3. *Allocation of Cost on Utilized Capacity*

	WEIGHT (LBS.)	VOLUME (CU. FT.)
Vehicle	2000	200
Product A	300	20
Product B	425	45
Product C	775	35
	1500	100

$$\frac{\text{Actual Weight}}{\text{Weight Capacity}} = \frac{1500}{2000} = .75$$

$$\frac{\text{Actual Cubic Volume}}{\text{Cubic Capacity}} = \frac{100}{200} = .50$$

Cost will be distributed on weight proportions.

A point of indifference will be reached, using this method, where the values exhibited in the ratios are equal. Here a purely arbitrary judgment decision must be made. It has been previously stated that costs will vary with order combinations, physical location or distance traveled, and/or physical accessibility. Thus, any changes in the factors must be integrated into the cost formula and reflected in the resulting costs.

Order combination refers to the number of selections made while completing a load. One would expect that as the number of picks increases, the cost must necessarily increase. This does not necessarily hold true in all instances. This factor, at this point, ties in with physical accessibility. This introduces the concept of handling times, which may vary between products. So the actual case may show that four picks took longer to handle than did three other selections. A gradation, then, that would describe handling costs as a function of the number of order picks would not be accurate. The costing technique presented here describes handling costs as a function of time and, therefore, is more accurate in its assessment of the effects of the factors causing cost differences.

Distance traveled is measured in time expended, as is handling cost. When depicted in time, distance traveled reflects variations in speed due to maneuvering, etc., so that distance is not directly a function of time. The average speed figure then will successfully reflect the factors causing the cost difference.

SUMMARY OF INPUTS FOR WAREHOUSING COST FORMULA

Step 1: Determine standard operating cost for vehicle hour.

Step 2: Establish actual distance traveled in the operation.

Step 3: Establish the vehicle's average speed in feet per hour.

$$\frac{\text{Two-way distance}}{\text{Time of operation}} = \text{average speed}$$

Time of operation inputs:
1. Time at maximum speed
2. Time for accelerations and decelerations (may use standards for turning movements, etc.)
3. Stop time
4. Maneuver time (loading and unloading)
5. Load and unload time (actual performance)

Step 4: Determine the utilization of the vehicle on an hourly basis.

$$\frac{\text{Actual distance}}{\text{Average Speed}} = \text{utilization}$$

Step 5: Determine cost for load (or trip).
Vehicle operating cost × Vehicle utilization = cost of trip per hour.

Step 6: Establish physical limitations of vehicle.
1. Weight_____Given
2. Volume_____Height × Width × Depth

Step 7: Determine actual weight and cubic measurements of products comprising the load.

Step 8: Determine the ratio of actual weight to optimum weight capacity and actual volume to optimum cubic capacity.

Step 9: Compare ratios and allocate costs based upon the variable which comes nearest 1.00.

EFFICIENT DISTRIBUTION WAREHOUSING

Distribution warehousing is too complex to attempt to compile a single check list to exhibit all the warehousing principles that would result in the most efficient warehouse. This section, however, states a few major propositions on the subject of efficient distribution warehousing.

1. Construction costs are lowest for square buildings.[18]
2. In construction, one should make allowances for expansion.
3. If building costs are not excessive, an enclosed dock is advantageous.[19]
4. The distance between the stock bins and the shipping dock should be minimized.
5. Stock should be shelved according to sales velocity. Figure 11-4 shows a model relating sales turnover and volume to placement position.
6. Narrow aisles should be utilized wherever the building construction allows. Narrow aisles conserve valuable floor space.[20] They also permit the order picker to select from both sides of the aisle without having to make a return trip on the opposite side. Narrow aisles reduce criss-crossing distance in relation to the use of that pattern with width of the aisles.
7. One way aisles reduce congestion, thus facilitating the movement flow.

[18] U.S.D.A., "Grocery Warehouse. . . ." op. cit., p. 4.
[19] Ibid., pp. 10. The advantages of this enclosure are:
   (A) Protection from weather extremes.
   (B) Dock need not be cleared at day's end to avoid pilferage.
   (C) Dunnage and trash least likely to accumulate inside building.
   (D) Improved employee health and productivity.
[20] A technical analysis of space economics is presented by Joseph E. Wiltrakis, "Unlocking Space Economies by Formula," Materials Handling Engineering, September 1962, Vol. 17, No. 9, pp. 58–62.

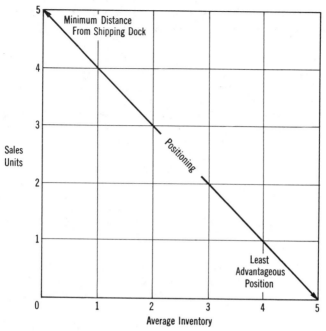

Figure 11-4. *Stock Positioning.*

8. Mechanized equipment results in greater efficiency, resulting in lower unit costs.
9. If expansion room is needed, vertical expansion uses the third dimension of the cube. The cost of additional concrete flooring and roofing for horizontal expansion is more expensive than placing merchandise higher in the building.[21]
10. Pallets should be stored at angles if the savings in handling costs exceed the corresponding space diseconomies.[22]
11. Temporary storage areas should be located close to the actual stocked items, minimizing distance.

EXPANDING THE MARKET AREA SERVED
BY A DISTRIBUTION WAREHOUSE

The policy problem to be discussed in this section is the determination of methods to serve customers located in a market area ex-

[21] U.S.D.A., "Grocery Layout. . . .", *op. cit.,* p. 9
[22] If space economies are conceived as being of higher priority, reference should be made to a fine discussion on the maximization of space utilization in the use of pallets appearing in Reed, *Plant Layout, op. cit.,* pp. 230–232.

clave[23] from an existing distribution center warehouse. In order to simplify the problem, the following basic assumptions are made:

1. Management has made a long term decision that expansion in the direction of the market area exclave is desirable.
2. The specific problem will last until expansion of the market justifies a second distribution warehouse.
3. Not more than one distribution warehouse enters the analysis at the beginning of the time period.
4. The number of customers comprising the exclave is relatively small at the beginning of the time period. The number is far too small to consider the immediate addition of a second distribution warehouse which could operate at a sufficient scale to economically serve the exclave. This assumption may reflect the tendency of management to enter new markets gradually, foregoing some possible profits in order to minimize the possible loss should the expansion decision prove to be the wrong one.

A simplified diagram may be helpful in visualizing the problem, although it omits certain theoretical considerations and involves certain unrealistic assumptions. In Figure 11-5, length BD represents

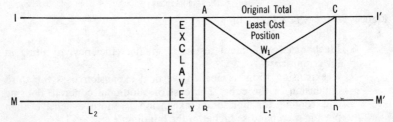

Figure 11-5. *A Market Exclave in Relation to An Established Warehouse.*

that portion of all total market areas served by the firm from the existing distribution center, In other words, BD is the market area served by the existing distribution center located at L_1 at a cost of W_1L_1. The limits of the market area BD are determined by the points at which W_1A and W_1C cross the indifference line II'. Beyond points A and C on II', the costs of the distribution center would be such that, under normal operating procedures, it could not compete evenly on a strictly cost basis with equally efficient warehouses at other locations.

[23] Market area exclave is that area which is outside of, and not necessarily directly adjacent to, the present market area of the existing distribution warehouse.

The area represented by the distances EX on the MM' line is the market area exclave. EX is clearly outside of the defined market area of the existing distribution center. The problem, then, is how best to serve EX until a new distribution center is established at some location, L_2. Presumably, the second distribution center would be located so that L_1 and L_2 shared a common boundary.

THE REQUIREMENTS OF A SOLUTION

The following basic criteria or requirements have been established for evaluating a course of action. These requirements merely represent one set of criteria; a particular firm might desire others.

First, a course of action should provide the desired level of service at the total least cost. Second, the solution should be a subsystem which fits into the over-all physical distribution system of the company as well as other systems. For example, inventory control for serving the exclave must be integrated with the present inventory control system. The form of ownership of the distribution center could also affect the feasibility of integrating a course of action into the original system. Third, the course of action must enable the customers to compete with customers in the market area of the exclave. These units must be competitive not only on a price basis, but also in terms of variety, service, dependability, and other bases of non-price competition.

Fourth, the course of action must offer flexibility. The expansion process is viewed as an evolutionary one in which change is constantly taking place. The specific problem is defined as temporary, and therefore requires a temporary solution. To solve a temporary problem by creating a permanent one is defeating the long-run strategy of the company. Several possible courses of action will be examined in the light of these requirements.

POSSIBLE COURSES OF ACTION

Several alternative plans other than the normal method of serving the market area could be used to serve the market area exclave. By projecting cost data of each of these plans, or some combination of them, a decision can be made. Among the courses of action available to the company are:

1. Less frequent delivery and larger safety stocks.
2. Spotting of trailers.
3. Simple subwarehousing.
4. Subwarehousing at a store site.
5. Use of local sources of supply.
6. Possibility of return loads.

LESS FREQUENT DELIVERY AND LARGER SAFETY STOCKS

From the standpoint of the distribution center warehouse management, the simplest method of serving the market exclave may be to reduce the frequency of deliveries. Outlying customers within a market area often receive less frequent deliveries than those near the distribution center. Whether or not the frequency of delivery could be reduced even further as the distance increased beyond the market area to the exclave is questionable.

The further economies of less frequent delivery than presently given to outlying customers would be small. Offsetting these economies would be the costs of carrying increased inventory. A fundamental cost of this increased inventory would be the interest cost to finance the additional safety stock necessary to maintain the desired service level. Additional space would also be required. Reduced inventory turnover would probably increase losses from spoilage and damage. Other costs such as insurance, labor, and taxes would also be increased at the retail level.

In terms of the four basic requirements of the previous section, this course of action would under most circumstances probably fall short on the first and third requirements; that is, on the total least cost and the retail competitive requirements. This course of action would, however, fit into the present system, and would offer considerable flexibility.

SPOTTING OF TRAILERS

The spotting (or dropping) of trailers is a method of delivery whereby the tractor and trailer leave the warehouse, travel to some point, and are unhitched. Usually the tractor will pick up another trailer at this point. The unhitched trailer will then be hauled by another tractor for the remainder of the journey, if it has not been completed. Spotting better utilizes the time of the driver and/or tractor. A trailer may be dropped either at the destination store or at some intermediate point between the distribution center and the store. If the trailer is dropped at the store, it may serve as a temporary storage place until the merchandise is unloaded, marked, and stocked in a continuous operation. Intermediate spotting is probably more applicable in serving stores which are distant from the warehouse.

Spotting may be used to serve the market area exclave. Additional economies may be obtained if double trailers are permitted for the first portion of the haul. Spotting would require some additional investment in movement equipment, but economies would be gained by reducing overtime pay to drivers.

In terms of the four basic requirements, the spotting of trailers (1) may or may not prove to be the lowest total cost method, (2) will fit into the system, although a degree of control will be lost over the driver(s) and equipment which are no longer based at the distribution center warehouse, (3) will enable the retail units to be competitive only if a sufficient number of deliveries are made, and (4) will offer a very high degree of flexibility for future changes in the market and, consequently, in the distribution system.

SIMPLE SUBWAREHOUSING

Simple subwarehousing is not used here to mean the same thing as branch warehousing. The functions performed and the number of items carried are different. Subwarehousing is the temporary storage of a limited number of items at a point for the purpose of more fully utilizing the movement capacity of the individual units. An example should help to explain this more fully.

In serving the market area exclave, a very small warehouse would be located early in the route, somewhere after delivery to at least one customer but most likely within the exclave. This small warehouse would serve as a depository for the few items which were to be subwarehoused. Assume that the requirements of the exclave stores are as in Table 11-4 over a period of time.

The customers in the exclave required $2\frac{1}{2}$ loads of merchandise on the first delivery date. This means that under regular delivery methods a half load of capacity would be wasted on the first day. Likewise, three-fourths of a load would be unused on dates 3 and 4. However, if subwarehousing were used, the excess capacity on delivery date 1 would be filled with items destined for the subwarehouse. Then, on

306 MICRODISTRIBUTION SYSTEM POLICY

TABLE 11-4. *Requirements of Exclave Stores*

DELIVERY DATE	NUMBER OF TRUCKLOADS	REGULAR DELIVERY UNITS REQUIRED	DELIVERY UNITS REQUIRED UNDER SUBWAREHOUSING
1	$2\frac{1}{2}$	3	3
2	2	2	2
3	$2\frac{1}{4}$	3	2
4	$2\frac{1}{4}$	3	2
	9	11	9

delivery dates 3 and 4, only two trucks would be dispatched. At least one of these trucks would not carry items from the distribution center which were ordered by the stores but were on hand in the subwarehouse. Upon unloading a significant portion of the load at the first store, the truck would pick up the necessary items at the subwarehouse and complete its route. The example is much simplified, and does not make the necessary allowances for leakages in the system.

Some practical problems involved in such a system are the size of the subwarehouse, its location, the specific items and the number of items to be subwarehoused, and the control of the subwarehouse. As regards size, generally the lower the cost can be kept the better. The ideal location will in many instances be adjacent to the first delivered customer, as will be seen in the next section. The specific items to be warehoused should move in large volume, be low in value, be quickly and easily loaded and unloaded, and not easily damage or deteriorate. In general, the fewer the number of items the better, down to about ten items. The entire operation should be controlled from the distribution center warehouse.

The principal advantage of subwarehousing is that it more fully utilizes the movement capacity of each truck, consequently requiring fewer trucks. The same number of tons is shipped, but the number of total miles traveled is reduced, resulting in a reduction of total ton-miles. However, the total cost may not be reduced, since certain costs are involved in using subwarehousing. The operation of the subwarehouse will involve some costs and some additional inventory, and the time of the driver may be increased.

In terms of the four requirements, subwarehousing fares as follows. It may reduce costs, but may not necessarily be the least total cost method by itself. Some adjustments of the total system would be necessary for subwarehousing to fit into it. However, these adjustments should not seriously affect the rest of the distribution system. Customers would be adequately served, and the method could be implemented so as to allow a great degree of flexibility for future change.

SUBWAREHOUSING AT A CUSTOMER'S SITE

This course of action is merely a modification of the previous method. It does, however, involve the following advantages: (1) operation and control of the subwarehouse may be facilitated, (2) an additional stop is eliminated by the driver, and (3) the subwarehouse space may be easily converted to use by the retail unit when the customer requires more space and/or the subwarehousing plan is no longer needed.

There are certain conditions under which subwarehousing may be carried on at the customer's site. First, the customer should be the first stop in the exclave route. Second, he should be in a location that may require expansion in the future, or one at which the subwarehouse space could be advantageously leased or sold to another customer once the subwarehouse plan was discontinued. Third, the subwarehouse should be constructed so as to facilitate loading and unloading for the present and provide for easy conversion to a different use in the future. Fourth, the subwarehouse should be located in a fringe, rather than in a high cost central, location. Fifth, the subwarehouse should not be regarded as a part of the customer's business for control purposes, but should be under separate and coordinate control.

The first requirement may be better achieved by subwarehousing at the customer's site if conditions are nearly ideal. The fulfillment of the other three requirements will be similar to those mentioned for simple warehousing, and will ultimately depend upon the degree to which conditions are suitable.

USE OF LOCAL SOURCES OF SUPPLY

Local sources of supply may be used in combination with some other course of action, or the firm may decide to depend entirely upon such sources for the temporary time period. The most likely use of local sources would be to supplement deliveries from the distribution center for perishable items.

A principal reason for using local sources of supply is that customers will be better served on those items without the firm's carrying an excess of inventory. Thus, the customers will be better able to compete in the non-price areas. The requirements of the systems of the entire company may necessitate a rigid policy for controlling purchases from local sources. This would be particularly true for centrally controlled organizations.

POSSIBILITY OF RETURN LOADS

The use of return loads to the distribution warehouse from plants in the market area exclave is not a complete course of action in itself. It is mentioned here only because it represents one method whereby an area may be served profitably which would otherwise be served at a loss.

CENTRALIZING AND REDUCING THE NUMBER OF DISTRIBUTION WAREHOUSES

A number of firms have found it practicable in recent years to centralize and reduce the number of their distribution warehouses. Such moves have been made possible largely through improved intercity transportation, information flows, and handling methods.

Improvements in intercity transportation have lessened the time required for movement of both freight and people, thereby lowering the amount of inventory required in the pipeline. Lower transit times have been a result of new technology creating higher movement speeds and improved means of transfer of lading between forms of transportation. For example, air freight can be moved in jet planes at speeds in excess of the speed of sound and delivered by truck at destination; the transfer of lading between the two agencies is easily accomplished by mechanical handling of the goods on pallets. Thus, both terminal and transit times are reduced.

Improved data collection has led to more timely and accurate information regarding inventory and sales. One of the main reasons for decentralization of distribution warehouse systems was that the central office could not acquire and process inventory and sales information fast enough to use it in decision making. Therefore, in order to have stocks readily available, the distribution system had to be constructed to allow for the time lag in data collection and analysis. The development of electronic data processing machines has made it possible to collect sales, inventory, and production data quickly and synthesize it for quick use in business decisions. Centralization of data collection has also made it possible to centralize the distribution warehouse system.

Improved handling methods often facilitate central warehousing. Such improvements as unitized loads and standardized package sizes lead to fewer, more efficient handlings throughout the entire distribution system, reducing the need for decentralized break-bulk and reassembly operations. Coupled with such moves may be the fact that with more centralized operations, the advantages of scale may permit the introduction of mechanical handling systems in the warehouse in an effort to lower operating costs.

The opportunities for reducing distribution costs through the centralizing or reducing the number of distribution warehouses are rather substantial. Inventory costs are a large part of the costs of distribution, and a reduction of such expenses could result in important gains for the firm.

There are two important limitations to the tendency toward distribution warehouse centralization. These are: first, availability of adequate movement facilities to provide rapid transit to the firm's markets from a centralized warehouse location; and, second, the extent to which the customers demand services or the extent to which competitive firms make such services available. The limitation of rapid transit to the market is self-explanatory. Customer service requires a little explanation.

Service to the customer has many connotations. It may be quick replacement of inventory, carrying a full selection of a narrow product line or a broad group of products with a narrow selection in each line, or special handling for small orders.[24] Inventory requirements are also rarely stable; demand may be irregular, cyclical, or seasonal, and stocks may have to be decentralized to meet demand if the fluctuations are of short duration. In any event, if the customer requires service attainable only through decentralized warehousing operations, the vendor firm must attempt to meet such requests, taking into

---

[24] There are also other connotations of service, such as repair facilities and credit. The above factors are the principal ones that would affect inventory level as it relates to the centralization of warehousing facilities.

account the cost involved. The firm must also be aware of the strategy of its competitors in meeting the customers' requirements, which may force decentralization. In this type of situation, computers and simulation techniques are very useful in showing the results of competitive strategy.

CHAPTER TWELVE

INVENTORY MANAGEMENT

Inventory costs are one of the major expenses of a business enterprise, with a resulting emphasis on management decisions in this cost center which will maximize use of assets and yet minimize costs. The purpose of this chapter is to present the economic justification for inventories, the need for control, the components of inventory costs, the use of statistics for effective control, and the use of simulation in inventory decisions.[1]

ECONOMIC JUSTIFICATION FOR INVENTORIES

Inventories are important in the economic system, enabling business to (1) optimally locate production, warehouse, and retail facilities, (2) purchase and produce at the most economic rate, (3) hedge against shortages, price changes, and uncertain demand, and (4) produce seasonally to meet a continuous demand or produce continuously to meet a seasonal demand. Each of these reasons alone may justify carrying inventories; taken in combination, they represent a critical area for business decisions.

OPTIMAL LOCATION

Initial production, final fabrication, and ultimate consumption often are most economically carried on at different locations for a wide variety of reasons, including location of natural resources, weight loss or gain in production, and population density. Thus, a movement

---

[1] This chapter was written in conjunction with Mr. Stanley Hardy, Graduate School of Business, Michigan State University.

inventory is required to overcome geographical separation of the operations. The movement inventory (I_t), is a function of the average sales, production or consumption rate (S_r) and the average transit time (T); this can be expressed as $I_t = S_r \times T$.

ECONOMIC PRODUCTION AND CONSUMPTION

Each unit in the economic system is both a consumer and a producer. The economic rate of consumption for a particular unit is determined by its economic rate of production. Only by chance would the rate of production of one unit be the same as the economic rate of consumption of the next unit. Inventories allow each unit to operate separately, and to produce or consume at its own economic rate.

HEDGING

A firm hedges to protect itself against some possible future loss. Often certain goods become scarce for one reason or another, and the lack of these goods critically affects the sales or production needs of the firm. Therefore, whenever there is a possibility of goods becoming low in supply a firm often increases its inventories of those goods. A good example of this is the steel inventory accumulations prior to expected steel strikes.

Price changes also affect inventory policies. If a price rise is predicted with some degree of certainty and the amount of the rise is reasonably well known, the firm can calculate the extra amount of inventory it should purchase. The marginal savings from the extra purchase should be equal to the marginal cost of holding the extra inventory.

Generally, demand is uncertain, and the firm wishes to be able to meet this demand but does not want to hold excessive stocks. Again, the solution lies in equating the expected gain with the expected loss. Solutions of this type will be covered in more detail later in the chapter.

SEASONAL PRODUCTION AND/OR CONSUMPTION

Seasonal production and/or consumption is really a special case of economic production and consumption. Agriculture is a good example of seasonal production and continuous consumption; inventories are obviously needed to tide us over from one growing season to the next. An example of seasonal consumption is Christmas specialties, such as toys and decorations, which are often produced continuously and inventoried until the Christmas season, permitting the firm to produce at an economical rate. A side effect of this is continuous employment of labor, which has social and economic benefits.

THE NEED FOR INVENTORY CONTROL

If inventories were free until put into use, the only control objective would be to have enough on hand. Unfortunately, inventory costs money in the form of interest, taxes, insurance, space cost, deterioration, obsolescence, labor-clerical salaries, labor-handling, ordering costs, and lost profits from lost sales. Controls need to be devised to hold such costs at a minimum consistent with the objectives for which the inventories are acquired.

In most inventories, a very small percentage of the total inventory accounts for a high percentage of dollar investment. The balance will be large in numbers, but will add up to only a small amount of investment. Therefore, the inventory may be stratified, with the strictest (and most expensive) controls put on that part that accounts for the high dollar investment. The remaining inventory may then be controlled with the more routine, less expensive type of controls.

Some pressing inventory control problems arise from a fundamental conflict of interests between the customers, suppliers, and employees. The production department looks for long manufacturing runs, with lower setup costs and steady employment. The sales department philosophy looks for quick delivery and service to the customer; they contend that customer goodwill can only be attracted through quick reaction to the customers' requests. There is also a conflict between the financial department and inventory. The comptroller often sees inventory as an idle resource, making no apparent contribution towards output or sales; to him, the tie-up in capital without satisfactory output is a drain on the company's funds. Of course, the basic problem is that each group does not recognize the costs outside its own operation. This problem is intensified because each group has a different answer to the question of how large inventories should be.

It takes a strong administration to reorient the various departments to view their subsystem in the light of requirements of the total firm.

INVENTORY COSTS

Inventory costs can be divided into costs associated with ordering and costs associated with holding and handling the inventories. The costs associated with the ordering process are illustrated in Figure 12-1, a flow chart of the total processes involved in placing an order for items in the general storeroom of a typical manufacturing plant. There are 17 different operations and 21 separate pieces of paper or records involved in the placing of one order. By studying this process, one can develop the average cost of placing an order. Total order costs for a firm will vary directly with the number of orders placed.

Holding and handling costs are generally called *storage costs*. The factors involved in handling and storing inventory include capital (interest) cost, storage costs (rent and heat), insurance and taxes, obsolescence and spoilage costs, and associated labor costs. The capital, or interest, cost is a product of the capital value of a unit in inventory, the length of time in inventory, and the interest rate placed against the invested capital. The capital value includes the cost of raw materials; the length of time in inventory depends upon the average order quantity, reorder level, and lead time. Several different interest rates can be used, including the prevailing bank rate, although this ignores the entrepreneur's compensation; a rate equal to the rate of return on the firm's common stock; a rate based on the average cost of capital used by the firm. Since the selected rate becomes a function of the cost in inventory levels, its definition will affect the level of inventory and must be selected wisely.

Space or storage costs are incurred because of the time between receipt of material and its movement to the next step in the business process. The cost is simplified if rented facilities are used, since this cost generally is directly related to space used. If the space is owned, items such as depreciation, taxes, heat and light, alarm service, and other utilities must be delegated to space costs.

Inventory obsolescence and spoilage costs may take several forms: (1) loss due to scrappage because of damage to the product, (2) spoilage due to deterioration of the product, and (3) the product's becoming unsalable due to technological innovation or style changes. All of these costs are related to time in inventory. Scrappage may be related to movement, but the longer the product is in inventory, the greater the possibility of damage because of movement in the storage areas.

Insurance and taxes on the inventory will be related to the product of the average inventory and the value of the assets in inventory. The insurance premium is generally based on the monies required to replace the inventory in case of loss. The tax rate is based on some fixed percentage of the value of the material in inventory. Thus, insurance and tax cost will generally vary directly with the level of the investment in inventory.

The labor costs involved in inventory levels includes stock maintenance, supervision, and paper supplies. These costs will generally vary as a combination of step functions and direct ratios. Normally, addition or reduction of labor is not directly proportional to inventory level (at least in the short run), but changes in discrete steps. The level of supplies used (record keeping) will vary much more directly with the inventory level.

BASES FOR INVENTORY COST DETERMINATION

These costs may be combined into the following groups: (1) the cost of money tied up in inventory and insurance plus taxes on items in inventory, which concerns average investment in inventory and interest, insurance, and tax rate; (2) the cost of storage space, which concerns volume and density; and (3) the cost due to obsolescence and deterioration, which concerns time in inventory.

In item (1), the cost of the money tied up in the inventory or the interest on the investment in the inventory usually comprises the highest percentage of over-all inventory costs. The interest rate selected is essentially an opportunity cost, and may be based upon the cost of borrowing money, the current rate of profit of the company, or some other figure. The opportunity cost concept is based upon the assumption that if this amount of money were not tied up in inventory, it could be invested in other activities which would return the assumed rate of interest or profit.

Insurance and taxes on inventory can be determined by an analysis of cost-accounting data. Specifically, taxes and insurance are paid by the company periodically, based on the inventory capital. These costs are reduced to an average percentage of the capital in-

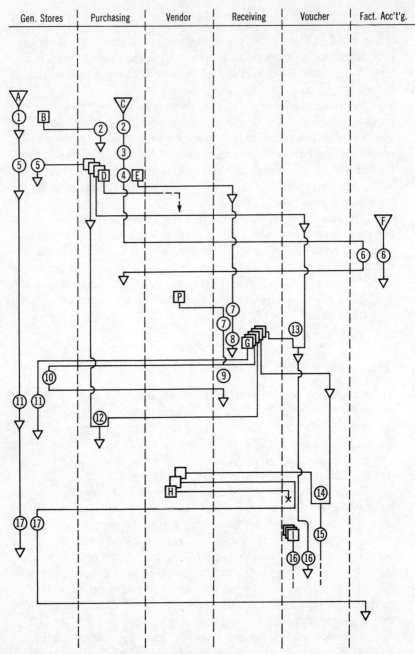

Gen. Stores | Purchasing | Vendor | Receiving | Voucher | Fact. Acc't'g.

Figure 12-1. *A Flow Process Chart.*

316

1. Write requirements (taken from General Stores Record) on 8½ x 11 paper. (B) Send to Purchasing.
2. Pull traveling requisition (C) from file, record requirement, file 8½ x 11 paper.
3. Negotiate price and delivery with vendor, assign purchase order number.
4. Type four copies of purchase order (D), one master receiving report (E). This is all done with a single typing. Send purchase order copies as follows:

      (1) To General Stores   (1) To Vendor
      (1) To Voucher   (1) To Buyer
      Send master receiving report to Receiving

5. Record in General Stores record purchase order information. File purchase order.
6. Send traveling requisition to Factory Accounting. Record price in General Stores Cost record.
7. Goods and packing slip are received—the information is posted to the master receiving report.
8. Five ditto copies of the receiving report are run off.

      (2) To General Stores   (1) To Purchasing
      (2) To Voucher

9. One copy of the receiving report and the packing slip are combined and sent to General Stores.
10. Receiving report and packing slip are signed, sent back to receiving, and filed.
11. Information from receiving report is posted to General Stores record. Receiving report is then filed.
12. Receiving report is attached to purchase order and filed.
13. Three copies of invoice are received from vendor—one is destroyed, one is sent to General Stores, one is attached to a receiving report.
14. The voucher is made up from information on receiving report and invoice.
15. Payment is recorded on copy of receiving report and purchase order.
16. The price is posted from the invoice to the General Stores record. The invoice is sent to Factory Accounting and filed.

CODE FOR VARIOUS FORMS AND RECORDS USED ON FLOW PROCESS CHART—
GENERAL STORES PURCHASING

A. General Stores Records
B. Standard 8½ x 11 Paper—indicating General Stores requirements
C. Traveling Requisition
D. Purchase Order
E. Receiving Report Master
F. General Stores Cost Records
G. Receiving Report
H. Invoice
I. Voucher
J. Packing Slip

vested in inventory, which would be added to the primary cost of the capital invested in inventory.

The second cost component contributing to total inventory level cost is storage. Either private or public warehousing can be used for inventory storage. The private warehouse is owned or rented by the company. The cost of renting or owning these buildings must be included in the cost of storage. The cost of insurance for the buildings and of light, depreciation, heat, maintenance, etc. must also be included. In the public warehouse, space is rented at a nominal cost which includes the warehouse insurance cost, warehouse company profit, and the cost of associated maintenance. Whichever method is used, the associated cost must be included in the total inventory costs.

The third component, deterioration and obsolescence, depends upon the type of products in inventory and the length of time that they remain there. These costs are usually very small in comparison to the over-all costs, unless perishable products are considered. In many cases, these costs are assumed to be negligible. However, cost accounting information would furnish data necessary in determining whether this assumption is valid. If not, they would have to be accounted for in determining the total costs.

GENERAL MODEL FOR DETERMINING TOTAL STORAGE COSTS

Let us attempt to construct a general model for determining total storage costs. A single expression would be as follows:

$$\text{Total Cost} = \sum_{i=1}^{n} C_i = C_1 + C_2 + \ldots + C_n$$

where C_i = total storage cost of good i
  = interest, insurance, tax cost + space cost + labor cost + obsolescence and wastage cost for good i

This can be expressed as

C_i = (average dollar inventory for i)(interest + insurance + tax rates)
  + (warehouse costs)(percentage space for i)
  + (labor cost)(percentage labor for i)
  + (total obsolescence cost)

$$\times \frac{\text{(total dollar inventory for } i)}{\text{(total dollar inventory for all goods)}}$$

Using mathematical notation, we can express the above as

$$C_i = (Cg_i)\left(\frac{\sum_{t=1}^{365} Il_{it}}{365}\right)(Ir + Irr + Tr) + TwSp_i + TlLp_i$$

$$+ (To)\left[\frac{(Cg_i)\left(\frac{\sum_{t=1}^{365} Il_{it}}{365}\right)}{\sum_{j=1}^{n} (Cg_j)\left(\frac{\sum_{t=1}^{365} Il_{it}}{365}\right)}\right]$$

and Cg_i = unit cost of good i
 Il_{it} = units of inventory of good i on day t
 Ir = interest rate
 Irr = insurance rate
 Tr = tax rate
 Tw = total warehouse cost
 Sp_i = percentage of warehouse space devoted to good i
 Tl = total labor cost (clerical, supervision, paper supplies)
 Lp_i = percentage of labor attributed to good i
 To = total obsolescence cost

ECONOMIC ORDER QUANTITY

The two main components of inventory costs—ordering, and holding and handling—are now analyzed to determine the economic order quantity and the reorder level. To do this, the following equations are used:

EOQ = Economic order quantity, the order quantity producing the lowest total cost
 I = Interest and holding cost storage costs as a percentage of unit cost
 P = Unit cost
 HC = Total holding cost
 Q = Annual demand
 C = Ordering cost per purchase order
 OC = Total ordering cost
 TC = Total cost

Total cost is equal to the sum of the total order costs and the total holding cost expressed as

$$TC = HC + OC$$

and total holding cost equals the average inventory, $\dfrac{(EOQ)}{2}$, times the unit holding costs, $(I \times P)$,

$$HC = \frac{EOQ}{2} \times I \times P$$

Also, total order cost equals the number of orders per year, $\dfrac{Q}{EOQ}$, times the ordering cost per purchase order

$$OC = \frac{Q}{EOQ} \times C$$

Therefore, the equation for total cost is:

$$TC = \frac{EOQ}{2} \times I \times P + \frac{Q}{EOQ} \times C$$

This function, as shown in Figure 12-2, indicates that cost is high for small orders because of the order costs involved and for large order quantities because of the holding costs. The object is to determine the order quantity where total cost is at a minimum, indicated as point L.

There are two ways to determine this minimum point. First, one can start with a low value for EOQ and successively increase it by small steps. At first the value of TC will fall, but at some point it will

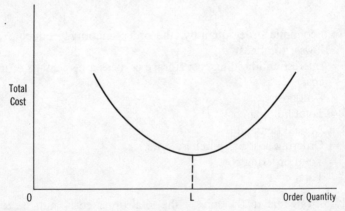

Figure 12-2. *The Order Cost Curve.*

begin to rise; this would indicate the minimum point. Second, one can use calculus and differentiate the function with respect to the order quantity. This would provide us with the equation for the slope or tangent of the function at any point. We know that the slope is equal to zero at the minimum point. Therefore, we would set the equation to zero and solve for *EOQ*.

$$\frac{d(TC)}{d(EOQ)} = \frac{d}{d(EOQ)} \left(\frac{EOQ}{2} \times I \times P + \frac{Q}{EOQ} \times C \right)$$

Differentiating the above results in

$$\frac{d(TC)}{d(EOQ)} = \frac{I \times P}{2} - \frac{2Q \times C}{EOQ^2}$$

Set the above equal to zero and

Then

$$\frac{I \times P}{2} = \frac{2Q \times C}{EOQ^2}$$

$$EOQ^2 = \frac{2Q \times C}{I \times P}$$

$$EOQ = \sqrt{\frac{2Q \times C}{I \times P}}$$

As an example, assume the following values:

$$Q = 1825 \text{ (5 units per day for 365 days)}$$
$$C = \$2.46$$
$$I = 20 \text{ per cent}$$
$$P = \$50.00$$
$$\text{Lead Time} = 3 \text{ days}$$

Solving for *EOQ*, we get 30 units (to the nearest whole unit). We know that demand during lead time is 15 units (3 days lead time times 5 units demanded per day). Therefore, the reorder level is 15 units. The maximum planned inventory is 30 units, the same as the order quantity.

With the foregoing in mind, a static inventory is presented in Figure 12-3. When the firm runs out of stock at the end of the sixth, twelfth, and eighteenth days, new stock arrives. Thirty units are re-

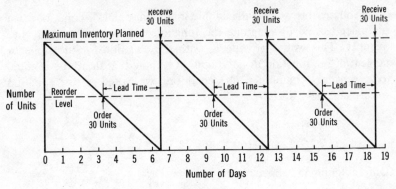

Figure 12-3. *A Static Inventory Model.*

ceived, bringing the inventory level up to the maximum planned level. These units were ordered when the stock level fell to 15 units, at the end of the third, ninth, and fifteenth days.

STATISTICS FOR EFFECTIVE CONTROL

In this section, we will discuss a variety of statistical tools that can be used to gain more effective control over inventories. This will include such tools as probability, model building, expected value, conditional probability, forecasting, and time series.

PROBABILITY

Much business activity occurs by chance. For example, the number of customers desiring a particular product on any one day, the number of those customers who are financially able to make the purchase, and the number of those who visit a particular store on the day in question are all based upon chance. The study of such chance occurrences is the study of probability.

The object of probability studies is to build some mathematical model that will depict the chance occurrences of the real world. There is no such thing as a "correct model." It is just that some models are more correct than others. The model to be chosen at any particular time is the one that is best supported by empirical evidence. An example of models and how we might chose the most "correct" one follows.

Suppose we toss two identical coins one at a time. The probability model of such an experiment might be Table 12-1, Model I or Model II.

TABLE 12-1. *Probability Model A*

MODEL I		MODEL II	
Outcomes	Probability	Outcomes	Probability
2 Heads	1/3	2 Heads	1/4
1 Head, 1 Tail	1/3	1 Head, 1 Tail	1/2
2 Tails	1/3	2 Tails	1/4
	1		1

Here we have a choice of models. Which one is more "correct?" If we examine the possible outcomes in more detail, it should be possible to make a choice. The first coin tossed will be a head or a tail. If it is a head, then the second coin tossed also will be a head or a tail. If the first coin is a tail, then the second can still be a head or a tail. Let us construct a model showing these outcomes rather than the simple outcomes that are listed in the first two models.

TABLE 12-2. *Probability Model B*

OUTCOMES	1ST COIN	2ND COIN	PROBABILITY
2 Heads	Head	Head	1/4
1 Head, 1 Tail	Head	Tail	1/4
1 Head, 1 Tail	Tail	Head	1/4
2 Tails	Tail	Tail	1/4
			1

It is obvious that Model II is more correct than Model I. In any probability model where it is possible to list all the outcomes, a more correct model will generally result from doing so.

The applicability of the above models to business can be seen if we take sales data from a firm and try to develop the probability of sales for any given day. Suppose the data may be arranged as in Table 12-3:

TABLE 12-3. *A Probability Table for Sales Data*

SALES PER DAY	FREQUENCY	PROBABILITY
0	0	0/60 = 0
1	10	10/60 = 1/6
2	15	15/60 = 3/12
3	25	25/60 = 5/12
4	10	10/60 = 1/6
5 or more	0	0/60 = 0
TOTAL	60	60/60 = 1

After arranging the sales per day and the corresponding frequencies in Columns (1) and (2), we can then determine the probability of sales per day in Column (3). The total sample size is determined by the number of observations, in this case 60. To find the probability of an event, divide the frequency of the event by the total number of observations. The event of two units of sales per day occurred 15 times in a total number of 60 days observed. The probability of that event is $3/12$. It should be noted that probabilities are stated in fractions or decimals less than one, and that the sum of the probabilities for all possible events must total one.

CUMULATIVE PROBABILITY

Quite often one needs to know the cumulative probability of an event. By rewriting Table 12-3, this type of information can be provided easily. For example, the probability of selling two or more units per day is $5/6$.

TABLE 12-4. *A Cumulative Probability Table*

SALES PER DAY	PROBABILITY SALES $= X$	PROBABILITY SALES $\geq X$
0	0	1
1	1/6	1
2	3/12	5/6
3	5/12	7/12
4	1/6	1/6
5 or more	0	0

EXPECTED VALUES

The term *expected value* is the same as a weighted average. The weights applied are the probabilities of the events occurring. Suppose that we are interested in the average or expected sales per day for the system we have just been studying. The procedure is to multiply the number of sales per day times its probability, then add this column of figures. The total will be the expected sales per day.

TABLE 12-5. *Expected Value*

SALES PER DAY	PROBABILITY	COLUMN 1 $\times$ COLUMN 2
0	0	0
1	1/6	1/6
2	3/12	3/6
3	5/12	15/12
4	1/6	2/3
5 or more	0	0

Expected Sales Per Day $= 31/12 = 2\frac{7}{12}$ Units

Often the businessman must decide between two courses of action. He is interested in the expected payoff or losses. If he can predict the probabilities of events which might occur and the gains and losses associated with the decisions and the events, he can determine the expected value of each decision. Suppose there are three possible events, a, b and c, and that the probabilities of these events are $\frac{1}{8}$, $\frac{1}{2}$ and $\frac{3}{8}$ respectively. Also there are two possible decisions with payoffs as listed in Table 12-6.

TABLE 12-6. *Assumed Alternative Payoffs*

EVENT	DECISION 1	DECISION 2
a	($1000)	$ 0
b	$2000	$2000
c	$4000	$2500

This can be put into the form of Table 12-7 to determine the expected values of each decision.

TABLE 12-7. *Expected Values of Alternative Decisions*

Event	(2) PROBABILITY	(3) DECISION 1	(2) TIMES (3)	(4) DECISION 2	(2) TIMES (4)
a	1/8	($1000)	($125)	$ 0	$ 0
b	1/2	$2000	$1000	$2000	$1000
c	3/8	$4000	$1500	$2500	$ 937.50
	EXPECTED VALUE		$2375		$1937.50

It is clear that Decision 1 has a higher expected value than Decision 2 ($2375 as compared to $1937.50). Then the businessman must decide whether he wants to gamble the possible loss of $1000 for an expected gain of $434.50 ($2375–$1937.50) over Decision 2.

CONDITIONAL PROBABILITY

Conditional probability comes into play whenever there are two sets of events and the probability of an event's occurring in the second set depends upon the outcome of the first. Suppose that there are three urns; one green, one yellow and the other blue. The green urn contains five white balls and five black balls. The yellow urn contains five white and ten black balls. The blue contains ten white and five black balls. The model of conditional probabilities would appear as in Table 12-8:

TABLE 12-8. *Model of Conditional Probabilities*

URN	PROBABILITY	BALL	CONDITIONAL PROBABILITY	GENERAL PROBABILITY
Green	1/3	White	5/10 = 1/2	1/2 × 1/3 = 1/6
		Black	5/10 = 1/2	1/2 × 1/3 = 1/6
Yellow	1/3	White	5/15 = 1/3	1/3 × 1/3 = 1/9
		Black	10/15 = 2/3	2/3 × 1/3 = 2/9
Blue	1/3	White	10/15 = 2/3	2/3 × 1/3 = 2/9
		Black	5/15 = 1/3	1/3 × 1/3 = 1/9
				TOTAL = 1

The general probability of picking a white ball is $\frac{1}{2}$ whenever we do not know the urn from which the ball is to be drawn. However, if we do know which urn is used, we can give the conditional probability of drawing a white ball. Given the yellow urn, the probability of a white ball is $\frac{1}{3}$. Given the blue urn, the probability of a white ball is $\frac{2}{3}$. The above model allows us to make more accurate predictions, given prior information as to the urn to be used.

JOINT PROBABILITY

The business world is often interested in joint probability distributions, particularly the probability distribution of demand during lead time. Demand may have a certain probability distribution and lead time another. Let us examine the case where lead time can be 1, 2 or 3 days, with a probability of $\frac{1}{4}$, $\frac{1}{2}$ and $\frac{1}{4}$ respectively. Demand can be 1 or 2 units per day, with a probability distribution of $\frac{2}{3}$ and $\frac{1}{3}$ respectively. Table 12-9 is a complete table of events (see p. 328).

To use the information in the above table, it is necessary to construct another table. The necessary information is the probability distribution of demand during lead time. To get this information, add the probabilities for each demand possibility. For example, the demand of two units during lead time has a probability of $9/108 + 24/108$ or $33/108$. Table 12-10 shows demand for the other possibilities:

TABLE 12-10. *Probability of Demand during Lead Time*

DEMAND DURING LEAD TIME	PROBABILITY OF DEMAND $= (x)$	PROBABILITY OF DEMAND $> (x)$
1	18/108	90/108
2	33/108	57/108
3	32/108	25/108
4	18/108	7/108
5	6/108	1/108
6	1/108	0

This table also has the cumulative probability distribution of demand during lead time, which is useful when one is considering safety stocks or service levels.[2] If the reorder point is established at 5

[2] The idea of safety stocks in inventory management stems from the inability of the firm to accurately predict demand during any reorder period. The firm is attempting to hedge against greater than average demand during lead time by adding some arbitrary extra amounts to its inventory. A more sophisticated method of hedging is to establish a service level to set the reorder point.

TABLE 12-9. *Model of Joint Probabilities*

LEAD TIME	PROBABILITY OF LEAD TIME	DEMAND	PROBABILITY OF DEMAND	DEMAND DURING LEAD TIME	PROBABILITY OF DEMAND DURING LEAD TIME
1	1/4	1	2/3	1	$1/4 \times 2/3 = 18/108$
		2	1/3	2	$1/4 \times 1/3 = 9/108$
2	1/2	1, 1	$2/3 \times 2/3 = 4/9$	2	$1/2 \times 4/9 = 24/108$
		1, 2	$2/3 \times 1/3 = 2/9$	3	$1/2 \times 2/9 = 12/108$
		2, 1	$1/3 \times 2/3 = 2/9$	3	$1/2 \times 2/9 = 12/108$
		2, 2	$1/3 \times 1/3 = 1/9$	4	$1/2 \times 1/9 = 6/108$
3	1/4	1, 1, 1	$2/3 \times 2/3 \times 2/3 = 8/27$	3	$1/4 \times 8/27 = 8/108$
		1, 1, 2	$2/3 \times 2/3 \times 1/3 = 4/27$	4	$1/4 \times 4/27 = 4/108$
		1, 2, 1	$2/3 \times 1/3 \times 2/3 = 4/27$	4	$1/4 \times 4/27 = 4/108$
		1, 2, 2	$2/3 \times 1/3 \times 1/3 = 2/27$	5	$1/4 \times 2/27 = 2/108$
		2, 1, 1	$1/3 \times 2/3 \times 2/3 = 4/27$	4	$1/4 \times 4/27 = 4/108$
		2, 1, 2	$1/3 \times 2/3 \times 1/3 = 2/27$	5	$1/4 \times 2/27 = 2/108$
		2, 2, 1	$1/3 \times 1/3 \times 2/3 = 2/27$	5	$1/4 \times 2/27 = 2/108$
		2, 2, 2	$1/3 \times 1/3 \times 1/3 = 1/27$	6	$1/4 \times 1/27 = 1/108$
					TOTAL $= 108/108 = 1$

units, the probability of not meeting demand would be 1/108, and the service level would be 99+%. If the reorder point is 4 units, the probability of being out of stock during the reorder period would be 7/108, or the service level would be 93+%.

The lead time and demand possibilities that were used in the last table are not representative of the real world. A three-day lead time is rather short, and demand is often in units of hundreds or more. Because of the larger numbers found in real life, the construction of a table showing probability distribution becomes a physical impossibility using manual methods (see a later section on simulation). Fourteen separate events were analyzed in the simple example. An actual problem might run into the millions. The formula for calculating the number of events is:

$$\sum_{L=\text{Lower lim } L}^{\text{Upper lim } L} (D\text{ Max} - D\text{ Min} + 1)^L$$

where D max is maximum demand per day
        D min is minimum demand per day
        D is continuous in integer form
        L is lead time days
        (D max − D min + 1) could also be stated as the total number of different possibilities of demand per day

FORECASTING

A good forecast is the key to effective inventory control. If management knows with some degree of certainty the expected demand upon the inventory, customers can be satisfied and costs can be minimized. It is important that a forecast cover the time lapse required for decision-making and the necessary time to allow the decision to become effective. In other words, the forecast must cover the total lead time period. It should also cover the expected time lapse between ordering periods.

A forecast, as used here, is an objective analysis of past data projected into the future. It may be modified by a prediction based

---

Service level is a term used to indicate the probability of meeting or servicing the customer demand. A 90% service level means that demand will be met 90% of the time during the reorder periods. The firm must attempt to determine the out of stock costs for a particular item and balance this with the costs of holding the extra inventory.

upon a subjective evaluation of the future. A firm may be planning some special promotion or selling campaign which should be subjectively evaluated in order to modify the sales forecast. Many such other events fall into this category of prediction. It is not the purpose of this section to discuss this type of subjective analysis; we will be concerned with forecasting.

TIME SERIES ANALYSIS

The definition of forecasting leads directly into time series analysis. A time series is an arrangement of statistical data in a chronological order. Analyses of this data are made in order to describe and measure the changes or movements in the series during a period of time. There are four different classifications of change or movement:

1. Trend—a secular movement, a long time growth or decline.
2. Seasonal pattern—an almost regular movement within the 12 month period which occurs every year and is caused by the changing seasons.
3. Cyclical patterns—these patterns are generally caused by the business cycle, and swing from prosperity through recession, depression, recovery, and returns to prosperity. Cyclical patterns are irregular and vary in length and intensity. As such, they are beyond the scope of this text.
4. Non-repetitive movements—such movements are caused by accidents or unusual conditions such as strikes, wars, disasters, or other non-recurring conditions. Generally, these observations are removed from the data when trends are being analyzed.

The most commonly used methods to analyze data for trends are: freehand, semi-average, moving average,[3] exponential smoothing, and least squares. Each of these methods will be examined briefly, with comments on their respective advantages and disadvantages.

FREEHAND METHOD

The freehand method fits a trend line by eye to data plotted on a graph. Transparent straight-edges or "French" curves are often used

---

[3] The moving average is the most commonly used method for forecasting business trends.

for neatness. The obvious advantages of this method are its speed and simplicity. Another advantage is that some data are not susceptible to mathematical description of the long-time trend. The freehand method is not limited to such mathematical models. However, the method is not entirely objective, and much practice is required to become accomplished.

SEMI-AVERAGE METHOD

In the semi-average method, the data is split into two halves. An average is found for each half and is plotted at the midpoint of its respective period. A straight line is then drawn between the two points and this represents the trend. This method also possesses relative speed and simplicity. A major disadvantage is that it uses the arithmetic mean, which is greatly affected by extreme values. Also, it is slow to react to change; a good forecasting device should be able to detect a change in trend rapidly.

MOVING AVERAGE METHOD

The moving average method of trend analysis is a series of successive averages determined by averaging successive groups of data. The first item in a group is dropped, and the next item not in the group is added to it. Suppose we are interested in analyzing the trend in the data found in Column 2 in Table 12-11, using a three period moving

TABLE 12-11. *The Use of Moving Totals and Averages*

1 TIME PERIOD	2 OBSERVATIONS	3 3-ITEM MOVING TOTAL	4 3-ITEM MOVING AVERAGE
$t+1$	3		
$t+2$	5	12	4
$t+3$	4	15	5
$t+4$	6	21	7
$t+5$	11	27	9
$t+6$	10	33	11
$t+7$	12	36	12
$t+8$	14	39	13
$t+9$	13		

average. The first three numbers (3, 5, 4) are added together. The total is entered in Column 3 and the average is entered in Column 4. Next (3) is dropped from the group and (6) is added. The total again is entered in Column 3 and the average in Column 4. This continues until all the data is used.

An advantage of this method is that only simple computations are used. The disadvantages are numerous: (1) moving average always underestimates an upturning trend and produces a higher estimate than the true trend in a downturn; (2) the average is arithmetical and greatly affected by extreme values; and (3) it is not quick to spot a change in the trend.

EXPONENTIAL SMOOTHING METHOD

Exponential smoothing is a refinement of the moving average method. It fits a trend to the most recent data, and can be thought of as a weighted moving average method.

If S_t is the current forecast estimate, it can be found from the following formula:

$$S_t = \alpha x_t + (1 - \alpha)S_t - 1$$

where α = the smoothing constant
         x_t = actual current demand
   $S_t - 1$ = previous forecast estimate

TABLE 12-12. *Equivalence Table*

α	EQUIVALENT NUMBER OF PERIODS IN A MOVING AVERAGE
.500	3
.400	4
.333	5
.300	5.67
.286	6
.200	9
.154	12
.105	18
.100	19
.080	24
.050	39
.038	52
.010	199

The smoothing constant may be chosen in the same manner as one chooses the number of periods for a moving average. See Table 12-12.[4]

The advantages of such a method are ease of computation and speed in spotting changes in the trend (for a function of α, the larger the α, the faster a change is noted). The method lacks complete objectivity because of the subjective choice of α.

LEAST SQUARES METHOD

This is a method of fitting a straight line to the data in order to indicate the trend. The principle underlying the least squares method states that a line of best fit to a series is a line about which the sum of the squares of the deviations will be a minimum. There can be only one line with this characteristic. The deviations that concern us are the differences between the observed (actual) values and the line, or forecasted, values.

A straight line may be algebraically described as $Y = a + bX$. The X value in this particular equation is a time period, and Y is forecast as the value for that particular time period. The constants a and b are found by solving the following set of simultaneous equations:

(1)
$$\Sigma(Y) = Na + b\Sigma(X)$$
(2)
$$\Sigma(XY) = a\Sigma(X) + b\Sigma(X^2)$$

A sample problem is presented to demonstrate this method. Suppose the data resembles that in Table 12-13.

This trend line has been plotted on Figure 12-4. Note its relationship to the observed values.

There are certain advantages to this method. One is that the trend is expressed in a mathematical formula which can easily be interpreted. Others are that it is objective and a convenient form for extrapolation into the future. Some of its disadvantages are: (1) it is more difficult to compute: (2) it is based upon the assumption that the trend is linear; and (3) it is not quick to note changes in the trend.

---

[4] R. G. Brown, *Smoothing, Forecasting and Prediction of Discrete Time Series* (Englewood Cliffs, N.J.: Prentice-Hall, 1962), p. 108.

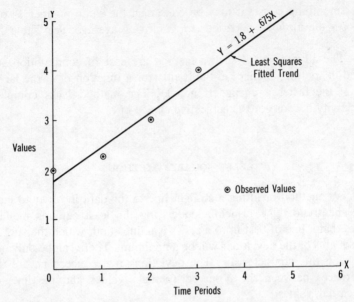

Figure 12-4. *Least Squares Method of Fitting Trends.*

TABLE 12-13. *Least Squares Method*

X	Y	XY	X^2
0	2	0	0
1	2.25	2.25	1
2	3	6	4
3	4	12	9
6	11.25	20.25	14
$\Sigma(X)$	$\Sigma(Y)$	$\Sigma(XY)$	$\Sigma(X^2)$

$N = 4$ (number of observations, time periods). Then by

(1) $$11.25 = 4a + 6b$$

and

(2). $$20.25 = 6a + 14b.$$

Then from (1)

$$a = \frac{11.25 - 6b}{4}$$

and substituting in (2)

$$20.25 = \frac{6(11.25 - 6b)}{4} + 14b$$

$$b = .675$$
$$a = 1.8.$$

Therefore

$$Y = 1.8 + .675X$$

Forecast error involves consideration of how far wrong the estimates are from reality and the probability of being off by any given amount. The forecast error may be computed in one of two ways. The most commonly used method is to compute the standard error of the forecast. The other method is to compute the mean absolute deviation. Both methods are equally acceptable. The first has the advantages of precalculated tables and common usage. The latter is easier to compute.

The standard error of the forecast(s) is obtained by the following formula:

$$s = \sqrt{\frac{\sum_{i=1}^{N} (\hat{x}_i - x_i)^2}{N}}$$

where $\hat{x}_i$ = the estimate (forecasted value) for time period i
x_i = the actual (observed) value for time period i
N = the total number of time periods observed

The mean absolute deviation (MAD) can be obtained by using the formula below:

$$MAD = \sum_{i=1}^{N} \frac{|\hat{x}_i - x_i|}{N}$$

The mean absolute deviation is considered to be approximately equal to 0.8 of the standard error of the forecast.[5]

The deviations about the estimated (forecasted) values generally tend to have a normal distribution, even though the deviations about the mean of the data are not normal.[6] This bit of information can be a guide in solving inventory problems. In a normally distributed random variable, two-thirds of all values fall between the points plus and minus one standard deviation from the mean. We also know that between plus and minus three standard deviations from the estimate, we will find 99+% of all the values. In this particular case, we would substitute the estimate for the mean. There are tables available

[5] R. G. Brown, *op. cit.*, p. 283.
[6] This is not always true. A check on the data should be made before using this assumption.

that give the probabilities for any range of deviations. Figure 12-5 presents this visually.

Since there are no tables readily available that give the same type of information for the mean absolute deviation it will be neces-

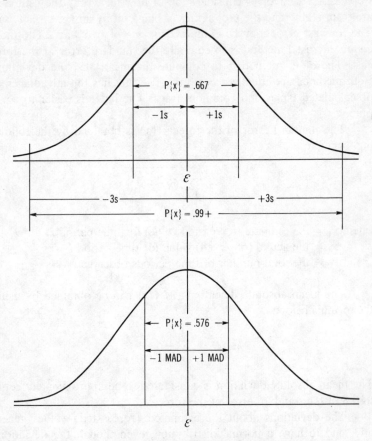

$\mathcal{E}$ = the estimate (forecasted value)

Figure 12-5. *Values in a Randomly Distributed Variable.*

sary to convert to standard deviations. This becomes a rather simple task, since s = 1.2 (*MAD*). As an example, suppose that the forecast for the next time period is for 50 units, and that we have found that the *MAD* from our past observations is 3 units. We can convert the *MAD* into a standard error and find that s = 3.6. By checking a table of normal values, we find that, if we are interested in the 90%

confidence interval of the demand for the next period, the range will be ± 1.65 standard errors. When we say 90% confidence interval, we mean that we have confidence that the values will fall within this interval 90% of the time. This could also be stated as $P\{x$ falls within the interval$\} = .90$. Therefore, we will have a 90% confidence that demand for the next period will be $50 \pm 1.65s$ or 50 ± 5.94 units.

DYNAMIC INVENTORY CONTROL

The economic order quantity model discussed earlier in the chapter was a static model in which the factors did not vary. Static analysis is often the only convenient way to handle a business problem. The complexities facing the decision maker may be too great, and this approach becomes the only way out. Also, a static approach often leads to the real essence of the problem, in which the relevant issues stand out clearly. Often many of the variations cancel each other out and, through the use of averages, the solutions have a good probability of being correct. Static analysis may also be used to obtain a first approximation answer and to lead to a better dynamic analysis.

Dynamic control of inventory involves consideration of exogenous and endogenous variables. *Exogenous variables* are the result of the forces which originate outside the firm's control but affect the firm's activities, and *endogenous variables* are those under the control of the firm. The exogenous variables are treated as random forces to which probability techniques may be applied. Endogenous variables are treated as non-random.

Two exogenous variables are demand for the company's products and lead time on purchase orders. The firm aspires to a certain growth in the demand for its products. Some of the growth can be attributed to the demand creation activities of the firm, the balance to the general acceptance pattern for the product. This demand fluctuates by day, week, month, season, and year; thus, the number of customers deciding to buy a particular product is different at any moment. Demand may be treated as being randomly variable.

Lead time on purchase orders is another exogenous variable. The two factors which affect lead time are the time at which the order is placed and the status of current orders at the vendor. Time of order placement is important since, in some companies, a run of a particular size and specification of product (for example, steel) is scheduled for a particular time of the month; proper order scheduling will often reduce lead time. Status of orders is important, since a backlog of orders will tend to increase lead time. For the most part, lead time may be considered a random variable affected by many diverse elements such as weather, mechanical and technical delays, scheduling difficulties, transportation, and labor difficulties. Generally, the random elements that the firm cannot control are those external to the firm.

Two examples of endogenous variables are inventory levels and lead time to the customer. Inventory levels, a function of demand and lead time, both exogenous random variables, may be controlled within certain limits; i.e., the firm is capable of establishing policies governing inventory that will control the levels. If the firm is able to determine the probability distributions of demand during lead time, the costs of being out of stock, and the costs of ordering and holding stock, it may be able to adjust its ordering policies to get the most profits from the sale of inventory.

Lead time to the customer is another internal random variable. The time that a customer must wait for service, delivery or backorders, or the time that a truck must wait to be loaded, is connected with the arrival rate of customers, orders, or trucks and of the service time required. Waiting line or queuing theory has been developed to help solve problems of this nature.[7]

THE DIFFERENCE BETWEEN STATIC
AND DYNAMIC MODELS

Let us compare the difference between static and dynamic conditions by looking at two inventory models. Figure 12-3 represents the static model, and Figure 12-6 the dynamic.

Figure 12-6 shows an inventory model that more closely approaches the dynamics of the real world. The average demand and lead time are the same as in Figure 12-3, but demand has been allowed to vary, as in Table 12-14.

The effects are immediately obvious. On the 7th day there was an excess of 5 units over maximum planned inventory. On the 12th

[7] Philip M. Morse, *Queues, Inventories and Maintenance* (New York: John Wiley & Sons, Inc., 1958).

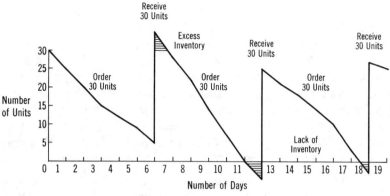

Figure 12-6. *A Dynamic Inventory Model.*

and 18th days, the firm was unable to meet the demand by 5 and 3 units respectively.

Now consider what might have happened if lead time were also variable. If, on the first order, lead time were shorter than average, the

TABLE 12-14.   *Assumed Demand over Time*

DAY	DEMAND	DAY	DEMAND
1	5	11	7
2	5	12	5
3	5	13	4
4	3	14	3
5	3	15	4
6	4	16	4
7	7	17	7
8	6	18	6
9	8	19	2
10	7	AVERAGE	5

excess inventory would have been even greater. And if, on the second and third orders, it were longer than average, even more demand would not have been met. If the reverse had occurred, there would have been a dampening effect. A sudden surge of unplanned inventory can be quite expensive. Sometimes the expense is demurrage charges, and at other times it is the cost of public or rented warehouse space, with its attendant extra handling charges. The inability to meet demand can be very serious. The firm's product may have many good substitutes, and the unfilled demand may be lost. If nothing else, the customers are certainly inconvenienced.

There are two approaches to solving dynamic problems. One is *analysis,* and the other is *simulation.* Both are based upon probability, statistics, and mathematical relationships. Analysis attempts to seek out the various relationships and interactions, to develop statistical distributions in the system, and to solve mathematically for optimum solutions. Simulation involves the recreation of the firm and its relevant environment into a mathematical model. The model is then operated under various decision rules seeking some optimization.

ANALYTICAL METHODS

Analytical methods stress an effort to discover the relationships of the variables in the situation being studied, and then the best solution is sought. Generally, the solutions are based upon equating the expected gain with the expected loss.

A simple problem will demonstrate this method. Suppose we have the hot dog concession for the local college football games. Further, suppose that the only relevant costs are the costs of the hot dogs and the buns. The sale price of each hot dog is 15¢, and the cost is 10¢. If we do not bring enough hot dogs to the game, then our loss is the profits on the lost sales. If we bring too many, our loss is the cost of the extra hot dogs. This problem can be set up in the following manner.

The expected gain equals the profit per hot dog (G) times the cumulative probability of selling the hot dog (p).

$$E(\text{Gain}) = Gp$$

The expected loss equals the cost per hot dog (C) times the cumulative probability of not selling the hot dog $(1 - p)$.

$$E(\text{Loss}) = C(1 - p)$$

Then by equating the expected gain with the expected loss we get

$$E(\text{Gain}) = E(\text{Loss})$$
$$Gp = C(1 - p)$$
$$Gp = C - cp$$
$$Gp + Cp = C$$
$$p = \frac{C}{G + C}$$

In other words where the cumulative probability of sales is equal to $\dfrac{\text{Loss}}{\text{Gain} + \text{Loss},}$ then that number of hot dogs will be the optimum number of hot dogs to bring to the game. In the example, the probability would be $\dfrac{10}{5 + 10} = \frac{2}{3}$. If the cumulative probability of sales is as represented in Figure 12-7, we should bring 3800 hot dogs.

It should be recognized that this is a very simple model, and that every situation calls for a model to fit its own particular characteristics. A general dynamic model would be rather difficult to construct, and it would be too abstract to do much good. An example of a general model for inventory problems is shown in Footnote 8.[8]

Simulation assumes a set of relationships between selected variables and then proceeds to a calculation of results. The major reasons

[8] The following total cost inventory model might be considered a general model, with the idea in mind that it must be modified to fit a particular situation. Total cost is equal to the order costs plus the holding costs plus costs due to stock outs.

Let TC = Total Cost

and $\dfrac{SC}{Q}$ = Order costs where total annual sales (S) divided by the order quantity (Q) gives total number of orders per year. Multiply this by the cost per order (C) to get total ordering costs.

Let $\dfrac{QI}{2} + (R - M)I$ = Holding Costs where the order quantity (Q) divided by 2 gives the average inventory due to order quantity. Multiply this by holding cost per unit (I) to get partial holding costs. ($R - M$) gives the number of units in the inventory due to the reorder quantity being greater than the expected demand during lead time.

Let $\dfrac{S}{Q} \Lambda \sum\limits_{d=R}^{\infty} P(d > R)$ = Stock out costs where $\dfrac{S}{Q}$ gives the number order periods per year (or the number of times that stock out could occur).

Λ is the stock out penalty per unit.

$\sum\limits_{d=R}^{\infty} P(d > R)$ is the expected stock out per order period.

$P(d > R)$ is the probability that demand (d) will be greater than the reorder quantity;
Therefore:

$$TC = \frac{SC}{Q} + \left[\frac{Q}{2} + (R - M)\right] I + \frac{S}{Q} \Lambda \sum_{d=R}^{\infty} (d > R)$$

The solution is found by an iterative method due to the discontinuity of the function.

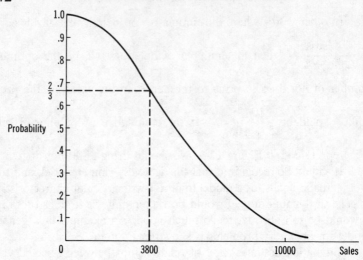

Figure 12-7. *Cumulative Probability of Hot Dog Sales Per Game.*

for simulation are time and complexity of relationships. Simulated time has two important characteristics: it may be compressed to speed solutions, and lead or lag times may be extremely important in the interdependent relationships of factors in the firm or system. Computers make it possible to obtain in a few minutes the experience of several years, a virtual impossibility with solely analytical techniques. The complex interrelationships in a system also make simulation desirable. Often analytical methods are impossible or impractical, and simulation is the only way to even approximate the best solution. An obvious advantage of simulation is that experimentation can occur without jeopardizing the firm in the market place.

Most simulations employ the Monte Carlo technique to simulate the chance or probability elements common to most dynamic situations. The elements or events that occur at random must be studied in order to determine their probability distributions. Then, as the time comes to check on the occurrence of the event, some random device is used along with the probability distribution. This makes the simulated event occur with the same frequency as the real event.

EXAMPLE OF A MONTE CARLO SIMULATION

Let us consider a particular problem involving the effects of ordering policies on inventory levels under uncertainty conditions of demand

and lead time. A firm's historical records indicate that demand has an average of five units per day and lead time has an average of two days. Further examination shows that the probability distributions of demand and lead time are as in Table 12-15.

The object of the Monte Carlo simulation will be to trace the day-to-day transactions of the firm as it is operating under the above

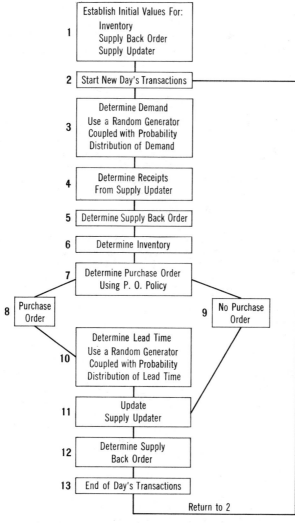

Figure 12-8. *Diagram of a Monte Carlo Simulation of Inventory Operation.*

TABLE 12-15. *Probabilities for Demand and Lead Time*

DEMAND		LEAD TIME	
Amount	Per Cent	Amount	Per Cent
4	40	1	30
5	30	2	40
6	20	3	30
7	10		

uncertainties. A diagrammatic sketch of this simulation is presented in Figure 12-8. Each of the steps is outlined below to allow manual operations.

1. Establish initial values for the system as follows:
   Inventory = 25 units
   Supply Back Order = 15 Units

   Supply Updater:

   > Supply 1 day away = 5 units
   > Supply 2 days away = 5 units
   > Supply 3 days away = 5 units

2. Start day's transactions: indicate day number.
3. Determine demand for the day:
   This requires the use of some random generating device to simulate the probability distribution of demand. As mentioned before, the distribution was as follows:

   > 4 units 40 per cent
   > 5 units 30 per cent
   > 6 units 20 per cent
   > 7 units 10 per cent

   In the computer, it is possible to construct a random number generator that will give a uniform distribution of numbers between 1 and 10. Therefore, we could assign the numbers 1-4 to a demand for 4 units, the numbers 5-7 to a demand for 5 units, the numbers 8-9 to a demand for 6 units, and the numbers 10 to a demand for 7 units.

   The same thing could be accomplished by putting numbered slips of paper in a box, the numbers ranging from 1 to 10. Drawing the numbers at random and replacing them will produce the same demand distribution as above. A spinner with equal divisions numbered 1 to 10 will do the same.

4. Determine the receipts from the supply updater: the receipts for the day are those that were in the supply one day away position the day before. Therefore, just transfer that value to receipts.

5. Determine supply back order:
Here we are interested in the balance on order with the supplier after receipts but prior to making a purchase order. To find this quantity, subtract receipts from the old supply back order.

6. Determine inventory:
Add receipts to the old inventory and subtract demand.

7. Determine purchase order:
The ordering policy must be predetermined. As an example, we might use the following policy:
Purchase order = 3 times current day's demand, less the total of inventory and supply backorder
and if the above is negative, Purchase Order = 0

8. Determine lead time:
Use a similar random generating device as in 3, but adjust it to the probability distribution of lead time.

9. Update supply updater:
Supply 1 day away = Supply 2 days away
Supply 2 days away = Supply 3 days away
Supply 3 days away = 0
Then add the purchase order quantity to the proper supply by days away according to lead time from 8.

10. Determine supply back order:
We now adjust the supply back order to pick up the purchase order and add the purchase order quantity to the supply back order.

11. End of day's transactions:
Start a new day by returning to 2.

To run this simulation by hand, set up a series of columns to record the transactions. Appropriate column headings are as follows:

Demand
Receipts
Supply back order (before purchase)
Inventory
Purchase Order
Lead Time
Updated Supply
  1 day away
  2 days away
  3 days away
Supply Back Order (end of day)

Experimentation may be carried on by varying the ordering policy. The resulting change in inventory levels can be noted. As an exercise, one might seek the policy that provides the lowest over-all level of inventory and runs out of stock only five per cent of the time.

Appendix to Chapter Twelve

A Simulation Problem

The ABC Company is negotiating for a contract to sell a certain bulk product to a customer in the United Kingdom. The customer has a fixed daily demand rate of 100 units of the product which is expected to remain constant for the duration of the contract. The customer requires a guarantee that its inventories will not fall below 250 units more than five per cent of the days in the year.

The ABC Company obtains its supply from a single source in Africa, which produces at a constant rate of 110 units per day. Three company owned ships, with a capacity of 625 units each, will be used exclusively for transport to the United Kingdom. The company owns a fixed storage with a capacity of 2100 units in Africa and 1250 units in the United Kingdom. There are two berths in Africa, where the ships can take on cargo, and one in the United Kingdom, for discharging cargo. The harbor facilities are large enough in both locations so as not to be considered limiting factors.

One full day in berth is required to load or unload a ship. A ship can neither enter nor leave a berth during a storm. Otherwise, the weather is assumed to have no effect upon the movement of the ships. Movement between ports is at a constant rate of one-eighth of the distance between the ports. Storms are seasonal; from April 1 to September 30 the probability of a storm in Africa is 0.2, and in the United Kingdom it is 0.1. During the remainder of the year, the probability of a storm is just reversed: 0.1 in Africa and 0.2 in the United Kingdom.

The company is faced with the problem of determining whether it can fulfill the terms of the contract without increasing its capacity at either port or adding more cargo vessels.

This is an ideal problem for simulation techniques. The situation can be visualized as in Figure 12-10. The circles numbered 1–7 indicate daily positions of the ships at sea going to the United Kingdom.

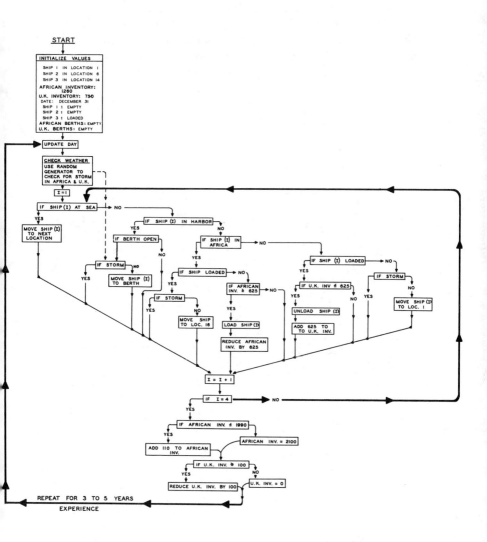

Figure 12-9. *Simulation Problem Chart A.*

Numbers 8 and 9 are the harbor and berths in Africa, and 17 and 18 are the harbor and berth in the United Kingdom.

To start the simulation, assume that all the ships are at sea in locations 1, 6 and 14. Also assume that the African inventory is 1260 units and the U.K. inventory is 750 units. The date is December 31. A diagram of the simulation appears in Figure 12-9.

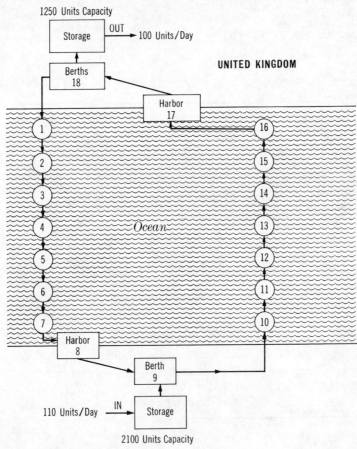

Figure 12-10. *Simulation Problem Chart B.*

This simulation can be carried on by using pennies for the ships. Daily movements can be simulated on Figure 12-10 and records kept indicating the inventories at each port. Storms can be generated using any of the manual random generators previously mentioned. What is your answer to the ABC Company's problem?

Appendix A

Carrier Pricing Theory and Policy

Carrier pricing theory and policy is curiously ambivalent. It possesses a great attraction because of its importance and the amount which has been written about it. Yet it seems almost impossible to agree on a definitive, universally accepted delineation of its significance, its manifestations, and its similarities to industrial pricing and policy.

Eliot Jones and others have said, "Carrier services are supplied under conditions of common costs[1] and the costs of transporting a particular commodity is therefore not ascertainable. . . . The apportionment can only be made on an arbitrary basis." [2]

Without making an actual check, it would appear that all texts and discussions in the field of economics since Adam Smith and before have stated that the two main elements in rate-making (carrier prices) or industrial pricing are cost of service, or what it costs the producer of the service or the goods to make these available, and what the customer or user of the goods or the service is willing or can afford to pay for it.

The cost of a specific part of the production of a transportation service, just as is the case with a commodity under common cost conditions, cannot be separated with precision and allocated to that service in accordance with the share of costs for which it is responsible. This has greater pertinence in railroad pricing than in motor carrier pricing; with the latter being a variable cost industry, it is easier to determine the out-of-pocket cost of transporting a particular truckload lot which moves by itself than that of a number of carload units moved at one time in a train.

When different commodities of different natures and values are in a train for varying distances, it has, heretofore, been most difficult

---

[1] The term "common costs" refers to non-separable costs accrued in the task of producing common transportation service for different commodities.

[2] Eliot Jones, *Principles of Railway Transportation* (New York: The Macmillan Company, 1929), p.85.

to develop an accurate pro rata allocation,[3] although more precise costing procedures and techniques may change this before long.

Competition, whether intramodal or intermodal, prevents rates from necessarily reflecting differences in the efficiency of the management of the carrier, in the economic prosperity of a particular territory covered, or in the number of firms with sidings on the carrier, either within urban centers or elsewhere on the line. A carrier cannot be bound by abstract theories of rate-making. If it is alert, it knows its total costs, although their allocation to commodities may be uncertain. It is becoming increasingly aware, through intensified marketing research, of what the shipper is willing to pay. Further, it has some idea of whether the regulatory agency will permit a base rate which covers all variable costs and contributes to overhead. Such a rate, which a lower cost carrier cannot meet, is often an inherent advantage. But the carrier's problem up to this point has been uncertainty as to whether this rate may be ruled to be a destructive rate practice by the Interstate Commerce Commission, violating the National Transportation Policy, with a resultant order to raise the rate to a basis on which the competing carrier can obtain a portion of the traffic.

A term which requires definition is *differential pricing,* which means discriminatory pricing which does not transgress the regulatory agency's interpretation of the standards of reasonableness which are included in the governing enactment. The term is not used in the sense of an unlawful rebate or some other concession from the published rate.

FULLY DISTRIBUTED COSTS

The term *fully distributed costs* is a difficult one, for it carries a different significance for different people. Ordinarily, it means that constant or overhead costs have been computed exactly, and that each commodity bears the same proportion of these costs, regardless of its ability to do so. It makes a nice neat formula to say that rate-making consists of adding to (A) the average variable cost (B) the amount derived from equal proration of all constant or overhead costs, with

---

[3] Even if possible, competition may well prevent the same rate's being applied for the same service in different areas where the commodity is the same, let alone where it is one of different value.

each ton-mile taking the same rate. Such is not the case. Ford Edwards, one of the outstanding transportation economists of our time, says that "nothing moves at fully distributed costs." [4]

The investment in railroad plant which is necessary before any traffic can move is so great at the start of the operation that no goods would be moved under any system of distributed costs, because of their cost being so great per unit.

Fully distributed costs, in effect, soak the present traffic with the cost of idle capacity. These abnormally high costs, when erroneously used as a rate floor, prohibit utilization of excess capacity by building a prohibitive wall around it. The assumption in using fully distributed costs as a rate floor is that there will always be the same ratio between traffic volume and plant capacity, regardless of the increase in volume. This is an untenable assumption. [5]

The conception of rate changes is that they will better volume. Should this be true, fully distributed costs will be higher per unit than warranted by the new traffic volume. Under the ICC formula, constant costs are allocated on the basis of weight. A heavily loaded car, more efficient and more productive, would be penalized if the program for increasing the weight per car is successful. The market place is the only reliable allocator of constant costs, since there is no one, universally-agreed upon basis for such allocation.

In addition, fully distributed cost pricing is unrealistic because of the failure to recognize that a low value commodity cannot absorb the same amount of constant costs as can a high value commodity, as for the one of low value the equivalent amount is a higher percentage of the market value. Such pricing policy also does not recognize that if the low value commodity is so over-priced that it cannot move, the rates which the high value commodities must pay may be even higher to make up for the revenue lost.

SIGNIFICANCE OF FULLY DISTRIBUTED COSTS

Generally speaking, economists use the term fully distributed costs in the sense of such costs being of long-term significance. The courts

---

[4] Ford K. Edwards, "Transportation Costs, Value-of-Service and Freight Rates," 21 *ICC Journal* 495. This is one of the best discussions on this subject which has come to our attention.

[5] John W. Ingram, "Fully Distributed Nonsense," *Railway Age,* Vol. 151, No. 23, December 4, 1961, p. 125.

follow this line of thought. For example, in *Dixie Carriers v. United States*,[6] the High Court said, ". . . the inherent advantage of lower costs refers to the long-run or fully distributed costs of carriage." We cannot concur with this if it relates to the rates on individual commodity movements, although we support this insofar as it relates to aggregate rates.

In *Air-Freight Investigation*,[7] the Civil Aeronautics Board said:

> We are of the opinion that *economic considerations do not demand that at all times the rates* for any class of traffic or type of service *must cover the fully allocated cost of carrying that traffic or providing that service; rather that rates at all times must reasonably be related to costs.* The test of reasonableness must include variations in the ability of traffic, the effect of new rates in generating new traffic and the resultant effect of increased volume in the reduction of unit cost. (Emphasis supplied)

The words emphasized signify that, while rates in the aggregate over a long term must cover all costs, they do not have to cover, at the time of movement, full average or fully distributed costs, in view of the varying ability of different commodities to stand the impact of freight rates. This conforms not only to current pricing application, but also to the realities of our economic structure, in reference to both carriers and industries. The carriers who contend so fervently that the railroads should be forced to rectify current pricing discrepancies and apply the fully distributed cost principle in their pricing should themselves apply the principle in their own pricing. Whenever they publish a special commodity rate, for example, they depart from the principle of fully distributed costs as they advocate it.

In spite of the fact that fully distributed costs has a well-defined meaning in economics, we submit that it is something of a misnomer if "fully" and "distributed" are intended to convey their normal meaning. The words, standing by themselves, seem to signify that costs must be "fairly apportioned" [8] so as to recover all money spent in providing the transportation service. They do not (or should not) denote that the rates for the transportation of a particular commodity have to bear the same proportion of variable costs and make the same

[6] 351 U.S. 56 (1956).
[7] 9 CAB 340 (1948). The same opinion was voiced by the Interstate Commerce Commission in *U.S. Sugar Corporation v. Atlantic Coast Line Railroad Company*, 277 ICC. 193 (1950).
[8] *Northern Pacific Railway v. North Dakota*, 236 U.S. 582 (1915).

contributions to constant costs and to profit as any other commodity, regardless of value. If we apply them to specific movements, we mean that "average pricing," which is unrealistic, would be disrupting to our economy, and would be against current practice. To apply differential pricing is not to denigrate the economic principle of resource allocation.

If this classic principle of resource allocation is to operate effectively, it would seem equitable to make certain that the present market mechanism is not disturbed, but that the recovery of full costs of providing the transportation services continues to be our aggregate long-run policy. This concept meets substantially the present definition of long-term, fully distributed costs, but if it is to be applied consistently, it should be extended beyond the current application to include the full cost of the services provided in substantial part by government aid. How can economists or others advocate "full costs of providing the service" and be so inconsistent, in some instances, as to fail to admit the necessity of recovering the full costs of services made possible through government appropriations? How far may "social responsibility" be allowed to trespass on the equity of transportation competition?

Rates are based historically; in other words, on past experiences, although they are intended for future use. Rates reflect the judgment of carrier pricing experts in evaluating the elasticity of demand, just as industries' prices reflect similar evaluation by their pricing specialists. Since demand over the long run varies, reflecting a variety of factors, freight rates may not, over the long term, be on a constant or relatively unvarying level. Further, can we estimate with any accuracy what long-term costs will be and, therefore, what rates based on such long-term or fully distributed costs may feasibly be?

POLEMICS IN FULLY DISTRIBUTED COSTS

Inasmuch as various individuals and groups are contending currently that rates for the future should be based on long-term, fully distributed costs, as advanced by the Supreme Court in the *Dixie Carriers* case, we would like to advance the following polemics:

1. The term fully distributed costs should, so far as past costs are concerned, only have a long-term significance in relation to aggregate costs.

2. For future application, fully distributed costs should only be considered significant for a relatively short term so far as rates covering costs on individual commodities are concerned, or for the long term in the sense of the aggregate of such short-term applications.

3. The term fully distributed costs for either long or short term application should not connote any necessity of having the rates on any commodity based only on the assumption of average costs plus average contributions to constant costs and to profits.

CARRIER PRICING THEORY.[9]

In this section on carrier price theory, consideration is given to railroad rate theory, the imprecision of rate making, and a reappraisal of traditional railroad pricing policy.

RAILROAD RATE THEORY

It has been stated that competition is not a regulator of the rate level, since "competition does not keep the earnings of the industry at a normal level." [10] This is true to the extent that competition does not make certain that the earnings are a satisfactory level above costs, but competition often does result in rates' being forced down to an unsatisfactory level. Accordingly, it seems appropriate to say that competition is a regulator, whether or not the results are satisfactory. Actually, our regulatory system does not permit free competition.

Since the railroads, as a constant cost industry, are better able to apply marginal pricing or lower rates on new business than on business already secured, they are in an area of increasing returns (the revenue derived is greater than the cost of handling) when business is good. When business is declining, this feature of the railroads makes them suffer disproportionate declines in revenue, since they cannot adjust so readily to such conditions as can variable cost carriers.

It is more productive for a railroad to set a lower rate on a com-

---

[9] Newton Morton, "Carrier Pricing Theory," *Delta Nu Alphian*, Vol. XXII—Number 3, January, 1963. Used by permission.

[10] D. Philip Locklin, *Economics of Transportation* (Homewood, Ill.: Richard D. Irwin, Inc., 1960), p. 129.

modity which will not move at the higher, prevailing rate, for the lower rate theoretically covers the extra expense and makes some contributions to overhead or constant costs. With these tendencies to cut rates having been in evidence when the competition was largely intramodal (i.e., when the railroads were concerned primarily with their share of traffic compared to that of other railroads), they are accentuated at the present time when the railroads are also suffering from intermodal competition—the motor carriers and the comparatively new barge lines, as well as increasing amounts moving by private carriers, and by the shippers themselves. A similar tendency to take some traffic at rates lower than those maintained where there is less competition is found in these other transportation modes also.

Economic classicists holding to the principle of free competition would say, "Let the rate cuts fall where they may," with the carriers of lesser efficiency or lesser revenue reserve falling by the wayside. Our national adherence to the principle of regulated competition presently prevents such a ruthless elimination. The intensified intramodal and intermodal competition tends to reduce rates to the basis of variable (out-of-pocket and intermediate variable) costs, in the desire to utilize the railroad plant to capacity. Our administrative agencies in transportation should prevent a rate level below the out-of-pocket cost basis. Some feel that discriminating rates would not continue in the presence of real competition. Others hold that competition forces the discrimination where it is encountered, while maintaining a higher basis where there is no competition. We must recall continually that discrimination is not a violation of our regulatory safeguards unless our administrative agencies see it as sufficient to be considered as "undue" discrimination.

It is not necessarily true that, in the absence of probative cost data, a conclusion on the reasonableness of a specific rate would be impossible. If the proposed rate and revenue therefrom compare favorably with the rates and revenues on similar commodities between the same or other points, the rates should be approved,[11] provided the compared rates are not depressed.

A rate which is compensatory and no lower than necessary to meet competition should, according to the ICC, be approved, provided the proponent carrier is in fact meeting competition and not creating it. The rail carriers feel that if they are only allowed rates which will meet competition, this amounts to allocation of the traffic by the ICC,

---

[11] Bakery Goods and Chemicals, Eastern Points, 34 M.C.C. 551, 561.

and that they, the rails, should be allowed a fully compensatory basis (not necessarily fully distributed rates) which may result in their beating competition. They further feel that denying them this right prevents them from benefiting from their advantages, which is one of the salient points involved in the National Transportation Policy. Those who disagree with the railroads advance another tenet of the same National Transportation Policy when they contend that establishing such a rate, which a higher cost carrier cannot meet, is a "destructive rate practice."

System averages have little probative value in determining the compensatory character of the rates on a specific commodity. In other words, average truckload costs, for example, do not necessarily reflect the truckload costs of handling a specific commodity.

IMPRECISION OF RATE MAKING

It is difficult for the student of transportation and traffic management to realize that rate-making is not a precise process, where a slide rule is moved a certain distance to reflect the influence of each particular factor, and where the summation reflects accurately the influence of each factor. However, reasonable rates have been determined in the past, not by close adjustment to any finely-calculated cost of service, but by the exercise of experienced judgment after consideration of all the pertinent factors.[12] In determining reasonable rates, the value of the service, as reflected by the ability or inability of the traffic to bear relatively high rates, has been considered. This has meant, according to the ICC, that the economic life of the nation may require continued application of the principle that, for the good of the whole, the burden of maintaining carrier services must be distributed in part in disregard of relative cost and in proportion to the ability to pay. Of course, this results in the low rates on the low value commodities' being less than those based on fully-allocated costs, while the rates on the high value commodities are above those based on fully-allocated or fully-distributed costs.

This works out well for the low value commodities, which can continue being marketed where the particular rates apply, and it does enable the carriers concurring in this realistic pricing to continue their participation in the traffic. This holds true although the shippers of

---

[12] Charges for Protective Service, 241 ICC 510 (1940).

the high commodities do not feel elated at the social contribution they are making when their own rates are forced higher than a compensatory basis. In relation to these high value goods, such as tobacco,[13] the ICC has held that they are not contributing their fair share toward the transportation burden when they do not give consideration to the value of the service. When this happens, rail and truck rates, while reasonably compensatory in themselves, but lower than comparable rates, may be found to be unreasonably low.

In one recent case, the ICC validly and concisely met the argument that rates should be based on fully allocated costs by saying:

> If rates were made in this manner, it would result in reducing the rates on much of the high grade traffic transported by the carriers. At the same time, however, it would bring about increases in the rates on most of the low-grade, volume moving traffic. Rates on the latter have been made in the past under a continuous interplay of economic forces to permit such traffic to move with reasonable freedom and thus to contribute as much as possible to the carrier's overhead of fixed costs. To revise all rates so as to make them reflect exactly or approximately the fully distributed costs, if such a thing were practicable, would tend to dry up much of the traffic moving in large volume, with a consequent reduction in the contribution which this traffic now makes to the carriers' general revenue needs. Such a change would increase rather than reduce the portion of the general transportation burden to be borne by the higher-rated traffic.[14]

The ICC is quite consistent in adhering to its position that its function is not to act as an automatic adjustment valve to influence some aspect of economic or social welfare. It has also stated that "it is not the province of the Commission to determine the relative merits of different sales methods or by rate adjustments to perpetuate any particular system, or sales pattern of distribution.[15]

Another rate-making guide is that whether or not rates are reasonable should not depend on the commercial exigencies of the shippers. The ICC has held that it has no authority to equalize fortunes, opportunities or abilities.[16] Rate control, therefore, is not to be used as a universal adjustment to compensate for all differences in abilities to meet competition. Differences in transportation charges from com-

---

[13] Tobacco from North Carolina Points to Southern Points (Rail), 280 ICC 767 (1951).

[14] *U.S. Sugar Corporation v. Atlantic Coast Line* R. Co., 277 ICC 193 (1950).

[15] Transit and Mixing Rules on Foodstuffs, 270 ICC 157 (1948).

[16] Livestock to and from the South, 253 ICC 250 (1942).

peting producing points are to be based solely on differences in the circumstances and conditions surrounding the transportation of the competing products. Nevertheless, considerable attention is given to competition, for a fundamental objective of regulation is to preserve the benefits of competition in the public interest. Cases involving the consideration to be given to this element, however, do not indicate clearly the ICC's policy in respect to its importance.

REAPPRAISAL OF TRADITIONAL RAILROAD PRICING POLICY

The need for the railroads to reappraise and revise their pricing policies and techniques is emphasized by the decentralization of economic activities. As the longer railroad hauls are curtailed, the shrinking of transport distance converts the former rail advantage, always greater on longer hauls, to one of narrower favorable differentials, if not one of unfavorable differentials where the trucking costs and pricing may be lower than those of the rails.

As our foregoing discussion has indicated, the former and largely continuing policy has been based on differential pricing, with higher value goods absorbing the impact of a greater share of costs than is borne by the low value goods. Motor carriers, particularly for-hire, common carriers, are much more interested in these high value goods than in low value goods, partly because the shippers' interest in truck movement, in the face of rates which are in many cases higher than the rail rates, is due to the fact that trucking service may effect considerable savings in inventory costs.

Across the board horizontal or general price increases were not new with World War II, but since that time they have certainly distorted former relationships. These flat or percentage increases have had a greater effect on the high value goods, widening the disparity on these goods which the trucks want and having a lesser effect on the low value goods which the trucks want to haul only for short distances.

The basic factor of what it costs the carriers to provide the service is the lower limit of rate-making, while the old idea of what the shipper is willing to pay has been modified. He pays up to the level at which he may secure equivalent service from some alternative mode of transport, and it is becoming increasingly true that his own, private transportation constitutes this alternative.

When the railroads had a relative monopoly throughout most of the country, the pricing restraints were provided in the main by government regulation. If the rates charged were, in the minds of the shippers, excessive, they had two alternatives—not producing or not shipping.

Whenever there is room for discretionary pricing between the rate ceiling and floor, as there almost always is for some length of haul and some weight of shipment, the objective should be to set rates that will maximize total dollar contribution over incremental cost. This objective is often swayed by a rate structure going below that needed to merely undercut costs of alternative modes of transport.[17]

The two most likely ways to induce shippers to increase their use of the railroads are to give a lower rate for shipping during off-peak periods or, more likely, to provide incentive rates for loading cars more fully. These incentives would be alternating minima or sliding scale rates used in the *Paint* case, with rates for a certain minimum and a declining rate for the various levels above this. An example of such rates might be $.90 per hundredweight on a 30,000 pounds minimum, $.82 per hundredweight for weights in the 30,000 to 40,000 pounds range, $.75 per hundredweight for weights above 40,000 pounds, and so on.

There are various other ways to apply new rate-making concepts, such as so-called contract or loyalty rates. However, these attempts have lost effectiveness because carriers of other modes, particularly motor carriers, have petitioned for Investigation and Suspension procedure, the final result being that the ICC has refused, in some instances, to permit such rates to become effective. Because of sheer necessity, historical rate relationships (lower rates for raw materials than for finished products, preservation of relationship of competing producers, etc.) may have to be abandoned.

SELECTIVE RATE CUTS [18]

The reappraisal of traditional pricing policy has led to selective rate cuts. The significance of such action is followed by a discussion of differential pricing in class and commodity rates, marginal pricing,

---

[17] Joel Dean, "Competitive Pricing in Railroad Freight Rates," *Transportation Journal*, Vol. No. 3, Spring, 1962, p. 11.

[18] Based on Newton Morton, "Selective Rate Cuts—Yes or No?" Vol. 100, No. 1, *Traffic World*, September 7, 1957, pp. 69–74, *passim*. Used by permission.

what the traffic will bear, industry use of differential pricing, and the public interest as it affects selective rate cuts.

SIGNIFICANCE OF SELECTIVE RATE CUTS

Selective rate cuts, contrary to fairly general opinion, are neither a new policy or a new suggestion. They are simply one variation of the old idea of differential pricing, in which constant and common costs are distributed, not on a pro-rata, average or fully distributed basis, but, rather, with a most careful regard for the demand factor. Under such average pricing, each commodity would bear the share of costs for which it is responsible, plus the same contributions to other than out-of-pocket costs as are made by all other commodities. Under pricing application in selective rate cuts, rates are lowered in selected situations to meet and, if possible, beat competition. Commodity A (low value) bears a lesser share of such contributions than does Commodity B (high value). To say that the bearing by high value goods of a greater share of the costs than can be borne by low value goods is improper is to fail to recognize that the value of service cannot be eliminated entirely as a rate-making factor.[19]

Carriers—rail, motor and others—are endeavoring to give greater recognition to out-of-pocket or short-term variable costs in rate-making in establishing more precise costing, in order to make their pricing more productive where these selective rate cuts seem necessary.

DIFFERENTIAL PRICING IN CLASS AND COMMODITY RATES

Even basic rail and motor carrier pricing reflects differential pricing, in that the class rates are based on the assignment of the innumerable commodities shipped to a class or "rating" which bears an increasing relationship (e.g., three times first) to first class (the basic grouping) or a declining relationship to first class (e.g., second class). Various factors, including value, density, liability to damage, etc., may cause a commodity to be assigned to a lower class which bears a lesser proportion of costs per unit than do commodities in the higher classes. This was the way rail pricing evolved in the 19th century, and it was followed by the motor carriers subsequent to the Motor

[19] Cf. Newton Morton, "Value of Service in Rate Making," *Traffic World*, Vol. 104, No. 10, November 14, 1959, pp. 33, 36–39, *passim*.

Carrier Act of 1935, which became Part II of the Interstate Commerce Act in 1940.

Motor carriers[20] publish, as do the rails, special treatment (commodity) rates which reflect, not a preferred treatment to favored concerns, as some may imagine, but recognition of traffic which is particularly attractive because of its volume, its regularity of movement, or the element of competition involved. Approximately 90 per cent of rail traffic moves on such special treatment rates (commodity, or exceptions ratings, a heritage of the structure before the uniform class rates took effect in May, 1952). That the motor carriers employ selective rate cuts is not negated by the fact that a small percentage of their total traffic[21] moves on their special treatment rates.[22]

MARGINAL PRICING

The greatly intensified importance of competition in rate-making[23] is causing increasing deviation from the class basis, so much so that some say, with great validity, that class rates are already of much less consequence in carrier pricing and will be even less important as time passes. Motor carriers compete for business with the rails and other carriers and, so far as possible, establish whatever differential pricing on substantial volume movements is necessary to secure a respectable portion of the movement. The common carrier competition provided in the various media must also face, to an important and increasing degree, the accelerated competition provided by private carriage (shippers) and contract carriers.

[20] We must make certain to distinguish between motor common carrier rates and motor contract carrier rates, for the relative freedom in the matter of pricing and in other respects which the latter enjoy is not enjoyed by the former. The vital subject of the lesser regulation applied to motor contract carriers, as it affects both rail and motor common carriers, is beyond the scope of this treatment.

[21] A very important part of rail tonnage consists of low-value commodities which are given commodity rates in order to enable their continued movement in as great volume as possible. The motor carriers do not feel that it is worthwhile for them to give such low commodity rates, so if these commodities are to move via motor carriers, the applicable rate is raised to a grouping higher than is indicated in the classification. These rate "plugs" or "stops," result in raising the total percentage which moves on class rates.

[22] An Office of Defense Transportation study in 1945 estimated that 56 per cent of the total motor common carrier traffic moved on such special treatment rates, compared to the 90 per cent moving via such rates on the rails. There has been no later, similar study.

[23] Cf. The Doyle Report, Senate Committee on Commerce, National Transportation Policy. Preliminary draft of a report prepared for the Committee (Washington, D.C.: U.S. Government Printing Office, 1961).

The selective rate-cutting of differential pricing exemplifies marginal pricing, or the establishment in competitive situations of lower per unit rates for new traffic than those applicable to the traffic already secured. Marginal traffic is also defined as "added cost" or "incremental" pricing based on the costs of moving the additional traffic. The rails, as a constant cost transportation medium, are particularly susceptible to marginal pricing. The high cost of making the railroad plant available should make possible certain economies when it is used, provided the inherent advantages, under regulation, are permitted to be shown in fully-compensatory pricing. Accordingly, for every extra unit of traffic hauled, up to the capacity of the train (or plant), revenue will increase more than the cost of handling the extra traffic. An area of increasing returns exists in such a case.

Marginal pricing situations arise frequently when there is an imbalance, meaning that the return movement is not made with any freight or with insufficient freight to contribute properly to the round trip costs—a true joint cost situation. This situation frequently faces the motor common carriers. Under those circumstances, the carrier may well feel that any revenue it can obtain is a profit. Economic theorists who stress that marginal pricing is proper would probably agree with the carriers who, in many cases, may not be familiar with marginal pricing or differential pricing by name. This reasoning may, to the carrier, appear logical, and conceivably could be so if this particular traffic could be isolated and the rates applied without reference to other traffic. However, an interrelationship of rates is recognized by many of the carriers, and a change in one rate, however legitimate it may seem, involves many other changes. Competing carriers and other shippers will claim that rates so made give an undue advantage to the favored traffic and impose an unjust burden on other traffic. What they mean is that their ability to compete is lessened.

In advocating selective pricing, the rails propose to apply the marginal pricing and increasing returns concepts and, where they face competition, establish rate cuts which, while compensatory, result in their securing the traffic.

WHAT THE TRAFFIC WILL BEAR

It is not practical to present a detailed treatment of the many factors which management (either carrier or industry) must consider in establishing its prices. Both apply somewhat inexact estimates based on empirical knowledge (although we must not omit consideration of pricing refinements made possible by electronic computers) trying to maximize revenue through varying the contributions to constant costs and to profits to be made by each service or commodity, according to "what the traffic will bear." This principle denotes a pricing practice which goes back to the dim past. To many people, this principle, or even its more recent version in this country, "what the traffic will reasonably bear," as determined by the ICC, almost inevitably denotes shady practices. These were rampant when the rails were applying the idea in the grabbing, rugged, entrepreneuring period prior to and somewhat after the first federal regulation in 1887. The distinct imputation is that these attitudes carry over to this time, when conditions are totally different, and justify the attempts of other carriers to grab what they can from the federal government. This is not a fair charge.

INDUSTRY USE OF DIFFERENTIAL PRICING

Industry employs differential pricing in many ways, such as quantity discounts, trade discounts, cash discounts, geographical area price maintenance, area coupons in testing the market, different margins of profit and mark-up, different brands and prices for different units of the same product, etc. Pricing specialists (either carrier or industrial) must evaluate the elasticity of demand and decide whether greater revenue will be provided by the sale of more units at a lower rate per unit or fewer units at a higher rate per unit.

MOTOR CARRIERS AND SELECTIVE RATE CUTS

The opposition of motor carriers to the idea of selective rate cuts by the rails tends to obscure the fact that there are numerous instances where the motor carriers themselves have been permitted by the ICC to establish compensatory rates lower than the rails can meet. It is expected fully that such instances will continue. Every time motor carriers make a commodity rate, they are employing selective rate-cuts. In fact, the basic railroad system of class rates in which commodities of lower values are assigned to the lower classes, which bear a lesser percentage of first class rates than do higher valued goods, exemplifies differential pricing. When the motor common carriers follow the railroad class rate system, they are, accordingly, following this same system of selective pricing. Their apprehension concerning the use of selective rate-cuts by the rails depends on how much of such special pricing they can meet.

RAILROADS AND SELECTIVE RATE CUTS

The railroads are contending for equal competitive conditions, not government protection through umbrella rate-making or the provision of facilities. It is a question of whether final retribution for past sins or salvation through current competitive measures will arrive first.

The railroads would not be realistic if they did not recognize the importance of other carriers to our economy. Many railroad representatives admit quite readily that they often cannot equal motor carrier services. They do feel, however, that where they can establish fully compensatory pricing which will enable them to compensate for service inequalities and obtain the traffic, they should be permitted to do so. Neither rails, motor carriers, barge lines, nor airplanes can provide the entire range of essential services. The extremely difficult problem is to determine the field in which each, in the public interest, should function, and the share of traffic each should secure.

It would seem that a reasonable approach to the solution of this problem would be to permit costs of service, plus reasonable contributions to overhead or constant costs and to profit, to constitute the reasonable determinant. A great part of our perplexity at this problem is our inability to decide whether we want free competition or the present compromise of a continued, regulated competition which allocates shares of the traffic on the basis of factors other than true economic costs.

Industry, which is not subject to pricing controls as stringent as those applicable to the carriers, is free from public castigation for applying essentially the same differential pricing (selective rate cuts included) as the carriers. If this is proper for industry and other carriers, what is wrong with applying it to railroad pricing? Differential pricing is an ordinary characteristic of industrial pricing in allocating constant and common costs, and it is not necessarily confined to these. Carriers cannot price their transportation service at a figure which is greater than its customers are willing to pay. This is affected by the presence or lack of competitive transportation of the same or different media. Likewise, industry cannot price their products at a figure greater than the market value of the articles transported.

PUBLIC INTEREST AND SELECTIVE RATE CUTS

The issue crystallizes. The shipping public should be allowed the benefit of rates made by a carrier, when such rates more than cover the specific cost of producing those particular transportation services and make necessary contributions to constant costs and to profit, as previously discussed, and yet are lower than other carriers can meet. The chips should fall where they may, with the low cost carrier applying such rates under ICC sanction. This appears to be proper, even though it is extremely difficult to determine consistency in the application of the standards which determine sanction.

The motor carriers do not want any change in the present statement in the National Transportation Policy that the Interstate Commerce Act "be so administered as to recognize and preserve the inherent advantages of each" type of transportation. Yet to deny the railroads the right to carry additional traffic at rates which cover out-of-pocket costs and make reasonable contributions to overhead or constant costs, thus recognizing their natural advantages as a constant cost industry, is to fail to recognize and preserve their "inherent advantages" discussed in this policy. Motor carriers, insisting upon an unchanged National Transportation Policy, refuse to recognize these advantages, and the ICC has been unduly reluctant to recognize it in its administration of the Interstate Commerce Act.

WHAT FORMULA FOR RATES? [24]

Aside from political action necessary to equalize transportation, taxation and working rules, transportation people themselves (including their customers and regulators) could do much to improve present chaotic conditions. Take, for example, the painful slowness with which railroad rates are being revised to conform to present competitive con-

[24] "What Formula for Rates?" *Railway Age,* Vol. 149, No. 25, December, 1960, p. 54. Used by permission.

ditions. No malevolent devil is retarding the necessary modernization. The difficulty lies instead in getting agreement among the three parties—railroads, customers and regulators—as to the principles which revision should follow. If the parties could see eye to eye on the pattern, revision could come quickly, and the situation of the railroads would be greatly and instantly improved.

As a starter toward developing an acceptable pattern, we offer three suggestions, as follows:

1. Recognize the commercial uselessness of the class rates (and rates following the class rate pattern) and contrive substitutes which will give effect to rail costs as a "floor" and private truck costs as a "ceiling." All railroad rates which are unrealistically high in relation to railroad and truck costs are obviously useless.

2. Recognize that, for the shorter hauls where railroad costs and truck costs are close together, railroad rates must be held down to a small margin above direct costs.

Keeping railroad rates low in this area has encountered some criticism, to the effect that it amounts to undercharging the short hauls at the expense of the long hauls. It does nothing of the kind. Traffic will not move at all by rail in this area unless rates are kept realistically low. Even at a tiny margin above direct costs, this traffic will make some contribution to overhead costs, which would otherwise have to be borne entirely by the long-haul tonnage.

3. Recognize that, where truck costs exceed rail costs, it is economically justifiable for railroad rates to include a larger margin of profit than that expected from the shorter hauls.

Some have contended that such rates would "discriminate" against the long-haul shipper. A little reflection will quickly dispel such an illusion. The railroads have to collect their full costs or go out of business. They have no alternative but to collect these costs wherever they can be collected without losing tonnage. It is only recognizing the economic facts of life to give the railroads a restricted opportunity to practice "value of service" pricing, which most shippers favor. Railroads can still make some rate concessions to their customers' "market competition." It is still possible to charge the same rate from 900 miles to 1200 miles and not expose the tonnage to competition, or go below the railroads' own costs.

Appendix B

Constructive and Routine Duties

of the Traffic Department[1]

All of the functions and duties of the transportation or traffic department may be classified as either constructive or routine. Routine duties come up frequently and can be handled as a matter of course by the clerical personnel. Constructive duties involve analysis and corrective action. The time and attention of the transportation specialist and his higher ranking assistants should be concentrated on such duties. An example of these duties is in connection with freight rates; negotiation with carriers for proper freight rates is a constructive function, whereas the quotation of rates is a routine function.

FUNCTIONS PERFORMED WITHIN THE DEPARTMENT

1. Specification of routes on outbound and inbound shipments—The specification of routes on outbound and inbound shipments is one outstanding duty of a traffic department. Indication of a definite route removes all doubt as to the class of service or carriers desired. One of the obligations of a traffic manager is to minimize shipping costs; this involves a knowledge of the costs of shipping, time in transit via the various forms of transportation normally used over equipment entering the company's yards, and reciprocity. Control over equipment entering the yards is important in eliminating congestion and in routinizing the movement of goods into and out of the factory. Reci-

[1] Portions of Appendix B are adapted with permission of the publisher from F. H. Mossman and Newton Morton, *Principles of Transportation* (New York: Ronald Press, 1957), pp. 355–362.

procity is important in that carriers may require suppliers to route company material over not only their particular lines as a part of policy, but also the shippers will wish to maximize their control of tonnage in order to engender carriers' cooperation in effecting desired rate changes and other traffic matters.

The routing of inbound traffic requires close coordination with the purchasing department on movement costs from alternate sources of supply. The right to route inbound shipments should be reserved wherever possible as a means of minimizing movement cost. Where the industry functions as a private carrier, the traffic manager may also work with the purchasing department in instructing vendors to hold goods for the shipper's trucking returning to the plant, in order to mitigate the joint cost problem.

2. Negotiating with carriers for proper freight rates—This requires a knowledge of rates, rate comparisons, and the organization of rate proposals for progression through appropriate channels.

3. Maintaining records—Record keeping varies with the policy of the company and the desires of the traffic manager. Some of the most common records include: a daily record of truckload and carload movements by territory; monthly payment of freight to all leading carriers used, number of routings supplied, average cost of shipping each product per month or per year; amount of business given to the company by the carriers, number of freight bills preaudited, number of branch plant bills audited, number of rate quotations given, number of claims paid or filed, number of passenger reservations made, and amounts saved through correcting overcharges.

4. Arranging for consolidated shipments—Small shipments are often consolidated to obtain the benefits of carload and truckload movements and/or rates. A knowledge of the various carriers' services is necessary to effect such combinations.

5. Handling of claims—The traffic department handles undercharge, overcharge, and reparation claims as well as loss and damage claims. It is basic that the department clearly understand the terms of purchase and sale, and that all efforts be made to avert such claims.

6. Arranging equipment supply—The arrangement for the supply of proper equipment requires a thorough knowledge of a carrier's car supply rules and a motor carrier's equipment supply situation. The equipment must be ordered enough in advance of loading to avoid unnecessary delays.

7. Supervising local and/or plant transportation—In some cases, local transportation in the terminal area or short-haul in the contigu-

ous territory may be under the control of the traffic manager, while plant transportation may be under the maintenance superintendent or other official. There is a great variance in this practice and no typical arrangement in the field.

8. Managing exports and/or imports—In some of the larger companies, there may be a separate department to handle export and import traffic. In other cases, the traffic manager has charge of the shipment up to the port of exportation. The booking of space, clearance of the shipment, and other details of the shipment are quite often handled by a foreign freight forwarder.

9. Investigating distribution processes—The services of carriers may deteriorate, and it may be desirable to shift to other carriers or methods which may have become available. Such necessity may originate with a specific complaint and broaden into an investigation of greater scope. All distribution processes should be reviewed with changing conditions and in cooperation with the appropriate departments of the company.

In many cases, various parts of over-all distribution are assigned to different middle or top management people. The modern concept is that it is more efficient to have these various functions concentrated in one physical distribution manager.[2] Doing this will involve not only more knowledge and responsibilities than have been within the training and functioning of the transportation and traffic management specialist, but will also include some functions considered by other departments to be traditionally within their province.

Some of the operations, functions and responsibilities with which the specialist should be thoroughly familiar, for example, are budgetary control, cost accounting, machine data processing, integrated data processing, industrial relations, management development, sales, marketing, advertising, traffic, transportation, manufacturing, quality control, production control, inventory control and engineering.[3]

In recognition of this, the Delta Nu Alpha national transportation fraternity offers a program of training courses, and the American Society of Traffic and Transportation sponsors examinations in economics, traffic management, general business, interstate commerce law, and regulations. It has come as a shock to many traffic management men to realize that what they consider a standard and relatively

[2] Philip F. Cannon, *Organizing for Effective Physical Distribution Management*, AMA Report Number 49, *op. cit.*, p. 15.
[3] George V. Evans, *The Distribution Manager and His Place in the Organization*, AMA Report Number 49, *op. cit.*, p. 29.

complete training is only the beginning, and that the requirements of the "new frontier" in distribution are going to be considerably more demanding. The requirements for successfully filling a position as distribution manager makes mandatory a new analysis of goals and the training which will make possible the attainment of these goals.

THE BUYER OF TRANSPORTATION AND MODAL COMPETITION

In the period prior to the 1930's, the policy of the railroads was to adjust rates to facilitate the movement of low unit value commodities. This meant that there was internal subsidization, with the higher unit value goods absorbing a greater portion of fixed costs then did the low unit value goods. Carriers could do this with relative impunity, for the amount of tonnage they controlled would permit this. With the rise of competition, the situation changed considerably. The railroads lost a great deal of this higher unit value tonnage to the motor carriers, who concentrated on such business.

The buyer of transportation no longer depends on the railroads. The price basis which determines how he moves his goods is not that which the railroads have published and filed in their traffic. Often it is the basis which competing carriers, particularly the motor carriers, have filed or the basis which the transportation buyer is able to force from the motor common or contract carriers. More recently, the basis of price for a transportation buyer with fairly consistent volume tonnage has been his costs for hauling the goods by his own or leased equipment. In the latter case, there have been some questions as to whether he was making sufficient allowance for imbalance, labor problems, full costs of providing the service, etc. Nevertheless, the amount of such traffic has been increasing.

This has resulted in the following typical situation, in which the role of a traffic manager and his relation to competition among the modes can be depicted simply and clearly. The regulated, for-hire carriers who have been frustrated by the erosion of their traffic through just such manifestations can attest to its authenticity.

A manufacturer of television sets in the midwest had a good volume of freight moving by rail to a nearby large city. A common carrier truck line had roughly comparable rates but considerably faster service and was able to secure all of the business, which amounted to seven to twelve truckloads a week. This continued for a period of time, but if there were floods, so that the trucks could not operate, the railroad received the business. Subsequently, a contract carrier eyed the service of the common carrier truck line and entered into an arrangement with the manufacturer for seven loads a week to the city. This gave the contract carrier seven a week, the common carrier truck line none to five a week, and the railroad all of the business if any floods occurred.

After a period of time, a new traffic manager observed that about four truckloads of components came back from the city each week, so the manufacturer secured some truck tractors and trailers. This left the following distribution of business: the private trucking got four loads each way; the contract carrier got three loads each week one way; the common carrier got none to five each way; and the railroad got all of the business if a flood occurred. In this case, regulation will have a hard time altering the distribution very much, notwithstanding the distress in the situation.

RELATIONS OF THE TRAFFIC DEPARTMENT WITH OTHER DEPARTMENTS

The relations of the traffic department with other departments in the company are often just as important as its internal operations, for these relations may well determine the prestige of the department with the rest of the company. Good working relations are fostered both by regular personal contacts with heads and members of other departments and by observing due protocol in making suggestions on ways the traffic department can help others to perform their tasks more easily and quickly. The following are a few of the ways in which the traffic manager may help other functional divisions of the company.

EXECUTIVE DEPARTMENT

The traffic department can aid the executive department by furnishing:

1. Advice on the purchase of transportation equipment. This may mean the purchase of extra trucks, in order to permit the com-

pany to operate its own trucks rather than using commercial carriers. It may also include palletizing all shipments of the company.

2. Studies on new locations for plants. This would include an analysis, on request, of transportation costs to and from several prospective sites.

3. Advice on siding and other agreements with carriers.

4. Information on general transportation conditions. This might include new developments and trends, important court decisions, prospective changes in freight rates and what they will mean to the company, and changes in passenger service.

5. Smoothly functioning procurement of passenger reservations on the numerous trips which the typical executive makes.

SALES DEPARTMENT

The traffic department can aid the sales department by furnishing:

1. Quotation of freight rates via the various forms of transportation. The traffic department may determine the greater cost via certain routes and try to help the sales department give the customer improved transportation service.

2. Expediting and tracing service in order to help locate shipments for customers. Complete information, given promptly in response to a request from the customer, is of great assistance in developing the prestige of the sales department. Securing the record of the time in transit by the first shipments to a new sales area will aid in determining whether or not better service would be accorded by some other routing. There should be no change in routing on the basis of one complaint. Several shipments should be checked. There should be no useless tracing.

3. Help to the customers in the handling of claims. The traffic department may actually file the claims when the customer refuses to do this himself. (Most claims are settled on the basis of claimant-carrier negotiation, not court action).

4. Cooperation in routing. When a competitor is located nearer the customer, the traffic department may find it advisable to shift to truck movement, even though such a move may cost somewhat more on the average shipment to the customer.

5. Quotation of rates which a competitor pays for shipment from his production point to a common market, in order to determine if any adjustment in prices is necessary to meet the competition.

6. Ideas about the possible connection between sales and carriers' varying rates based on variations in weight ("break-down" and carload weights).

7. Negotiation of more favorable rates, where feasible, to markets where sales are experiencing difficulty.

PRODUCTION DEPARTMENT

The production department can be assisted by the traffic department in the following:

1. Location of lost or delayed inbound materials in order to avoid a production shutdown. If the supplies cannot be delivered in time, it may be necessary to arrange for purchase from a nearby source, possibly at a higher cost.

2. Suggestions for improvements in intraplant handling of materials.

3. Quotations of applicable rates in the determination of cost estimates; e.g., figuring full production costs on new products.

4. Work with carriers for the maintenance of an adequate car or truck supply.

PURCHASING DEPARTMENT

The traffic department can aid the purchasing department, which is responsible for locating sources of supply, through the following activities:

1. Giving advice on the minimum purchase necessary to get the lowest rate on shipments from vendors. The feasibility may depend on sufficient space to store the greater amount of goods.

2. Supplying rate quotations for the determination of purchase cost or for adjustment on invoices at the end of the month where purchases have been made on a "collect, freight allowed" basis.

3. Persuading the purchasing department to specify on its purchase orders the routes which, for service or policy, the traffic department prefers.

4. Tracing and expediting shipments.

5. Checking copies of invoices against goods received or conducting "blind checks."

6. Arranging indemnity on inbound shipments moving on order notify bills of lading.

7. On request, supplying information as to rates from possible new sources of supply.

8. Supplying information on prospective changes in rates or service.

9. Arranging pick-up of vendor traffic by company trucks.

ACCOUNTING DEPARTMENT

The traffic department can cooperate with the accounting department by:

1. Auditing freight bills.[4] The traffic department may also arrange a supplementary audit by an outside firm which may file the claims itself or may prepare them for filing by the shipper. The usual method of payment to the various bureaus is 50 per cent of the amount recovered. Agreements with such companies are usually on a contract basis for a year.

2. Maintaining bills of lading for a monthly check by the accounting department.

3. Sending preaudited bills to the accounting department for payments.

4. Arranging with the various carriers for credit accommodations in the payment of freight bills.

5. Linear programming.

6. Allocating freight charges to the department of the company for whose account the transportation is supplied.

LEGAL DEPARTMENT

The traffic manager should be very familiar with the federal and state laws relating to transportation. As a result of this knowledge, he can be particularly helpful to the legal department with respect to:

1. Developments in transportation legislation and their effects on his company (many members of the bar do not know transportation law).

---

[4] These audits by the traffic department may be made before payment of the bills or after payment. Where feasible, the former is preferable.

2. Transportation information on rate cases; in some companies, this may be the most important activity of the traffic manager.

3. Cooperation in the handling of claims if they involve court action. (As stated previously, however, all claims do not involve court action).

SHIPPING AND RECEIVING DEPARTMENT

If the shipping and receiving department is not included in the traffic department, the traffic manager should work with this department on the following:

1. Advising on the correct bill of lading descriptions.

2. Arranging for the best bill of lading forms; revision of old forms may be advisable in some instances to include new products.

3. Securing proper car or truck supply.

4. Supervising pool car shipments.

5. Cooperating in securing the proper notations on the delivery receipts in case of loss or damage.

6. Cooperating in cases of concealed loss or damage requiring inspection by the carriers.

7. Maintaining a record of receipts to indicate the necessity for filing a claim. In order to ascertain whether the entire shipment has been received in satisfactory condition, a check should be made against the invoice, or a "blind check" may be made by the receiving clerk.

8. Recording deliveries of goods to the stores or to other departments.

ADVERTISING DEPARTMENT

In some companies the advertising department is a separate department, and in others is included within the sales department. Wherever it is located, the traffic department frequently can aid advertising personnel the following ways:

1. Arrange for the movement of company exhibits. Special arrangements may be necessary for delivery to the exhibition hall, which may permit deliveries only at certain hours.

2. Give proper descriptions to be used in forwarding the exhibits. It may be necessary also to trace shipments in order to have

the exhibit available at the proper place prior to the start of the exhibition.

3. Furnish rate quotations on sample shipments.

4. Give advice on areas where the industry enjoys at least equal rates so that advertising campaigns are not started in disadvantageous territories.

BIBLIOGRAPHY

Adams, Walter and James B. Hendry, *Trucking Mergers, Concentration, and Small Business: An Analysis of Interstate Commerce Commission Policy, 1950–1956,* Senate Small Business Committee. Washington, D.C.: U.S. Government Printing Office, 1957.

Altazan, John E., *I.C.C. Policy Concerning Consolidations and Acquisitions in the Motor Carrier Industry.* New Orleans: Loyola University Press, 1956.

Ammer, Dean S., *Materials Management.* Homewood, Ill.: Richard D. Irwin, Inc., 1962.

Barger, Harold, *Distribution's Place in the American Economy Since 1869.* Princeton, N.J.: Princeton University Press, 1955.

Barlowe, Raleigh, *Land Resource Economics.* Englewood Cliffs, N.J.: Prentice-Hall, Inc., 1958.

Battelle Memorial Institute, *Development of a Framework with Which to Restructure the Regulated Carrier Freight-Rate System of the United States.* Columbus, Ohio: Battelle Memorial Institute, 1964.

Beckman, Martin, C. B. McGuire, and Christopher B. Winsten, *Studies in the Economics of Transportation.* Published for Cowles Commission for Research in Economics. New Haven, Conn.: Yale University Press, 1956.

Belson, Walter W., *Changing Patterns in Transportation.* Washington, D.C.: American Trucking Associations, Inc., 1960.

Berelson, Bernard, *Content Analysis in Communications Research.* Chicago: Free Press, 1952.

Berge, Stanley, *Railroad Passenger Service Trends.* Evanston, Ill.: Northwestern University Press, 1961.

Blaine, J. C. D., *Selected Cases and Case Studies in Transportation Regulation and Management.* Dubuque, Iowa: William C. Brown Company, 1963.

Bonbright, James C., *Principles of Public Utility Rates.* New York: Columbia University Press, 1961.

Bowersox, Donald J., *Food Distribution Center Location: Technique and Procedure.* East Lansing, Michigan: Bureau of Business and Economic Research, Michigan State University, 1962.

Brink, Edward L., "A Simplified Solution for the Location of Marketing Outlets Using an Analog Computer," *Marketing's Role in Scientific Management*. Chicago: American Marketing Association, 1957.

Caves, Richard E., *Air Transport and Its Regulators*. Cambridge, Mass.: Harvard University Press, 1962.

Cherington, Paul W., *Airline Price Policy*. Boston: Harvard Business School, Division of Research, 1958.

Cherry, Colin, *On Human Communication*. Cambridge, Mass.: The Massachusetts Institute of Technology Press, 1957.

Churchman, C. West, *Measurement-Definition and Theories*. New York: Financial Executives Research Foundation, Inc., 1962.

————, *Prediction and Optimal Decision*. Englewood Cliffs, N.J.: Prentice-Hall, Inc., 1961.

Clark, J. M., *Studies in the Economics of Overhead Costs*. Chicago: University of Chicago Press, 1923.

Clewett, Richard M., *Marketing Channels*. Homewood, Ill.: Richard D. Irwin, Inc., 1954.

Cohen, Saul B. (ed.), *Store Location Research for the Food Industry*. New York: National American Wholesale Grocers Association, 1961.

Colton, Richard C. and Edmund S. Ward, *Practical Handbook of Industrial Traffic Management*. Washington, D.C.: The Traffic Service Corporation, 1959.

Cookenboo, Leslie, Jr., *Crude Oil Pipelines and Competition in the Oil Industry*. Cambridge, Mass.: Harvard University Press, 1955.

Corwin, Edwin S. (ed.), *The Constitution of the United States of America*. Washington, D.C.: U.S. Government Printing Office, 1953.

Cost Finding Section, Bureau of Accounts, Interstate Commerce Commission, *Explanation of Automatic Data Processing Procedure of Rail Form A, 11-63 Using IBM 7090*. Washington, D.C.: U.S. Government Printing Office, 1964.

Cost Finding Section, Bureau of Accounts, Interstate Commerce Commission, *Rail Carload Cost Scales by Territories for the Year 1962, Statement 2-64*. Washington, D.C.: U.S. Government Printing Office, 1964.

Cox, Reavis and Wroe Alderson (eds.), *Theory in Marketing*. Homewood, Ill.: Richard D. Irwin, Inc., 1950.

Crisp, R. C., *How to Reduce Distribution Costs: A Practical Scientific Approach to Increased Selling Efficiency*. New York: Funk and Wagnalls Co., 1948.

Duncan, Otis D., *et al., Metropolis and Region.* Baltimore: The Johns Hopkins Press, 1960.

Epstein, Bart J. and Howard J. Green, "Store Location Analysis," *Marketing Research in Action,* Studies in Business Policy, No. 84. New York: National Industrial Conference Board, 1957.

"Factors in a Purchase Decision," *Convenience Goods Purchasing: Needed Research.* Ann Arbor, Mich.: Foundation for Research on Human Behavior, 1957.

Fair, Marvin L. and Ernest W. Williams, Jr., *Economics of Transportation.* New York: Harper & Row, Inc., 1959.

Fair, Marvin L. and John Guandolo, *Tedrow's Regulation of Transportation.* Dubuque, Iowa: William C. Brown Company, 1964.

Ferguson, A. R., *et al., Economic Value of the U.S. Merchant Marine.* Evanston, Ill.: Northwestern University Transportation Center, 1961.

Fine, Isadore V., *Retail Trade Analysis.* Madison, Wis.: Bureau of Business Research, University of Wisconsin, 1954.

Fite, Gilbert C. and James E. Reese, *An Economic History of the United States.* Boston: Houghton Mifflin Co., 1959.

Flood, Kenneth J., *Traffic Management.* Dubuque, Iowa: William C. Brown Company, 1963.

Frederick, John H., *Commercial Air Transportation.* Homewood, Ill.: Richard D. Irwin, Inc., 1961.

————, *Improving National Transportation Policy.* Washington, D.C.: American Enterprise Association, Inc., 1959.

————, *Using Public Warehouses.* Philadelphia: Chilton Company, 1957.

Friedrick, Carl J. (translated), *Alfred Weber's Theory of Location of Industries.* Chicago: University of Chicago Press, 1929.

Fulda, Carl H., *Competition in the Regulated Industries—Transportation.* Boston: Little, Brown and Company, 1961.

Germane, Gayton E., Nicholas A. Glaskowsky, and J. L. Heskett, *Highway Transportation Management.* New York: McGraw-Hill Book Company, 1963.

Gottman, Jean, *Megalopolis: The Urbanized Northeastern Seaboard of the United States.* Cambridge, Mass.: The Massachusetts Institute of Technology Press, 1961.

Greenhut, Melvin L., *Microeconomics and the Space Economy.* Fair Lawn, N.J.: Scott, Foresman, and Company, 1963.

————, *Plant Location.* Chapel Hill, N.C.: University of North Carolina Press, 1956.

Hall, Margaret, *Distributive Trading.* New York: Hutchinson's University Library, 1944.

Haning, Charles R., *Private Trucking Costs and Records.* College Station, Texas: Texas Transportation Institute, 1958.

Harper, Donald V., *Basic Planning and the Transportation Function in Small Manufacturing Firms.* Minneapolis: The University of Minnesota, 1961.

————, *Economic Regulation of the Motor Trucking Industry by the States.* Urbana, Ill.: University of Illinois Press, 1959.

Hay, William W., *An Introduction to Transportation Engineering.* New York: John Wiley & Sons, Inc., 1961.

Haynes, D. Oliphant, *Materials Handling Applications.* Philadelphia: Chilton Company, 1958.

Healy, Kent T., *The Effects of Scale in the Railroad Industry.* New Haven, Conn.: Yale University Press, 1961.

Hennes, Robert G. and Martin I. Ekse, *Fundamentals of Transportation Engineering.* New York: McGraw-Hill Book Company, Inc., 1955.

Heskett, J. L., R. M. Ivie, and N. A. Glaskowsky, Jr., *Business Logistics: Management of Physical Supply and Distribution.* New York: Ronald Press, 1964.

Hoover, Edgar M., *Location of Economic Activity.* New York: McGraw-Hill Book Company, 1948.

Hudson, William J. and James Constantin, *Motor Transportation.* New York: Ronald Press Co., 1958.

Hunter, Holland, "Resources, Transportation and Economic Development," *Natural Resources and Economic Growth,* J. J. Spengler, ed. Washington, D.C.: Resources for the Future, 1961.

Independent Offices Appropriation Act of 1952, House Report No. 383, 82nd Congress, April 27, 1952.

Institute of Internal Auditors Research Committee, *Internal Audit and Control of a Traffic Department.* New York: Institute of Internal Auditors, 1958. *Interstate Commerce Acts, Annotated.* Washington, D.C.: U.S. Government Printing Office, 1927–1959, vols. 1-18.

Isard, Walter, *Location and Space Economy.* New York: John Wiley & Sons, Inc., 1956.

————, *et al., Methods of Regional Analysis.* New York: John Wiley & Sons, Inc., 1960.

Johnson, William B., *Challenge to Transportation.* Stanford, Calif.: Stanford University Press, 1961.

Kansky, K. J., *Structure of Transportation Networks: Relationships Between Network Geometry and Regional Characteristics.* Chicago: University of Chicago Press, 1963.

Kelley, Eugene J., *Shopping Centers: Locating Controlled Regional Centers.* Saugatuck, Conn.: The Eno Foundation for Highway Traffic Control, 1956.

Kemeny, John, *A Philosopher Looks at Science.* Princeton, N.J.: Van Nostrand, 1959.

Knorst, William J., *Transportation and Traffic Management,* revised edition, four volumes. Chicago: College of Advanced Traffic, 1954–57.

Koontz, Harold and Richard W. Gable, *Public Control of Economic Enterprise.* New York: McGraw-Hill Book Company, 1956.

Kuhn, Tillo E., *Public Enterprise Economics and Transport Problems.* Berkeley, Calif.: University of California Press, 1962.

Ladd, Dwight R., *Cost Data for the Management of Railroad Passenger Service.* Cambridge, Mass.: Harvard University, Graduate School of Business Administration, Division of Research, 1957.

Laden, H. N. and T. R. Gildersleeve, *System Design for Computer Applications.* New York: John Wiley & Sons, Inc., 1963.

LaLonde, Bernard J., *Differentials in Supermarket Drawing Power.* East Lansing, Mich.: Bureau of Business Research, Michigan State University, 1962.

Landsberg, Hans H. *et al., Resources in America's Future.* Baltimore: Johns Hopkins University Press, 1963.

Lang, A. Scheffer and Richard Soberman, *Urban Rail Transit: Its Economics and Technology.* Cambridge, Mass.: Massachusetts Institute of Technology Press, 1964.

Lapin, Howard S., *Structuring the Journey to Work.* Philadelphia: University of Pennsylvania Press, 1963.

Lemly, James H., *Non-Vehicular Benefits from Utility Use of Streets and Highways.* Atlanta: Georgia State College of Business Administration, 1960.

Levy, Lester S. and Roy J. Sampson, *American Economic Development.* Boston: Allyn and Bacon, Inc., 1962.

Lochlin, D. Philip, *Economics of Transportation,* fifth edition. Homewood, Ill.: Richard D. Irwin, Inc., 1960.

Longman, D. R. and Michael Schiff, *Practical Distribution Costs.* Homewood, Ill.: Richard D. Irwin, Inc., 1955.

Losch, August, *The Economics of Location,* translated by Wolfgang F. Stolper. New Haven, Conn.: Yale University Press, 1954.

McDowell, Carl and Helen Gibbs, *Ocean Transportation.* New York: McGraw-Hill Book Company, 1954.

McGarrah, Robert E., *Production and Logistics Management.* New York: John Wiley & Sons, Inc., 1963.

Metcalfe, James V., *Principles of Ocean Transportation.* New York: Simmons-Boardman Books, 1959.

Meyer, John, *et al., The Economics of Competition in the Transportation Industries.* Cambridge, Mass.: Harvard University Press, 1959.

Miller, Ronald E., *Domestic Airline Efficiency: An Application of Linear Programming.* Cambridge, Mass.: Massachusetts Institute of Technology Press, 1963.

Miller, Sidney L. and Virgil D. Cover, *Rates of Return to Class I Line Haul Railways of the United States, 1921–1948.* Pittsburgh: University of Pittsburgh Press, 1950.

Morton, Newton, *Digest of Selected Cases on Interstate Commerce Regulation,* second edition. Washington, D.C.: The Traffic Service Corporation, 1963.

Morton, Newton and Frank H. Mossman, *Industrial Traffic Management.* New York: Ronald Press Co., 1954.

Mossman, Frank H. and Newton Morton, *Principles of Transportation.* New York: Ronald Press Co., 1957.

Mott, George Fox (ed.), *Transportation Renaissance.* Philadelphia: American Academy of Political and Social Science, 1963.

Myskowski, Walter, *Abstracts of Supreme Court Decisions Interpreting the Interstate Commerce Act.* Washington, D.C.: Association of Interstate Commerce Commission Practitioners, 1954 and supplement 1956.

Nale-Povic, Joseph G., *Traffic Patterns in Domestic Water Transportation of Farm Products and Supplies.* Washington, D.C.: Agricultural Marketing Service, U.S. Department of Agriculture, 1961.

National Petroleum Council, *Report of the Committee on Oil and Gas Transportation.* Washington, D.C.: National Petroleum Council, 1962.

Nelson, James C., *Railroad Transportation and Public Policy.* Washington, D.C.: The Brookings Institution, 1959.

Nelson, Richard L., *The Selection of Retail Locations.* New York: F. W. Dodge Corp., 1958.

Neuner, E. J., *The Natural Gas Industry*. Norman, Okla.: University of Oklahoma Press, 1960.

Norton, Hugh S., *Modern Transportation Economics*. Columbus, Ohio: Charles E. Merrill Books, Inc., 1963.

Oxenfeldt, Alfred R. (ed.), *Models of Markets*. New York: Columbia University Press, 1963.

Paranka, Stephen, *Urban Transportation Dilemma*. Atlanta: Georgia State College of Business Administration, 1961.

Pegrum, Dudley F., *Transportation Economics and Public Policy*. Homewood, Ill.: Richard D. Irwin, Inc., 1960.

Perloff, Harvey S. *et al.*, *Regions, Resources, and Economic Growth*. Baltimore: The Johns Hopkins University Press, 1960.

Poole, Ernest C., *Costs a Tool of Railroad Management*. New York: Simmons-Boardman Books, 1961.

Proceedings of Transportation Research Conference, *Transportation Design Considerations*. Washington, D.C.: National Academy of Sciences, 1961.

Railway Systems and Management Association publications—Chicago.
Research and Railroad Operations, 1955.
Integration of Information Handling, 1955.
Management Controls of Transportation Operations, 1956.
Marketing—The Future of the Railroads, 1958.
The Developing Transportation Revolution, 1960.
Economic Costing of Railroad Operations, 1960.
Large Scale Systems Study, 1962.
Railroad Management Strategy, 1962.
Transportation Marketing, 1963.

Report of the Interstate Commerce Commission to the Senate and House of Representatives. Published annually by the U.S. Interstate Commerce Commission. Washington, D.C.: U.S. Government Printing Office.

Report of the Special Committee to Study Railroad Problems, National Association of Railroad and Utilities Commissioners. Washington, D.C.: U.S. Government Printing Office, 1960.

Report Prepared for the Committee on Interstate and Foreign Commerce, United States Senate, by the Special Study Group on Transportation Policies in the United States (Doyle Report). Washington, D.C.: U.S. Government Printing Office, 1961.

Schiff, Michael and Martin Mellman, *Financial Management of the Marketing Function*. New York: Financial Executives Research Foundation, Inc., 1962.

Schramm, Wilbur, *The Process and Effects of Mass Communication.* Urbana, Ill.: The University of Illinois Press, 1955.

Seburn, T. J. and B. L. Marsh, *Urban Transportation Administration.* New Haven, Conn.: Yale University Press, 1959.

Sevin, Charles H., *Distribution Cost Analysis,* Economic Series No. 50. Washington, D.C.: U.S. Department of Commerce, 1946.

Shott, J. G., *Piggyback and the Future of Railroad Transportation.* Washington, D.C.: Public Affairs Institute, 1960.

Smith, Paul E., *Shopping Centers: Planning and Management.* New York: National Retail Dry Goods Association, 1956.

Smykay, Edward W., Donald J. Bowersox, and Frank H. Mossman, *Physical Distribution Management.* New York: The Macmillan Company, 1961.

Stevens, Hoy, *Line-Haul Trucking Costs in Relation to Vehicle Gross Weights.* Washington, D.C.: Highway Research Board, National Academy of Sciences, 1961.

Stocker, Harry E., *Materials Handling.* Englewood Cliffs, N.J.: Prentice-Hall, Inc., 1951.

Stover, John F., *American Railroads.* Chicago: University of Chicago Press, 1961.

Taff, Charles A., *Commercial Motor Transportation,* revised edition. Homewood, Ill.: Richard D. Irwin, Inc., 1961.

————, *Management of Traffic and Physical Distribution.* Homewood, Ill.: Richard D. Irwin, Inc., 1964.

Thompson, William H., *Transportation of Poultry Feed Ingredients from the North Central States.* Brookings, S.D.: Agricultural Experiment Station, South Dakota State College, 1960.

Transportation Design Considerations. Proceedings of Transportation Research Conference. Washington, D.C.: National Academy of Sciences, 1961.

Ulmer, Melville J., *Capital in Transportation, Communications, and Public Utilities.* Princeton, N.J.: Princeton University Press, 1960.

U.S. Department of Commerce (Office of Transportation), *Charges for Private Use of Federal-Provided Transportation Services and Facilities.* Washington, D.C.: U.S. Government Printing Office, 1953.

Vernon, Raymond, *Metropolis 1985: An Interpretation of the Findings of the New York Metropolitan Region Study.* Cambridge, Mass.: Harvard University Press, 1960.

Warner, Stanley Leon, *Stochastic Choice of Mode in Urban Travel: A Study in Binary Choice*. Evanston, Ill.: Northwestern University Press, 1962.

Webber, Melvin W., *et al.*, *Explorations Into Urban Structure*. Philadelphia: University of Pennsylvania Press, 1964.

Westmeyer, R. E., *Economics of Transportation*. Englewood Cliffs, N.J.: Prentice-Hall, Inc., 1952.

Wilcox, Clair, *Public Policies Toward Business*. Homewood, Ill.: Richard D. Irwin, Inc., 1960.

Williams, E. W., *The Regulation of Rail-Motor Rate Competition*. New York: Harper & Row, Inc., 1958.

Williamson, Harold F. (ed.), *The Growth of the American Economy*, second edition. Englewood Cliffs, N.J.: Prentice-Hall, Inc., 1951.

Wilson, G. Lloyd, *Traffic Management: Industrial, Commercial, Governmental*. Englewood Cliffs, N.J.: Prentice-Hall, Inc., 1956.

Wilson, George W., *Essays on Some Unsettled Questions in the Economics of Transportation*. Bloomington, Ind.: Foundation for Economic and Business Studies, Indiana University, 1962.

Wingo, Lowdon Jr., *Transportation and Urban Land*. Washington, D.C.: Resources for the Future, Inc., 1961.

Wolfe, Harry D., *et al.*, *Pretesting Advertising*. Business Policy Study No. 9, New York: National Industrial Conference Board, 1963.

Yaseen, Leonard D., *Plant Location*. New York: American Research Council, 1956.

INDEX

A

Accounting department, 374
Achter, Stephen B., 288
Act to Regulate Commerce, 146–147, 148
Acts:
  Act to Regulate Commerce, 146–147, 148
  Civil Aeronautics Act, 147, 162
  Clayton Act, 177, 178
  Commission Divisions Act, 150
  Delegation of Authority Act, 150
  Elkins Act, 148
  Emergency Transportation Act of 1933, 171
  Freight Forwarder Act, 147, 162
  Garfield Act of 1866, 146
  Hepburn Act, 146–147, 148, 191
  Interstate Commerce Act, 147–149
  Merchant Marine Act of 1936, 147
  Motor Carrier Act, 147, 162
  Sherman Antitrust Act, 176, 180
  Shipping Act of 1916, 147
  Transportation Act of 1920, 146, 149, 157, 162
  Transportation Act of 1940, 147, 162, 171
  Transportation Act of 1958, 160
Adaptability of agencies possessing high fixed costs, 43–44
Advertising department, 375–376
Affluence, 203–204
Air-Freight Investigation, 9 CAB 340 (1948), 352
Air transportation:
  application of capital, 54
  characteristics of, 29–30
Aitchison, Beatrice, 186
Alderson, Wroe, 6
Allocating functional costs to factors causing cost differences, 269–273
Almond, Edward L., 118

Alternative distribution systems, cost analysis of, 210–220
Applebaum, William, 230
Applicability of capital to movement, 51–55
Application of capital to distribution systems, 27–64
Assembly terminals, 32
Atlantic Coast Line Railroad Company v. United States, 284 U.S. 288, 295 (1932), 174
Average length of haul, 92
Average size of order, 266–267
Average total unit cost, relationships between factors causing cost differences, 273–278
Average-unit-cost pricing:
  causes of trend toward, 99–100
  illustration of, 278
  possible results of, 101–102

B

Bakery Goods and Chemicals, Eastern Points, 34 MCC 551, 355
Barges, 28
Basic-nonbasic concept, 117–118
Beckman, T. N., 46
Behling, Burton N., 182
Beverly, Phil C., 180–181
Bowersox, Donald J., 243, 291
Break-bulk terminals, 32–34
Bricker Report, 165
Brigantine William, 28 Fed. Cas. 16, 700 (1808), 144
Brown, R. G., 333–335
Brown Shoe Company v. United States, 370 U.S. 294 (1962), 178
Business firm as an adjustive subsystem, 199–200
Buyer of transportation and modal competition, 370–371

386

Jones, Eliot, 349
Jones, S. Richard, 285

K

Kearney Company, A. T., 61, 260–
 261, 290
Kefauver, Estes, 172
Kelley, Eugene, 261
Kemme, Randall T., 129
Klaasen, Adrian J., 265–266
Knorst, W. J., 94
Kohn, Clyde F., 117, 118, 122

L

LaLonde, Bernard J., 229, 237
Launhardt, Wilhelm, 105, 106–107,
 111
Lazer, William, 261
Least squares method, 333–334
Legal department, 374–375
Levels of crude petroleum traffic, 90–
 92
Lewis, Harold M., 127–128
Lewis, W. Arthur, 37
Life styles, changing customer, 200–
 206
Line-haul costs, 65–67
Livestock to and from the South, 253
 ICC 250 (1942), 357
Local sources of supply, 307–308
Locational orientation of terminal
 types, 235–237
Locklin, D. Philip, 140, 354
Logistics:
 definition, 3–4
 of movement, principles, 19–26
Logistics systems:
 customer life styles affecting the
  firm's, 198–206
 macrodistribution systems, 16–17
 microdistribution systems, 17–18
 model for discussion, 15–16
Longman, Donald R., 288
Losch, August, 75–76, 108
Louisville and Nashville Railroad, 42

M

McGarry, Edmund D., 6
Macrodistribution systems, 4–5, 16–
 17
Magnuson, Warren, 168
Marginal pricing, 361–362
Margolin, Edward, 182–183
Market area:
 Greenhut's study, 109–110
 Isard's study, 110–112
 Losch's theory, 108–109
 size and shape, 108–112
Market density, 266
Market planning and programming,
 207–210
Market research:
 relationship of approach, 278–282
 relationship of assumed costs, 278–
  282
Marketing approach, 245–246, 278–
 282
Marketing, transportation and, 138
Mass transmission, 204–205
Materials handling systems, 287–288
Mayer, Harold M., 117, 118, 122
Mechanization, 24–25
Megalopolis, 127–129
Merchant Marine Act of 1936, 147
Methods of cost determination, 56–69
Metropolitan area:
 decentralization within, 120–125
 growth, 114–117, 125–127
Metropolitan city-regions and distribu-
 tion structure, 125–130
Metropolitan traffic congestion, 161
Meyer, John R., 15
Microdistribution systems:
 adjustment to change, 197–224
 logistics of, 17–18
 policy, 287–344
 terminal location, 225–256
Mill, John Stuart, 7–9
Miller, Sidney L., 156, 181
Minimizing transport costs in terminal
 location, 237–244
*Minneapolis and St. Louis R. Co. v.
 United States,* 361 U.S. 173,
 187 (1959), 177
Mobility, 205–206
Model for discussion of the logistics
 system, 15–16
Morse, Philip M., 338

T